T0314133

Capitalism's Hidden Worlds

HAGLEY PERSPECTIVES ON BUSINESS AND CULTURE

Series Editor: Roger Horowitz

A complete list of books in the series is available from the publisher.

Capitalism's Hidden Worlds

Edited by
Kenneth Lipartito *and* Lisa Jacobson

PENN

UNIVERSITY OF PENNSYLVANIA PRESS

PHILADELPHIA

Published by
University of Pennsylvania Press
Philadelphia, Pennsylvania 19104-4112
www.upenn.edu/pennpress

Printed in the United States of America
on acid-free paper

10 9 8 7 6 5 4 3 2 1

Library of Congress Cataloging-in-Publication Data

Names: Lipartito, Kenneth, editor. | Jacobson, Lisa, editor.
Title: Capitalism's hidden worlds / edited by Kenneth Lipartito and
    Lisa Jacobson.
Other titles: Hagley perspectives on business and culture.
Description: 1st edition. | Philadelphia : University of Pennsylvania Press, [2020] |
    Series: Hagley perspectives on business and culture | Preface. | Includes
    bibliographical references and index.
Identifiers: LCCN 2019031230 | ISBN 9780812251814 (hardcover)
Subjects: LCSH: Capitalism—History. | Informal sector (Economics)—History. |
    Black market—History.
Classification: LCC HB501 .C24269 2020 | DDC 330—dc23
LC record available at https://lccn.loc.gov/2019031230

Contents

Preface   vii
Roger Horowitz

Introduction: Mapping the Shadowlands of Capitalism   1
Kenneth Lipartito and Lisa Jacobson

PART I. MEASURING AND UNVEILING MARKETS

Chapter 1. Lifting the Veil of Money: What Economic
Indicators Hide   25
Eli Cook

Chapter 2. Accounting for Reproductive Labor: Feminist Economists
and the Construction of Social Knowledge on Rural Women in
the Global South   44
Eileen Boris

PART II. WORKING THE MARGINS

Chapter 3. The Loose Cotton Economy of the New Orleans Waterfront in
the Late Nineteenth Century   67
Bruce E. Baker

Chapter 4. Jim Crow's Cut: White Supremacy and the Destruction of Black
Capital in the Forests of the Deep South   81
Owen James Hyman

Chapter 5. In the Shadow of Incorporation: Hidden Economies of the Hispano Borderlands, 1890–1930   99
Bryan W. Turo

PART III. THE LICIT AND THE ILLICIT

Chapter 6. Capitalism's Back Pages: "Immoral" Advertising and Invisible Markets in Paris's Mass Press, 1880–1940   119
Hannah Frydman

Chapter 7. Capitalism's Black Heart in Wartime France   139
Kenneth Mouré

Chapter 8. The Emergence of the Offshore Economy, 1914–1939   157
James Hollis and Christopher McKenna

PART IV. HIDDEN MARKET SPACES IN PLANNED ECONOMIES

Chapter 9. Comrades In-Between: Transforming Commercial Practice in the People's Republic of China, 1949–1962   181
Philip Scranton

Chapter 10. Hidden Realms of Private Entrepreneurship: Soviet Jews and Post–World War II Artels in the USSR   203
Anna Kushkova

Notes   223
List of Contributors   273
Index   277
Acknowledgments   285

P r e f a c e

The process leading to this volume began when Ken Lipartito and Lisa Jacobson contacted me to see if Hagley's Center for the History of Business, Technology, and Society would support their initiative to explore "the concealed, invisible, and underground dimensions of capitalist economies" as a way to understand how "a crucial part of what drives capitalism falls outside of waged relations and formal, visible exchange." I knew both well; they had conducted research at Hagley on their own insightful book projects, and I had worked with them in the Business History Conference, where Lisa served as a trustee and Ken as president while I was the organization's secretary-treasurer. This seemed a terrific idea for an initiative and completely relevant to Hagley's interest in promoting creative and original research into business history and the history of capitalism. I recruited Wendy Woloson to this effort, as I was familiar with her own highly relevant work through the collection she edited (with Brian Luskey), *Capitalism by Gaslight*, and her own ongoing research on the boundaries of capitalism that she was exploring through, among other sources, Hagley's ample collections.

Ken, Lisa, Wendy, and I commenced by recruiting papers via a call for proposals for a fall 2017 conference at the Hagley Library in Wilmington, Delaware, called Hidden Capitalism: Below, Beneath, and Beyond the Market. To move toward publishing a collection of essays, I asked Ken and Lisa to serve as volume editors and to assemble the chapters that would best engage with the crucial questions that lay behind their initiative. Six of the essays in this collection are revised versions of papers presented at the conference. The coeditors solicited four additional essays to broaden and diversify the methodological, geographical, and chronological scope of the volume. In all cases, the chapters are significantly revised, edited, and conceptually sharpened by the close involvement of the editors.

Taken together, the ten essays in this volume draw upon the methods of historians, economic anthropologists, and feminist studies scholars to illuminate the varied market subcultures that operate within capitalism, as well as the varied capitalist market subcultures that emerged within the socialist economies of the Soviet Union and the People's Republic of China. Spanning the century between the 1880s and the 1970s, the essays contained here examine the workings of hidden markets both within national borders and beyond them, from the economic borderlands of the U.S. South and the Rocky Mountain West to the liminal zones of offshore tax havens. Taken together, they show how diverse economic actors have used hidden markets to hide wealth, to redress inequalities, or simply to make ends meet. On the flip side, the essays also show how policy makers and regulators have exposed hidden markets to make the obscured transparent, to affix value to the unmeasured, and to seal the porous boundaries between the licit and the illicit, the legal and the illegal.

This is the twelfth volume in the Hagley Perspectives on Business and Culture series, now housed, very happily, at the University of Pennsylvania Press. I especially want to thank our editor at the press, Robert Lockhart, for his consistent support of the series as well as his incisive intellectual engagement with the development of these volumes. At Hagley, I want to recognize the indispensable role played by Carol Lockman, longtime manager of the Hagley Center for the History of Business, Technology, and Society, along with our staff more generally. These collections aim to bring cutting-edge research to the attention of scholars; I hope you will find these essays stimulating and useful.

Dr. Roger Horowitz
Director, Center for the History of Business, Technology, and Society
Hagley Museum and Library
Editor, Hagley Perspectives on Business and Culture

Introduction: Mapping the Shadowlands of Capitalism

Kenneth Lipartito and Lisa Jacobson

Ruthlessly exposed to the market. That might be the most common way of thinking about capitalism today. Many observers see free markets, the relentless pursuit of profit, and the unremitting drive to commodify everything as capitalism's defining characteristics. These most visible economic features, however, obscure a range of other less evident, often unmeasured activities that occur on the margins and in the concealed corners of the formal economy. Some of these activities may enhance capitalism's dynamism, while others may bolster its legitimacy. Still others provoke outrage and calls for regulation. The range of practices in this large and diverse hidden realm encompasses traders in recycled materials and the architects of junk bonds and shadow banking. It includes the black and semi-licit markets that allow wealthy elites to avoid taxes and to offshore assets or enable the marginalized and dispossessed to survive despite inadequate incomes. It also includes the unmeasured domestic and emotional labor of homemakers and home care workers. By some estimates, the unmeasured economic activity that occurs within the household, informal market, and underground economy amounts to almost 30 percent of the total U.S. economy and globally probably much more.[1] We do not know the full measure of these hidden features of capitalism because all these activities have one thing in common: they are not recorded in the economic statistics, stock indexes, tax registers, and account books that historians typically draw upon.

Capitalism's Hidden Worlds sheds new light on this shadowy economic landscape. In doing so, it also reexamines how we think about the market. In particular, it reveals the missed connections between the official, visible realm of exchange and the uncounted and invisible sectors that stand right next to it. While some hidden markets have emerged in opposition to the formal economy, much of the obscured economy we describe operates as the other side—and in some cases, as the dark underbelly—of the legitimate, state-sanctioned marketplace. A range of historical actors—from fortune-tellers and foragers to tax lawyers and black market consumers—have constructed this unseen world in tandem with the observable public world of transactions. Others, such as feminist development economists and government regulators, have worked to bring the darkened corners of the economy to light. By peering into these corners, we explore how the capitalist marketplace sustains itself, how it acquires legitimacy and even prestige, and how the marginalized and the dispossessed find ways to make ends meet.

Our point of departure differs from the typical way that scholars look at the market. Usually the market is treated as a place where wants, desires, resources, and opportunities are exposed and made visible, quantifiable, and graspable. As we show, however, no study of the market can stop there. In fact, the creation of legally sanctioned markets gives rise to the demand for invisible market transactions and privacy. The decision to hide assets from tax collectors, protect trade secrets and tacit knowledge from would-be competitors, or simply to limit the exposure of one's identity all constitute ways that people have found to obscure their economic visibility without withdrawing from economic activity. The most extreme cases take place in the shrouded realm of illegal activities, where smugglers traffic in prohibited or heavily taxed goods and sellers supply wants for banned substances and banned pleasures.

We should not rest with a simple opposition between the visible or sanctioned market and these sorts of black market activities. In fact, substantial economic activity takes place in the gray economy, where business transactions may be technically legal but not wholly respectable or may be formally illegal but widely tolerated. Often such activities occupy a liminal zone—being neither illegal nor legal because they have not yet come under juridical scrutiny. Sometimes innovations like shadow banking and financial derivatives that originate in the unregulated gray zone become widely embraced by the public marketplace. In fact, an important feature of the capitalist cycle of creation and destruction may involve just this move from gray market to white market. New products, techniques, and forms of competition may arise powerfully and suddenly in remote corners of the economy through social interactions, leisure activities, and hobbies. Students of innovation can find many examples—from the amateur labor performed by the early devotees of radio a century ago, to the hobbyist enthusiasm and information sharing about early personal computers, to the uncommercialized experiments with such social media platforms as Myspace and Facebook.[2]

The history of hidden economic activity also takes into account boundary zones where the formal and informal, visible and invisible meet. Perhaps the prime example is the family home, which functions simultaneously as a site of women's unwaged toil, a place of refuge, and a point of opposition against capitalism's advance. Feminist scholarship has long noted that in many periods of history, women's reproductive labor—the uncompensated work of caregiving, cleaning, cooking, and child-rearing—provided the support that allowed others (usually men) to work in the marketplace. Much of this unwaged activity goes uncounted in measures of GDP, yet it has bolstered capitalism's legitimacy by putting a floor under otherwise unsustainable family incomes. The cultural invisibility of women's reproductive labor made it easier to overlook inequitable wages even as it cemented women's disadvantaged position in both the family and the labor market.[3]

The visible and invisible marketplaces map onto each other in complex ways. Sometimes they intersect to their mutual benefit. Other times they collide on a path of conflict. Such complexity reminds us that no natural or preset border exists between the formal, legal, or visible market and the spaces where the hidden, obscured, and illegal market activity occur. At different historical moments different states and different actors have drawn the line separating the visible and the invisible market in different ways. Activity that may be formally illicit or prohibited can still enter the licit economy, as when entrepreneurs funnel the profits from illegal activity into the legitimate banking system. In other cases, features of the licit economy transform into outright exploitation, as when labor mobility becomes trafficking. Writing about the history of hidden markets invites us to explore these crevices in capitalism. It requires us to reconceptualize the relationship between the margins and the center—between the licit and the illicit, the waged and the unwaged, the public and the private—to better understand the mutual dependence of the visible and invisible markets.

Histories of Capitalism Old and New

The idea that capitalism has hidden dimensions is not new. Economists and historians have produced studies of black markets and illicit enterprises, underground economies, the informal sector, and smuggling and fraud—covering a full array of activities that slip beneath the radar of state surveillance and the state's taxing authority.[4] Traditional ways of conceptualizing capitalism and its origins, however, have largely ignored these hidden dimensions and the complex interplay between the formal economy and hidden markets. For Adam Smith and the neoclassical economists who followed, capitalism burst forth once markets were unshackled from restraints and brought into the open. Once societies freed the market, trade connections grew, incomes rose, demand for goods increased, and creative entrepreneurship flourished. It is no surprise then that many neoclassical economists can trace capitalism, in some rough form or another, all the way back to ancient Babylonia.[5] Karl Marx had a very different explanation of how capitalism emerged, but he too looked at the way the extension of the market and commodification of human activity provided the conditions for capitalism.[6]

Whatever model of capitalism one uses—and however one explains capitalism's origins—scholars all begin with the centrality of the market as the driving force that makes capitalism possible. Once the market is allowed to allocate labor and other resources, the pressures of competition and the imperative of profit take command. Owners of capital seeking profit under market competition must find ways to increase labor productivity by enlisting new technologies, creating new organizational efficiencies, and preying on the vulnerability of workers. Capitalism also thrusts outward, seeking fresh resources and markets, eventually engulfing the entire world in its tentacles.[7]

Missing from such accounts is the sense that capitalism is something that people and states had to create and that states and societies had to legitimize. Missing, too, is the sense that alternative institutions and modes of economic organization may persist alongside or in opposition to capitalism.[8] Taking a less deterministic view, the historical sociologist Karl Polanyi argued that this triumph of the market was actually a radical project, even a utopian one—just the opposite of natural and inevitable. It required great effort and the power of the state to pry market activity out of the matrix of social life and custom that had long governed the terms and meanings of economic exchange.

Polanyi called attention to the way that economic activity had throughout history been embedded in social relationships, religious norms, cultural values, and political institutions. Like Marx and Smith, though, he contended that capitalism had erased this earlier type of marketplace. While agreeing that capitalism represented a radical break from the past, Joyce Appleby, by contrast, recognized that capitalism was "as much a cultural as an economic system." It came into being when new ways of understanding human capacities and the wealth-generating effects of efficiency, ingenuity, and work discipline dethroned traditional society's emphasis on "status, stasis, and communal obligations."[9] More recently, however, economists, historians, and sociologists have called into question this idea of a radical break with the past. Mark Granovetter has proposed that even under capitalism markets are necessarily embedded in society and culture. Far from being holdovers or inefficient blockages to a free market, these social features promote trust and reduce risk, making them functional with respect to market operations. In Granovetter's conception, Polanyi's radical separation of the market from society never occurred, and markets could take different forms depending on how they were embedded in society.[10]

Granovetter and other institutional economists take a rather mechanistic view of embeddedness, but others have contended that the ends of economic action matter as much as the means when it comes to defining what separates capitalism from other economic systems. The economic historian Bas van Bavel, for example, argues that while product and commodity markets can be found throughout history, the factors used to produce commodities in capitalist societies—land, labor, and capital—become sites of intense conflict and controversy under capitalism. Markets are continually reembedded in various ways because both workers and capitalists find that too much market freedom can work to their disadvantage. It is not just that the social and political features surrounding markets are needed for market functioning; it is that markets themselves provoke conflicts, political reactions, and attempts to bring them under control.[11]

In the most recent attempt to understand the workings of capitalism, the so-called new historians of capitalism also start with markets. Their approach combines aspects of Marx's focus on commodification as the driving force behind capitalism's emergence and Polanyi's emphasis on the market's interaction with the sociopolitical matrix. Commodification turns everything into a saleable item and therefore a potential source of profit, the lifeblood of capitalism. While earlier historians paid close attention to workers, consumers, peasant farmers, and artisans who carved out spaces that resisted capitalism and capitalist values, the new historians of capitalism see commodification as a rolling tide that engulfs all and reformats politics, society, and culture in the process.[12]

Sven Beckert's global history of cotton shows the strengths and weaknesses of the new literature. Following the world-systems model of Immanuel Wallerstein, Beckert maps the process by which global production was reorganized along capitalist lines from the sixteenth century forward. Europeans structured the world into multiple spheres of labor, from peasant producers in India dependent on merchant credit, to landless workers in Manchester selling their labor power at the factory gate, to slaves in the New World bending to produce commodities on plantations. All of these parts came together in a global commodity supply-and-production chain by the nineteenth century, making modern capitalism. Yet when it comes to origins, it seems that capitalism starts by pulling itself up by its own bootstraps.[13] Beckert claims that an early "war capitalism" phase harnessed the power of the state to the interests of the merchant classes who were organizing the global production system. Within this system there was certainly violence and conflict but no real possibility of alternatives or agency outside of the European capitalists. As the Caribbean historian Trevor Burnard has pointed out, Beckert's history places the engine of all transformation in the hands of the West. The rest of the world is only present as its subjects and victims.[14]

In their sweeping approach to commodification, exploitation, and profit, the new historians of capitalism do not distinguish capitalism from what scholars had once seen as alternative forms of exploitation or noncapitalist modes of production. This is perhaps most evident in their treatment of slavery. Beckert stresses that slave-grown cotton was essential to British industrialization, linking the two into a single economic system. Others argue that slavery itself was a form of capitalism. Slave owners were relentless improvers of productivity, by whatever means necessary, including by forcing more work out of the enslaved through whippings, threats, and torture. As slavery expanded across the Americas and Caribbean, owners used the political system to protect their investment and increase its value, and they drew on the financial system to turn human property into liquid capital by mortgaging the bodies of slaves. With this financing they bought more land and more slaves, further increasing their profits. Slaveholders even used accounting technologies that Max Weber argued were the hallmark of capitalist enterprise to measure the productive potential of the men and women they owned.[15]

Powerful though this case is, lumping slavery and wage labor together as part of capitalism downplays points of fundamental conflict over what the market is, what it means, how people make and define profit, and what alternatives might exist.[16] One central feature of market-driven capitalism is its "progressive" impulse. It pushes the owners of capital to find new ways to profit and commodify—and to transform whole societies, if necessary—to get what they want.[17] Slavery lacked these "creative destructive" elements, as slave masters were much more concerned with maintaining control and preventing actions that would endanger their property or power. As a result, they underinvested in transportation and education and fell further and further behind the North in literacy and industrial development, a legacy that would keep the South the poorest region of the United States well into the twentieth century.[18]

Our work departs from both the model deployed by the new historians of capitalism and traditional Marxian models. For the new historians, capitalism resides in the networks that interconnect different forms of labor and production more than in the forms of labor and production themselves. Following the world-systems approach, they focus less on the internal workings of markets, labor processes, or production sites than on the ways different forms of each are brought into coordination. Thus, slavery becomes "capitalist" in part because of its function in a larger system connected to industrialization and mass consumption, even if slavery itself has features and aspects that do not seem fully capitalist.[19] The Marxian tradition, by contrast, focuses closely on the development of a capitalist class and transformations that commodify labor (and indeed capital). Both models, however, treat "the market" as a universal, unproblematic entity. Both view commodification as transforming society from a precapitalist state to a capitalist one, either by the qualitative linking of production sites through market expansion, as the new historians of capitalism see it, or by the commodification of labor, as traditional Marxists see it. In both cases, there is a rigid division between the precapitalist world and the capitalist one, with the former a stage on the road to the latter. By contrast, we are interested in the liminal spaces, interstices, and mixed market forms that do not fit neatly into either the capitalist or precapitalist category. Our cases involve types of market activity that cannot be simply reduced to commodification but should not be treated as nonmarket or communal or reciprocal either. Indeed, often they have both market and nonmarket characteristics, which involve a complex mixture of values and motives beyond those of pure capitalist profit.[20]

As this volume suggests, mapping the scope of capitalism's operations requires that we also examine the economic shadowlands where hidden markets and alternative economic practices often evade the capitalist state's regulatory gaze and measuring tools. Historians of the nineteenth-century economy have undertaken some of the most exciting work in this vein and have opened lines of inquiry that this volume also pursues. The contributors to *Capitalism by Gaslight*, edited by Brian Luskey and Wendy Woloson, examine a host of economic players and petty entrepreneurs—prostitutes, fraudsters, dealers in secondhand clothes, traffickers in stolen horses—who helped make the economy work for those who occupied its fringes. These seemingly marginal players, Luskey and Woloson argued, helped to create "capitalism as much as captains of commerce and industry did." Participants in morally and legally ambiguous businesses sparked debates and policy responses that eventually sharpened the boundaries between legitimate and illegitimate commerce.[21]

Like Woloson, Luskey, and others, we argue for a dynamic *social history of capitalism* that leaves room for bottom-up as well as top-down agency. While the new history of capitalism has mainly put agency in the hands of white male elites, many essays in this volume look at women and minorities who participated in far less visible sectors and spaces of the economy. The elites we discuss are ones who sought to escape the glare of the visible market to operate in its concealed corners. We adopt a perspective that examines the economy from the side, even more so than from the top or the bottom. We peer in from the borders and peripheries to understand the highly contingent, messy, and often contested processes by which capitalism took shape and acquired legitimacy.[22]

A social history of capitalism offers a way to think about how diverse actors—from capitalist elites and petty entrepreneurs to scavengers, home workers, and consumers of illicit goods—have created varied markets, generated new sources of profit, and cobbled together a living. We share with classic works of social history an interest in alternative economic forms and values that either persisted or faded into the background as capitalism ascended. We find, however, that many of these alternative forms were not holdovers from a precapitalist past but rather hidden or suppressed variants of market capitalism itself, present and active at the very moment the more public capitalist mainstream was asserting itself. When we look at capitalism sideways—and not solely from the vantage of capitalism's commanding elites or its resurgent resisters—we can better understand how capitalism thrives on, preys upon, and adapts to economic activities that fall outside the boundaries of the measured and the seen. We can see capitalism as a tangled hybrid of many forms. And we won't lose sight of women's crucial roles in sustaining those hidden and unmeasured economic worlds.[23]

Hidden Markets in the Capitalist Ecosystem: Toward a New Framework

Where *Capitalism by Gaslight* documented a period when "the rules of economic engagement were still being established," the essays in this volume span the late nineteenth and twentieth centuries, when corporate capitalism was ascendant and capitalist ways of doing business wended their way into socialist economies and free trade zones that operated beyond national borders.[24] Yet, even in the late nineteenth and twentieth centuries, when capitalism increasingly eclipsed other economic forms, hidden commerce continued to exert its influence on the economy and on economic development. If capitalism is fluid and ever changing—if it becomes something different when new technologies, new modes of production and distribution, and new systems of regulation displace older capitalist orders—we should pay more attention to how hidden markets shape these new permutations of capitalism.[25]

Instead of treating capitalism as a single, if multifaceted, system anchored by the market, we argue that markets with different features and ways of operating can coexist on the same plane. Sometimes even different economic systems can coexist on the same plane, as we see when communist societies permit private entrepreneurship in certain sectors of the economy. Instead of thinking in terms of "the" market, we acknowledge that markets of various arrangements appear in various social settings and times.[26] The question is, how should we understand these differences? Is capitalism a single structure with variant forms, or do capitalism and noncapitalism coexist as separable entities with different dynamics, histories, and futures?

Our position is that we should start by treating capitalism as a hybrid system—though not necessarily a single organic entity. In this way the story is not one of a global world system with differently positioned markets and economies. Nor is it a story of the "varieties of capitalism," each inflected by the particular sociopolitical circumstances of a nation. Nor is it the classical story of stages, from feudalism to capitalism, from liberal capitalism to monopoly capitalism, imperialist capitalism, or neoliberal capitalism. Finally, it is not even the older social-history formulation that pits capitalists against protestors and resisters sticking to a precapitalist past.

Elements of all these perspectives appear in this volume, but collectively the chapters push beyond them. Where most previous histories of capitalism have emphasized the uprooting of the past and the nakedness of the market, this volume stresses the mixed, partial, and embedded nature of markets even under capitalism. In contrast to the neoclassical model that sees people ready to join the market once the state removes fetters and puts proper institutions and property rights in place, we stress how institutions reflect different social and political conditions and cultural values. Rather than treat these social and political conditions as external to the market, however, we see them as mutually constituted: markets, values, and institutions coevolve. Finally, rather than seeing capitalism pushed by untrammeled market forces and endless commodification, we see an economy that spills outside the boundaries of formal markets, a subsurface of pipes, waterways, and sluices that constitutes a different economic hydrology.

Almost all of those who study capitalism embrace the idea that ruthless competition characterizes the system. Competition may drive innovation, focus profit seeking, or cause actors to recoil and seek protection from its destructive gales, but it is always there. It is a beneficial force for Adam Smith, but even Smith's opponent Marx admired Charles Darwin, whose ideas of competitive struggles for survival were just coming into vogue in Victorian England.[27] Rather than casting capitalism's ruthless profit seeking as a Darwinian struggle for survival of the fittest, we prefer Darwin's other image: the tangled bank. As Darwin observed, in any ecosystem there is not only competition but also complex and supportive interconnections among species. Likewise, the capitalist economy coexists with and even draws sustenance from many different forms of economic activity existing in the same space, even if they operate by different principles. We start with a view of capitalism as a complex ecosystem of institutions and actors that operates at different scales (international, national, regional, local) and in different temporalities. While the ruthless-profit imperative constitutes one defining feature, it does not fully capture the dynamics that animate capitalism and help capitalism achieve legitimacy.[28]

Our model of capitalism, resting on a broader engagement with the varied practices that constitute an economy, draws on the work of the social philosopher Dave Elder-Vass. Elder-Vass argues that economies are best described as collections of diverse appropriative practices.[29] He defines appropriative practices as socially and normatively structured interactions among people that influence who gets what. They are not confined to classic market activity and exchange but may include human interactions and transfers that provide goods, services, and other things of value: labor in the home, gifts, reciprocal exchanges, and the free exchange of knowledge.[30] While historians of capitalism are attuned to the different ways market appropriation may occur—through finance, slavery, property ownership, risk management, patents and royalties, corporate profits—they have not considered the ways nonmarket, semimarket, off-market, and alternative market economies may work. How these varied markets operate within the same capitalist ecosystem—and how capitalist-oriented markets function within socialist economies—is the focus of this volume.

Exploring the hidden precincts of capitalism brings to light a whole set of economic practices that originate on the margins of the formal market economy. In some instances, alternative forms of exchange create viable economic systems that work alongside mainstream capitalism rather than in direct opposition to it. Sometimes they even evolve into profitable multimillion-dollar businesses. Consider the place of secondhand goods in the U.S. economy. By the mid-twentieth century, for example, the once morally suspect business of selling junk and used clothes had become thoroughly integrated into U.S. middle-class life as consumers sought out thrift stores and garage sales for affordable secondhand goods. Typically run by women, suburban garage sales generated a billion dollars annually in the 1970s. They simultaneously challenged and buttressed mainstream commerce by enabling some buyers to resist marketing pressures to acquire the newest while generating income that sellers could use to justify their new purchases. The buyers, Jennifer Le Zotte has argued, could imagine themselves as "maverick consumers" while the sellers "operated as . . . lightly rogue capitalists, pursuing profit outside established and taxed corridors."[31]

Reciprocity, sharing, and recycling are all forms of production and exchange that can operate alongside and sometimes in conjunction with traditional market capitalism. Open-source software, bartering goods online, appropriating the trash of others, and sharing content on the web do not involve the traditional market, let alone the wage-labor relationship. There may be a monetary aspect to them, as when YouTubers gain advertisers, yet a large percentage of web content does not generate sales—nor does it intend to. Social media companies and data collection firms, on the other hand, benefit from just this sort of open sharing when they monitor social media accounts and internet forums to acquire free data for their advertising algorithms and mass marketing campaigns.[32]

Instead of viewing these diverse economic practices as a way station on the road to full capitalism or as appendages to the main capitalist economy, we see them as key elements of the complex capitalist ecosystem. Capitalism's veiled face can exist at the national or regional levels, within distinctive cultures, and even across nations within transnational communities. Sometimes hidden markets come together peacefully with the more visible features of capitalism in the mutually supportive way of the tangled bank. Sometimes they collide contentiously as mainstream capitalists seek to push aside or uproot alternatives. The different elements of the capitalist ecosystem will overlap, but they do not have to be subsumed into an organic whole. Nor does capitalism have to be defined by some essential feature like wage labor, commodification, or exploitation of the economically weak and marginal (although it contains all of these elements). If we instead treat capitalism as a field of analysis, our empirical and interpretive tasks must be redirected. We need to be more attentive to how capitalism changes over time, how it picks up different features and drops others, and how it relates its many assorted elements.

The essays here wrestle with all these issues. They address questions of power, agency, and contingency by interrogating the relationship between the manifest and the hidden, the mainstream and the marginal, and the licit and the illicit. They examine the conditions that enable the marginalized and the powerful to create concealed economic spaces and the circumstances that inhibit players (big and small) from using those concealed spaces to their advantage. As the essays in the volume show, policy makers and elites have deployed state power so that some markets can thrive unseen while others are constrained and subjected to tighter surveillance. Often the wealthiest and most powerful have used such devices as tax havens and offshore accounts to increase their wealth. In other cases, hiding can be a form of creative adaptation, as when smaller players learn to exploit the economy's interstices for modest gain or even just basic survival. In still other cases, racial minorities and outsiders enter shadow economies to participate in activities from which discrimination has excluded them.

One important implication of the research in this volume is that we cannot always find the answers to questions about the legitimacy of hidden markets in clear rules of law. Legality itself is a place where issues of power get played out. A banker might view the offshore tax haven as a legal instrument to preserve wealth, but other citizens might see it as a fraudulent tool that allows the wealthy to dodge their civic responsibility. A street peddler who sells fashion knock-offs might be condemned by high-end labels as a dealer in counterfeit merchandise, but to others he is simply a worker trying to make a living in an economy with limited opportunities. A dealer in black market goods might be condemned as a cheat or cheered for working the black market in opposition to an authoritarian regime. Many of the essays contained here highlight just these sorts of tensions and dualities.

Part I, "Measuring and Unveiling Markets," addresses a major methodological issue in policy studies and the histories of economic and feminist thought: How do we account for economic activity, and what gets lost in our accounting? How does such accounting render some activities visible and others invisible? The essays by Eli Cook and Eileen Boris both show how reliance on price-based metrics has tended to obscure inequality, ideology, and nonpecuniary values. Capitalist countries have long approached such economic indicators as GDP, the CPI, or the Dow Jones Industrial Average as objective metrics that ostensibly reveal the health of the economy and the progress of society. Cook's essay shows, however, that these statistical indicators were built out of an ideological project to efface questions of distribution and equality. He traces the U.S. origins of price-based economic metrics to the mid-nineteenth century, when statistics increasingly took stock of societal well-being by measuring the economy's capacity to produce income and increase wealth. The new interest in monied metrics departed from an earlier antebellum-era focus on "moral statistics" that linked social welfare to rates of pauperism, prostitution, and mental illness—all "important aspects of the human condition . . . that could not be measured in dollars and cents." Cook demonstrates how the increasing reliance on monetized economic metrics in the late nineteenth and early twentieth centuries privileged the interests and values of ruling elites by placing certain aspects of our modern lives on a pedestal, while covering others in a veil.

Eileen Boris examines how feminist development economists, working in conjunction with women lace makers in India, started to push back against the limits of such accepted metrics as market-based GDP. They created new forms of economic knowledge by bringing rural women's unmeasured and unremunerated labors to light. In the 1970s, pioneering feminist economists who studied rural women and development in the Global South identified a hidden market space overlooked in economics: the category of reproductive labor—the daily activities like cooking and care that sustain and socialize people. Development planners had long discounted the economic value of women's work because women's uncompensated family and farming labor went uncounted in official statistics and measures of GDP. As a result, poverty-reduction programs that focused on increasing employment and accelerating economic growth often intensified gender inequalities and the heavy burdens that reproductive labor imposed on women. Feminist economists called upon researchers to decolonize economic knowledge by enlisting rural women and scholars from the Global South in research that sought to identify and expose the exploitative conditions that impoverished women home workers. This collaborative research facilitated the creation of cooperative organizations that improved the Indian lace makers' earnings and helped to revise the ways economists have measured and conceptualized reproductive labor. The resulting economic knowledge laid the groundwork for the International Labor Organization's subsequent efforts to create labor standards for home-based and domestic workers.

The second part of the book moves from the macro level of knowledge creation to the gaps of the formal economy, where alternative economic practices thrived alongside the major corridors of capitalism. "Working the Margins" examines how men and women from working-class and minority communities, including African Americans in the U.S. South and Nuevomexicanos in the Hispano borderlands, set out to make a living at a moment after the abolition of slavery when the governing ideas about property were in flux. Bruce Baker's study of the trade in loose cotton, or "the city crop" as it was known in late nineteenth-century New Orleans, illuminates the difficulties of both sustaining and restraining an underground economy awash in legal ambiguity. In some cases, the dockworkers and scavengers who made their living around the cotton wharves gathered and then sold the cotton that had fallen out of the bales—a semilegal practice of recycling the cotton trade's "waste." In other cases, scavengers actively encouraged those leavings, committing what the New Orleans Cotton Exchange regarded as theft. The men who inspected bales to grade the cotton further delegitimized the loose cotton trade when they took overly generous samples and pocketed them for later resale to the junk shops and cotton pickeries that purchased low-grade cotton. Whether stolen or recycled, the city crop eventually found its way to the bottom layers of the legitimate trade, which sold it to regional and overseas markets for use in commodities that did not require high-quality fiber.

The close and functional relationship between the legitimate trade and the illegal or semilegitimate trade highlighted the challenge of regulating loose cotton. The very processes that made cotton profitable—measuring, weighing, and sorting cotton into grades—made it vulnerable to theft, but the marketability of low-grade cotton made the loose cotton trade difficult to eradicate. As studies of organized crime, counterfeiting, and knock-offs in fashion also show, formal and self-represented legal and legitimate enterprises often condemn these activities, yet the capital circulated by them often ends up in the legitimate market and can create profits even for those who condemn black and gray markets. Counterfeit merchandise can bolster the allure of luxury brands and may even serve as the gateway purchase to the eventual acquisition of branded luxury goods.[33]

While Baker highlights the mutual interdependence of gray markets and official markets, Owen Hyman and Bryan Turo turn our attention to the economic borderlands of the U.S. South and Rocky Mountain West, where corporate capitalism eroded but never entirely displaced alternative economies on the margins of the formal economy. Both study communities of racial minorities whose long-standing practice of sharing communally owned resources came under pressure from large, land-hungry corporations. Focusing on the decades between 1870 and 1940, Hyman examines black freed people who acquired land through the 1862 Homestead Act in the piney woods on the southern Mississippi-Louisiana border. Black and white small farmers both relied on shared access to the forests to provide for their own sustenance and raise cattle for the market. Many also grew sugarcane and processed it into bottled syrup—a valuable commodity that they marketed and offered as payment in kind to the hired hands who harvested the cane. At other times they took on work for wages. Operating in a complex economic ecosystem, black and white farmers combined small-scale industry with subsistence farming and processed cane syrup for both the market and the barter economy. Neither purely capitalist nor precapitalist, this interracial economy blurred the boundaries that traditionally divided the formal and informal markets.

As the lumber industry moved aggressively to clear the forests, it destroyed the varied sources of capital on which both black and white farmers depended. Contrary to many assumptions, farmers joined forces across the color line to beat back the advance of large-scale lumbering, sometimes making their land claims visible through violence and intimidation. Ties of interracial marriage and family and a common interest in preserving the ecology of the woods fostered cross-racial cooperation, but in the end many black farmers lost their property and livelihoods to outright land and lumber grabs. While environmental historians have seen the destruction of black capital as a byproduct of the capitalist drive to rapidly liquidate timber, Hyman recasts deforestation as a story of outright theft, legitimized by the culture of Jim Crow. Biased judges, the defunding of black education, and unaffordable court costs deprived African Americans of their ability to seek legal recourse when lumber companies took advantage of widespread black illiteracy to overstep their timber-cutting contracts. The theft of black capital undermined the material basis for small farming and interracial cooperation, leaving blacks more dependent on wage labor and alternative economies, including bartering, to piece together a living.

Bryan Turo's study of the Hispano borderlands in New Mexico and Colorado between 1890 and 1930 examines similar conflicts over land-use rights between large cattle companies and Nuevomexicanos, whose property claims dated back to the Mexican era. Nuevomexicanos pushed back against large cattle operators by reorganizing an assortment of previously legal economic practices into a shadow economy that existed alongside the more visible economy. Although Nuevomexicanos who continued to practice open-range herding risked prosecution as trespassers, they relied on their deep knowledge of the land and social networks to gather intelligence about places where their cattle could graze without detection. Such practices often enabled them to evade attempts to pin them down to the formal practices and legal documentation required by white society. Rather than viewing the alternative economy sustained by Nuevomexicanos as simply informal or subsistence-based practices, Turo stresses how multiple logics of capital came into play in confrontations over land use.

In attempting to explain how *fluid* economic systems hardened into one dominant form, the new historians of capitalism overlook these sorts of alternative economies comprising mixtures of practices. The networked relationships, embedded ties of material and symbolic resources, and common interest in sustainability found in the economic borderlands studied by Turo and Hyman seem, in fact, to operate much like the most advanced and innovative sectors of modern economies today. As Turo observes, the scope and significance of these older, alternative economic practices often remain hidden from public view and hidden in the historical record because the state typically only measures and records the economic activities and resource exploitation of economic elites. Instead, the older economic practices of

Nuevomexicanos and Native Americans came into public view as commodified attractions for Anglo-American tourists. After corporate capitalism uprooted their alternative economies, New Mexico built a profitable tourism industry around the crafts of Native American artisans and the pastoral rusticity of Nuevomexicanos. Both became emblems of the state's romanticized "precapitalist" past, ones that belied the actual dynamics of a now vanished economic world.

The third part, "The Licit and the Illicit," examines entrepreneurial men and women and ordinary citizens who created new opportunities and alternative paths for survival through their participation in black and gray markets. These essays do not tell a simple story of defying market controls but rather illuminate the mutual dependency of licit and illicit markets. In many instances, conventional business relied on officially prohibited commerce for revenue while the participants in shadow economies relied on the complicity of legitimate businesses for their survival. Hannah Frydman finds such complicity in her examination of classified ads for prostitutes, abortionists, and illegal or ostensibly immoral services in late nineteenth- and early twentieth-century Parisian newspapers. The market for these services depended on an interrelated series of changes in technology and business organization. Inexpensive printing led to a proliferation of low-cost newspapers, and the need for revenue led newspapers to create back pages for classifieds. The success of the classifieds hinged on one final factor: advertising copy clear enough to those who sought forbidden services yet coded enough that newspapers could still claim plausible deniability. Newspaper publishers left little to chance. Even as the front pages claimed the moral high ground by denouncing prostitution, their sensational reporting on crimes and the white slave trade taught readers how to decode the ads and discover subversive content hiding in plain sight. The market, in short, worked in chiaroscuro, blending light with dark. Indeed, trouble only arose when it became all too clear what was going on.

While Parisian newspapers and illicit entrepreneurs attempted to evade censors with a wink and a nod, the stakes were far higher for the Frenchmen and women who violated state controls on food and other essential consumer goods in Nazi-occupied France. As Kenneth Mouré's essay shows, frustrations with shortages and official market rules that set prices below producers' costs encouraged widespread participation in the black market by both French citizens and German authorities. These wartime black markets worked very much like any other, responding to supply and demand and adjusting prices accordingly. While the Vichy government took steps to punish egregious black marketeers and confiscate their unauthorized profits, it allowed low-level violations by individuals and businesses trying to provide for their families and employees. The black market was so pervasive, Mouré writes, that French citizens and Vichy authorities found it difficult to "separate 'gray' from 'black' markets, survival from profiteering, serving family and community needs from maximizing one's own personal advantage." Although many French citizens regarded their defiance of state controls as patriotic, they sharply rebuked merchants who collaborated with Nazis and profited at the expense of the public good. The "hidden" moral economy of the black market came into play when the wartime and postwar confiscation committees used their authority to exact retribution.

Mouré and Frydman, like Baker, illuminate the ways that official denotations of criminal market activities do not always align with the public's perceptions of illegitimacy. If one trades surreptitiously in defiance of a puppet regime, such as Vichy France, does that count as an "illegal" activity? If one engages in an ostensibly immoral activity to survive, is that necessarily wrong? In other cases, market activities that may be legal nonetheless provoke a deep sense of distrust. Some, for example, might accuse fortune-tellers of commodifying people's aspirations and anxieties and selling them back to the powerless and propertyless. Others, however, might see fortune-tellers as legitimate entrepreneurs who help their clients cope with the instabilities and dangers of the so-called real market.[34]

Similar questions about the boundaries between the licit and the illicit arise when the wealthy and powerful engage in formally lawful activities that provoke public suspicion and resentment. While many commonly imagine offshore tax havens as a post–World War II innovation, James Hollis and Christopher McKenna argue that the offshore economy emerged during the interwar period in reaction to wartime restrictions on trading and partnering with enemy nations and subsequent efforts to restrict capital flight and tax evasion. Whether through legal means or by illegal tax evasion, individuals and corporate executives in Britain, France, Germany, and the United States structured their financial relations to avoid the restrictions and exchange controls then being imposed throughout the world. At the same time, merchant vessels began to fly "flags of convenience" to avoid tax and maritime regulations, and the United States created "foreign trade zones" that suspended U.S. customs law, laying the foundation for the international banking facilities and export processing zones that emerged later.[35] As Hollis and

McKenna show, prior to World War II, national governments lacked the institutional capacity, and in some instances the attendant will, to effectively deal with such alternative offshore business models. As the global economy shrank between the wars, the growth of offshore economic activity helped to bolster the remaining remnants of global trade. State officials, business professionals, and corporate executives in offshore jurisdictions keenly appreciated this opportunity and deliberately amended their laws to increase their attractiveness to foreign capital. Moreover, large states sometimes permitted evasion and offshoring in the interest of gaining strategic advantage against rival states.

While much of the present volume analyzes how markets operate in capitalist societies, the essays in Part IV, "Hidden Market Spaces in Planned Economies," make the surprising case that even capitalist-type markets (ones defined by free trade and profit) could receive state sanction in socialist societies. In the 1950s and 1960s, both the Soviet Union and the People's Republic of China authorized delimited market spheres that permitted some degree of private entrepreneurship in the interest of promoting economic development, meeting basic consumer needs, and enhancing the legitimacy of the socialist state. Philip Scranton examines communist China's early experiments with markets and private enterprise before the Cultural Revolution shut them down. Eager to avoid the rigidities that had inhibited economic development in the Soviet Union, the Chinese Communist Party permitted state, individual, and private-public partnerships in retail stores, eating establishments, artisan and repair shops, and on the streets where peddlers sold their wares—the sorts of places and activities that central planning could not effectively manage. The Chinese communists were particularly careful not to eviscerate the managerial and entrepreneurial talent needed for economic development, as the Soviets had done after their revolution.

As it turns out, even the Soviet Union did not completely eschew capitalist-type markets. In her study of Soviet Jewish artels (artisans' cooperatives engaged in small-scale production), Anna Kushkova indicates that the Soviet leadership also supported market activity that could further the aims of the communist state. In the 1940s and 1950s, Soviet officials granted artels a temporary license to make a range of everyday consumer goods that the war-devastated economy could not produce. Though officially sanctioned, the artels created a quasi-autonomous refuge for private enterprise that operated in the spaces between the official and the clandestine spheres of production. Thanks to discriminatory occupational barriers that excluded Jews from work in heavy industry, the artels became an important Jewish economic niche in Moscow's suburbs. Jews also gravitated toward such low-prestige work because the artels created opportunities for otherwise banned entrepreneurship. Knowledge gained from long experience cultivating trade networks enabled Jews to effectively discern whom to trust, whom to compensate, and how to dispose of their profits without arousing suspicion. They transformed their ethnicity from a liability into an asset by forging trusted trade networks with other Jews. Like the essays by Turo and Hyman, Kushkova shows how disadvantaged minorities used kinship-based social networks to carve out hidden spaces within the dominant economy where they could make a living.

In both China and the Soviet Union, these early ventures with markets, while at odds with socialist orthodoxy, should not be dismissed as aberrations. Scranton argues that the market experiments of the 1950s and 1960s enabled Communist Party officials to create a "socialism with Chinese characteristics" that permitted flexibility in some economic sectors even as they maintained strict control over finance, agricultural purchasing, and larger industrial enterprises. As did the Jewish artels, the Chinese entrepreneurs found creative practices and work-arounds to operate capitalist enterprises in a sea of official socialism. By the 1970s, Marxist economists were arguing that markets could actually serve socialist ends, disputing the long-standing assumption that the two could never mix.[36] As these case studies show, the idea that the market inevitably leads to full-scale commodification does not account for the way markets can be deployed and embedded in different political and social systems to serve different ends.

The essays in this volume demonstrate that the conventional conception of the market as public, open, visible, and voluntary erases from view a wide array of obscured market activities that flourish within the capitalist ecosystem. The hidden economy exerts its influence by solving problems the official economy fails to address. It offers a place of escape and anonymity where creative or destructive innovation can occur away from the prying eyes of accountants, regulators, and incumbent competitors. It also enables the "losers" in the visible economy to hang on by supplying alternative means of financial survival. These cases call into question claims by such development economists as Hernando De Soto and Muhammad Yunus.[37] They argue that the poor suffer because they lack clear title to their assets and cannot turn them into capital, so greater visibility would help them get the capital they need to progress. While clear title to assets would certainly help in some cases, other times, as we have seen, the marginalized did better when they could hide from the more powerful economic interests bent on expropriating their resources. Capitalists like transparency when it can speed economic transactions, though they themselves may go into hiding when the state comes calling with taxes and regulations. As with everything else, the question of market transparency and invisibility often hinges on whose interests are at stake. To understand capitalism fully, we must continue to chart these hidden worlds.

PART I

Measuring and Unveiling Markets

Chapter 1

Lifting the Veil of Money: What Economic Indicators Hide

Eli Cook

"Climate change will affect the basic elements of life for people around the world," warned the Stern Review, a 2006 economic analysis of climate change. "Hundreds of millions of people could suffer hunger, water shortages, and coastal flooding as the world warms." In the very next paragraph of the executive summary, the report cautioned that "if we don't act, the overall costs and risks of climate change will be equivalent to losing at least 5 percent of global GDP each year, now and forever." To our modern ears, the report's easy shift from human suffering to GDP probably seems obvious, as we have grown accustomed to the notion that gross domestic product—an economic indicator that measures, in units of money, the annual amount of market goods and services produced and consumed in a given territorial area—is an accurate measure not only of the health of our economy but also the well-being of our society. Whether used in environmental studies, economic models, cost-benefit analyses, presidential tweets, corporate board rooms, World Bank memos, political stump speeches, to separate "developing" nations from "developed" ones or to determine the career path of Chinese Communist Party officials, monetized metrics like GDP have become central barometers of our everyday lives.[1] They also often serve as our modern kingmakers. When Americans were asked what the most important issue in the 2012 presidential election was, the most popular response was "the economy in general." But what is "the economy"? As many scholars have recognized, there is no "economy" without economic indicators. Ostensibly bringing the abstractions of capitalist modernity to life, such measures as GDP gave birth to the reified thing we moderns call "the economy," and it is these same economic indicators that allow us to "see" whether the economy is "sick," "healthy," "flourishing," or "shrinking."[2]

Serving as our market binoculars, whatever these monied metrics choose to enumerate becomes visible to us. Whatever they choose to ignore remains in the dark. A 2015 study by the Harvard Business School, for instance, demonstrated that a majority of Americans "vastly underestimated the levels of inequality" in the United States. This is not surprising when one looks at the economic indicators used by the mainstream media in 2015. Of the twenty-five indicators listed on the *New York Times* website at the time, not one measured wealth or income distribution. Imagine how different U.S. policy and society might have looked these past fifty years if "the economy" had been framed and measured with indebtedness, inequality, or working-poor rates rather than the usual mix of GDP growth, Dow Jones Industrial Average, and unemployment figures.[3]

Following the 2016 election, some pundits were quick to claim that the influence of such technocratic tools as economic indicators would wane in the wake of the anti-egghead wave and "postfact" sentiment that pushed Donald Trump into office. This, however, does not appear to be the case. As president, Trump has leaned hard on economic indicators to make his political case. For an alleged anti-elitist populist who supposedly spurns statistical facts and expert knowledge, Trump sure does tweet a lot of Bloomberg-console data on corporate profits, GDP, manufacturing indices, and business confidence. In his first year in office, his most recurrent tweet involved citing the stock market and how the continuous rise of corporate wealth undoubtedly reflected the equally improved state of the American people. "Since November 8th, Election Day," Trump tweeted out in typical fashion on July 3, 2017, "the Stock Market has posted $3.2 trillion in Gains and consumer confidence is at a 15 year high. Jobs!"[4]

Trump had good reason to turn to the likes of the Dow Jones or S&P 500 to prove his success as president: the stock market is essentially a sociopath. Unless social justice or human rights affects corporate bottom lines, "the market" does not usually care about them. The ethical controversies surrounding the Trump administration's actions regarding Russia, health care, race relations, sexual harassment, environmental deregulation, or immigration have made Trump one of the least popular presidents of all time. Yet these very issues become almost entirely hidden from sight if one uses GDP or the New York Stock Exchange to gauge the success of U.S. society. One poignant example of the Dow's propensity for obscuring some of capitalism's biggest blemishes occurred on June 1, 2017. This was the day Trump announced he was withdrawing from the Paris climate accord designed to slow global warming and hopefully save the planet. The backlash against this decision was immediate and widespread. That day, the Dow Jones Industrial Average went up 136 points. A few months later, GDP estimates for that quarter were revised higher, thus matching the highest growth rates since early 2015.[5]

Regardless of whether economic indicators are wielded by populist know-nothings or wonkish neoliberals, they provide a rare lens through which normal, workaday people might catch a seemingly objective glimpse of the broader economic and social forces that shape their lives. As such, they have proven to have immense social, cultural, and political power in large part because these measures place certain economic phenomena on a pedestal while concealing other aspects of the human condition behind a veil. What is more, in setting not only the benchmarks of society but also the economic frame of reference for its citizens, economic indicators—much like opinion surveys—can often dictate to "average Americans" whether their own personal financial suffering or success is "normal." If you feel as if your wages have stagnated, yet the media mostly ignores inequality figures while reminding you that "the economy" continues to "recover," you might very well reach the implicit conclusion that the main problem isn't with the economy—it is with you.[6]

The incredible power of money-based economic indicators to accentuate certain aspects of everyday life while downplaying others is a relatively novel development in human history. In his portrayal of the English working class in the eighteenth century, E. P. Thompson depicted how rioting peasants would oftentimes "set the price" of bread in instances where they believed they were being overcharged. Refusing to pay the merchant, miller, or baker what they thought to be exorbitant prices, the angry crowd would take the loaves of bread by force—but they would not steal them. Instead, they would leave behind what they felt was a fair price. While Thompson stressed that custom played an important role in this "moral economy," peasants did not use force every time prices rose. Along with notions of economic justice and tradition, there was a second trigger to these riots: peasants could lift up the bread market's veil of money and see what was really going on behind the scenes. "The poor had their own sources of information," Thompson explains. "They worked on the docks. They moved the barges on the canals. They drove the carts and manned the toll-gates. They worked in the granaries and the mills. They often knew the local facts far better than the gentry." As Thompson notes, peasants experienced the production chain of bread in their day-to-day lives. They could recognize instances where some link in the chain—be it the merchants, bakers, or millers—was attempting to grab a larger piece of the pie.[7]

By the mid-nineteenth century, however, few people in industrializing nations such as the United States were still able to peek into the proverbial village granary as the English peasants had done a century before to view the economic mechanisms that shaped their lives. In an attempt to gain control of their elusively interdependent environment in the midst of rampant market revolution, humans now living amid capitalism were forced to rely heavily on government-collected statistics that could relay information about economic activities that occurred outside their local communities. By the turn of the twentieth century, economic indicators had emerged as the main window through which Americans came to understand and subsequently try to take control of their social and economic world. "The economy" was emerging—and economic indicators were its maker. To see the economic pie, these Americans would have to look at a pie chart.[8]

Such economic indicators, however, can never reflect all the goings-on of a society. Choices must be made concerning what to explicitly measure—and what to implicitly ignore. In this chapter, I will try to grasp what exactly modern economic indicators hid in the mid-nineteenth century when monied metrics first took hold of the American imagination. By tracing the historical origins of these measures, placing them in their proper political, economic, and social context, and illuminating what alternative forms of quantification were cast to the side, one can uncover not only what these statistics disclosed but also what they downplayed.[9]

I will focus here only on the rise of economic indicators in the mid-nineteenth century northern United States. Two clarifications regarding this choice are in order: First, while I do believe that Americans have tended to have more of a penchant for pricing progress than other cultures or societies, I am not arguing here for any kind of American exceptionalism. The rise of economic indicators was hardly a uniquely American phenomenon. Second, I have chosen not to focus on the American South in this chapter not because elite Southerners did not share elite Northerners' enthusiasm for economic indicators but precisely because they very much did. The intertwined history of economic quantitation, human capitalization, and American slavery is simply too complex and important to cover in such a brief piece. I will only note here that in the eighteenth-century North—as well as the South—it was the enslavement of African Americans that inspired the creation of the first proto-GDP income metrics in U.S. history, thus setting crucial precedents for the future.[10]

In examining the rise of economic indicators in the second half of the nineteenth century in the northern United States, I argue that there are three main aspects of everyday life that economic indicators have tended to hide. The first was the non-pecuniary sides of the human condition that cannot be measured in dollars and cents. The second was the political goals, ideological leanings, class interests, and cultural values of the white, upper-class men (and they were almost entirely white, upper-class men) who developed, lobbied for, and institutionalized economic indicators. The third was closely related to the second, but in our own "Age of Inequality" and the "1 percent," it deserves its own category—the tendency of most nineteenth-century economic indicators to obscure inequality and great wealth disparities. Let us begin our statistical journey with the inability of nineteenth-century economic indicators to count that which cannot be priced.

What Money Can't Measure: The Fall of Moral Statistics

The United States underwent a statistical revolution in the mid-nineteenth century. In the early decades of the century, beginning around the mid-1820s, most Americans tended to turn to a collection of figures known as "moral statistics" to gauge the well-being and progress of their society. These metrics—which began to be collected by the federal census as early as the 1830s—measured such things as health, life expectancy, insanity, pauperism, prostitution, education, literacy, libraries, crime, incarceration, temperance, and disability. By the mid-1850s, however, a quantitative upheaval was underway as moral statistics began to take a back seat to an alternative form of social measurement that measured the progress of the United States by calculating the income-generating capacities of the American people in units of money—based on newly collected data from the groundbreaking 1850 census.

Moral statistics were not exactly innocent and should not be romanticized. Created by a nascent class of bourgeois elites in industrializing towns across the Northeast and Midwest, these figures were often wielded in Jacksonian America as disciplinary instruments of paternalistic social control designed to keep intransigent laborers (especially immigrants) in line. Nevertheless, these figures focused squarely on the physical, social, mental, and even spiritual well-being of the American people. They did not shy away from depicting the uglier sides of capitalist development, be it increased poverty, prostitution, incarceration, or mental stress. In focusing on the human condition, these figures differentiated themselves from future economic indicators that would treat the American people as income-generating means to a wealth-accumulating end. For better or for worse, moral statistics placed people at the center of their statistical vision. Their units of measure were bodies and minds—not dollars and cents. To gain a better sense of what became hidden in the turn to money-based indicators, we must, therefore, first take a closer look at three of the leading moral statistics of the 1830s and 1840s: pauperism, prostitution, and mental health.[11]

In 1836, pauperism statistics appeared for the first time in the *American Almanac*, the leading statistical gazetteer of the day. The initial figures the almanac cited were from Europe. By 1838, however, the almanac had added the number of U.S. paupers to the statistical tables it collected on each state, reaching the conclusion that "paupers in all the States are few, compared with the number found in most European countries." Such pauperism and poverty statistics quickly became a leading measure of societal well-being in Jacksonian America. In 1834, a popular labor newspaper edited by George H. Evans, of the Workingmen's Party, pointed to the degradation of U.S. society by showing how in one U.S. city of 80,000 people there were more than 5,000 paupers. For men like Evans, embedded in this view of pauperism statistics was a proto-Rawlsian theory of justice: a society should not be judged not by its aggregated wealth but rather by the fate of its poorest denizens. In other cases, pauperism figures became a euphemism for what many Americans viewed as the exploitative nature of English capitalism. "I should be very unwilling to make the British Government a model for our legislation in republican America," a young James Buchanan declared on the floor of Congress in 1839. "Where is the country beneath the sun in which pauperism prevails to such a fearful extent?"[12]

These pauperism statistics would often detail the perceived causes of poverty. An 1845 report of New York's secretary of state based on data collected by the various superintendents of the poor argued that pauperism was caused by "intemperance," "idleness," "idiocy," "lunacy," "blindness," "lameness," "sickness," "decrepitude," "old age," "destitution," "misfortune," "mute[ness]," "orphan[ed]," "illegitimate," "abandoned," "debauchery," "total debauchery," and "cause not given." Revealing the disciplinary goals behind many pauperism figures, such classification practices were often used to divide the "deserving" from the "undeserving" poor. The serial do-gooder and moral reformer Lemuel Shattuck divided the poor in such a manner in his 1845 city census of Boston, classifying paupers according to whether they could work or were "unable to labor." By the end of the 1840s, this approach was reaching the federal government as one Boston Brahmin wrote a letter to the Senate Census Committee suggesting that a table separating paupers with "physical disability" from those with "bad habits" should be added to the 1850 census.[13]

Another popular moral statistic was prostitution. A "census of prostitutes" became a frequent occurrence in cities such as New York, Cincinnati, and Philadelphia, whether they were carried out by government institutions such as the New York Board of Aldermen, moral reform organizations such as the Magdalen society, magazines such as the *Journal of Public Morals*, or crusading individuals such as John McDowall. For many elites, prostitution figures were viewed simply as indicators of "licentiousness" and "moral depravity," and the poor, working-class women were blamed for having "fallen." Other Americans, however, viewed prostitution as a metric that revealed structural social problems. One writer for *The Sun* newspaper linked sexual exploitation to economic exploitation, noting that the increase in prostitution was due to the low wages of female servants and the "unjust arrangement of remuneration for services performed." In *New York Naked*, George G. Foster voiced the same conclusion: "Female prostitution is the direct result of the inadequate compensation for female labor."[14]

The idea that prostitution could serve as an indicator of societal well-being led some reformers to greatly expand the scope of inquiry, in hopes of uncovering the reasons behind the disturbing social phenomenon. William Sanger's mammoth *History of Prostitution* included data on prostitutes' health, literacy rates, age, life expectancy, place of birth, average weekly earnings, trade or calling prior to prostitution, and even their father's occupation or business. Discovering that prostitution was the "only means of support" for 85 percent of the women he spoke with, Sanger turned prostitution statistics into an economic indicator of labor exploitation while placing the brunt of the blame on the importation of European forms of capitalist social relations to the United States. "Study the moral statistics of any of the manufacturing towns in Great Britain or on the Continent of Europe," he concluded, "and the same results are presented, but in more alarming degree." Yet here too, one must be careful not to overlook the underlying ideological world view of the middle-class men who often carried out such studies. As Michael Zakim has argued, talk of prostitution in Jacksonian America could also serve to implicitly legitimize, or at least underscore, the economic exploitation of working-class men.[15]

Last but not least, insanity statistics were also a central component of the moral statistician's toolbox. Mental health was a hot-button issue in Jacksonian America, as the establishment of dozens of asylums in this era would suggest. These figures packed a powerful punch in large part because there was widespread agreement in this era that mental illness was a by-product of the mental stress that accompanied the rise of market relations and the demise of traditional hierarchical societies. This reasoning caused quite a stir around the 1840 census in which it appeared at first as if free blacks in the North had far higher rates of insanity than enslaved blacks in the South. These figures were soon to be discovered as erroneous, but before they were, northern physicians such as Edward Jarvis viewed them as important indicators of the North's market revolution. While slaves did not supposedly need to worry about their own economic survival, Jarvis argued, free blacks were saddled with the "responsibilities which the free, self-thinking and self-acting enjoy and sustain."[16]

Psychological indicators of capitalist anxiety became especially prominent following the Panic of 1837, an event whose very name hints at the mental anguish that accompanied a sudden contraction in output. Samuel Woodward, a leading expert on insanity statistics, concluded that the United States was fourth among all the countries in the world in the proportion of lunatics because of "overtrading, debt, bankruptcy, sudden reverses, disappointed hopes." Jarvis again argued for similar causes. "In this country," Jarvis noted, "where no son is necessarily confined to the work or employment of his father, but all the field of labor, of profit, or of honor are open to whomever will put on the harness, all are invited to join the strife for that which may be gained by each."[17]

Pauperism, prostitution, insanity.—all three of these leading statistical indicators measured important aspects of the human condition in a capitalist society that could not be measured in dollars and cents. Even the biggest capitalists of the age thought this to be true. Horrified by the social dislocation he witnessed during a visit to manufacturing towns in England, the Lowell, Massachusetts, industrialist Nathan Appleton believed that social progress could not be measured in money, as it tended to obscure the true state of the poor. "'Tis true that in this country money will purchase a thousand conveniences and attentions we are without in America," he noted in his diary while in England, "but as these are in great measure the consequence of the debasement of the lower classes of society—for the happiness of our country at large I could wish it long without them." Small wonder than that Lowell's own textile factories often used an array of paternalist moral statistics to track, discipline, but also try to protect from "debasement" the women who toiled in their mills.[18]

Further evidence of this Jacksonian-era pushback against the pricing of everyday life can also be found in the sudden explosion in the use of the word *priceless* in the 1830s and 1840s, a linguistic development that reflected the widely held belief in the age of moral statistics that some things could not— and should not—be measured in money. Addressing a crowd of New York City Jacksonian Democrats in 1838 who feared that market relations were impeding their republican independence, one labor activist used the term in typical fashion when he rhetorically asked his fellow workers whether "the priceless legacy of a Jefferson [would] be wrested from us." Seeking to bracket off certain pockets of life from the cash nexus, the term was also used to frequently describe women, childhood, suffrage, democracy, virtue, love, and—especially by abolitionists of the era—human bodies. Clearly, the term struck a nerve during an era of market revolution. According to one historical database, the frequency with which the word appeared in published texts quadrupled from 1810 to 1840. According to another, the term appeared 29 times in American newspapers between the years 1805 and 1815 and 668 times between the years 1835 and 1845. Between 1815 and 1825, not a single article in the *New Hampshire Sentinel* contained the word *priceless*. In the 1840s, the word appears 21 times.[19]

Yet as U.S. capitalism—especially long-distance capital investment in real estate, railroads, banks, and government bonds—ramped up in the mid-nineteenth century, unpriceable moral statistics began to lose their grasp on elite U.S. culture in the North. Many of the social ills they measured would soon become buried under a steady flow of dollar-denominated statistics. A new national investor class was emerging that, unlike the small-town bourgeoisie of the Jacksonian era, did not take interest in the number of paupers in Sheboygan or prostitutes in Toledo. Coming to view their society and its inhabitants as a series of income-generating investments, what mattered most to these men of capital was the American people's capacity to generate money.

The Men Behind the Numbers

Due in large part to an increase in capital investment and an intensification of market relations, economic indicators really took off in the years leading up to the Civil War. One of the first sparks that lit this flame came in the form of Hinton Helper's best-selling antislavery book *The Impending Crisis in the South*, which was published in 1857 thanks to the generous support of New York City's leading businessmen. In Jacksonian America, abolitionists had often used moral statistics to demonstrate both the social backwardness of the South and the terrible suffering of the slaves. Helper, on the other hand, turned to a series of monetized wealth, income, and output statistics to prove that the North was by far the more advanced society. Explaining in his preface that he did not intend to "display any special friendliness to the blacks" but rather focus only on the "economic aspects [of slavery] as regards the whites," Helper contended that slavery should end not because it was immoral and inhumane but rather because it was inefficient and unproductive. Seeking to show that the United States could get more bang for its buck under a system of free labor, Helper's first chapter compared the "progress and prosperity" of the North and the South by tabulating the cash value of agricultural produce that both regions had extracted from the earth. In so doing, he calculated that in 1850 the North had produced $351,709,703 of agricultural goods, the South only $306,927,067. Throughout the rest of the book, Helper supplied a steady stream of similar progress-pricing indicators.[20]

Other men in the North during this era were also coming to measure the well-being of U.S. society in accordance to its capacity to produce income and increase wealth. "The prosperity of any people, the comforts they enjoy, and their wealth and power, depend entirely on their productive industry," declared Ezra Seamen, the chief clerk of the first comptroller of the U.S Treasury, in his 1852 book *Essays on the Progress of Nations*, which would go on to see numerous future editions. Now able, thanks to new data collected by the 1850 census, to add together the total dollar value of such products as cotton, fabrics, hats, boots, pork, beef, wheat, rye, milk, cream, and eggs, Seaman priced U.S. "prosperity" at $865,269,561, or $59 per person. An 1856 article in *Hunt's Merchants' Magazine* went even further by pricing the social gains from educating New York children at $500 million. "The brain is . . . an agricultural product of great commercial investment," explained the author of the article, and "the great problem of political economy" was "how most economically to produce the best brain and render it most profitable."[21]

No antebellum periodical did more to push the gospel of statistical growth more than *Hunt's Merchants' Magazine* and its longtime founder and editor Freeman Hunt. Proclaiming that his goal was to "construct the Science of Business," by the 1850s, Hunt had filled the pages of his journal—the first truly national business magazine of its kind in the United States—with an array of economic charts, graphs, tables, and statistics designed to help businessmen best allocate their capital and maximize their investments. In these years, *Hunt's* also became a key platform for businessmen to lobby for the benefits of unbridled capitalist development while proving that it was commerce and capital, not agriculture and labor, that made the United States flourish. Hunt also taught his audience that money could serve as the ultimate measure of not only commodities but also the self. "In a republic," Hunt declared in his self-help business manual fittingly titled *Worth and Wealth*, "there remains but one basis of social distinction, namely, wealth. . . . In society at large, gradations of social position are measured by stock-certificates, rent-rolls and bank-accounts." Sure enough, each weekly edition of *Hunt's* was filled with various stock, manufacturing, real-estate, and banking statistics to allow U.S. capitalists to constantly track what they and their investments were worth.[22]

Along with Freeman Hunt, another leading disseminator of economic indicators in this era was Thomas Kettell—a fellow financial journalist who wrote the "money column" in the *New York Herald*. In this capacity, Kettell—like Hunt—educated businessmen in the importance of using economic data when investing their capital or lobbying the government. As one nineteenth-century Wall Street investor later recalled, it was Kettell "who gave that journal [the *Herald*] a reputation among financial men." Kettell became increasingly known for using monied metrics in much of his writings—including his strident defense of slavery and its great profitability. Particularly fond of per capita wealth statistics, Kettell would frequently use such figures in a before-and-after comparison to prove the benefits of a bank, railroad, or cotton plantation to a community. "The railroads of Massachusetts have cost $50,000,000, and the wealth of the state has increased $300,000,000 or six times the amount in ten years," Kettell gushed in a typical article. "That is to say, from the land at Plymouth to 1840, two hundred years elapsed, in which the wealth of Massachusetts reached $299,878,327. Ten years of railroads have added a sum equal to the whole results of those two hundred years. Is that not a rail-road pace?"[23]

The railroad revolution played a central role in the sudden rise of economic indicators in the 1850s, a decade that saw a sharp uptick in railway investment and construction. As William Cronon has recognized, railroads "generated vast new quantities of statistics which themselves helped revolutionize the American economy by making possible increasingly intricate analyses of trade and production." No one took advantage of the railroad's ability to produce market statistics more that Henry Varnum Poor, editor of the *American Railroad Journal*. A magazine devoted to providing financial statistics to help investors decide in which lines they should invest their monies, the *Journal* was chock-full of data on the railroads' freight traffic, operating costs, net earnings, and dividend rates. Reflecting how elites of the era were shifting much of their investment portfolio to railroad securities, Poor's subscription list increased from 12,000 in 1849 to 30,000 in 1854.[24]

Northern capital's need for information regarding their own specific investments, as well as broader economic conditions, brought economic indicators to the fore in the 1850s. Yet—and this is a crucial point—they did not remain solely in the sphere of business. Men like Helper, Seaman, Kettell, Poor, and Hunt all utilized market statistics—particularly economic output, growth, and income figures—not only as indicators of profit and gain but also as markers of progress and well-being. Transitioning from a specific profit analysis on certain railroads to a far more general statement regarding national wealth and well-being, Henry Varnum Poor came to believe that "the railroad system may be regarded as the barometer of the entire industrial system." While admitting that he dealt "with but one subject or department of national industry or life," Poor argued that this one "department, however, goes far to include all as the greater part of the products of our industries are moved from producer to consumer by our railroad. The amount of such movement is consequently a pretty accurate measure of the productiveness of the industries of the country, of the progress made in them from year to year and of the national wealth." In similar fashion, while Helper and Kettell were polar opposites when it came to the question of slavery, both men wielded wealth and income data to demonstrate not only profit—but also progress.[25]

These economic indicators appeared before the American people as objective fact. Hidden beneath these figures, however, lay the subjective interests, world views, and values of those who created them. By briefly tracing the lives of the antebellum men who stood behind the vast amount of economic data that began to circulate throughout the northern United States in the mid-nineteenth century, we can once again lift the veil of money from economic indicators and witness the often overlooked social and power relations that undergirded them. The white, elite men who stood as the vanguard of economic quantification made sure to frame their statistical data as measures of collective, national progress. In reality, however, they were often universalizing specific class interests. Measuring prosperity according to corporate income, industrial output, or per capita wealth made a good deal of sense for the United States' upper classes, since they were usually the ones who possessed the stocks, owned the factories, and held the wealth.

Deeming the maximizing of market output as the main goal of U.S. society and life, as well as the ultimate "barometer" of both personal and social success, was not an impartial assumption but rather a deeply cultural and political one. While such attitudes may have seemed obvious to businessmen, it was hardly that for the men and woman who actually built the railroads, paid the rent, or worked in factories. "The real and ultimate value of [manufacturing] to the true prosperity and abiding good of the commonwealth," Boston labor activists would note in their typical rejection of the pricing of progress, "can only be learned, by placing money in one scale, and man in the other." The cultural values and class interests of these labor leaders led them to ideological assumptions that were diametrically opposed to the likes of Helper, Hunt, or Kettell. "Although manufacturing undoubtedly increases the material wealth of the nation," they noted, "it does it, as now managed, at the expense of its manufacturing people."[26]

Crucially, however, the interests, values, and ideology of the elite men who gave economic indicators life remained hidden from sight. As a result, monied metrics often served as stealth ideological carriers, subtly injecting certain political views, racial prejudices, class interests, or cultural preferences wherever they might be implemented. The more these statistics circulated, the more the hidden world view that shaped these statistics circulated with them, reproducing the ideology that had first given them life. The more these seemingly apolitical figures were used to value U.S. society, the more the hidden capitalism that undergirded these figures exerted social power and became cultural common sense.

Taking a final look at where these 1850s economic statistics came from and how they were collected offers further evidence of how such figures concealed class dynamics in particular. In 1851, a group of wealthy New York businessmen founded the American Geographical and Statistical Society (AGSS). In the upcoming years, it became the meeting point for data-minded businessmen. The membership list reveals a who's who of midcentury U.S. business and media elites and includes not only the likes of New York merchants such as Henry E. Pierrepont, Alexander Cotheal, Henry Grinnell, and S. DeWitt Bloodgood or newspaper editors such as the *New York Times'* Henry Raymond, the *New York Evening Post's* Hiram Barney, and the *New York Sun's* Charles Dana but also the top business journalists in the country such as Edward Mansfield, Freeman Hunt, and Henry Varnum Poor.[27]

AGSS members, many of whom were heavily invested in western railroads, would come to society meetings to hear talks titled "Statistics of Agriculture," "Growth, Trade and Manufacture of Cotton," "Railroads from the Atlantic to the Pacific Ocean," or "Statistics and Geography of Iron." This, however, was not the only service supplied by the AGSS. Perhaps more importantly, it also served as a powerful statistical lobbying firm. For example, it managed to persuade the New York state legislature to add industrial and agriculture statistics to the 1855 state census. Judging by the society's library catalog from 1857, which is filled with an assortment of novel statistical reports by banking comptrollers, canal commissioners, and state treasury departments, it appears that the AGSS had a great deal of success convincing other state governments (especially midwestern states such as Wisconsin and Ohio) to increase their data-collecting capacities. Along with the 1850 federal census (whose designer, Archibald Russell, was a founding member and leading activist of the AGSS) this government-collected data enabled the rise of economic indicators in this era. But you would not, of course, know any of this just by looking at the statistics themselves.[28]

Erasing the 1 Percent

Charles Barzilai Spahr was a PhD student at Columbia University in the early 1880s. In his dissertation, later published as a book titled *An Essay on the Present Distribution of Wealth in the United States*, Spahr used tax data to measure U.S. wealth inequality. "Seven-eighths of the families [in the United States] hold but one-eighth of the national wealth," Spahr concluded, "while one per cent of the families hold more than the remaining ninety-nine." More than a century before economist Thomas Piketty's groundbreaking study of inequality, Spahr had discovered the "1 percent." Unfortunately, unlike Piketty, almost no one ever heard of Charles Barzilai Spahr.[29] While a few socialists would go on to cite his book in the early twentieth century, his findings went mostly unnoticed. A nasty review by the Columbia professor Richmond Mayo-Smith in a leading academic journal helps explain not only Spahr's historical obscurity but also how mainstream academic economists actively came to marginalize economic indicators that measured not only the size of the economic pie but also how it was sliced.[30]

An enthusiastic advocate of U.S. industrialization, Mayo-Smith had written his own book on economic statistics in 1888, filling it mostly with indicators that made capitalism look good. He made clear that he did not support statistical investigations of wealth distribution, since "the only share of the product that we can follow out statistically is wages," and "all attempts to get at profits by estimating the total value of the output and comparing with the sum spent on raw materials and on wages are fallacious because they do not take into account risk." Unwilling to measure inequality, Mayo-Smith criticized Spahr for collecting such figures. "Having shown that property and incomes are unequally distributed and that (in his opinion) the inequality is increasing," Mayo-Smith wrote, "Dr. Spahr seems to think that his task is ended. But that is only the beginning. The real question is whether such a concentration of wealth is not a good thing for the whole community." Mayo-Smith went on to suggest that cost-of-living statistics served as a far better benchmark of social progress than wealth distribution, since "the happiness of individuals is measured not according to their ownership of property . . . but according to their command of the enjoyments of life."[31]

It is not a coincidence that Mayo-Smith pointed to cost-of-living figures as the ultimate measures of social progress. By the end of the Gilded Age, such "standard-of-living" indicators had joined the likes of the Dow Jones Industrial Average (invented in 1889), market output, and aggregated wealth figures as the premier economic indicators in the United States. In fact, the goal of the largest statistical project ever undertaken by the U.S. federal government in the nineteenth century was to calculate the historical "cost of living" in the United States by comparing the wages of workers across the century with the costs of basic consumption goods. Initiated by (millionaire) Senator Nelson Aldrich, head of the Senate Finance Committee in the early 1890s, government bureaucrats were instructed "to ascertain through accurate and adequate statistics of prices and wages, the changes which have taken place in the condition, as shown by the relative purchasing power of their earnings, of the great mass of people in the country for the half century which has just closed." Imagining Americans—not only in 1890 but also in

1840—strictly as market consumers and wage laborers, the basic premise of the Senate Finance Committee's "Aldrich Report" was that in order to measure the prosperity of the American people, all one had to do was compare wages to cost of living.[32]

Much like the wealth and income figures of the 1850s, the cost-of-living figures of the 1890s presented themselves as not only objective measures of progress but also obvious ones at that. "The relative standard of life at the different periods," the final Aldrich report on cost of living explained as if it were obvious, "can, of course, be obtained only from a combination of prices with average earnings or wages." Yet these economic indicators, like wealth and income figures, also hid a slew of class interests, cultural values, and ideological assumptions. For example, in choosing to measure the social "condition" by calculating whether wages purchased more consumer goods than before, the Aldrich Report reflected the consumerist turn that had overtaken Gilded Age thought. In contrast to the producerist theories that had previously dominated the nineteenth century, the Aldrich Report cared little about whether U.S. laborers had control over their work breaks or daily output, whether they were bosses or bossed, whether they received a full return on the fruits of their labor, or whether wage labor was even a legitimate institution in a nation that placed the ownership of property at the center of its theories of freedom. Rather, the report was animated by a rapidly growing consumerism that deemed the good life—just as Mayo-Smith had done in his critique of Spahr—simply as the ability of permanent wage laborers to consume more goods for less money.[33]

In this final section, I want to briefly focus on one specific aspect that these cost-of-living figures hid and what Spahr had tried in vain to bring to the fore: the prickly issue of economic distribution. Another hidden subjective assumption implicit in the Aldrich Report was the construction of a conceptual barrier between labor and capital. In U.S. producerist thought, wages and profits flowed out of the same pool of wealth created during the production process. According to this zero-sum world view, wages and profits were in an inverse relation to each other, since capitalists accumulated wealth by expropriating much of the surplus. To determine whether wage levels were just or fair, therefore, required an examination of profit rates as well as wage rates. In the Aldrich Report, however, capital was all but invisible. By examining the hundreds of pages of wage tables in the Aldrich Report one can glean a great deal of insight into labor costs—but little about capital gains.

Much like Spahr, other Gilded Age activists also failed in their attempts to use statistical data to raise awareness about rising economic inequality. Taking a careful look at Boston savings bank records in 1871, the labor-led Massachusetts Bureau of Labor Statistics discovered that over 50 percent of the deposits were for more than three hundred dollars—a sum that clearly no wage laborer could have attained. Aggregating these mysterious deposits, the bureau calculated that one-seventh of the savings accounts in the state held around half of the total wealth deposited in the banks. I believe this to be the first modern example of inequality statistics in U.S. history. It was also the last report that these bureau heads would ever make. After Boston businessmen pressured the legislature, they were let go and the bureau was put in the hands of Carroll Wright, who went on to be the most important labor statistician in U.S. history. He explored many aspects of industrial life, but inequality was never one of them.[34]

Moving into the early 1880s, the Knights of Labor statistician Leona Barry sought to use data to measure not only gender inequality but also class exploitation. Poverty-stricken, Barry had gotten a job at a hosiery mill, where she made eleven cents a day. It was while working at the mill that she joined the Knights of Labor. She was soon made head of the new Woman's Work Department. Her main mission was to traverse the country, collecting statistics on women's labor that would not only reveal "the abuses to which our sex is subjected by unscrupulous employers" but also the need "of equal pay for equal work." Unlike cost-of-living statistics, Barry's reports focused not only on labor's wages but also on employer's profits, which enabled her to measure the level of inequality and exploitation at the U.S. workplace. "The contractor who employed five operatives made 30 cents per unit, or 1.50 a day," she noted in one example, "while each worker received only 30 cents for the entire day's work." By the 1890s, however, the Knights of Labor had crumbled and Barry was forced to return to the factory, never to collect inequality statistics again.[35]

In the 1890s, Henry George's followers tried to raise the issue of inequality once more. Two pro-George activists from the Saint Louis Single Tax Club led the charge, circulating thousands of petitions demanding that the census acquiesce to their demands to measure the distribution of debt in the United States. "There is a growing feeling that the farmers and other wealth producers do not receive an equitable return for their toil . . . that 95 percent of the wealth is the hands of less than 30,000 persons; and that the sturdy self-respecting farmer is becoming the American peasant." The petition went viral. Within a few months, the census was flooded by hundreds of letters from across the country requesting that the demands made by the Saint Louis men be met. While some small victories were had, the government never turned to the measure of income inequality.[36]

Reclaiming the Priceless

These nineteenth-century activists have been all but forgotten and their ideas for alternative forms of economic and social quantification mostly marginalized. As with the case of moral statistics, I tell their stories here to stress not only what past economic indicators overlooked or obscured but also to emphasize what still remains hidden in our modern mix of GDP, Dow Jones, and cost-of-living statistics. Be it income inequality, gig-economy anxiety, debilitating poverty, gender exploitation, or severe indebtedness, these are the types of statistical measures that Americans today rarely hear on their daily commute, see on the nightly news, or read in presidential tweets. In an era when stock market indices have never been higher, unemployment is at an all-time low, and growth estimates have been trending upward—yet 72,0000 Americans overdosed in 2017, the life-expectancy gap between rich and poor keeps getting disturbingly wider, and debt per household is back to pre-2008 levels—we need to recall and reclaim these forgotten nineteenth-century metrics more than ever as "the economy" keeps "recovering" from the Great Recession but the average U.S. family does not.[37]

Telling the history of such alternative measures of society can also serve as an important reminder that nineteenth-century Americans did not simply accept the pricing of progress with open arms. The term *priceless* took off in the age of moral statistics as Jacksonian Americans pushed back against the pricing of everyday life. This trend only ramped up in the Gilded Age and Progressive Era, as many Americans continued to challenge the notion that everything could or should be measured in units of money. Yet by the end of the Progressive Era, as the Google Ngram below shows, the use of the term *priceless* began to rapidly decline.

While Ngram is not without its faults, I nevertheless believe this chart helps us see the hegemonic rise of economic indicators and the pricing of everyday life in the twentieth century. (The term *the almighty dollar* shows a similar rise-and-fall pattern.) As monied metrics rose, the idea that some things should not be measured in money fell. While Americans in the nine-

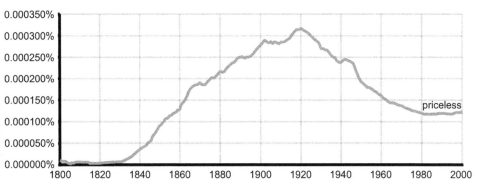

Figure 1.1. Google Ngram of the word *Priceless*, 1800–2000.

teenth century still challenged monied metrics by demanding that certain pockets of society be shielded by the cash nexus and remain "priceless," such pushback seems to have dwindled in the 1920s—just as such corporate-backed institutions as the National Bureau of Economic Research were inventing the national income accounting techniques that would, in time, lead to the epoch-making invention of GDP.[38]

To conclude, in briefly historicizing social measurement and the rise of economic indicators in the nineteenth-century American North, my hope is that this chapter can serve as a usable past that will help us reclaim the priceless, thus not only pushing back against the pricing of everyday life but also pushing the many hidden sides of our current capitalism and its discontents into the light.

Chapter 2

Accounting for Reproductive Labor: Feminist Economists and the Construction of Social Knowledge on Rural Women in the Global South

Eileen Boris

In 2013, the Conference of International Labour Statisticians recognized unpaid reproductive labor as "work" in recommending the inclusion of "own-use production" in official statistics. It offered a wide definition of such labor as work "that produces goods and services for household consumption," such as "collecting firewood and fuel, fetching water, cooking, cleaning and also providing care for children, the elderly and other dependents." Under these criteria, women toiled longer than their male counterparts everywhere, with women in "developing" countries working three hours more than men.[1] This recalibration of what constitutes work moves toward fulfilling the "long-term aim" of feminist economists some forty years ago "to abolish the separation of the so-called 'productive' work from 'reproductive' work, eventually resulting in defining 'housework' as work."[2]

This chapter examines the pioneering thought of feminist economists associated with the International Labour Organization (ILO), whose investigations on rural women and development in the Global South in the 1970s conceptualized reproductive labor—that is, daily activities like cooking and care that not only sustain people but socialize them—as essential to economic life. In the process, these researchers and others like them helped shape the policy-making agendas of international agencies, in this case that of the ILO, the specialized agency of the United Nations devoted to work, labor, and employment.[3] Development planners long had overlooked the economic value of women's work because women's uncompensated family and farming labor lay outside of the GNP and other statistical measures. Development programs that aimed to reduce poverty by increasing employment and accelerating economic growth often intensified gender inequalities and the heavy burdens that reproductive labor imposed on women without proper resources, like cook stoves and water, to perform such tasks. Eager to bring women's hidden economic activities to light and better understand the effects of industrial development on rural women's lives, feminist economists called for disaggregating the household and counting unpaid family and subsistence labor as work. While the more radical among them argued that capitalist accumulation increased women's domestic workload, most agreed that development gave wage-earning men new ways of asserting dominance over women through control of family income. Gender equity demanded a new approach.[4]

Defining work never was a semantic enterprise. As Eli Cook emphasizes, the construction of economic indicators embodied gendered, class, and other assumptions about worth. The very concepts of productive and unproductive labor, use, and exchange value contain judgments beyond the economy, even as such terms seek to explain the replacement of labor power or the accumulation of profit. Household labor, we might say, was hidden in a double sense: behind the doors of domiciles or the threshold separating household from street and apart from recognized outputs. Making people through making goods for family consumption rendered the productive qualities of household labor invisible. Accounting for such labor denaturalizes—indeed, historicizes—much of the work undertaken by women across time and space.[5]

The ILO was not the only UN agency seeking to generate income from women's reproductive labors, but it proved a generative space in the late 1970s into the 1980s. The UN Food and Agricultural Organization (FAO), for example, provided food for family consumption if women would use family lands to produce for the market as part of its World Food Programme (WFP).[6] But the architects of the ILO's World Employment Programme (WEP)were skeptical of such exchanges as a form of welfare. They insisted on employment as the surest path to ending poverty. The problem came from undermining women's traditional subsistence labor, thus deteriorating their economic position and status even further by encouraging sectors dominated by men.

Documenting the work of poor women was the task of a related ILO unit: the Programme on Rural Women. The effort to decolonize knowledge distinguished the program within the ILO, an institution that generated "facts" about the world of work. The program would enlist rural women and scholars from the Global South to ask women about their conditions and then seek improvement through women's organizations. Exemplifying such collaboration, the German scholar Maria Mies, with local assistants Lalita and Krishna Kumair, captured the predicament of Indian lace makers who made luxury goods for the Western market at pay levels that deepened their impoverishment but maintained their status as housewives. Program-sponsored reports, like Mies's pathbreaking *The Lace Makers of Narsapur*, bolstered claims for treating home-based laborers as workers.[7]

ILO Development Feminists

The Programme on Rural Women offered an institutional context for reconstituting the subject of development. Through research, project construction and evaluation, training, and other assistance activities, it sought to counter impediments toward women's advancement. The program formed a key component of the ILO's response to the 1975 UN World Conference on Women, particularly the "Employment and Related Economic Roles" section of the *Plan of Action* that included the increased participation of rural women in national development.[8] Its immediate genesis came from implementing the WEP, which cast the labor of women as central to obtaining "basic needs." Meeting basic needs involved the provision of "certain minimum requirements of a family for private consumption: adequate food, shelter and clothing, as well as certain household equipment and furniture" and "essential services provided by and for the community at large, such as safe drinking water, sanitation, public transport and health, educational and cultural facilities."[9] That is, reproduction was central to enhancing income-generating production. As one staff member explained, "Basic needs strategies, in particular, should by definition be women-oriented strategies."[10]

The Programme on Rural Women was a prefigurative initiative that could operate below the radar precisely because its small staff in Geneva belonged to a larger section of the ILO, the Employment/Rural (EMP/RU) branch, and had the support of the head of the Employment Department (EMPLOI), a key technical department of the organization. It sought to change projects "from planning development *for* a target population (in this case, women of the poorest strata, especially landless peasants) to the active *involvement* of these groups in the design and implementation of income generation and employment schemes." Added to social or communal services—including child care, laundry, food processing, and health and family planning—such projects could counter the usual "overwork" that modernization brought when "women are obliged to combine wage or self-employment with their already very heavy burden of domestic responsibilities."[11] Program staff insisted that "technical assistance without the necessary knowledge base can be disastrous."[12]

These women constituted a group that I call the ILO development feminists. To understand this group requires taking their ideas seriously.[13] During the program's first decade, most of them—Ingrid Palmer, Lourdes Benería, Zubeida Ahmad, and Martha Loutfi—were economists, a group that, with lawyers, dominated the ILO workforce. Economists, it was believed, were scientific and the least subjective in the positivist framework of post–World War II / Cold War social science, compared to anthropologists or sociologists. In the early 1970s, modernization theory still held sway, but theories of underdevelopment from the likes of Andre Gunder Frank and Walter Rodney were challenging its reign. As with many fields, a radical branch from the left asserted itself, drawing in feminists and New Leftists and reviving different strains of Marxism. Though some economics departments—notably at the New School, American University, and University of Massachusetts in the United States—became known for their heterodox approaches, they were a distinct minority. Institutional economists and political economists with a theoretical bent found their foothold in the profession unstable with the prominence of monetary and rational-choice theory. Tensions within the field of economics played out in debates over development.[14]

Development economists and practitioners had identified the rural woman as a drag on production and sought to reach her.[15] But they got it all wrong, according to the Danish civil servant Ester Boserup, whose *Women's Role in Economic Development* (1970) served as a touchstone for UN efforts. She argued that it was the development policies themselves, rather than the backwardness of women, that placed barriers to integrating women into economic modernization.[16] Boserup accepted the inevitability and benefits of the transformation from subsistence to industrial and export-oriented economies, but new technologies benefited men's work over women's work in the sexual division of labor, which was culturally specific but persistent across societies. Despite her gender analysis, Boserup remained a neoclassical economist who stressed the operation of markets through supply and demand based on rational individual choices. She conflated capitalist development with economic growth by accepting a modernization theory that turned technology into a heuristic device to make inevitable the direction of economic change. Her goal was to provide education and training and access to credit and technology, so women could benefit from such development rather than transform the contours of development itself or reconfigure household power relations, an arena she ignored.[17]

A growing number of women working within the UN system, inspired by Boserup, defined women in development (WID) as "simply the taking of women into account, improving their status, and increasing their participation in the economic, social, and political development of communities, nations, and the world."[18] They pushed for legal equality, equal rights in divorce, child custody, property holding, credit, equality, voting, and civil rights. A focus on women, however, could let men ignore the ways that gender operated, relegating women's issues to a separate box, while the equality approach did not necessarily reduce poverty without tackling other structural factors.[19]

WID, according to the U.S. development expert Irene Tinker, derived from initiatives in the early 1970s that linked women like herself who had engaged in fieldwork for various international and national agencies in the Third World. These networks solidified in Mexico City at the UN World Conference on Women.[20] There women researchers and practitioners shared the understanding "that globally most women, especially poor women, work. But this economic value of women's work was overlooked because subsistence and farming activities . . . or processing food, are not paid and so are not included in national accounts."[21] To development planners, women were invisible, so often projects made their situation worse by increasing men's power over them and removing their access to income generation. That was Boserup's lesson. With the notion of inclusion, liberal feminists rarely disavowed modernization; they wished to move its boundaries to encompass women. Critics questioned existing global power relations, championing women and development (WAD) rather than WID. They charged that WID failed to account for the roots of women's subordination in the sexual division of labor and the gendered discourse of development itself. A later generation questioned both WID and WAD from the standpoint of gender and development, reflecting a shift away from Marxism to poststructuralism. In the

2000s, holders of a critical transnational feminism, which has returned to a materialist analysis, have questioned the disembodied form of gender and development.[22]

These critiques began in the 1970s with feminists who sought women's liberation from traditional patterns of male dominance in the private, as well as the public, sphere, including in the household, marriage, intimate relations, and sexuality. Such scholars and activists situated the position of women in terms of larger socioeconomic forces. Left feminist scholars questioned the legacies of dispossession and appropriation, the theft of primitive accumulation, from colonialism and imperialism. The Subordination of Women Workshop (SOW), located around the Institute of Development Studies at Britain's University of Sussex, offered a feminist analysis that found Marxism inadequate by itself to explain women's status. According to SOW, "the theoretical object of analysis can not be women, but rather the relations between men and women in society," which required analysis of marriage as well as the market.[23] The Bielefeld School of radical feminist thinkers, to which Mies belonged, emphasized the interaction between patriarchy, capital accumulation, and colonialism.[24]

ILO development feminists built upon Boserup's analysis, even as they found it ultimately unsatisfactory. The Spanish-born Lourdes Benería, who left Rutgers University for an eighteen-month stint at the ILO in 1977–1978, offered a truculent critique of Boserup in coauthored articles with Gita Sen, an Indian feminist economist then teaching at New York's New School for Social Research. Sen would become a founder of the Third World feminist Development Alternatives with Women for a New Era (DAWN). Benería and Sen were heterodox economists (that is, not neoclassical); they were among a growing feminist contingent within the Union of Radical Political Economists (URPE). After giving Boserup her due, the two concluded, "Teaching the women better techniques in subsistence cropping . . . would have been like treating cancer with a bandaid."[25]

According to Benería and Sen, Boserup blamed culture rather than political economy for women's loss of economic independence with modernization. She thus ignored the dispossession and appropriation of land and rights to its cultivation under conquest, as well as subsequent processes of capital accumulation. For Benería and Sen, "women's loss of status" came "from the interweaving of class relations and gender relations" rather than "European patriarchal culture."[26] That is, capitalist accumulation separated women from their means of survival and control over resources. In many cases this process increased their workload and intensified the difficulty of providing for the household. Capitalism reorganized the division of labor, sometimes sending men to the town and other times turning unmarried women into migrant laborers themselves. Men's control over women changed, sometimes loosening their power, but more often male dominance became reconfigured through the wage rather than land rights or marriage rules. Boserup suggested outcomes that later researchers found, but she lacked the accumulation framework to interpret her findings.

Especially annoying to Benería and Sen, Boserup missed the differential impact by class that such processes had on women, particularly the landless in contrast to landed peasantry. Even polygamy varied by class. "Forms of appropriation of land, of surplus, and of women's reproductive capacity" shaped the division of labor, they argued, appearing as "the distinguishing factor" rather than whether an area used hoes or plows, as Boserup had claimed.[27] Similarly, not all men benefited from the monetary rewards of commercial crops. Benería and Sen concluded, "The problem for women is not only the lack of participation in this process as equal partners with men; it is a system that generates and intensifies inequalities, making use of existing gender hierarchies to place women in subordinate positions at each different level of interaction between class and gender." If capitalism liberated women by removing them from the household into waged labor, a debate that historians were conducting in the mid-1970s, it also generated "new forms of subordination."[28]

At the heart of subordination for Benería and Sen was women's reproductive labor, the absence of which in Boserup reflected a lack of feminist perspective. By looking beyond the household, Boserup ignored the social relations between the sexes and "the material base of [women's] oppression."[29] In contrast, Benería and Sen turned to household and domestic labor, work usually not monetized or counted, a type of labor that merged into agricultural production and sustained other activities, including the transformation of raw materials into consumable items for the family and field hands. In rural societies, especially subsistence ones, the line between domestic and other labor blurred, unlike formal sectors dominated by the wage as with factories and many urban occupations. Studying rural societies outside of commodity production implied that reproduction was a form of production, though Benería and Sen did not explicitly make that point in discussing Boserup's neglect of reproductive labor.[30]

A double perspective, grounded in the relation between production and reproduction, served as their alternative. Unlike what came to be called dual-systems theory, Benería and Sen never relegated reproduction to patriarchy and production to capitalism.[31] But they maintained a separation between the two. They deployed this perspective to explain sex hierarchies within production, the elimination of which even in a reformist sense required the reorganization of reproductive labor. That is, policies, whether based on workers' control (radical) or affirmative action (liberal), that sought increased women's labor force participation and placement in higher-paying positions would flounder because they neglected who does the reproductive labor. In this regard, Benería and Sen showed the flaws in Frederich Engels's classic analysis that sought to emancipate women through wage labor, moving them from the home to the factory. (Benería pointed out that Boserup seemed to support Engels but failed to engage with him.)[32] However, Benería claimed that "this double focus on production and reproduction" actually did not "invalidate the argument of Engels and the traditional left about the need to transform and do away with exploitative and hierarchical productive structures, and about the need for women to participate in paid production in order to deal with women's oppression." For "this transformation needs to be accompanied by other fundamental changes . . . beginning at the household and ideological level."[33]

The real problem with Left discussions of the time came from condemning population control without fully recognizing that it was women who undertook childbearing. Benería and Sen recommended more grounded research on what poor women wanted and thought about pregnancy, birth control, and related issues, on who made the decisions and why, on what kinds of family limitation women practiced, and on the consequences of childbearing on other aspects of a woman's work and life. Programs for infant and maternal health, sanitation, and health facilities could "give poor, rural women more options than having to resolve class contradictions through their own bodies," they observed. But such mainstays of development projects could not substitute "for the basic problems of extreme poverty and inequality in land holding: the contradictions of class and capital accumulation in the countryside [that] can be resolved only through systemic social change."[34]

In concluding one article, Benería and Sen returned to the inadequacy of Boserup's strategy of women improving individual human capital through education. Throughout the Global South, education had proven to be no protection against unemployment. As the examples of China and the Soviet Union implied, it took more than education to correct for women's responsibility for child care and household labor; even socialism had not fully liberated women from reproductive labor. In the short term, Benería and Sen found the expansion of health, transport, water, and electricity systems (that is, the provision of basic needs then promoted by the ILO) more promising for the alleviation of women's overwork than training schemes—if women could control such programs. The self-organization of the poor was thus a necessity. In a utopian leap, they declared, only "the elimination of class and sex hierarchies through a radical transformation of society" could usher in permanent change.[35]

Going to the Women

Before Benería, first shaping the Programme on Rural Women in 1975–1976 was the Australian development economist Ingrid Palmer, who recently had been a fellow of the Centre for South East Asian Studies at the University of Hull.[36] Interested in women's health, Palmer had specialized in Indonesia and the effect of changes in rice varieties on nutrition. She would spend her career consulting on development issues for international agencies and organizations. During her time in Geneva, Palmer laid the basis for the program through concept papers, proposals, commissioned research, and overtures to scholars in Africa and Asia. (Benería would extend contact with Latin American women researchers.) After a year, she returned to Brighton, in the United Kingdom, apparently because she wanted to finish other projects.[37]

Palmer provided a new twist on the equal-versus-special-treatment debate that had cast the ILO, with its lingering women-specific standards, as an obstacle to women's equal rights—despite its commitment to equal remuneration and nondiscrimination. She contrasted the "*majority of women* in developing countries" from the minority in the "formal, highly-visible employments where the employer is easily identifiable and can be influenced by the law." Equal rights legislation, which included "equal remuneration, maternity leave, anti-discrimination, and other protections," she argued, came from "the natural demands of women who are in calling distance of conferences, ministries and the judiciary system." But they were inappropriate for those in the informal sector or self-employed. She claimed that "if the majority of African women are agriculturalists self-provisioning for the family from land husbands own or have the usufruct of and are struggling to meet their family responsibilities, then it is difficult to see how this kind of legislation is a priority at all for them until other things have happened." Palmer would graphically portray rural women as drudges, burdened by overwork and incessant childbearing—that is, intensive reproductive labors, what she named "physical oppression."

Relying on a sensibility central to 1970s radical feminism, Palmer would analogize the relation of men to women within the household as a "'north-south' situation of unequal exchange" similar to the "dichotomy . . . existing between the developed and developing worlds."[38] In this context, relief for rural women in the Global South required additional effort, including access to cash income. It belonged to the fight for world employment rather than the struggle to end discrimination on the basis of sex that dominated most universalist agendas, which conflated demands of women from industrialized nations with women's demands. During a period when ILO standard setting was breaking down under employer intransience, Palmer argued "the solution to . . . distress lies in devising a new strategy of development rather than in enacting legislation."[39]

Such an analysis could be both patronizing and realistic. As a later debate between the gender theorist Judith Butler and philosopher Martha Nussbaum underscored, just because poor women in the Global South struggled to fulfill their basic needs, that did not preclude their right to rights, including sexuality and gender identity.[40] Likewise, equality should apply to the rural women no less than the urban ones. The question revolved around what path led to equality, and was equality enough when the goal was a higher standard of living and collective determination of social life?

A critique of the ways that the ILO and other agencies generated knowledge, both in terms of methods deployed and the people wielding them, informed Palmer's position. The ILO needed one unit to facilitate the exchange of ideas for integrating "investigation and action" through pilot projects that could provide models, be a center for information for nations and within the ILO, and identify areas for legislation. The EMPLOI, Palmer insisted, was the place to do this because it combined research and action projects, covered central specialties (such as migration, technology, and fertility), and housed the basic needs strategy, "which must of necessity include women's welfare and work conditions."[41] However, the unit suffered from "ethno-centrically based desk research" that could not truly capture women's situation. Economics, reliant on data sets and official statistics and GNP measures that excluded much of women's labor (for not being monetized), undercounted women's work and its value. Required was fieldwork and the evaluation of development programs with yardsticks derived from women's expressed concerns. Palmer was calling for economists to become ethnographers to develop frameworks based on going to and listening to the women involved. They should engage in investigation rather than research.[42]

There was much to investigate. Most international efforts sought to lower fertility, improve skills, and instruct women in nutrition and health. Instead, Palmer proposed to go to the women to discover the impact of multiple factors: commercial crops on their economic role, technology on their agricultural work, migration and absence of men on their resources, water-carrying and food-storage practices on family labor, their own organization and social activities in villages on status, and the introduction of commercialized products, like baby foods, on work and quality of life.[43] Research could consider women's place in basic needs strategy, the role of land inheritance and other factors in agricultural work, discussions of family planning, and women's place in urban and informal sectors. She recommended the evaluation of ongoing projects in handicraft and rural development programs, the establishment of cooperatives, monitoring legislation, and assessing the UN Decades of Development. She wanted not "flat vignettes of kinship relations and some of their effects" but "what it is like to be a poverty-stricken, tired, anemic, overburdened rural woman, and how this woman sees her options." Elsewhere Palmer insisted that women's "physical conditions of work, which need to be appreciated and which are the proper concern of the ILO, have not been described in developmental literature." Needed was "authentic material . . . straight from the mouths of rural women" to overcome existing stereotypes and avoid creating new myths.[44]

This position held two basic tensions. First, Palmer devalued reproductive labors in the process of insisting on their value. Women's provision of food, water, and fuel were productive, economic acts, she insisted, but she then went on to name them as burdensome. The rural women required better means to carry out such tasks. Palmer, like Boserup, would redirect technology to lighten women's work, distributing solar cook stoves for more efficient and productive labor—and thus freeing women's labor power to be redeployed for earning income. Second, Palmer pointed to rural women as producers of knowledge yet still dictated the terms of the discussion. Certainly Palmer wanted to understand these women as full people, how they looked when talking, whether they laughed, what they thought, and what ideas they had for improving productivity.[45] With the overall basic needs approach, Palmer recommended participation by those involved in decision making. Yet she did not wait for the women to enunciate what needed to be done. She questioned the feasibility of reaching that goal unless power relations within the household were equalized.[46] Rejecting integrating women into men's interests, she argued for placing women's interests alongside men's "in the *design* of higher productivity employment."[47] Allegiance to the goals of neoclassical economics remained.

Women investigators were best positioned to carry out the proposed research. "The ability to identify with a group of persons comes from experience of common discrimination," Palmer claimed. A development scholar like herself should have known better than to deploy this universalist rhetoric, which, like an earlier generation of women reformers, held that women on the basis of their gender would devote themselves to service to other women. "While many men are sympathetic to the relief of women's extra physical and social oppressions, far fewer men are committed to doing anything about it," she asserted. "In the absence of appropriate intellectual training," Palmer noted, "hunches have to be played and a real use of imagination and empathy made. Those who are merely sympathetic have a much harder time doing this than those who are committed." While the ILO should recruit qualified women, going beyond the usual channels to feminist professional associations of anthropologists and economists, "it will not be easy to find suitable women." Indeed, her letter writing to international agencies, university departments, research centers, and government ministries generated only scattered interest.[48]

Nonetheless, Palmer began the process of commissioning research from women through contacts in Nairobi, Manila, Dakar, Copenhagen, Stockholm, and London, as well as India and the Philippines.[49] She attended conferences abroad, including Women and National Development at Wellesley College in June 1976, papers from which appeared as the autumn 1977 issue of *Signs*, the foremost journal in women's studies. That conference exposed U.S. researchers as focused on the Third World but, to the chagrin of women from those regions, as not serious about addressing "the third world within."[50] Despite proposing a multiyear program with an increasing budget for field studies, consultants, and seminars totaling around a million dollars, the Programme on Rural Women would operate on a cobbled combination of donor monies and meager regular budget allocations.[51] Only two of her projects—one on Bangladesh, the other on Nigeria—gained funding.[52]

Palmer remained self-reflective. She was well aware of the dilemma of whether they were "studying what women can do for development or what development can do for rural working women."[53] To a colleague studying Ghana, she lamented the possibility of moving women out of the home would lead to a backlash from their men: "For *us* to burn *their* fingers would create extra obstacles for the second time around. And quite right too! After all, they have to work out their own economic and emotional survival tactics in a situation over which they have precious little control."[54] As she advised a graduate student from London, off to conduct research in India, "I am convinced that the difference lies in the way (male) economists have always looked at household work. In the end, of course, it doesn't matter a hoot what you call an activity, but raising consciousness about concepts of production and clarifying ideas of individuals contributions to the total supply of wanted goods and services help to change developmentalists' ideas on what development is all about."[55]

Without using the term *feminism*, Palmer crafted an approach that would define feminist methodology in the social sciences by refusing to see subjects as objects and creating a participatory process. She spoke of "the feminization of the development process."[56] Those committed to transforming rural women's lives claimed to begin where the women were and promised substantive improvements by taking domestic labor seriously even when regarded not as subsistence production, as it usually was, but as household work. Palmer may have lacked the language that Benería would bring from involvement with women's groups in New York City, but she understood the necessity of recovering the economic contribution of reproductive labor, empowering women themselves. Feminist theorists soon dropped the concept of women as a sex class, a term describing Palmer's analysis, but the idea of the sexual division of labor remained central to studies of gendered class relations.

Fostering Research that Mattered

The ILO taught Lourdes Benería the inadequacy of economics "to ask and analyze questions that I felt were important for a program on rural women."[57] She would reflect, "It was not enough to look at labor market factors to understand women's incorporation in the labor force; other aspects of this process needed to be taken into consideration, such as the limitations placed on women by cultural practices affecting gender constructions, women's and men's work and women's mobility." Like Palmer, she turned to anthropology, sociology, and other interdisciplinary approaches for answers.[58]

The reproductive labor of rural women, their everyday tasks, framed Benería's effort to expand the Programme on Rural Women. She lamented, "Rural women are often the most forgotten participants in the economy." However, "rather than being 'marginal' participants in the stream of economic activities, they are an 'integral' part of it." After all, "they work long hours in domestic and agricultural jobs, and . . . perform *essential* activities to the economic system, namely those related to production of foods and services, either in the fields or at home, and those related to the reproduction of the labour force."[59] Toiling fifteen to sixteen hours daily at tasks that in industrial settings occurred away from the home and belonged to the market, they combined agricultural labor of all sorts with family provision. Benería reached out to the authority of the International Women's Year and the ILO's World Employment Conference to underscore the necessity to study "women's participation in domestic production . . . the subsistence sector and family agricultural production," "rural women and wage labour," and "rural women's organisations."[60] Her proposals to ILO superiors became less academic, more specific and policy oriented, generally feminist without using explicit Marxist feminist terms.

With funds from the Netherlands, Benería organized a consultants meeting that brought together individuals whose work became foundational to the field of women and development. Sen and Mies, still researching in India, came. So did the Moroccan sociologist Fatima Mernissi, who had published *Beyond the Veil: Male-Female Dynamics in Modern Muslim Society* in 1975.[61] Neither Mernissi nor Filomina Steady from Sierra Leone, who taught at Boston University at that time, or Marie-Angélique Savené from Senegal ended up contributing to the resulting book, *Women and Development: The Sexual Division of Labor in Rural Societies.*[62] Best known for her cross-cultural analysis of black women, Steady would chair the Africana Studies Department at Wellesley College between 1999 and 2009; she also held a number of UN positions.[63] Savené, a founder of the Association of African Women for Research and Development (AAWRD), would produce a report for the program in 1983. The Ethiopian development specialist Zenebeworke Tadesse published in the collection; she served as the first executive secretary of the AAWRD and had a prominent career with the United Nations.[64] Also present but not in the collection were Eastern European researchers: Barbara Tryfan, who became the long-term head of the Department of Rural Sociology at the Institute of Rural and Agricultural Development of the Polish Academy of Sciences, and Ruza First-Dilic, a sociologist from the University of Zagreb.[65] Contributing was Kate Young, a social anthropologist focused on Mexico who was a mainstay of the Institute of Development Studies at the University of Sussex. She eventually would leave for foundation work in London.[66]

Other participants remained in academia. The New Zealander Elizabeth Croll, having just completed a PhD in anthropology, ended her career as vice principal of the School of Oriental and African Studies at the University of London. Her work on women, feminism, and socialism in China was pathbreaking.[67] The agricultural economist Carmen Diana Deere, also having recently completed her PhD, became an important figure in feminist economics. In 1978, she was beginning a distinguished career studying rural poverty, peasantry, and women and land rights at the University of Massachusetts, Amherst, where she remained until moving to the University of Florida in Latin American studies in 2004. Her collaborator, the Colombian sociologist Magdalena León de Leal, became a prize-winning author of books on Latin American women, the sexual division of labor, and the new international division of labor. Her studies on domestic workers would form the basis for their inclusion in Colombia's social security system.[68]

Along with sharing empirical research, the consultants grappled with four central topics. "Modes of Production, Agrarian Structures, and Women's Work" addressed the question, "should we expect that more equalitarian productive structures will automatically result in equality between the sexes?" Croll argued that socialism had facilitated "women's access to productive resources," but other factors within the household division of labor still led to a subordinate position. A case study on Yugoslavia agreed that women remained in a "marginal" position outside of capitalist relations. The second set of discussions, "Sex Roles and the Division of Labour in Rural Economies," emphasized the "under-rated" quality of women's agricultural and domestic labors. Other sections included "Effect of the Penetration of the Market on Women's Work Load" and "Rural Development and Women." León de Leal and Deere traced the ways that capitalist agriculture affected the labor process and the sexual division of labor, creating a reserve army of female labor that still performed subsistence and family maintenance. Capitalist penetration meant that women in India lost control over their crafts production, Mies showed. Most significantly, the gathering questioned the meaning of the "integration of women in development" because women already were part of communities and economic life. The real issue was "how" and under what sorts of conditions did their participation occur. Participants wondered whether Bangladesh or China would set the course for the future: the former generated low-wage incorporation; the latter sought economic transformation.[69] In the late 1970s, China still appeared as an alternative socialist formation in which women held up "half the sky."

What kinds of women workers emerged from these case studies? The ILO cast "women in developing countries" as a special kind of woman worker, as the Other to the Western women, already judged as different from the white male industrial norm. A synthesizer like Palmer portrayed the rural woman as a drudge, whose reproductive tasks became more difficult with technological changes that redistributed control over the means of production to men. Structural analysis, in contrast, predominated at the workshop and subsequent anthology. Researchers sought the facts of women's work over their subjective experiences. Chapters presented matter-of-fact findings without emotive language, but contributors on occasion managed to highlight the dignity and agency of women over their subordination. The rural woman emerged as a resourceful survivor, willing to perform tasks necessary to maintain her household. During a time when some Western feminists were celebrating women's culture, in these accounts the Third World woman worker maintained her own admirable sphere. Scavenging for fuel and water in lieu of purchase took the women farther away from home, "involving more labor, time, and effort." Women became the most militant agricultural workers; they "both suffer and organize against their oppression," as Sen found.[70]

At the end, the meeting offered a set of proposals that supported the work of the program. Attendees predictably validated the promotion of research to develop "clear analysis" and as a prelude for action, on specific topics, such as control of labor in agrarian production, both legal and de facto; women as agricultural wage workers, even if seasonal or part-time; nature of wage discrimination; activities of traditional women's organizations; estimates of women's economic contributions in and away from the home; and women's own responses to forms of oppression.[71] This agenda shared with Palmer's a focus on the household and women's reproductive labors; it differed from her—and Boserup—in its concern with the accumulation process. Continuing discussion—and dissemination of research—occurred at regional workshops in Latin America, Africa, and Asia over subsequent years.

Decolonizing Knowledge

Benería actively participated in "the decolonization of research," a phrase from African scholars who organized a workshop around this theme in Dakar, Senegal, in December 1977. She sought to "establish contact with them [the researchers] in order to (a) know what they are involved in (note the very interesting objectives of the programme); and (b) investigate the possibilities of co-operation."[72] On her way, she attended another meeting organized by the FAO in Accra, Ghana, where around twenty-five traders, though illiterate, "participated very actively by explaining their own problems and commenting on some of the papers which were translated to them into their two local languages." In contrast, those who came to Dakar for African Women and Development: The Decolonisation of Research were well-known and respected researchers, like Savené and Tadesse. So many women expressed interest in collaborating with the Programme on Rural Women that Benería judged the problem would be finding funds, not researchers from the continent.[73] A 1985 compilation showed the majority of the seventy-five publications of the program involved women from the Third World, including Africa.[74]

Continuing Palmer's task of expanding the network of researchers, Benería explained to Mies that the program sought "to facilitate and promote the functioning of women's organisations so that women can collectively express *their own* vision of what they need and organize their actions." Evaluating Mies's research proposal, "Market Economy on Women's Productive and Reproductive Work in the Rural Subsistence Sector in India," Benería admitted, "I am writing to you about a problem that we are facing. We are in the process of reaching as many women from third world countries as possible in our research programme on rural women. In your case, would it be possible to include one (or more) collaborator(s) in your study? Or could a part of the study be carried out say by an Indian woman?" The funders wanted "as many non-Western women as possible" involved.[75] Zubeida Ahmad, a Harvard-trained Pakistani economist who spent thirty years at the ILO, reported, "The main problem, if there is one, concerns her [Mies] nationality. As far as I know she is a German married to an Indian, a professor at Hyderabad University." But Mies spoke Hindi "well so that during our field trip in the tribal areas in India she was questioning the women in the villages without the use of intermediaries."[76]

Mies found local collaborators. She reported to the ILO, "It was absolutely necessary that the field investigators and research assistants were women, because rural women will not speak freely and openly to male investigators from the city." An additional problem stemmed from the reduced mobility of middle-class women with academic credentials, still subjected to "patriarchal norms that women have always to be under male protection."[77] At the end she recruited "two young women, Lalita and Krishna Kumari who were courageous enough . . . to live in the villages among the lace-making women and share their life." A founder of a pioneer feminist organization in the area, Lalita spoke the local language; she communicated politics through a gift of song, a medium that has proven quite powerful among workers and peasants of all types. These students "had enough enthusiasm, empathy and commitment to the cause of women's emancipation to be able to establish a relationship of trust and friendship between the lace makers and ourselves."[78]

Going to the women, sitting "with them in front of their mud houses," Mies and her collaborators sought to close the gap between researcher and researched. "First the lace making women did their own research on us," she recalled. "'Who are you? Are you married? Do you have children? Where do you come from?' They began to talk about their work, the lace making as well as their housework. . . . Several of them also told us freely about their husbands and men in general." Over thirty years later, Mies remained "impressed . . . by the openness and clarity of their thinking" reflected in the life histories they gathered.[79] The separateness of men's and women's work and social lives allowed her team to chat with the women. When the men were around, "they either acted as mouthpieces or as interpreters for the women."[80]

Mies was forthright on how "women's work in the informal sector . . . feeds the process of capital accumulation." Lace makers, invisible as housewives, produced not only for family survival but also for the world market. Through a political economy charting increased pauperization and landlessness, despite the rich soils in the area of Andhra Pradesh and a history of lace making connected to colonization, she traced the transformation of lace making from "pastime" to "necessity." Undertaken between morning and evening cooking and then resumed by oil lamp, this form of crocheting became naturalized, even as male merchants and middlemen, who favored women from their caste, came to control a vast putting-out system.

The "non-separation" of production and reproduction, despite the ideology of separate spheres, set "the precondition for the exploitation."[81]

Deepening Marxist feminist theory, Mies exposed a central paradox: the primitive accumulation process extracted from the subsistence production of the lace makers depended on maintaining these "housewife-workers" as outside of wage labor as usually configured. Capital flowed to the informal sector. The entire strategy of profits from self-employment rested on "a patriarchal and sexist division of labour."[82] Campaigns to improve homework thus had to confront women's status within as well as outside the household, which would become a central contention of feminist development thought. Evidence from Latin America underscored the power of this analysis. By bolstering the role of wife and mother, a later survey of the literature found, the home location of the labor encouraged "increased patriarchal control of homeworkers by husbands, intermediaries and employers."[83]

The lace makers had their own instrumental goals; they "were very keen themselves to discuss their situation and their problems with us and asked for our help," Mies recalled. A 1985 report on the program boasted that "dissemination of the ILO's research findings" on their exploitative conditions— that is, Mies's work—had led the National Union of Working Women to organize the lace makers.[84] Some 3,000 women decided to form their own cooperative organization and secured 1,000 loans; with access to credit, new designs adapted from Chinese samples, and direct marketing to Western consumers, they improved their position in relation to the middlemen contractors who previously had rewarded their labor with a pittance. In referring to what the woman decided to do, Ahmad countered a critic who proposed placing the women in workshops under formal labor standards to gain the identity of worker as a first step toward collective action. The women, Ahmad noted, already were acting collectively.[85]

Conclusion

The attempt to decolonize knowledge, however incomplete, perhaps was the most important legacy of the Programme on Rural Women. As Ahmad explained to Benería in late 1982, "Slowly we are succeeding in winning over a few colleagues to questioning the basis of the existing sexual division of labour," while pinpointing the "elimination of women's subordination."[86] Ahmad would attend the preliminary meeting of DAWN and was on its initial steering committee. Aided by the Ford Foundation, DAWN was a

South-South initiative, that is, a project enhancing ties within the Global South rather than one connecting the Global North to the Global South. It brought together many of the researchers supported by the program. Ahmad helped to forge a "post-Boserup Manifesto" for the 1985 Nairobi UN meeting, "reconciling feminism and development" that would address women's situation in terms of the global political economy, critiquing growth without environmentalism, and repositioning the rural woman as "a symbol of strength rather than submerged under exploitation."[87] As one DAWN founder announced, "unless there is a better understanding of how patriarchy and economic systems propagate oppression, no effective or inclusive work on bringing about a new order can be done." Feminism provided the basis for a global solidarity among women in the fight against all forms of domination.[88]

Accounting for reproductive labor meant expanding the concept of work to include nonmonetized subsistence and family activities crucial for daily life. It challenged economic planners to not only consider the household but also notice the woman within as a distinct social actor. It asked the researcher to become an investigator who facilitated a community project through participatory involvement to address concerns defined by the women themselves. Subjects rather than objects, rural women emerged as historical actors demanding better work and better lives. The Programme on Rural Women promoted approaches that were priceless in an effort to make visible labors that made all other work possible. It set the ILO on a road that would extend labor standards to home-based and domestic workers and transform women's work into a key component of its agenda for the twenty-first century.

PART II

Working the Margins

Chapter 3

The Loose Cotton Economy of the New Orleans Waterfront in the Late Nineteenth Century

Bruce E. Baker

When statisticians for the New Orleans Cotton Exchange examined the figures for the 1872 season, they discovered that New Orleans had shipped out 23,594 more bales of cotton than it had received, about 1.75 percent of the total receipts. This discrepancy was a standard feature of the cotton trade and was referred to as the "city crop."[1] Of course, everyone knew that these bales did not spring up from the neutral ground of Canal Street. Instead they were "made up from excess of receipts, pickings, stealings and coonings at large" plus "samples and borings."[2] The problem the city crop raises sheds light on a part of the cotton trade that existed mostly in the shadows in the late nineteenth century. The cotton trade of the United States as a whole dealt with millions of bales moving all around the world, from farms and plantations across the South to cotton exchanges, rail depots, docks, and eventually mills from New England to Britain to Europe. Contemporaries gathered and circulated information about the scope and shape of the trade, but alongside that central part of the cotton trade existed an underground cotton economy. Cotton in the late nineteenth century was a ubiquitous physical presence, and it was a valuable commodity, so it naturally became the target of theft. Some cotton was stolen right out of the boll, picked secretly at night and traded at country stores for whiskey, and sometimes entire bales were stolen.[3] What this chapter focuses on, however, is the trade in loose cotton around the waterfront of New Orleans, small portions of ginned cotton that came loose from bales (one way or another) circulated through a complex and shadowy local economy and then were reintegrated into the mainstream cotton economy.

While in the 1850s cotton was king, these days we might say that it is the history of cotton that sits on the throne. There has long been a rich literature on the growing of cotton (the central economic activity of a large portion of the United States for well over a century) and the manufacture of it (the first, most important, and vanguard aspect of industrialization) but significantly less on the parts in between, with the notable exception of Harold Woodman's *King Cotton and His Retainers*, researched as a dissertation in the early 1960s, published as a monograph in 1968, and republished as a "classic" in 1990.[4] Recent "big books" on cotton, such as Giorgio Riello's *Cotton* and Sven Beckert's *Empire of Cotton*, cover vast sweeps of time and space and make convincing arguments for the importance of cotton in the global history of capitalism, but there remains plenty of scope for studies understanding various aspects of the business of the cotton trade along the lines of work by Robert Bouilly, John Killick, Tuffly Ellis, Kenneth J. Lipartito, and others, especially in the period after the Civil War.[5] Once we have a more thorough understanding of such basics as the development and role of cotton exchanges, examples of the practices of particular firms, and the uses within the trade of such instruments as futures contracts, through bills of lading, and free-on-board shipping, for instance, we can begin to integrate what we could consider the "noise" in the system: the economies that sprang up on the basis of these formal, standard practices of the cotton trade.[6]

Examining the loose cotton economy of New Orleans is worthwhile not for novelty or antiquarian interest but because it tells us something fundamental about how the economy of that city and the cotton trade functioned. The story of how the cotton trade came to be interested in tiny scraps of cotton fits into a narrative of the relentless revolution of capitalism's expansion, but it is also a story of the relationship between business practices and the large abstractions of the trade and the minutiae of the daily scramble of the poor for survival. It illustrates Peter Linebaugh's contention that "the forms of exploitation pertaining to capitalist relations caused or modified the forms of criminal activity, and . . . the forms of crime caused major changes in capitalism."[7] To understand it all, we must appreciate the material reality of cotton: how it was processed, how it was handled, its varying quality and qualities, and what it could be used for.[8]

Cotton, wherever it was bought and sold, did not simply float into New Orleans and then float right out again. Eric Arnesen provides a lengthy but useful account of the bales' peregrinations through the city:

> For Mississippi River steamboats collecting cotton from Louisiana plantations, African-American roustabouts physically carried bales of cotton on their backs onto the boats over simple gangplanks. Arriving in New Orleans, that cotton became the responsibility of more highly skilled cotton screwmen, the "aristocrats of the levee" who earned the port's highest wages. These men transferred the cotton to longshoremen, the largest category of waterfront labourers, who delivered it to draymen (also known as teamsters), who, driving horse-drawn carts, then transported the bales to cotton yardmen in the nearby cotton compresses. (Longshoremen loaded and unloaded all round freight, such as molasses, while a distinct category of round freight teamsters moved these goods through the city.) In the cotton yards, the bales were moved by yardmen, were sorted by quality by white classers and markers, were placed on the scales and then removed by the scalehands, and were weighed and reweighed, not surprisingly, by weighers and reweighers. After the bales had been compressed by large hydraulic presses to about a third of their original size by pressmen, yardmen delivered the compacted bales to draymen, who returned them to the wharves, where longshoremen manually and with winches loaded the bales onto the deck. Screwmen next assumed control: utilising jackscrews, they carefully compacted the cotton into the ships' holds.[9]

Arnesen's summary points toward another aspect of the cotton trade that we must recreate in order to understand the loose cotton economy: the actual mechanics of how bales were handled, since it was this handling that created the conditions for removing loose cotton from compressed bales. An article from 1888 gives some sense of this, though more descriptions are needed for a fuller account. In an attempt to test an alternative to expensive jute bagging, employees in a New Orleans pickery put three cotton-bagged bales through their paces. Cotton hooks were used to move the bales onto the scales for weighing and then to reposition the bales on the scales to be sure an

Figure 3.1. Ragged cotton bales on the docks at Norfolk, Virginia. Library of Congress.

accurate weight was recorded. The usual jute bagging would have been likely to tear under this treatment. From here, the bales "were then taken to the compress, were jerked from the dray by two powerful colored men, veteran knights of the cotton hook." In short, for bales of cotton weighing just over five hundred pounds and more or less rectangular in shape, every time they were moved, it was by digging a hook into them and "jerking and tossing them around," all of which tended to leave bales ragged.[10]

Photographs of cotton bales on the docks at Norfolk, Virginia, around 1890 give a good idea of how loose cotton entered the informal economy (see Figure 3.1).[11] The planks are littered with small bits of cotton, including a particularly tempting chunk in the foreground. All this was fair game for whoever could be bothered to pick it up, perhaps the two men lounging against the bales on the right. The compressed bales were covered with jute bagging and held by about eight iron bands. Numerous cuts in the bagging are visible, where samplers had to cut the bagging to remove a sample and failed to resew it securely. Especially interesting are the tufts of cotton hanging from some of the bales. What is their status? The process of repeated loading and unloading between the docks and the bale's ultimate destination was almost certain to dislodge these bits—the purchaser was never going to get those tufts anyway, so what was the harm in pulling them loose and taking them away?

Just as historians have urged us to think not of "cheap labor" but of the mechanisms by which labor is cheapened, we need to consider not just loose cotton but how cotton was loosened.[12] It is important to realize that this was not simply the result of theft, at least not always. Instead, loose cotton existed within the same sort of customary moral economy as the wood scraps known as "chips" in the London shipyards of the eighteenth century.[13] A couple of the early definitions of the city crop in 1866 include the phrase "stealings and coonings."[14] The term *cooning* is significant. According to Clarence Major, the term "cooning . . . originated among white speakers meaning stealing as opposed to robbing."[15] A survey for the *Dictionary of American Regional English* in the late 1960s found that *cooning* meant "to take something of small value that doesn't belong to you," which is a very good description of the acquisition of loose cotton on the waterfront.[16] While some loose cotton came from unabashed theft (though seldom outright robbery from a person), much came from what we might call (as some contemporaries did) *gleaning*, and much came from the sort of overly exuberant gleaning encompassed by the term *cooning*.

As far back as 1839, observers in New Orleans had complained,

> Every one knows that there are hundreds of women and small girls in this city regularly engaged in the business of picking up cotton and coffee about the streets and on the Levee; and that when they find the picking rather dry they even go so far as to steal it from the bales and sacks. They go in gangs, have their sentinels out with as much system as a flock of crows, and while one is on the lookout for the Commissary or whoever is appointed to watch, the rest will huddle around a bale of cotton or sack of coffee, fill their aprons or baskets, and be off in no time.[17]

Sometimes thieves made off with entire bales—four men in 1870 bought a couple bales of cotton cheaply from a ship's mate (who did not own the cotton) and found themselves arrested—but more often cotton was stolen a pound at a time, and the opportunities were endless.[18] Men whose business was moving bales around carried cotton hooks, and the hook an honest docker used to wrestle a bale around for loading looked exactly the same as the one a thief carried to pry out chunks of cotton that belonged to someone else.[19] Many cotton thieves were women and children, who blended in among those involved in the legitimate practice of "glean[ing] all the loose cotton or sugar which may be lying around, and which there is no objection to their taking." Women thieves would wear a false underskirt, slowly stuffing it full of the valuable commodity. "Coming out in the morning, looking as thin and skimp as possible, she will, in a couple of hours, acquire a proportion approaching that of the fat girl; having under her dress some fifty pounds of cotton," complained one observer.[20]

It is difficult to reach any clear conclusions on just which sort of people were stealing cotton. Newspaper reports are anecdotal, and it is impossible to know whether the thieves mentioned are entirely characteristic of the full range of those actually stealing cotton. Mary Sullivan, for instance, was either one of the most prolific cotton thieves on the New Orleans docks in the 1870s or one of the most incompetent (or both). She was arrested in December 1873, November 1874, January 1875, March 1875, February 1876, November 1877, and possibly on other occasions.[21] In general, cotton thieves reported in the newspapers tended to be men more often than women, and African Americans were disproportionately represented in the years immediately after emancipation. In a few cases, where it was possible to find other newspaper accounts of cotton thieves, they did have criminal histories. In December 1874, "Pat. Kennedy, Sarah Jones and Henry Lewis, well known Levee thieves, were arrested yesterday at the head of Gravier street, charged with pilfering cotton and cotton ties."[22] Earlier newspaper accounts suggested that Patrick Kennedy (if, indeed, it was the same Patrick Kennedy) had a long history of fighting, drinking, and going to jail, while Sarah Jones seemed to specialize in working with other disreputable women to lure men into dangerous places where, instead of being entertained, they were robbed.[23] However, the rarity of this sort of background information suggests that cotton pilfering on the waterfront was an activity conducted by everyone from amateurs to hardened criminals; for some it was a way of life, and for others, an opportunistic crime.

Pilfering contributed considerable amounts of cotton to the underground economy of the New Orleans waterfront, but by its nature, pilfering was intermittent. A larger amount of loose cotton almost certainly entered the underground economy through the hands of those employed in the legitimate cotton trade, especially samplers. Cotton may look like cotton to the amateur eye, but variations in grade and quality were important to the buyers who acquired the raw material for the spinning mills. Factors, and later brokers, selling cotton had to examine each bale to determine its grade and price. Rather than dash around from one cotton press or warehouse to another, sorting through heavy bales, they hired samplers to do the legwork for them. The sampler cut a hole in the jute bagging, twisted a hook into the compressed cotton, and removed about six ounces of cotton, roughly a large handful, in order to inspect it and determine its grade. Samplers generally employed a laborer to handle the bales and a sewer to repair the cut in the bagging once the sample was taken, and with these assistants, a sampler could examine about two hundred bales a day. Later, when badly packed bales, perhaps with lower grade cotton in the interior or wet cotton that deceptively added weight, became a problem, samplers on behalf of buyers would also use an auger to sample the interior of the bale, and this cotton could not then be added back to the compressed bale.[24] Many samplers got into the habit of taking samples that were a bit bigger than they needed and then trimming these down to the required size. This was faster than being too precise and maybe having to resample a bale, and it also gave them a few ounces of cotton per bale, which could cover the expense of hiring an assistant and maybe pay for lunch.[25]

Loose cotton entered underground economies elsewhere through similar channels. Setting aside the illicit traffic in unginned seed cotton that was a ubiquitous feature of rural life in the Cotton Belt and a particular point of conflict during Reconstruction, loose cotton economies developed in all of the South's cotton ports and interior transshipment centers to some degree. In Charleston, a problem of stolen samples and loose cotton developed by at least the beginning of 1868 and continued through the early 1870s.[26] In Wilmington, North Carolina, cotton thieves also disposed of their goods at junk shops.[27] In Fayetteville, North Carolina, in October 1865 "a negro boy was caught in the act of cutting open a bale and stealing cotton," and an African American man was arrested for pilfering cotton from a commission merchant's office in Memphis in March 1868.[28]

Bags of loose cotton could easily be turned into money in New Orleans, partly because there was also a sizable market for cotton of lesser quality or mixed grades. We are accustomed to thinking of raw cotton as the input for textiles for clothing, and while that was indeed the primary use for the fiber, in the nineteenth century cotton found its way into a wide variety of other products as well. The market for cotton waste and damaged cotton was complex and has been much less studied than the main cotton market.[29] One source estimated that a full third of all cotton wound up in some part of the cotton waste trade.[30] When cotton had too much "country damage" from mud, rain, and the thousand insults a cotton bale suffered between the gin on the plantation and the security of a ship's hold, or when it was damaged by fire or falling in the river, it could still be used. Low-grade and short-staple cotton, as well as cotton that had been damaged by water, sometimes went to Europe to make cheap quality goods or to the mills of the Rossendale Fells in Lancashire to be spun into short-staple yarn and then woven into sheetings.[31] Burned cotton could be sold for felt.[32] Felt was primarily made with wool for technical reasons about how the fibers behaved, and in the nineteenth century, felt was increasingly important for lining the hulls of ships to waterproof them, for carpets, and for roofing. In 1839 there was a breakthrough in the manufacturing of felt impregnated with asphalt for use in roofing, and this felt sometimes used vegetable fibers, presumably including cotton. The felt industry took hold strongly in Leeds and also in Rossendale, the same area that was already a center of the cotton waste trade.[33] Upholstered furniture in homes and also carriages and trains all used batting or wadding, much of which was made of cotton.[34] Mattresses, such as those made at the Louisiana Mattress Manufacturing Company on Camp Street or the Donahoe Mattress Manufacturing Company on Baronne Street, often used cotton as the stuffing.[35] Paper had traditionally been made from cotton rags rather than raw cotton, but some raw cotton could be added to make coarse printing paper or wrapping paper.[36] Some cotton from sources such as this could have been used in the nitrocellulose industry as well. Smaller fibers actually worked better for the production process.[37]

Cotton pilfered by the pound usually began its journey back into the legitimate trade in one of the fifteen "junk shops" scattered across New Orleans in 1879. About half were within a square or two of the waterfront.[38] While they did buy and sell secondhand goods of all kinds quite legitimately, everyone knew that junk dealers played a key role in the city's network of fences. Junk shops, according to a detailed account of the city's stolen goods markets, "are found in vast numbers on the streets near the river and basins. Here the property taken from the vessels and piers . . . is readily disposed of. . . . In these places vast amounts of stolen cotton are sold."[39] An 1873 newspaper described a typical transaction at one of the "hole in the wall" establishments:

solid line   – boundary of loose shop zone
dotted line – pickery locations
dashed line – main ship landing

Figure 3.2. "Pickeries, Loose Cotton Shops, and the Ship Landing." Base map from *Appletons' Hand-Book of American Travel. Southern Tour* (New York: D. Appleton, 1874), 192.

the proprietor "weighs the bag, cheats in the weight about one-half, allows one-half the price the cotton is worth, pays cash, asks no questions, and keeps no books."[40] At these rates, and with cotton going for ten cents a pound, a twenty-pound bag of loose cotton might bring its seller fifty cents. There were at least six such "loose shops" in 1873, located in the area bounded by Felicity, Magazine, and Erato, handy for the pickeries and the main ship landing that ran from Thalia Street to Felicity Street.[41] At that time, they were "all . . . do[ing] a thriving trade."[42]

It is hardly surprising that pickeries would be located close to the main ship landing where most of the cotton was loaded for export. Loose shops set up nearby as well since those who gathered loose cotton from the waterfront or the warehouses or cotton presses could dispose of it more easily, and the buyer of the loose cotton could get it to a pickery to be rebaled and made marketable again. It was also safely away from the place where those who controlled the cotton trade did business at Carondelet and Gravier Streets.

The loose cotton economy of New Orleans (and, to a lesser extent, other cotton shipment centers at the periphery of the South) is related to and yet distinct from the circuits of waste and recycling that were a feature of domestic and industrial life in the nineteenth century. The sociologist Zsuzsa Gille has argued that waste scholarship has operated at the micro level, understanding how waste is produced, and also at the macro level, tending to overlook how waste becomes waste and emphasizing its role in larger social and economic processes.[43] Starting from the domestic side, Susan Strasser examined how Americans went from reusing and recycling household goods of all kinds to producing ever greater amounts of trash as mass production led to greater packaging of goods and use of materials that could not easily be recycled. She emphasized, as did Wendy Woloson in an article about child junk collectors, that material recovered from waste, especially rags and iron, was an important input into the manufacturing process.[44] This was also the case to some extent for cotton, in the form of linters gathered from the ginning process and waste recovered during spinning, which was generally reckoned to be around 15 percent.[45] The cotton gathered one way or another from the waterfront, however, was neither a recycled part of the waste stream nor a byproduct of the manufacturing process. Instead, it was somewhere in between agricultural waste (like grain that falls to the ground during harvest) and stolen property, but because it had fallen out of the regular processes of sorting by quality and sometimes sustained damage, it could not be seamlessly reintegrated into the mainstream trade and, like stolen goods often do, tended to sell at a discount from its usual value.

Bales of damaged cotton often made their way to one of the city's twenty cotton pickeries, where the bales were torn apart, the usable fiber sorted from the trash, and the cotton rebaled.[46] Breaking down and rebaling cotton made it easy to sneak in illicit loose cotton since unlike a warehouse or cotton press, no one expected the number of bales coming out of a pickery to equal the number going in. A pickery was typically a structure about 130 feet wide by 150 to 190 feet long, configured as one large room with an office for the bookkeeper and clerks. Most also had a yard where bales of cotton would generally be stored, though the bales were broken down and "picked" inside. Many also had platforms for drying damp cotton before it was rebaled. Some pickeries had steam-driven presses for compressing bales, but most had "an ordinary plantation press which is worked by hand power."[47] Pickeries served an important function in a cotton port, but they were often viewed with suspicion since the cotton that was sold in junk shops usually came to pickeries for baling. In fact, in 1873, Peter Jones ran a junk shop along with a pickery.[48] An 1885 business directory made a point of describing one pickery as "entirely responsible" and described "the credit and responsibility" of another as "far above the average," suggesting others failed to meet such a standard.[49] Most of the pickeries were located along Orange Street within a few squares of the river, along Religious Street near Felicity, and along Tchoupitoulas between Erato and Terpsichore.[50] Other cities with a less extensive cotton trade tended to have establishments that combined the function of gin and pickery.[51]

By the early 1870s, snide comments from cotton men in other ports about the size of the New Orleans city crop and complaints from Liverpool about the raggedy and noticeably underweight bales they received prompted the organization overseeing the New Orleans cotton trade to make reforms. The New Orleans Cotton Exchange (NOCE) came up with a couple of strategies to improve the reputation of New Orleans for the careful and responsible handling of the cotton it exported by reducing the amount of loose cotton that leaked out of the legitimate trade. After the egregious city crops in the 1872–1873 and 1873–1874 seasons (24,431 and 34,508 bales, respectively), the NOCE decided to establish "some general system for the protection of this vulnerable article of merchandise in its transit through this city," and they focused on the cotton presses. Hiring a chief supervisor, twenty-six assistants, and around fifty laborers, the NOCE posted an assistant supervisor in each of the city's twenty-four presses and two railroad depots.[52] All "bales controlled by members of the Exchange"—the vast majority of the cotton in the presses—were monitored, and the loose cotton removed from these bales for samples was noted. Any excess was "kept securely under lock and key by the supervisors in the various presses (who make daily reports of the weights of the same to their chiefs) until sufficient to bale, and in that form it is disposed of."[53]

Buyers in Liverpool had long complained about the "country damage" to cotton shipped from New Orleans after being rolled through the mud or left in the rain.[54] This became such a problem that an international meeting in Liverpool in 1874 led to the NOCE creating a levee inspection system to prevent mishandling of cotton and provide clear documentation of who was liable for damaged cotton that arrived in Liverpool.[55] After some delay, the levee inspection system went into operation at the beginning of the 1875–1876 season.[56] The levee inspectors observed the condition of bales being loaded and provided captains with certificates attesting to the state the bales were in when they left New Orleans.[57] The NOCE took the opportunity to expand the remit of the new system to controlling pilferage in order to drive the junk shops out of business.[58] "Police commissions were procured for the inspectors," the NOCE explained, "and they [were] authorized to make arrests wherever necessary to protect the bales from being robbed." Shippers paid a penny a bale to the NOCE, which provided for one chief inspector and five assistants, but this force was spread thin on the New Orleans waterfront.[59]

The new arrangements did seem to have the desired effect on the infrastructure of the loose cotton economy. Between 1870 and 1876, the number of pickeries increased steadily, rising from eleven to twenty-two. That number began dropping in 1877, and by 1881 it was down to nine. Since the amount of cotton moving through the port was increasing, the declining number of pickeries suggests less need for their services dealing with damaged cotton because of better handling practices—but also quite possibly less loose cotton in circulation to be surreptitiously baled so it could rejoin the legitimate trade. Junk shops were in decline as well. In 1870 there were twenty-three and in 1871 fifteen, but by 1876, this number had grown to thirty. They, too, began going out of business in 1877, leaving only fifteen operating by 1881.[60]

Even after the NOCE systems of supervising the presses and the levee were in place, the loose cotton economy remained to some extent, though perhaps not on the scale of the early 1870s. In July 1885, the New Orleans *City Item* ran a series of articles criticizing the practices of the city's cotton trade.[61] The writer alleged that "two pounds of cotton are taken out of every bale, ostensibly for sampling purposes, but really for profit," and "other charges of a similar nature [were] made."[62] A New Orleans insider writing under the moniker "Facts & Remedy" argued that the situation was actually quite complicated and was primarily the result of an inadequate and out-of-date infrastructure that could not keep up with the current needs of the trade. He suggested that New Orleans should adopt the practice of examining bales once and issuing a certificate for their grade, which "diminished [the] handling occasioned by such a system. Repeated turning out, repiling, resampling and consequent thereupon loss in weight, natural and artificial, weighing and reweighing would be avoided."[63] Continuing his defense, "Facts & Remedy" minimized the seriousness of whatever abuses existed:

And what, pray, is all this defamation about? Mainly about "loose shops," a couple of ounces the sampler takes and two pounds per bale the factors loose is said to amount to. Relative to the first, why grudge them their existence! If they can exist legitimately, let them; it is a business to buy cotton in the loose form as it is to buy old gold or silver, or other second-hand goods. If they overstep their mark, we have laws for buying stolen goods, and a good detective employed by the parties thinking themselves injured will soon set the matter right; but it is certainly neither right nor just to strive to break up a business because there are "possibilities" of it being conducted dishonestly. The loose shop in itself does not injure anybody, particularly not the planter. Now to the sampler. Granted he takes two ounces out of the six to sell to the loose shop, the injured party is the buyer of the cotton, who now only gets four ounces. But it ought to strike everybody that the buyer, being on the spot, can easily cope with the abuse.[64]

A more characteristic New Orleans response cannot be imagined. As Scott P. Marler has demonstrated, in this period New Orleans was infamous in business circles for not keeping up with the times.[65]

Recent historians such as Sven Beckert have made it clear how important the cotton trade was to the development of global capitalism, and while we have an impressive grasp of many of the broad outlines, when we zoom in, there are still glaring gaps in our understanding. Most of the lacunae that Harold Woodman identified in the 1990 introduction to the reissue of *King Cotton and His Retainers* remain: "Despite their importance, the large cotton merchants who helped to transform the trade in the late nineteenth and early twentieth centuries have not been studied in detail," and "no one has undertaken a scholarly treatment of these newer and more successful merchants . . . and similar firms that came to dominate the trade in the United States and abroad beginning in the late nineteenth century."[66] Woodman's claim that "the history of the futures system remains largely unstudied" is still mostly accurate.[67] But if historians have not yet reckoned with the large structures of the cotton trade, the firms and institutions whose comings and goings were noted in newspapers, whose trading went on in grand buildings in the commercial districts of cities such as New Orleans, Memphis, and New York, whose participants often earned fortunes and left records and legacies, then they have certainly not begun to consider how this fiber "that made the modern world" (to adopt a publisher's overexuberant description) was entangled with secondary and underground economies from the fields where it grew to the ports where it was shipped, through the mills that spun it and the factories that wove it, all the way to the humble ragpicker's cart.

More broadly, paying attention to what became of the loose cotton that circulated in its own economy on the New Orleans waterfront suggests new ways of understanding capitalism itself. Clearly, not all the risk-taking entrepreneurs in the cotton trade wore fine suits and worked at the New Orleans Cotton Exchange. Poor women, bored sailors, and loafing longshoremen were perfectly capable of creating their own economic institutions and exploiting gaps in the market and ambiguities in the law. This example also demonstrates the interplay between illicit and mainstream economies, which is probably a feature of capitalism more generally, where crime and underground economies can point out flaws in existing systems and practices and even pioneer new opportunities that are later assimilated into the mainstream economy by those with greater capital and power.

Chapter 4

Jim Crow's Cut: White Supremacy and the Destruction of Black Capital in the Forests of the Deep South

Owen James Hyman

On September 13, 1874, the New Orleans *Daily Picayune* reported "an outrage . . . committed by a gang of negroes at St. Tammany," on the north shore of Lake Pontchartrain opposite New Orleans, Louisiana. A group of African Americans warned Poitevent and Favre Lumber Company teamsters to stop hauling timber in the vicinity of Bayou Bonfouca, on what the newspaper called "some indefinite pretenses." The teamsters refused. At nightfall the group returned to the Poitevent camp, where they found the company supervisor alone, beat him with a club, and left him for dead. The violence escalated the following evening, when two men intercepted twenty-year-old Samuel Poitevent at his residence as he was leaving to investigate the beating. Seeing that they were armed and recognizing he was about to be attacked, Poitevent fired both rounds from his double-barreled shotgun at his assailants. One man was knocked down from the blast. Both managed to escape. The *Picayune* noted an air of "intense excitement" in St. Tammany Parish, with whites and blacks arming themselves in preparation for a riot that never came.[1]

While the *Daily Picayune* interpreted the attack as senseless violence, it would not be the last conflict between African Americans and the Poitevent

and Favre Lumber Company at Bayou Bonfouca. The waterway was con-
nected by Lake Pontchartrain to a thriving intracoastal and circum-
Caribbean trade network spanning from Mexico to Cuba (see Figure 4.1).[2]
Much of south Mississippi's contribution to that commerce came from the
Poitevent and Favre mills, which sat on the east bank of the lower Pearl River
along the Louisiana-Mississippi border. Like Lake Pontchartrain, the Pearl
River emptied into Lake Borgne and the Gulf of Mexico beyond, allowing
ships plying its waters to bypass the port of New Orleans in search of foreign
markets. Poitevent and Favre exported timber directly to Tampico and
Havana, relying on the labor of skilled African American carpenters, caulk-
ers, sailors, and captains to maintain its fleet and navigate its vessels. The
men who attacked the Poitevent and Favre teamster most likely performed
similar work, albeit in the employ of another company.[3]

What transpired at Bayou Bonfouca was not the product of some corporate rivalry or labor dispute though; it was about land and timber. The community there included a number of African Americans involved in the coastal
trade, as well as agriculture, some of whom had owned property in the area
since at least the 1850s. To risk death by attacking a member of a powerful
industrial family, the men who tried to bushwhack Samuel Poitevent must
have felt their livelihoods were at stake. Examining why they did this—and
why they were not met with immediate reprisals from an armed gang of white
folks—highlights the shared interests white and black landowners held in
protecting one another's forests. Probing the company's subsequent actions
at Bonfouca also reveals an important interface between the South's culture
of Jim Crow segregation, discrimination, and violence and the collapse of the
region's forests in the half century after Reconstruction. Given their vulnerability before the southern judicial system, African American landowners
found themselves with little recourse when lumber firms harvested timber
on their property without their consent. Some, like those on the north shore
of Lake Pontchartrain in 1874, took matters into their own hands.

The black vigilantes who took on Poitevent and Favre in the woods of
St. Tammany were hoping to forestall what I call "Jim Crow's cut," the share
of the South's forests taken by lumber firms operating under the cover of
white supremacy.[4] The connections between Jim Crow and deforestation have
been obscured by a narrative of timber extraction that lumbermen, forest-
ers, and historians alike have referred to as the "cut out and get out" phase of
southern lumber production.[5] In this telling, the debt on investments in land
and machinery, coupled with high taxes for standing timber, forced south-

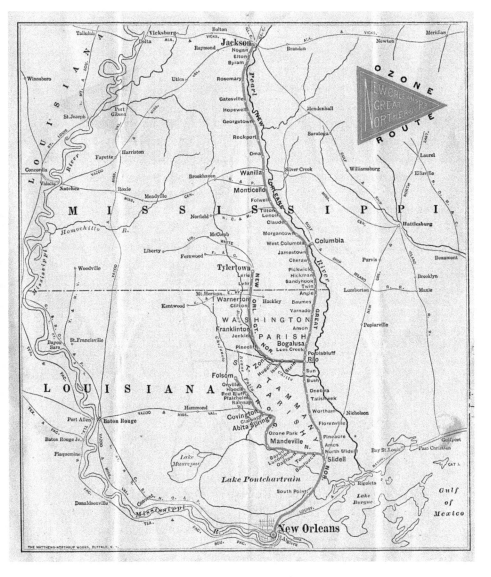

Figure 4.1. Lake Pontchartrain and its environs (Buffalo, NY: New Orleans Great Northern Railroad, 1910).

ern manufacturers to liquidate their timber as soon as possible—even when doing so came at a loss. Such interpretations follow what William Cronon called "the logic of capital"—that is, the ways in which fixed costs for manufacturers and transporters perpetuate, accelerate, and expand commodity flows.[6] While the "cut out and get out" framework rightly emphasizes the devastation wrought by the rush to convert trees into capital, it sacrifices an understanding of the complex interactions between lumber companies and smaller landowners for a sweeping tale of environmental collapse driven by economic imperatives. Incidences of trespassing, the undermining of cross-racial alliances, and the discriminatory use of timber-cutting contracts (a practice African Americans could do little about after Reconstruction) find no place in this story.

Like much of the new history of capitalism, this chapter relies on legal instruments like contracts and land conveyances to analyze how southern lumber companies and small black and white farmers reordered the rural landscape.[7] By insisting on seeing the forest before the trees, it trades a singular view of timber as a commodity for a richer understanding of the diverse economic activities that sustained black landowners in a period of widespread violence, intimidation, and fraud.[8] Scholars of the Deep South's Piney Woods have long treated industrialization and herding culture as mutually exclusive patterns of land use.[9] Yet the boundaries between formal and informal markets were not so clearly drawn. Black landowners combined work in small-scale industry, regional and transnational shipping, and cash-crop production with subsistence farming and herding on the forest commons. The cattle they ran on the open range moved freely across property lines and alternately served as part of the region's subsistence culture and as an agricultural product that could be sold for cash. Black farmers likewise drew upon interracial alliances with white neighbors and white kinfolk to provide alternative sources of credit, to support land transactions, and to assist in the processing of cash crops like cotton and sugar cane as well as timber. Understanding their experiences sheds light on the intersectional interests of race and class that informed the attacks at Bayou Bonfouca—interests that remain hidden in many studies of the Piney Woods region.[10]

Paying attention to Jim Crow's cut means stepping outside of the mills and taking stock of the opportunities for capital accumulation and community development the first generation of freedpeople found in the South's forests after the Civil War. These opportunities for freedpeople included using the 1862 Homestead Act to acquire land—a process that persisted well into the twentieth century. As was the case at Bayou Bonfouca, kinship connections born of antebellum miscegenation allowed for significant economic cooperation across the color line. White relatives helped former slaves process homesteading paperwork, offered their own lands for sale, and provided credit for land transactions. Although these relationships were without question unequal, they created a shared stake in the open range herding culture that characterized much of the South. Because white and black herdsmen relied on each other's forests to support their own livestock, any damage to black-owned land diminished the range for the white community as well. While the competing claims stockmen and industrialists made on the forest are well known, the stakes African Americans held in this conflict have been largely ignored in favor of a scholarly focus on the white majority that lived and worked in the Piney Woods.[11]

By moving beyond the most visible aspects of the market for land and timber, the present essay offers insight into the ways in which white supremacy hastened the collapse of the South's forests. Lumber companies didn't always purchase land outright in order to acquire wood. They signed rights of way and timber-cutting contracts with small landowners as well. These instruments provided a convenient way for farmers to clear a portion of their land for farming, retain some of their forests for herding, and gain ready cash while retaining title to their property. Yet they also created an opportunity for lumber companies to overstep the bounds of their contracts, to deceive illiterate or poorly educated farmers, and to trespass in search of ever more timber. African American farmers became particularly tempting targets for such abuse. Reconstructing their experiences reveals the racial consequences of the unmitigated pursuit of the "logic of capital" that have elsewhere been rendered invisible. In creating a threshold for corporate predation with few legal repercussions, the South's culture of white supremacy accelerated an environmental disaster that was at once a crisis in black capital. Moreover, Jim Crow's cut demolished the forest commons for all farmers.

Interracial Economies in the South and in Southeast Louisiana

After the Civil War, a constellation of forces both for and against black landowning played out in similar ways across multiple southern subregions. In the Yazoo-Mississippi Delta, a tangle of swampy bottomlands and rivers that yielded some of the most productive cotton fields in the nation, African

American land acquisition followed a pattern one scholar has described as being "away from the riverside." During the last two decades of the nineteenth century, freedpeople became the majority landowners in the Delta's backcountry, where less fertile soils prevailed. Under the patronage of former enslavers, prospective black farmers received cash and credit for clearing forests on the margins of the region's plantation districts and gained the opportunity to purchase land there as well.[12] In the Georgia Piedmont, which consists of a mix of rich plantations, erosive hillsides, and rocky, unproductive soils, white landowners offered marginal fields for sale to African American buyers with whom they were well acquainted. In North Carolina's turpentine belt, an area characterized by pine forests interlaced with riverine swamps akin to those in southeast Louisiana, poor black and white farmers found the opportunity to purchase deadened forests left behind by turpentine production. Throughout all of these different landscapes, white assistance proved critical to help forestall the legal manipulation of deeds and debt, as well as to prevent physical intimidation of black farmers.[13]

All of these patterns held true for the community at Bayou Bonfouca, where the hostility that fueled attacks against Samuel Poitevent and the Poitevent and Favre teamsters in the fall of 1874 resurfaced again the following summer. On July 10, 1875, the Republican newspaper editor John E. Leet wrote to the *New Orleans Republican* describing conditions in the southern part of St. Tammany Parish between the north shore of Lake Pontchartrain and the Pearl River. Leet had been traveling the area with census enumerators; as he saw it, "fully one-half the wealth is in the hands of the colored people. They own schooners on the lake and brickyards, and large herds of cattle." Their wealth was a product of the capital flowing through the region's lucrative coastal trade and the commodities that moved along Bayou Bonfouca to Lake Pontchartrain and beyond. These resources were a prime example of the potential the Piney Woods held for black community development, and they were under attack.[14]

Leet alerted readers that "Mr. Poitevent, the noted mill owner of Pearlington, Mississippi," was poaching timber from public land along Bayou Bonfouca and on property owned by the African American community there. According to the folks Leet spoke to, "Mr. Poitevent" carried with him "a contract for sixteen thousand pilings" to build jetties at the mouth of the Mississippi River. He justified his actions with a permit "from the United States government to cut timber not only on public land subject to homestead entry, but also on the homesteads which the colored people have entered and are occupying." Leet was incredulous. He incorrectly argued such actions would have nullified the homesteading contracts of local landowners because many of them had not yet occupied their property for the five years necessary to certify their deeds. Yet removing the valuable timber on their land without compensation would have amounted to an illegal taking on the part of the government. In other words, the actions he attributed to the lumber firm were outright theft that damaged the forest commons on which black and white residents at Bonfouca ranged their cattle.[15]

Poitevent and Favre did have an agreement with James B. Eads and Company to provide the lumber for jetties Eads was building at South Pass on the Mississippi River. Eads had also received authority to "use any materials on the public lands of the United States" for that purpose in the River and Harbor Act of 1875.[16] As for his company's activities on private land at Bayou Bonfouca, Poitevent and Favre scion John Poitevent invoked plausible deniability. In a rebuttal printed in the *Republican*, he stated he was the only Poitevent residing at Pearlington, had not acquired any timber for his contract with Eads in the state of Louisiana, and had not visited Bayou Bonfouca in more than two years. He left both the presence of his younger brother in the area in question and the previous year's conflict with members of the Bonfouca community unstated in his reply.[17]

Leet interrogated these silences in his own rejoinder a few days later. It didn't matter to him if John Poitevent hadn't been to Bonfouca in two years, for someone bearing the name Poitevent was there. Nor did it matter if the timber was cut for the jetties, as much of what the Poitevent crews were cutting came not from public lands but private property. In returning to the area after his initial letter, Leet actually spoke to a Poitevent steamboat crew traveling up the bayou to supply more than one hundred men cutting trees in the surrounding hills. The journalist admitted he might have erred "from a Southern point of view . . . in making a publication based on the statements of colored men." He therefore supplemented his earlier comments with the assessment of a white man of French descent named Terrence Cousin, "the oldest and richest citizen of that section." According to Cousin, "Mr. Poitevent was cutting timber not only on public land and homesteads but also on private land that had been in the possession of a single family for more than a century." Like his neighbors, the elderly brick manufacturer and merchant found the collapse of the nearby forest troubling.[18]

Although the precise details of what transpired at Bayou Bonfouca are unclear, the war of words between Leet and Poitevent, taken together with the black Bonfoucans' attacks, reveal much about the cut-over color lines in the Gulf South's forests. In Leet's estimation, black and white landowners were "interspersed together . . . upon the most neighborly and friendly terms . . . acting together for the mutual protection of their stock." Free people of color in the shipping industry had owned property in the area since the 1850s, while a number of black laborers took up homesteads there in the 1870s.[19] As suggested by the assaults on the teamsters and Samuel Poitevent, this integrated community's willingness to protect each other's cattle extended to protecting the pine hills in which they foraged their stock. The use of cudgels to enforce union discipline was an important part of the political style on the docks in New Orleans, indicating that it may very well have been local sailors who administered the beating.[20] In any event, black and white seafarers with shared French surnames like Cousin and Pechon lived together in mixed communities where they ran cattle on their own land and on the public domain—precisely those lands Poitevent and Favre threatened with its indiscriminate cutting.

The misrepresentation of contracts Leet described helps situate African American landowners' experiences within our broader understanding of how deforestation played out in relation to public policy. Scholars have long recognized the ways by which lumber manufacturers abused the Homestead Act of 1862, both by filing "dummy" claims through individuals who eventually renounced the property and by clearing out the public domain around those claims.[21] This narrative of wholesale environmental loss and the erosion of the national trust cuts over individual stories of abuse in which manufacturers and railroads took advantage of widespread African American illiteracy to overstep their contracts. Leet understood that education was critical. His first complaint on behalf of the black community at Bayou Bonfouca began with a cry for schools. In 1875 black citizens could still take advantage of statewide Republican organizations to press their interests. Folks like those at Bonfouca could also turn to their neighbors to support them when they took matters into their own hands. As Jim Crow hardened in the following decades—as funding for black education became even more scarce, as lynching exploded across the region, and as judges turned their backs on black litigants—industrialists found an opportunity to harvest landed black wealth for their own ends. This problem would only accelerate as railroads pressed ever deeper into the woods.

In 1874 and 1875, the Poitevent and Favre Lumber Company was already taking steps that would dramatically expand the presence of rail transportation and railroad logging in southeast Louisiana. By that time, the Mississippi firm was beginning to shift its center of production into Louisiana as it exhausted its original holdings. It would eventually build a mill on the north shore of Lake Pontchartrain at Mandeville, just west of Bayou Bonfouca. The logging road where Poitevent teamsters met the harsh discipline of African American landowners quite possibly served as the precursor to the company's East Louisiana Railroad. Within four years of the line's establishment in 1884, the *Daily Picayune* was praising Poitevent and Favre for opening up "new towns in the wilderness" across St. Tammany Parish. To be sure, much of the land in the area was sparsely occupied. Yet as the case of the communities at Bayou Bonfouca shows, farmers, sailors, and even manufacturers had lived along its waterways for decades. Each of these groups—white and black— relied on what the *Picayune* defined as a wilderness to range their cattle.[22]

By calling the thinly settled forests north of Lake Pontchartrain a "wilderness," the *Daily Picayune* touched on one of the most important dimensions of class conflict in the postbellum South: the open range. For most of the nineteenth century, the term *wilderness* denoted an unimproved and barren landscape. In mobilizing the term, the *Daily Picayune* author was dismissing both the natural resources of forage and water cattle found on the open range and the lifestyles of the families who raised those cattle. In contrast, fences and the enclosure they made possible signaled improvement and civilization.[23] In the antebellum period, political debates over fencing laws in the South most often revolved around conflicts between herdsmen and planters who chafed at the expense of fencing their crops to protect them from loose livestock. Instead, they called in vain for new laws that would eliminate the traditional use of unoccupied land as a commons and force cattle owners to fence their animals. After the Civil War, as railroads began to penetrate the Deep South's forests, industrialists joined the fight. Their concern lay with the high costs of compensating farmers for livestock hit by trains.[24]

The question of fencing and the open range thus pitted small farmers against planters, rural folk against townspeople, and agrarians against industrialists. All across the South, planters saw fencing as a way of forcing freedpeople back onto the plantation after emancipation. The forest commons provided freedpeople without land an opportunity to hunt game in the woods and run cattle on other people's property rather than return to work for their former enslavers. Yet the protracted battle over fence laws also held the potential to bring white and black farmers together over their shared class interests—just as the loss of timber had done for the families at Bonfouca.

The concerns were in fact the same, given that fences limited animals' access to forage nearly as effectively as eliminating the environmental basis for that forage. As long as African Americans held the franchise, their votes helped ward off the widespread adoption of new fencing laws meant to keep cattle, hogs, and other livestock sequestered. As the region's black farmers lost access to the ballot, though, white livestock owners proved unable to withstand the combined lobbying of planters and railroad operators for enclosure.[25]

Of course, railroads destroyed forests too. Poitevent and Favre's sale of the East Louisiana Railroad highlights industrialists' understanding of the threat their infrastructure posed to standing timber. It further shows the steps companies took to protect their own holdings from the actions of other firms. In 1906, Poitevent and Favre sold the East Louisiana Railroad to the New Orleans Great Northern Railroad (NOGN), a company established by Frank and Charles Goodyear of Buffalo, New York. The line became the foundation of the NOGN's passenger and freight service along the north shore of Lake Pontchartrain and the western banks of the Pearl River. At the same time, Poitevent and Favre granted a right of way across its lands in St. Tammany Parish to another Goodyear firm, the Great Southern Lumber Company. The agreement stated Great Southern could "lay and maintain and operate railroad tracks . . . and to take up and remove the same at pleasure" so long as it compensated the Mississippi firm for all damages to timber "resulting from skidding or lumbering operations."[26] Left unstated in the contract but protected against in its language was the fact that rights of way themselves became inducements to sacrifice other people's timber to the "logic of capital."

Subsistence Farming, Small-Scale Industry, and Lumber Production in the Piney Woods

Although observers at the *Daily Picayune* might have seen large firms like Poitevent and Favre as the leading edge of industrialization in the Piney Woods, the process was instead multivalent across the nineteenth and into the twentieth centuries. Planters had long maintained investments in small-scale industrial operations, such as steam-powered sawmills, grist mills, and sugarcane presses and boilers. Once the "cut out and get out" phase of timber production wound down in the 1930s, portable "peckerwood" sawmills run by individual operators cropped up across the region. Just like cattle herded on the open range, all of these activities sustained an interracial economy that blurred the boundaries between subsistence farming and production for the market.

In 1935, the sociologist Horace Mann Bond found just such an economy in operation along the Bogue Chitto River in Washington Parish, Louisiana, just a few dozen miles north of Bayou Bonfouca. Bond's primary informant was John Wilson, the son of a slave who had just lost two of his sons to a gunfight and subsequent lynching initiated by an argument with local officials regarding compliance with Washington Parish's stock-dipping ordinance. John was married to Tempie Magee, the granddaughter of the former Democratic state senator and planter Jacob Magee and a slave named Minerva. Tempie's father and uncle were both Republican Party leaders in Washington Parish during Reconstruction. Despite their political opposition, Jacob Magee and his brother Fleet proved willing to sell land to their black descendants at fair prices and almost certainly helped them navigate the homesteading process as well. John parlayed his own connections to white Washington Parish planters into a successful farm before "the first lynching of 1935" decimated his family.[27]

In a set of ethnographic interviews conducted with Bond, John Wilson laid out a richly detailed narrative of African American communities along the Bogue Chitto River, which flows into the Pearl River on the Louisiana-Mississippi border. In describing the movement of black farmers out of the bottomlands of the Bogue Chitto after emancipation, he told Bond, "The people settled up and down the creek for the benefit of the water, both white settlers and Colored." A parallel pattern of emigration marked African American settlement of the Yazoo-Mississippi Delta backcountry in the same period. Wilson defined the surrounding forests as "ranges" where cattle were allowed to "roam out in the hills" just like at Bonfouca. African American communities fanned out to the east of the old Bogue Chitto plantations, occupying the upland soils stretching along Hays Creek, Jamieson Creek, and Lawrence Creek. There they adopted the culture of free-range herding and subsistence farming that had sustained white residents in the region since the middle of the eighteenth century.[28]

White assistance was a critical element in the process of black land acquisition in Washington Parish. Describing the homestead claims of Jimmie Hart and George Magee outside the small town of Hackley, Wilson noted, "The white people were interested in them and told them how to homestead land." A June 23, 1896, patent issued to Jimmie Hart under the terms of the Homestead Act of 1862 lists 121.77 acres of land above the headwaters of

Jamieson Creek. George Magee received a patent for 120.55 acres near Hays Creek on October 22, 1896.[29] Wilson was thus describing a tendency within the white community that could never fully mitigate white supremacy but that did run counter to the depredations of greedy landlords and the political violence that marked the South after the Civil War. Far from being a contradiction, this current reflected entangled economic interests, as well as ties of friendship and family.[30]

Racism coursed through the structures of governance both inside and outside Washington Parish, making the support of powerful white planters all the more valuable. In his study of homesteading in the South after the Civil War, the historian Claude F. Oubre found the registrar in the General Land Office in New Orleans held little regard for the claims of aspiring black landowners. Freedpeople with clerical errors on their paperwork found their certificates invalidated without warning, robbing them of a year or more of work on the land even when the error was the registrar's own. Those facing trespassers who claimed to have homesteaded the land in their own right could expect little more than a letter certifying their claim was correct because the land office had no authority to adjudicate disputes. "Things like that happen to impede the progress of the Colored people," John Wilson lamented. He told Bond, "The land I live on now was once owned by a Colored man," but "white folks homesteaded him out of it."[31] In these cases, illiteracy and an inability to pay for court costs could leave black claimants with nothing to show for what may have been years of effort.

John Wilson's description of a one-mule farm in the Piney Woods drives home just how important forest land and railroad access was to the region's farmers. He began working his own property in 1899, planting his first crop on a fifty-acre tract of "green pine woods" he purchased from a white man he had known since childhood. Outlining the fruits of his first year on the property with his new wife, Wilson said, "I grew plenty of corn and sweet potatoes and I had plenty of syrup. In the Fall I would split rails and clear up the land." He took advantage of the logging railroad the Great Southern Lumber Company built nearby a few years later to clear his property, as it gave him access to a ready firewood market in New Orleans.[32]

The Wilson family nonetheless retained a significant amount of forest cover on their land. The typical forty-acre farm John outlined for Horace Mann Bond based on his family's plot contained thirty acres of farmland for cotton, corn, and a small garden, three acres of pasture, and seven acres of woodland. He explained that hogs "run in woods—anybody's woods" while farmers supplemented their forage with corn. To accommodate two milk cows and a mule on three acres, he recommended oats or "clover sown in oats." Production of the "600 to 800 pounds" of meat he deemed necessary for a family of eight thus required the careful use of each element of the farm and the open range. Changes in the scale and scope of lumbering, particularly the introduction of railroad logging with massive steam skidders that dragged entire trees through the forest, circumscribed these practices by transforming the open range into a wasteland. This problem was exacerbated for black farmers, who could rarely sue for damages.[33]

Our understanding of the viability of African American agriculture in the Piney Woods and the consequences of Jim Crow's cut have become a casualty of the "cut out and get out" narrative that dominates discussions of the region's environment. Yet contemporary agricultural research on the cut-over lands east of the Pearl River demonstrated exactly how men like John Wilson managed to thrive. In 1902, the agricultural chemist Eugene Beverly Ferris established the Piney Woods Branch of the Mississippi Agricultural Experiment Station at McNeil, Mississippi, some thirty-odd miles east-southeast of Wilson and his neighbors. Across two decades of work, Ferris discovered that many of the best practices for agriculture in the Piney Woods were already in use. After experimenting in vain with augurs, elaborate stump pullers, and dynamite, Ferris concluded that the local tradition of burning stumps and simply plowing between them on cut-over land represented the most cost-effective strategy for converting former forests to fields.[34]

Ferris found that sugarcane, which formed the basis of the informal exchange economy John Wilson tapped to manage his labor, remained one of the most valuable crops in the region. Wilson acquired hundreds of acres of land in Washington Parish while hiring workers with a combination of cash and agricultural goods like syrup made from cane. In describing how his family managed the labor necessary to harvest their cotton crop, he stated: "I grew a lot of corn, made syrup, sell meat and get work done like that. Instead of paying the labor off with cash I would pay them off with syrup, corn or meat and things like that. I would give children 50¢ and a man $1.00." George Foils, one of the white men John hired to bring in his cotton, faced greater difficulty securing labor to pick his own crop. As John put it, "Folks wouldn't hire to him because he was a poor man." For Foils, cattle offered an alternative solution. In describing his stint as a cattle buyer for a Washington

Parish rancher, John recounted an exchange with Foils in which the white farmer was eager to sell a set of yearlings to gain cash to pay for cotton picking.[35]

John Wilson's ability to pay off workers with cane syrup offers a sense of the quality of the land he was putting into production. Despite its status as the "best paying crop that could be planted" in Washington Parish, Ferris discovered sugarcane was most profitably grown on the best soils, "preferably well drained bottom lands." Again, Ferris deferred to local environmental knowledge. He recommended the crop be grown "as it has been grown in the past, in small quantities on each farm by a large number of small farmers."[36] As the Wilson case demonstrates, those small quantities per farmer nonetheless circulated widely throughout the region's broader agricultural economy.

The long history of plantation agriculture along the Bogue Chitto made Wilson's use of cane syrup as payment for farm labor possible. The planters in Washington Parish established a well-developed infrastructure for processing, storing, marketing, and financing the production of cane syrup. This formal economy allowed for the informal relationships of payment in kind that John Wilson used to finance the labor he needed to bring in his other cash crops like cotton and corn. Planters in both St. Tammany and Washington Parish promoted sugarcane cultivation as part of a wider program of agricultural diversification in the region. Their activities, in turn, helped build a market for bottled syrup. In 1907, for example, cane syrup was selling for forty cents a gallon in Abita Springs, northeast of Bayou Bonfouca in St. Tammany. In 1921, the farmers of Washington Parish built "a central boiling station for the standardization of cane syrup" to fetch the best price possible. Their goal was to create a high-quality product that would increase the demand for syrup from Washington Parish across the region.[37]

By paying workers to pick cotton using syrup that could then be sold for processing into sugar, John Wilson was participating in a form of "neighbor-to-neighbor capitalism" rooted in Washington Parish's interracial economy.[38] Tracing that network highlights the interrelationship between subsistence farming, small-scale industry, and black landownership. Wilson most likely pressed his sugarcane into syrup on the farm of Bennie Graves. As Wilson stated to Horace Mann Bond, Graves "lives not far from where I live. He has the syrup mill. They seem to be very fine people." Bennie's father, Willie Graves, was an industrialist too. Wilson remembered that Willie "owned a saw mill, a store and nearly all the niggers up there. The old man nearly about owns them and raise them too. When he became old he began to sell to these niggers. He didn't think they wanted to pay for it but they did." The property in question was almost certainly cut-over land left treeless by Graves's mill. As such, it followed the pattern of white residents selling less desirable land to African Americans in the Yazoo-Mississippi Delta, the Georgia Piedmont, and elsewhere across the South. If John Wilson's language is any indication, it is also quite possible that Graves's black customers were also his relatives.[39]

Although the black farmers of Washington Parish relied on small-scale industry to support effective agriculture on cut-over lands, intensive timber harvesting proved fatal to their livestock operations. As with Poitevent and Favre at Bayou Bonfouca, Washington Parish lumber firms took advantage of some black landowners' illiteracy to scalp their land of far more timber than their contracts stipulated. "Some of the old folks did not know one letter from the other," Wilson said. "[If] you do not know they would do you the same thing." Even those with the resources to defend themselves were at risk. A man listed in Bond's notes as Jake Elder, for example, owned "160 acres of pine timber" on which he raised what Wilson praised as "fine steers." After agreeing to sell forty acres of timber, he found the firms' crews actually harvested trees from eighty acres. When the company argued the land in question had not contained forty acres of timber, thereby necessitating the extra cut, Elder spent his payments in a failed suit for restitution. For farmers that depended on their woodlands to provide forage, such a loss could prove devastating, particularly as clear-cutting lowered the carrying capacity of the surrounding countryside.[40]

As Wilson recalled, transactions like these were part of a broader pattern of cheating on the part of what he called "the syndicate" working for "the lumber interest" and railroads. While no record for Jake Elder exists in Washington Parish's conveyance documents, Wilson was probably talking about Jacob Elzey and his son Eli J. Elzey. In 1890 Jacob Elzey homesteaded 160 acres along "a little old creek" that flowed into Hays Creek. Nine years later, he signed a timber-cutting contract with the Banner Lumber Company of Tangipahoa Parish, Louisiana. Elzey's agreement was one of dozens of contracts and rights of way Banner signed with black and white landowners. Taken together, the conveyances ran through the heart of Washington Parish's black landowning community.[41]

Jacob Elzey's contract with the Banner Lumber Company confirms at least some of Wilson's description. Elzey's mark, for example, demonstrates that he was illiterate. The agreement gave Banner Lumber Company the right to all of the timber on Elzey's 160-acre homestead together with a right of way for railroad construction in exchange for one hundred dollars. It is unclear exactly where and how much timber actually stood on his property. Nonetheless, the differences in language between the property description in his homestead patent and the property description in the contract could have certainly confused an individual who did not know one word from another. Elzey's patent assigned him the "southeast quarter of the southwest quarter" and the "northeast quarter of the southwest quarter" together with the "northwest quarter of the southeast quarter" of section twenty, township one south, range eleven east. Each of these one-sixteenth sections amounted to forty acres. The contract described the same property as the "east half of the southwest quarter" and the "northwest quarter of the southeast quarter." If Elzey's timber was concentrated on the western edge of his property—and if he or a semiliterate associate missed the distinction between the words *half* and *quarter*—then the difference would have been eighty acres cut over instead of forty. Such a mistake would not have protected him in court.[42]

To be clear, firms related to the Banner Lumber Company did have a history of abusing rights of way. If this was part of a broader pattern of behavior, it certainly could have produced the devastating results for Washington Parish's African American community that John Wilson outlined for Bond. Wilson further described "one man who homesteaded 160 acres of land" with the "finest timber that ever grew in that section and the K. and E. Railroad put a railroad through his place of business." The "K. and E." referred to the Kentwood and Eastern Railroad, a subsidiary of the Banner Lumber Company and its successor, the Brooks Scanlon Lumber Company. The farmer in question was a white man named W. J. Alford. Unlike Jacob Elzey, Alford prevailed in a lawsuit against the firm. Besides highlighting the ways in which lumber companies could abuse their contracts with small landowners, it also demonstrates the keen environmental awareness of Piney Woods farmers.[43]

In 1903, Alford sold a parcel of timber along with a right of way to secure it to M. M. Sanders and Son for two hundred dollars. Sanders and Son subsequently sold the contract to the Brooks Scanlon Lumber Company. In 1909, in conjunction with the Kentwood and Eastern, the company harvested his timber and built a permanent line across his fields, by which the firms began transporting "many millions of feet of timber" from tracts outside Alford's property. Alford's 1910 and 1911 lawsuits against the firms were extraordinary for their time. In a period when many companies were still debating the relative merits of reforestation, Alford argued the land had "been cut over about two years and the same would have made some progress toward reforestation, but the ground used by the said railroad has been kept clear of all timber." He also demonstrated a keen perception of the seasonality of fire, stating fires started by locomotives had burned "over his land so often and out of season killing many young trees that any reforestation has been prevented." Alford sued for $250 but estimated that his total damages were closer to $2,000. These values had nothing to do with the acre of property taken by the railroad but instead the future value of his forest holdings. Judge Thomas Burns concurred, ordering Brooks Scanlon to pay for damages and cease operating the railroad.[44]

Conclusion

By privileging the conflict between subsistence agriculture and industrialization, historians have perpetuated the corporate narrative of deforestation in the Deep South at the expense of a deeper understanding of white supremacy. To be sure, the physical evidence of clear-cutting can be overwhelming. Images of the horizon visible in every direction, with hundreds of acres of burned-over stumps or cattle grazing through tick-infested switchgrass where forests once stood, certainly verifies the dissolution of traditional rural life. The lumber industry in fact created similar landscapes in every region of the country. Yet assigning these outcomes to an autonomous logic hides the particular ways in which Jim Crow inflected the market for land and timber in the South. As Michael Zakim and Gary J. Kornblith put it, flattened economic narratives like that of "cut out and get out" simply "reproduce capitalist ideology itself."[45] Small farmers appear first as an obstacle and then as a casualty of economic modernization. Yet an overemphasis on the incompatibility of timber production and free-range herding cuts over the many ways in which small farmers of all races relied upon a matrix of small-scale industry, cash crop production, and running cattle in the forest commons.

That same versatility helped Washington Parish's black farmers as they struggled with the consequences of deforestation. They overcame the erosion that so often accompanied clear-cutting with support from Louisiana's Cooperative Extension Service, which rented heavy equipment like land levelers to African American self-help leagues. As the Extension agent Myrtis Magee noted in 1931, "Hill land in 1927 that had gullies 4 ft. deep . . . is now in good condition." Yet Jim Crow's cut was followed by still more manifestations of discriminatory land use. Although the Extension Service offered black farmers recommendations for crop rotation and agricultural diversification, by 1931 all forestry work with African American communities in Washington Parish came to a halt.[46] As such, they were locked out of state and federal supports for reforestation just as cut-over landscapes all across the South were coming back into timber production.

Lumber company predations carried out under the cover of white supremacy threatened the material basis for small farming and interracial cooperation at the same time. That a white man like W. J. Alford could expect to seek compensation against powerful lumber firms where a black man like Jacob Elzey could not is a prime example of the social and environmental blowback of Jim Crow.[47] In a shared agriculture in which white and black herdsmen both felt the loss of open woodland, the entire community was damaged when firms could prey upon black landowners with impunity. This is not to suggest that the suffering was similar. It was not. African Americans found misplaced justice before the bar in a way that was routine, and all too often when their lives were at stake. Moreover, the threat lumber firms posed to African American landownership was simultaneously a threat to their autonomy and basic citizenship rights in a way that was incomparable for white folks. These obstacles—the social consequences of Jim Crow's cut— played out across the South in ways that have largely escaped the attention of environmental and civil rights historians alike.

Chapter 5

In the Shadow of Incorporation: Hidden Economies of the Hispano Borderlands, 1890–1930

Bryan W. Turo

In late January 1905, amid the pressures of a booming decade of growth on the eastern rangelands of New Mexico, the MaCormick Cattle Company of Cimarron leased the northeastern corner of the 827,000-acre Mora Land Grant from Thomas B. Catron, the landowner, and the largest individual landowner in territorial New Mexico. With assurances from Catron's agent William E. Gortner that title to the Mexican-era land grant was then free and clear, the company's overseer, Mr. Strahan, moved to relocate five hundred head of cattle. But when Strahan attempted to run the herd on the designated lands, two competing ranchers, Mr. Montoya and Alberto Valdez, aggressively chased him and his stock away.[1] Both Montoya and Valdez claimed the use of these grant lands for their sheep, and even though they lacked fences, they protected their boundaries and their right to graze. When confronted, Montoya, who ran between seven thousand and seventy-five hundred head of sheep in partnership with his brother-in-law, explained to Mr. Strahan that he had a standing oral agreement with Catron, the grant owner, and so ordered Strahan off the premises. Such informal arrangements were quite common in the region, the expedient byproducts of the drastic change in landownership but not land residence, which unceremoniously made "squatters" of thousands of dispossessed Nuevomexicano land-grant heirs.[2] Still, Montoya's oral agreement was just as likely a savvy bluff. Whether or not Strahan could confirm or deny it, Montoya could rely on his own social networks to evade the formal economy and its contractual pasture fees. Valdez proved less diplomatic. Every time Strahan crossed cattle onto the land, the sheep rancher set his men and dogs upon the intruders. The MaCormick Cattle Company quickly tired of the disagreeable competition, sending word to Gortner that they would remove Strahan and their cattle from the Mora grant.[3] It was one less paying account for the grant's corporate ownership.

In the aftermath, Gortner lamented that the continued presence of the sheepmen on these valuable lands prevented more lucrative grazing leases, especially to "good" (white) cattlemen. As a well-connected attorney from nearby East Las Vegas, New Mexico, he was surely sore at missing out on some easy seasonal revenues. The uncompensated depletion of the overcrowded rangelands compounded the frustration. As one of New Mexico's preeminent land barons, Thomas Catron shared these sentiments. But what vexed him most was his inability to complete the sale of the enormous tract with any of the eastern buyers to which he marketed it. Uninhibited grazing lessened the property's value and created thorny questions as to clarity and strength of title. For the owner and his agent, replacing the sheep ranchers with the MaCormick Cattle Company was a step in the right direction.[4] As an incorporated entity with documented charter, fee-simple property, established valuation, and stock subscriptions (and therefore stockholders), the company participated in the state-sponsored economy and presented a clear example of capitalist development in the region.[5] Alternatively, the operations of Montoya and Valdez pointed to the types of economic activity that, while collectively significant, went largely overlooked and unaccounted for in terms of the territory's and later the state's development. Their labor, as well as that of thousands of "illegible" Nuevomexicanos and Native Americans, constituted a hidden economy throughout the rural expanses of northern New Mexico, especially where land-grant heirs faced high levels of dispossession and economic marginalization.[6]

Amid larger processes of market and political incorporation, shadow economies like sheep ranching and timber cutting on the contested spaces of the Hispano borderlands sustained themselves. Logics of rationalization steeped in liberal capitalism brought about new opportunities, especially for corporate entities, but also a new era of market rupture for rural Hispano and indigenous populations. As a result, the economic lives of these populations increasingly existed outside of, at odds with, or parallel to the formally tracked and measured economy. As part of this restructuring, many New Mexican communities lost legal access to the lands and resources that supported their village economies.[7] The ranching practices of Montoya and Valdez then, like so many of their contemporaries, represented a pragmatic response to shifting power dynamics.[8] Because the land they ranged on did not legally belong to them, because they held no formal leases or contracts, and because the final results of their labor—ewes and wool—were introduced into the market indirectly, these ranchers' operations likely showed up on someone else's balance sheet, if at all. Their labor was somehow simultaneously illegal, invisible, and productive. Their clandestine use of land and resources was quite literally a hidden economy.

Though often overlooked, the mixed economic activity of Nuevomexicanos and Native Americans is essential for proper consideration of New Mexico's twentieth-century development and notable lack thereof.[9] This oversight stems, in part, from the awkward fit with the normative boundaries of capitalism, a result of national prerogatives and the modern organization of economic data, compounded by rural marginalization and ethnic stigmatization.[10] A guiding question for this chapter, then, is how this region and its nonwhite majority, instead of becoming a center of population and trade in the twentieth century as it was in the nineteenth, faded in importance. After functioning as a hub of transnational trade and commerce, why did New Mexico, especially the trade area centered around Santa Fe, stultify so quickly as compared to its neighboring states? Of equal importance, how did the continued presence of alternative economies and economic logics influence New Mexico's marginal status and the choices available to its diverse residents? To answer these questions the chapter will consider the ways that pluralism framed the economy for many of the inhabitants of the region, the transformative influence of state and market incorporation, and how the resultant hidden economic activity occurred within the context of dispossession and marginalization.

Of interest here are the uneven results produced by the absorption of the borderlands and its variegated economies into the nation-state through modern forces of economic, juridical, and political incorporation. Full integration of the Hispano borderlands obscured the continued coexistence of alternative markets and alternative organizations of economic behavior. Federal and state bureaucrats' increased attention to formally conceived data meant that much of the economic activity enacted in the region existed apart from the state-sponsored economy. Although economic logics and practices with roots in the eighteenth and nineteenth centuries—the family, the land, and the seasons—continued, communities' access to resources fundamentally changed, thus recasting their work as outside of or distinct from the market and often even as illicit. And yet, with no little contradiction, the burgeoning tourism industry of the 1910s and 1920s reaped huge profits by relying upon commoditizing the very same "premodern" economic behaviors, such as the skilled crafts of Native Americans and the pastoral work of Nuevomexicanos. In this regard we see how corporate logics simultaneously moved forward a precapitalist imaginary and used that very same narrative to discount alternative forms of production and labor.

Economic Pluralism in the Hispano Borderlands

During the nineteenth century, the Hispano borderlands stood at an intersection of North American peoples, cultures, and economies. Centered in northern New Mexico, the area represented the largest concentration of demographic and market activity in the Rocky Mountain West.[11] Quite literally a continental crossroads, the trade that flowed through key places, such as Taos, Santa Fe, and Las Vegas, linked New Mexico to Saint Louis, Philadelphia, Baltimore, and New York; to Chihuahua, Zacatecas, and Mexico City; to the Great Plains, the Rocky Mountains, the Great Basin, and the California gold fields; and even to Europe as both the point of origin for many of the goods that filtered across North America and the terminus for much of the capital that facilitated this intricate web of commercial relations.[12] The region hosted multiple overlapping, intersecting, and competing economies as enacted by its diverse populations of Native Americans, Nuevomexicanos, and Euro-Americans.[13] The trade and exchange that funneled to and through the area took many forms, demonstrating the region's social and cultural diversity, as well as its economic potential.

For historians of capitalism, this dynamic economic borderland presents an example par excellence of the ways that multiple market logics interacted, coexisted, and competed amid a broader context of state and market penetration and incorporation. In this regard, strict distinctions between formal and informal sectors made little sense for most of its inhabitants. Instead, throughout the nineteenth century, Native American, Nuevomexicano, and Euro-Americans all practiced some degree of economic pluralism, meaning that individuals, households, or communities provided for their livelihood and sustenance by relying upon more than one ecological, spatial, or market niche.[14] While uniquely adapted to the mountains, valleys, plateaus, and plains of the southern Rockies, this diversified strategy had much in common with the several subsistence or makeshift modes of production considered by historians of agrarian societies, whether in England, Appalachia, or Southeast Asia.[15] Its implementation afforded residents of borderland communities the flexibility to adapt to rapid economic transformation and the practicality to look to the past, present, and future in determining options for market engagement.

By the late nineteenth century this fluid economic ecosystem hardened (though incompletely and with plenty of cracks), forged in the process with state-sponsored capitalism and Anglo-American fee-simple property rights.[16] Nuevomexicano claims affixed to lands granted by Spain or Mexico felt the brunt of this mostly nonviolent and often covert transformation. The products of colonial New Mexico's need to incentivize frontier settlement, Spanish and later Mexican authorities awarded several types of Mercedes Reales to individuals, families, and communities. For all but a select few, these grants included *ejidos*, or mixed-use spaces held in common by the residents and protected by law.[17] After U.S. military conquest in 1846 and the installation of a territorial government in 1850, however, these Spanish- and Mexican-era grants entered a state of legal ambiguity. Through the U.S. Office of the Surveyor General, the New Mexico Territorial Courts, and later the U.S. Court of Private Land Claims, U.S. civil servants, lawyers, and judges acted in concert with speculators and politicians to steadily strip Nuevomexicano owners and residents of their lawful protections, usufruct rights, and even ownership itself.[18] By the time New Mexico earned the distinction of the forty-seventh state in 1912, total grant land loss reached over 80 percent.[19] Of significance for this discussion, an associated 80 percent of Nuevomexicanos did not then, nor ever, relocate their villages in response to the sweeping cycle of legal dispossession.

In a plan designed in 1900 by the delegate to Congress Pedro Perea, the well-connected Nuevomexicano politico proposed legislation that would ease the plight of those dispossessed land-grant heirs while subtly aiding land speculators as well. Basing his idea on the Homestead Act and the use of land scrip by the federal government, Perea argued in his "Free Home Bill" that alienated Nuevomexicanos deserved 160 acres of public land in exchange for their lost or soon-to-be-lost grant lands. He lamented the "hardships in our

Territory, to many poor families, on account of our grants. For instance, people who lived for many years on the Maxwell Grant, on the Mora Grant, and perhaps on the TA, and many others, [who] never could, and never can get title to their lands. They have only possession, of which in many instances they have been ousted, and in others, they will be ousted at a future time." Perea continued, "Now, my idea is, that people who have lost, or who may hereafter lose their homes, in cases as above stated, should be allowed, to take 160 acres of Government land, and the years they were in those Grants credited to them, so that they can get free homes."[20] Although the "Free Home Bill" never received serious consideration by the U.S. Congress, Perea's statements show great awareness of the structures of immiseration leveled against Nuevomexicano "squatters," as well as the most direct solution, title to land.

For their part, the Nuevomexicanos on the Maxwell, Sangre de Cristo, Tierra Amarilla, Mora, Preston Beck, Eaton, Chavez, Las Trampas, Antonio Ortiz, Town of Anton Chico, and San Miguel del Vado land grants (among many others) often refused to concede ownership to private or corporate interests, even when those interests were backed by the law and the state.[21] In March 1907, for example, the land agent Frank Clark wrote to Thomas Catron to explain that the residents of the Antonio Ortiz grant categorically refused to pay any rent for pasturage.[22] Likewise, many Nuevomexicanos avoided paying regular leases or fees on grant lands even as they continued to run enormous flocks. As a case in point, during the fall of 1902 alone William Gortner repeatedly complained about the fifty to sixty thousand animals found on a 130,000-acre section of the Mora grant.[23] The ranchers who owned them proved difficult to track down. They obscured their activities, movements, and livestock ownership and, when cornered, often explained (truthfully or otherwise) that the grant owner bestowed personal allowances. They utilized mobility, clouded boundaries, and feigned ignorance to graze their herds, support their villages, and avoid formal leases. The rural, pastoral landscape allowed these ranchers to fly under the radar as a means of resistance, a practice that they carried out to a modicum of success during this period of heightened attention to land management by capitalists and federal bureaucrats alike.

Evasion and misdirection represented only part of the resistance equation for Nuevomexicano ranchers, however. They also asserted usage and possession by their continued presence on and defense of common lands. If the rangelands of eastern New Mexico provided a place to avoid oversight, they

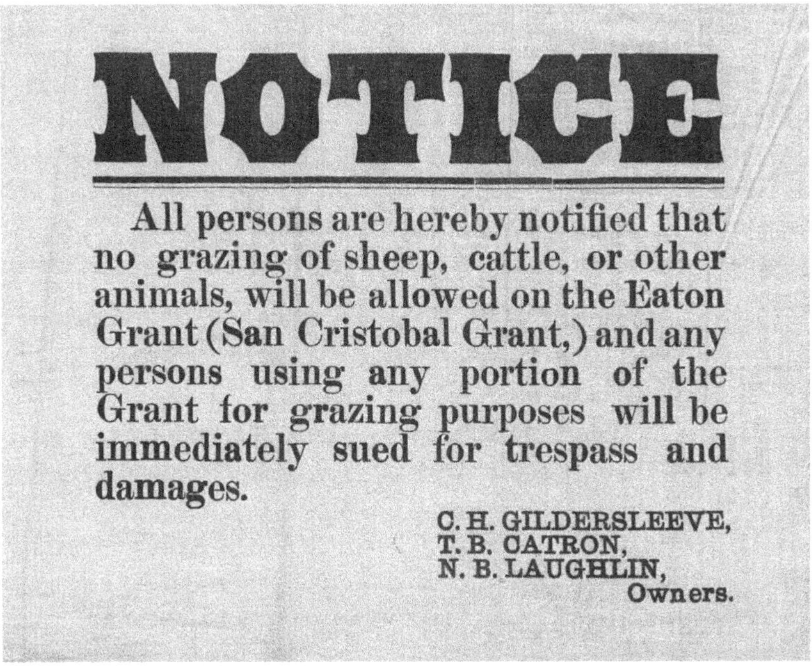

NOTICE

All persons are hereby notified that no grazing of sheep, cattle, or other animals, will be allowed on the Eaton Grant (San Cristobal Grant,) and any persons using any portion of the Grant for grazing purposes will be immediately sued for trespass and damages.

C. H. GILDERSLEEVE,
T. B. CATRON,
N. B. LAUGHLIN,
Owners.

Figure 5.1. "Notice" of ownership of Eaton grant by C. H. Gildersleeve, T. B. Catron, and N. B. Laughlin, c. 1903. Thomas B. Catron Papers, Center for Southwest Research, University Libraries, University of New Mexico.

also attracted cattlemen in droves. By the early twentieth century the environment already showed signs of overgrazing.[24] The economic and cultural contest that resulted fused the issues of ownership and allocation with race and labor. Euro-American cattle ranchers grew increasingly frustrated by the continued presence of "squatters," while the residents grew increasingly aggressive toward the protection of their available range and their interests.[25]

Another manifestation of this hidden economy appears in the widespread use of private property (mostly ex-grant lands), the national forests, and the public domain by rural households of all backgrounds. As with their practice of grazing livestock on lands held in common (*ejidos*), villagers of the Hispano borderlands collectively benefitted from their access and usufruct rights to neighboring forests and wooded lands. An important component of the economic pluralism practiced by Nuevomexicano grant residents, communal rights to forest ecologies served family and village priorities for the self-provisioning of building materials and fuel, alongside the gathering of supplemental foods and medicinal roots or herbs.[26] These practices continued and in places expanded or took on market dimensions internal to the local villages. Even as speculators bought up grant interests, lawyers moved forward with partition suits, and the Court of Private Land Claims cleaved off *ejidos* from approved and unapproved grants alike, the multipurpose use of the wooded lands persisted unabated throughout the borderlands. By the legal redefinition of the land's ownership, however, the meanings attached to those persistent activities altered drastically.

From the perspective of the state, Nuevomexicano utilization of forested lands shifted from inconsequential to illicit. This was especially true as the need for railroad ties and mine supports heightened capitalists' interests in the forests of northern New Mexico.[27] The state opened the door for "corporate predation" of the region's critically important wooded lands while railroad directors, sawmill operators, mercantile managers, and land agents voiced their collective displeasure at any circumstance that led to their unremunerated depletion.[28] Deforestation was not seen as the most injurious end. More disturbing to state and corporate interests was use of the forests in ways that were not formally productive.

On the Mora grant, for example, the Mora Timber Company manager Richard Dunn fumed about parties engaged in uncontrolled and illegal timber cutting. Providing a list with seven names, he explained to Thomas Catron that these men would all be considered trespassers and subject to legal action should they continue their activities.[29] A few months later Dunn complained again, except this time naming a whole new set of "squatters."[30] It's unclear whether those originally listed stopped their activities, decided to cut elsewhere on the grant, or, just as likely, had other community members take a turn to present a constantly changing set of faces and names. This scenario found repetition on many of the land grants of northern New Mexico, especially those near rail terminals or mining centers. Besides erecting fences, posting formal notices, and threatening suit or arrest, there was little that these company men could do to effectively quell the entrenched behaviors of villagers who scoffed at the idea that they were in any way trespassing. In the face of sweeping social and economic transformation, their hidden economy functioned to empower Nuevomexicanos, particularly when it facilitated continued attachment to the land and its resources.[31]

The presence of an extensive social network proved critical to Nuevomexicano villagers' capacity to effectively maintain their livelihoods through economic pluralism.[32] Based on kin and community reciprocities, households could mobilize support from formal and informal sectors, thus providing access to a variegated economic infrastructure. Especially as set against the backdrop of a diminishing land base and constraining political pressures, the system of social ties empowered individuals and communities alike. In this sense, networks not only collectivized Nuevomexicano interests, made that much more salient through real and symbolic ties, but facilitated the connection to and distribution of key resources. Multivillage networks gave cover to the hidden economy of northern New Mexico through the sharing of valuable intelligence regarding the best free lands, their current occupants or owners, opportune trails and routes, and people or places to avoid. As business-minded residents sought to rationalize the territory's economy in the late nineteenth and early twentieth centuries, these Nuevomexicano social networks proved invaluable time and again for the protection and even proliferation of villagers' economic pluralism.

Formalizing New Mexico's Incorporation

Meanwhile, the reigning class of rentiers, machine politicians, and territorial boosters directed their attentions to the enduring obstacles supposedly blocking progress. For the Catrons, Gortners, and Dunns of the region, the continued presence of "squatters," "trespassers," and the like prevented them from actualizing on their land-grant dreams. Early setbacks of the 1890s only made the situation worse for many who speculated in the Hispano borderlands. To begin the decade, popular defeat of the Republican-dominated Constitution of 1890 stopped a statehood surge dead in its tracks. Resuscitation would have to wait for the period of national recovery following the Panic of 1893.[33] Contrary to the widespread notions of southwestern isolation, the depression years demonstrated how New Mexico was already well incorporated into the rhythms of national markets. Multiple sectors, including mining, ranching, and banking, felt the pain quickly and acutely and were slow to recover. By the middle of the decade, the territory itself had defaulted on several bonds and racked up just shy of one million dollars in debt.[34] The usual scarcity of currency compounded the cycles of debt that ensued, as the lack of cash and falling land values made collections—even of interest charges—futile.[35] Held up on land deals, behind with their eastern creditors, and hamstrung by political scandal in Santa Fe, many New Mexican capitalists found themselves in a state of arrested development. To make matters worse, ethnic competition reached a crescendo in the early 1890s as Nuevo-mexicano resentment toward the Anglo-dominated system congealed in the forms of racial politicization, community retrenchment, and bursts of anger. One popular group, Las Gorras Blancas, most clearly expressed this politically and economically motivated rejection of the new order of things. They tuned in to extant ethnic and community networks to lead secretive gatherings, including at times the destruction of fences, barns, and other symbols of social intrusion.[36] It was against this backdrop then, of a region already burned over by the energies of nationalist and capitalist advances and the resultant backlash, in which calls for progress and order took root.

Led by politicians, professionals, entrepreneurs, and bureaucrats (themselves divided by competing regional, policy, and business interests), turn-of-the-century reform efforts shared a fundamental desire to bring a market rationality to the drivers of New Mexico's growth—its lands and natural resources. Capitalists and government officials alike aspired to establish a system defined by transparency of titles, documentation of holding and transference, and fee structures for land access and resource use. In an attempt to finally resolve the long-standing issue of Spanish and Mexican land-grant boundaries and ownership, the U.S. Congress created the Court of Private Land Claims (CPLC). From 1891 to 1904 the special court for the New Mexico District met in Santa Fe, where it held over 272 hearings and decided on 231 Spanish and Mexican land grants representing 35,491,020 acres.[37] It rejected 32,718,354 of those acres.[38] The CPLC applied an exceedingly rigid formula to heirs seeking to prove grant existence, size, and continued community residence. Its influence was especially deleterious to grantee's claims to *ejidos*, considered an anachronistic affront to ideas of fee-simple property ownership. It was aided in this regard by an 1897 decision by the U.S. Supreme Court in the case of *United States* v. *Sandoval*, which ruled that land-grant commons remained the sole property of the sovereign and therefore transferred to the U.S. federal government upon the signing of the Treaty of Guadalupe Hidalgo. As applied by the CPLC, the new rule itself resulted in the substantial reduction, outright elimination, and governmental appropriation of over one million acres of Nuevomexicano commons.[39]

Private developers, attorneys, the public domain, and the national forest system made up some of the most significant beneficiaries for those acres divorced from land grants.[40] For Nuevomexicano villagers with cultural and productive attachments to their *ejidos*, these losses painfully diminished their economic potential. Though the size, distance, and rural setting made them practically impossible to regulate and police, national forest lands carved from grants gained the early ire of Nuevomexicanos as direct symbols of subjugation and dispossession.[41] With origins in the Forest Reserve Act of 1891, the network of federally owned and controlled forests, which included thousands of acres of good grazing land, grew rapidly. The National Forest Service set aside the Pecos, Jemez, Taos, and Manzano reserves by 1906 before adding the Carson, Chiricahua, Datil, Durango, Gila, Lincoln, and Zion National Forests. By 1920 the system totaled over 9.5 million acres overseen by the chief forester, who administered the collection of grazing and timber-harvesting fees.[42] These forest lands evolved into spaces of intense contestation as Nuevomexicanos sought their unmolested access and use while forest rangers attempted to more scientifically manage the land through quantification and documentation, which included the assessment of fines for "trespassers." Over time, the distrust that developed between Nuevomexicano ranchers and government agents only helped to drive a wedge between the two groups, deterring local Hispano villagers from filing ranging leases and instead leading them to continue to practice an economy based in part on hidden land usage.

The territory and later state of New Mexico also sponsored economic growth by strategically investing in its legal and bureaucratic infrastructure, especially as related to business development. Incorporation laws, first passed by the Territorial Assembly in 1867, privileged and protected capitalist enterprise by establishing corporate personhood.[43] Additions, such as the 1875 Act Granting to Railroads the Right of Way Through the Public Lands of the United States indicate early attempts to use corporate law to attract desired industry.[44] Comprehensive reappraisals of the incorporation laws in 1897, 1905, and 1910 continued each time to point the needle in favor of big-business interests. The General Corporation Act of 1905, for instance, provisioned utility and transportation companies with new rules to appropriate and value lands through an eminent domain statute.[45] It also served state interests in that it required each for-profit corporation in New Mexico to file an annual report with the secretary of the territory, thus providing a checklist of data relevant to its legal status and financial solvency.[46] Corporate laws such as these constituted the binding agents of a hardening formal economy, helping to affix the correct types of business enterprises to the state. In return, the state sought to empower entrepreneurs by creating more robust legal tool sets for them to access and activate the productive powers of crucial resources, such as water, minerals, and oil.

The achievement of statehood in 1912 further solidified New Mexico's economic hierarchies, embedding a big-business agenda into the legal framework of the new state through its Constitution of 1910.[47] Although Nuevomexicanos represented their interests during the convention, most directly those of the well-to-do *rico* class, the resulting constitution provided few stopgaps against the economic decline of the village economy. On the contrary, the strong ranks of land-grant lawyers, prominent landowners, and urban professionals most successfully asserted their needs and protected their interests.[48] Major reclamation projects of the early twentieth century diverted the region's watercourses to drive the formal growth of the agricultural sector. At the same time, state resources were focused on support of the commercial classes, especially in city spaces, and gave decreased economic and political attention to the Nuevomexicano village networks of the borderlands. Though demographically significant, rural residents relied on an economic pluralism that placed much of their productive activity outside the quantifiable marketplace. And so rural Nuevomexicanos held an increasingly weak position under the new state framework, especially as compared to the evolving agribusiness and commercial sectors supported by the newly created State Corporation Commission.[49]

While the rationalization of hinterland spaces through federal courts and agencies accommodated the growth of the formal sector in New Mexico, significant changes in the territory's demographics also served to harden boundaries between modes of production and livelihood. Most dramatically, the first decade of the twentieth century featured a 67 percent increase in the territory's population, led by a wave of Euro-American immigrants. New arrivals filled in both rural and urban areas, though settlement patterns focused outside the Nuevomexicano heartland. Led by the Bureau of Reclamation, newcomers filed an abundance of homestead claims, which rapidly outpaced the total number of nineteenth-century entries and tripled the acreage of farmland under cultivation.[50] Ranching operations likewise recorded a period of expansion, leading to the heightened competition with the Nuevomexicano ranchers. With the arrival of statehood in 1912, the mixed-market economy that characterized the territorial period constricted, as did the available options for Nuevomexicano and Native American communities.

One result was that Nuevomexicanos too began entering the cities and urban spaces of New Mexico alongside throngs of mostly white, middle-class Americans. As railroad and banking hubs, the growing cities concentrated professional activity, commercial enterprise, and political influence. For places like Albuquerque and Las Vegas, the additions mostly occurred in "new" urban spaces that sprung up adjacent to but separate from the existent plazas of Spanish and Mexican origin.[51] The new city leaders organized chambers of commerce, commercial clubs, fraternal societies, water users' associations, sheep and wool growers' associations, fruit growers' associations, and even annual fairs and expositions, which doubled as events to promote civic pride and economic development.[52] That this round of urban growth overlooked core Nuevomexicano municipalities is evident when considering the 1912 list of towns and cities powered by electric utility companies. The clear preference for the newer, Anglo-dominated centers of activity and enterprise, not to mention the actual boost gained from connection to the electrical grid, further imbalanced the social and economic scales for New Mexico right as it entered its statehood phase.[53]

Evidence that ambitious New Mexicans were aware of and anxious about the territory's public image during the buildup to statehood can be found right in the title of a Ralph E. Twitchell advertorial. Published in Santa Fe in 1900, *Progress of New Mexico. Some Figures that Serve to Correct False Impressions. Fine Showing of Bank Deposits—Prosperity of all Classes—Business Conducted on a Cash Basis—Plea for Statehood*, spoke directly to the loudest economic arguments against admittance. To right the regrettable situation in which "New Mexico has been the most maligned, the least appreciated and the poorest understood portion of Uncle Sam's domain," Twitchell went on to provide pages filled with formal, quantifiable data to unambiguously demonstrate the territory's certainty of success.[54] Based on the belief that "your true-blue Yankee has a mania for figures and statistics," he reasoned the best way for New Mexico to convince the nation of its readiness was to let the numbers lead. A 1907 letter from the acting U.S. secretary of the interior to New Mexico governor George Curry requesting official data covering such items as taxable property, commerce and the progress of railroad enterprises, mining, forests, production of lumber, and undeveloped resources indicates that Twitchell understood the weight assigned to quantitative measures.[55] And so he included official totals from 1900 for such matters as bank deposits by industry, the average household's savings, the strong returns on territorial bond issues, the good progress made from investment in public buildings, and the actual ($125,000,000) rather than the assessed ($40,000,000) property values. "Surely," he ruminated in closing, "if intelligence, patriotism, and business capacity are the measure by which we are to be judged, there can be no doubt of our success."[56]

As a capable lawyer, historian, and Republican politician, Ralph Twitch-ell intentionally left out those more awkward figures that pointed to the enduring presence of alternative social perspectives and economic trajec-tories—to the realities of the hidden economy. New Mexico underper-formed in public education and literacy rates. The number of unadjudicated land claims remained quite high, and lands without proper title could not be formally transacted by the owner(s) nor properly taxed by the territory (much to land speculators' benefit). Hence another alarming figure—that well over one-third of the territory's land base went untaxed.[57] Even after the proceed-ings of the special Court of Private Land Claims, too many properties stood in title limbo while too many residents continued to live on lands without formal deed. Understandably, Twitchell would probably not want to include the number of "squatters" in his official-looking tables drawn up for those "true-blue" eastern investors and power brokers. Selling a narrative of New Mexico's advance toward order required the casual discounting of those unquantified figures and often the discounting of the human figures themselves.[58]

Incorporation's Hard Lessons for Hidden Economies

Set against these mounting changes, the Nuevomexicano economic logics of the nineteenth century proved unsustainable. The reality of widespread dis-possession alongside declines in the output of the agricultural and rangelands of the Hispano borderlands set the tone for the steady erosion of the village economy, including some, though not all, of its hidden elements. For Nuevo-mexicanos, a pluralist framework remained, but its component parts evolved, increasingly structured by a growing profile of corporate capitalism's more formal options, especially wage labor.[59] Since most formally contracted op-portunities existed outside of the Hispano villages of the region, Nuevo-mexicanos by necessity traveled to surrounding cities and states to find wage work, remitting their pay to their families. The resulting remittance econ-omy injected much-needed cash into the villages of northern New Mexico. As the population continued to grow, practices of equal inheritance for all children led to smaller and smaller family farm plots, further incentivizing younger generations to find work outside of the village. Seasonal migration away from the village for wage labor represented an increasingly common response. Though usually segregated into second-tier labor pools, Nuevomex-icanos found work across all major industries of the region, including ranches, railroads, mines, lumber yards, beet fields, and, increasingly, southwestern tourism.[60]

As wage labor incentivized the movement away from home, the rapidly growing tourism industry reaped profits by relying upon commoditizing the very same "premodern" economic behaviors of the village, like the skilled crafts of Native Americans and the pastoral rusticity of Nuevomexicanos.[61] For populations facing dwindling alternatives, this opened a viable strategy involving the daily maintenance of the old for the enjoyment of outsiders. Alongside new opportunities, the tourism industry fostered a mind-set of colonization and dependence for a new generation of economically marginalized residents of the mountains and plains of northern New Mexico. An important consideration asks how it was that within the limits of this story Nuevomexicanos went through at least two seismic identity shifts.[62] The first involved a deracination in the name of statehood; the second a reracialization to evoke a compelling (exotic) past to attract tourists and adventurers. Indeed, the adoption of racial tropes by the emerging tourism industry hints at the social factors set into the very bedrock of the borderlands' economic divide.[63] The popular narrative of "tricultural harmony"—that is, the peaceful coexistence of Indian, Hispanic, and white populations—powerfully and persuasively explained away the reality of racial and social tensions that continued to simmer throughout the marginalized communities of northern New Mexico.[64]

Euro-American logics steeped in the scientific management and corporate capitalism of the era viewed preindustrial work as inimical to progress. But, once harnessed by the corporate engine, the same work took on new meanings as its value could be more readily affixed and negotiated and therefore commodified and commercialized.[65] While many of the crafts marketed to tourists, such as Navajo blankets, Pueblo pottery, or Hispano *bultos* (wood-carved images of saints) had origins in the folkways of the region, their rise in production in the early twentieth century took place within a context of the solidification of corporate capitalism as the cornerstone of the tourism industry for the Hispano borderlands. Indeed, publicized attractions like the Santa Fe Fiesta and Indian "detours" helped to make tourism New Mexico's second-ranked sector by 1930. Their success relied heavily upon public perceptions of unabated premodern populations and cultures. To market "enchantment," for example, the Santa Fe railway and the Fred Harvey company needed their guides, performers, and craftsmen to be authentic—or at least the company's version of authentic—in their appearance, behavior, and labor.[66] Of no little contradiction, the same lifeways delegitimized by the state-sponsored capitalism of the territorial period gained newfound acceptance by that of the early statehood period. Clearly, ethnic behaviors and rustic wares meant something different when suffused with an increased flow of tourist dollars to a capital city or commissioned by an interstate corporation.

Unfortunately, even the addition of seasonal wage labor and the influx of tourism dollars proved insufficient to support the Nuevomexicano community and its hidden economy. The author of an urban-planning report for the capital region referenced such stark conditions when they found that between the years 1910 and 1960 the economic zone surrounding Santa Fe—inclusive of Colfax, Los Alamos, Mora, Rio Arriba, Sandoval, San Miguel, Santa Fe, and Taos Counties—recorded its strongest growth rate during the decade of the 1930s.[67] How could the period framed by the debilitating onset of the Great Depression be the region's best decade in New Mexico's first half century of statehood? The unfortunate answer lies in the overlapping contexts of economic, political, social, and ecological transformations that destabilized the communities of northern New Mexico during its territorial days, changes powerfully influenced by flows of international capitalism and market incorporation, and that fundamentally marginalized Nuevomexicano villages and communities.[68]

Ultimately, even those Nuevomexicanos who successfully sidestepped grazing leases, timber fees, property taxes, or national forest dues found that they could not dodge the harsh realities of an environment in decay. Severe drought in 1917 and 1918, for example, crippled the livestock and ranching industry, leading to calls for federal aid and the abatement of grazing fees for the entire state of New Mexico.[69] Ranchers of all backgrounds struggled to compete and survive, leaving even fewer options and less land to those operating outside the state-sponsored economy. By the 1920s the countryside of the Hispano borderlands represented one of the most impoverished, unhealthy, and undereducated regions in the United States. During the 1930s, the influx of federal spending as part of the New Deal injected much-needed funds. Spending on civil and military programs continued to represent the number one source of jobs and income for the Santa Fe Trade Area throughout the remainder of the twentieth century. Tourism ranked a distant second. Well removed from New Mexico's days as a southwestern hub for continental trade and commerce, modern capitalism, for all its rationality and order, presented far fewer options for the Nuevomexicano and Native American populations. Waves of dispossession and environmental degradation chipped away at the communities' economic and social bedrock, leaving them fundamentally vulnerable until their greatest value was found in their continued existence as precapitalist societies arranged and marketed for Anglo-American "enchantment."

New Mexicans grew increasingly dependent upon a next best option: federal monies and work programs. With the state economy depressed already by the 1920s, New Mexico transitioned to a net recipient of federal aid. By 1926, though ranked forty-third in terms of its population, New Mexicans collected the sixteenth most federal dollars per capita.[70] Nuevomexicanos of the Hispano borderlands gained particular attention during the New Deal era as national observers noted the reality of their situation. Indeed, by 1930 they were one of the poorest subgroups in the nation, with the highest rate of deaths to births and the highest infant mortality rates.[71] Educational attainment remained tragically low, with under 20 percent of Nuevomexicanos graduating high school. Though agriculture and ranching remained the basis for many villagers' livelihood, after generations of family inheritance the average household worked just six acres of land. These small plots produced insufficient yields to permit their owners to escape the debt cycles stemming from both mercantile-offered crop liens and *partido* contracts (essentially a sharecropping agreement) for sheep.

In this fragile economic ecosystem, characterized by a dearth of cash, tax levies alone could and did produce foreclosures and tax sales.[72] Avoiding the tax collector further incentivized Nuevomexicanos to seek redress through shadowy market activities, such as gathering wood from private property or the unpermitted grazing of their sheep within the national forests. In this context Nuevomexicano land loss stands out time and again as one of the clearest culprits for the economic malaise that hung about the Hispano borderlands and the people's continual turn toward informal market activities. An evolved pluralism with links to both wage labor and hidden economies presented a practical response, especially when supported by a culturally and socially cohesive village network.[73]

How do the experiences of the inhabitants of the Hispano borderlands inform our historical understanding of capitalism's unfolding? New Mexico's fitful relationship with the forces of the free market sheds light on the dynamic linkages between economic development and dependence. Though a crossroads of North American trade and commerce for the majority of the nineteenth century, New Mexico was churned through capitalism's creative destruction at an alarming pace, leaving a trail of economic fallout across the region. And it was only within the context of formal state and market incorporation that Nuevomexicanos most strikingly felt the brunt of systemic social and cultural marginalization. Full consideration of this economic slide proves relevant for the twenty-first century as access to opportunity and social mobility has significantly diminished and fewer places represent areas of core growth, almost all of them major urban centers. Alternatively, more rural places across the United States and the globe are moving further from economic stability and security. The ranks of marginalized communities, populations, and geographies are steadily growing.[74] Investigating the reasons for capitalism's scorched-earth campaign in New Mexico's Hispano borderlands has much to offer those looking for insights on how to reinvigorate burned-over rural economies. In this regard, attention to the role of hidden or shadow economies, as well as their reliance upon cooperative social networks, deserves continued scholarly attention, especially as we are confronted with the new reality of a denationalized globalization poised to power new rounds of worldwide economic incorporation and marginalization.[75]

PART III

The Licit and the Illicit

Chapter 6

Capitalism's Back Pages: "Immoral" Advertising and Invisible Markets in Paris's Mass Press, 1880–1940

Hannah Frydman

Classified advertising in the age of the mass press has been treated as an object of curiosity, the stuff of fluffy novels—missed connections and covert trysts—rather than as worthy of sustained analysis. An incomparable window onto the workings of capitalism on a human level, this heterogeneous form of advertising has been consistently overlooked by historians.[1] The classifieds seem too sexual, too textual, too marginal, for some, and too transactional, too abbreviated, too money-driven for others. In short, they seem to be an *improper* object of study.[2] Moreover, the mass press's classifieds have failed to spark scholarly interest, given that these ads look much like those printed in the seventeenth century, making them seem stagnant and distinctly less dynamic than the papers in which they circulated.

Much, however, was happening through—and between—the banal lines on the newspapers' back pages. In this essay, I use the sexual history of the Parisian classifieds in the late nineteenth and early twentieth centuries—a history peopled with masseuses, prostitutes, midwives, and abortionists—as a case study. Within the classifieds, sex and sexuality undergirded new, intimate forms of entrepreneurship—omnipresent but hard for scholars of "legitimate" commerce to see, and not only because many of the ads were written in code. The sexual, "private," or illicit nature of this work served to disconnect the ads from their economic foundations and import. The classifieds thus show how ideas of legitimacy and formality have shaped (or skewed) histories of capitalism, both global and local, and have masked the importance of women's labor and entrepreneurship in the process.[3]

Paying attention to the classifieds and their sexualization is crucial for understanding the (capitalist) civilization the newspaper made in nineteenth- and early twentieth-century France.[4] In what follows, I perform a careful reading of the discursive making and unmaking of the sexual classifieds from the fin de siècle to the interwar period, focusing on the constitution and deconstruction of markets through binary distinctions—such as center and margin, moral and immoral, licit and illicit, formal and informal. Before considering how classified advertising might serve as the basis for a different history of capitalism, one that confronts the historical functionality of these binaries instead of using them as transparent categories of historical analysis, let's first look at the previously untold history of France's sexual classifieds and their promising and problematic place in the French Republic.

Sex in the Classifieds

In 1880, an article by Jean Frollo[5] in the mass-circulation daily newspaper *Le Petit Parisien* lamented that many women who supported themselves by engaging in wage labor ended up with nothing but "the opportunities that present themselves—once night falls—to avoid dying of hunger." Even those who had not yet succumbed to prostitution had to brave the streets all the same in order to find employment because job postings were often found in dark corners of the city and, even worse, on or near urinals. One woman had complained to Frollo that if she stopped in these places, for even two seconds, she would find herself accosted by men and their "obscene propositions." She and other women workers demanded a safer way to learn about job openings— their survival (and, even more importantly to some, their morality) hung in the balance.

Le Petit Parisien presented an elegant solution to their problem. They created a "work column" in which bosses and foremen who employed women could publish free want ads in the back pages of the newspaper. This scheme would simultaneously benefit employers and save women workers from the necessity of wandering the streets, where they were easy prey for men who exploited their economic precarity.[6] Advertising columns were productive for newspapers as well. In late 1883, a more capacious classified section joined this philanthropic "work column," supposedly at the readers' request. "Employee wanted" ads remained free, but readers could now pay 1.50 francs per line of forty-five letters to place any other kind of ad. According to the newspaper's editors, these ads were simply too numerous to be printed for free.[7] After February 1884, the free column disappeared altogether, leaving only the venal marketplace behind. The drive for money won out over the "useful and good work" of helping women find employment safely. Employers could still post want ads, but they would now have to pay.

Le Petit Parisien was in good company in its search for new forms of advertising revenue. During the 1880s and 1890s, the majority of periodicals— including each of the four giants of this golden age of the press (*Le Journal, Le Matin, Le Petit Journal*, and, of course, *Le Petit Parisien*)—created weekly or semiweekly paid classified advertising sections (*petites annonces*[8]) on their back pages. The classifieds were thought to help "readers address themselves directly to the public for any communication, for any purchase, sale, or rental, or to display or offer a job or position."[9] With Parisian dailies reaching a circulation of two million copies around 1880, the development and spread of the classifieds through the mass press led to a spectacular renaissance of the small ad format at a moment when newspapers sorely needed the revenue.[10] By 1900, daily newspapers were each receiving dozens—and in many cases hundreds—of ads per week. Located under popular columns with such titles as Help Wanted, Position Sought, Classes and Lessons, Agencies, Capital Loans, Used Goods, Property for Rent or Sale, Wellness, and Marriages, the ads brought in a relatively small but steady stream of revenue at a franc or two per line.[11]

What exactly was being advertised on these large, densely printed pages? What were newspapers helping to sell? Frollo originally introduced *Le Petit Parisien*'s back-page advertising as a force for good, helping to clear a moral space for affordable, personal advertising in the newspaper. This battle, however, was an uphill one. Despite such claims to moralization, these ads were known to promote immoral commerce. Indeed, the best-known small advertising at the time, the personal *petite correspondence* column of the *Figaro*, was, from its inception in 1875, widely decried as a site of prostitution and described by one early opponent as "amorous, libertine, [and] adulterous." For this very reason, readers avidly combed the column, eager to find or imagine "real" sexual intrigues between the lines.[12] Throughout the 1880s and

1890s, the number of personal ads in Parisian newspapers steadily rose. Although most were less sexual—explicitly or implicitly—and, at least initially, written in clearer prose than those in *Le Figaro*, critics increasingly decried the sexual content encrypted in the back pages.[13]

As the number of ads rose, pronatalists, moralists, and feminist activists expressed concern that the mass press's back pages were dangerous for women. They claimed that these pages encouraged prostitution and exposed even the most honest men, women, and children to commercial sex, turning the act of reading the classifieds into a sexual one. Given the anonymity and paradoxical privacy of this very public medium, critics worried that classified exchanges would be conducted from a woman's boudoir. By the interwar period, this concern had become an erotic and satirical commonplace (see Figure 6.1).

Featured on the back cover of a July 1924 issue of the illustrated magazine *Le Sourire*, the image "La Lecture des annonces"—depicting a scantily dressed pinup girl "reading the advertisements"—makes plain that the flipside of moral concern is always erotic fantasy.[14] This pinup girl would have been at home among *Le Sourire*'s more or less overtly sexual advertisements, a small portion of which were accompanied by similar illustrations of seminude women. The newspaper she holds, however, is not an illustrated magazine but rather resembles a mass-circulation daily.

While mass-circulation dailies were less overtly sexual than the average illustrated weekly, many, including *Paris-Soir*, nonetheless made use of the principle that sex sells, just in a less immediately visible way. *Paris-Soir*'s writers knew that, at first glance, the classifieds could seem boring, like a "drab desert" dominated by apartments for rent, job openings, and cars for sale (see Figure 6.2).[15] In February 1924, to whet their readers' appetites and keep them from putting their papers down when they got to the classifieds, the editors ran a narrative advertisement among the classified ads in which the narrator convinced a fictional newspaper reader, M. Gobineau, of the (erotic) interest of *Paris-Soir*'s back page. "To read the Classifieds," they argued, was to "psychologically probe all of these hearts [of people who cross each other on the boulevards] . . . to discover a sort of summary of social life. What dramas are not revealed within certain appeals in the *Personals* or in the *Marriages* section?"[16] In this argument, sex was presented as a—or perhaps *the*—reason the classifieds were worth reading. By the 1920s, the ubiquitous marketplace of classified advertising, which in *Paris-Soir*'s own language "penetrate[d] everywhere" and was "read by all," was so thoroughly associ-

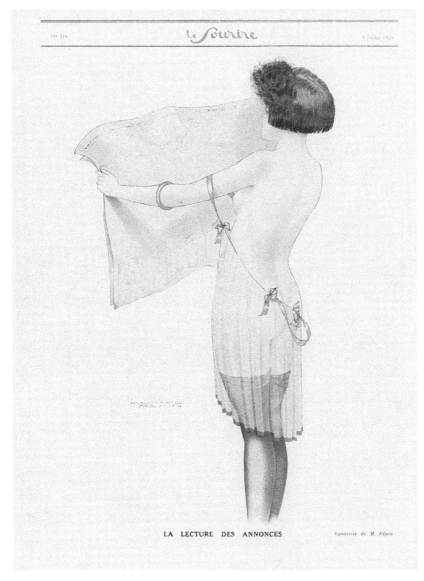

LA LECTURE DES ANNONCES   Aquarelle de M. Pépin

Figure 6.1. Reading the advertisements. Maurice Pépin, "La Lecture des annonces," *Le Sourire*, July 3, 1924. Source: Bibliothèque nationale de France.

Figure 6.2. Classified section. *Paris-Soir*, December 3, 1924. Source: gallica.bnf.fr / Bibliothèque nationale de France.

ated with (extra)conjugal intrigue that less intimate ads were described as the chaff to be separated from the wheat.[17] Frollo's fleeting dream of recreating the classifieds as a safe haven for honest working women had not come to fruition. They instead remained a site of imagined sexual maneuvering, even in papers like *Paris-Soir*, where looking for sex was more or less akin to looking for a needle in a haystack. What mattered was that people were *looking.*

Such accounts of a sexually saturated marketplace were not unrelated to the ways in which these ads created economic opportunities for women on the ground—ostensibly one of the moralizing possibilities of the classifieds (at least for *Le Petit Parisien*). From the late nineteenth century onward, these affordable *annonces* were an important technology for women's economic independence. The classifieds made it possible for women to quietly and privately overcome a well-entrenched, gendered division of labor that, across the nineteenth century, had made the "woman worker" a paradoxical term. By the end of the nineteenth century, the "woman worker" was a morally suspect category that represented first and foremost the unwelcome effects of industrial capitalism, namely, the moral degradation of France's women.[18] According to this discourse, there was no such thing as a "moral woman worker" in the urban marketplace.[19] By the late nineteenth century, the "virtuous woman" was firmly associated with consumption, reproduction, and the home.[20]

In the space between the immoral woman worker and the moral homemaker, however, much was conspiring. Early twentieth-century newspapers offer evidence of the emergence of new forms of entrepreneurship undertaken by women on the edges of these apparently opposed domains. This work could not easily be categorized as industrial or domestic and thus as immoral or moral. Through small ads, women asked for loans when in need, looked for well-paying work from the safety of their own homes, and ran lucrative businesses from their apartments. These private locations allowed them to mix the commercial with the domestic and make ends meet, often without a boss or pimp (or perhaps by taking up these roles for themselves). Women advertised a variety of services, such as language lessons, massages, fortune-telling, midwifery, and marriage brokerage. Unsurprisingly, as was the case with industrial labor, the mere mention of women in the marketplace was enough to render an ad questionable, if not clearly condemnable. Cultural commentators wielded sexual morality as a weapon against women who entered the marketplace, rendering them suspicious and their expulsion a convenient means of making market society "virtuous"—discursively speaking, at least.[21] As such, it did not take long for critics to call out ads for "massage" as prostitution and those for "midwifery" as abortion.

Ironically, the discourse that sought to exclude women from the classified marketplace because they *might* be selling their bodies alongside market goods also made it possible for more or less invisible, illicit markets to flourish in *plain sight*. Driven out of "licit" markets-in-formation by the specter of the prostitute, the woman-as-commodity, many women used legitimate advertising to earn a living wage. Only this time, they did so in a murky market of their own creation, away from urinals but not at all in the "moral," paternalistic way Jean Frollo had imagined. For some, the individualized, independent indoor sexual labor they pioneered by means of the classifieds paid better than almost any other work a lower- or middle-class woman could find.

A Republican Conundrum: Money and Definitions of Freedom in the Mass Press

To account for how the lucrative "immoral" classified marketplace was used to create the boundaries of the "visible" market, we need to zoom out and locate the newspaper, which housed and disseminated it, within a broader economic and political field. More specifically, we must analyze the conflictual relationship between the idea of the (financially disinterested) press as democratic technology and the (financially interested) press as capitalist business par excellence. Analyzing the classifieds, in other words, allows us to engage and complicate Habermas's classic narrative of the corruption of the high-minded public sphere by mass media.[22] In the next section, we will examine how the stabilization of the French Third Republic (1870–1940) in the 1880s changed the symbolic power of the press and made its venality— represented most visibly by newspaper advertising and understood through the metaphor of prostitution—newly problematic.

After a decade of turbulence marked by attempts to instate a conservative political program of "moral order" following the fall of the Second Empire (1852–1870), republicans solidified their power and stabilized the fledgling Third Republic in the early 1880s. Their victory was crowned by the passage of the law declaring the freedom of the press on July 29, 1881. For republican legislators, this law was the central pillar of the new regime, a symbol of the republic itself. The press was imagined as a mobile, moralizing force that would educate men to be good, informed citizens and stand as a safeguard for all other republican freedoms, as a place to speak truth to power. The 1881 law, however, came forty-five years after the first media revolution, led by Emile de Girardin in 1836 when, thanks to extensive advertising revenues, he created *La Presse* at a subscription price of forty francs instead of the traditional eighty. A second media revolution came with the launch of the French penny press by Moïse Millaud and his *Le Petit Journal* (1863), which made the press even more dependent on advertising. Mass-circulation dailies all soon adopted the affordable price of one sou. When paired with improvements in train travel and literacy, Parisian newspapers became national: they reached the majority of French citizens in a timely manner and made it possible to imagine the newspaper as knitting the republic together into a democratic community. While they could serve this political function, these same newspapers were, more than ever before, commercial objects. Their owners were industrialists, and the system ran on advertising revenues of all kinds. Speaking truth to power or diffusing moral ideas might happen in the mass press but only if it was good for the bottom line. Their publishers realized that disseminating what many described as "vice" was more lucrative than high-minded politics. Was this still freedom? What kind?

In the decades following the 1881 law, advocates of press freedom began to lament that, even though the press appeared to "enjoy unlimited freedom," it was "not genuinely free."[23] In 1897, in response to a survey on "The Responsibilities of the Press," created by the ambitious author and literary critic Henry Bérenger, the weekly *Revue bleue* published letters from government officials, sociologists, and journalists concerning the relationship between money and the freedom of the press.[24] Maurice Talmeyr, a journalist for *Le Figaro*, responded that the problem was that the press was ruled by money and therefore interested in pleasing the largest number of readers in order to do the most business possible. "Money being the goal," he wrote, "everything will necessarily be sacrificed to money. Go to the most honest or even the most literary newspaper; give it a choice between a nice little page of content and a good advertisement, and it certainly won't take the nice page." Talmeyr saw no way out of this situation under a democratic regime (many of the survey responses were unabashedly elitist) and told his readers that they needed to resign themselves to the spread of "demagogic enthusiasm and pornography" throughout the populace "because you will never stop a carnival barker [*un barnum*] from speculating on desire or vice."[25] Deputy Jean Jaurès likewise responded that "the press is deplorably pornographic. It solicits [*racole*] imaginations, and public corruption has become a source of profit."[26] That is to say that, far from moralizing the public, the newspaper, under the influence of money, was a vector for immorality, like pornography or prostitution.[27]

If the dreams of the legislators behind the law on the freedom of the press were naive, based on a press that had never existed outside of philosophers' minds, the newspaper was nonetheless endowed with new symbolic weight in response to their actions. Advertising, long a target of critique and cause of suspicion, now seemed even more dangerous.[28] The questions that underlay everything in Bérenger's survey were "How much freedom is too much?" and "What is the *moral* responsibility of the press?" Both questions implicitly called attention to the propagation of sexual content in the press and the profitability of this content, which ran counter to the republican desire to see the newspaper as a bulwark against the spread of vice of all kinds. Talmeyr and Jaurès both made clear that sex sells and that this fact corrupts the newspaper, which, in turn, corrupts society. They also argued that, like it or not, this was part of what the freedom of the press allowed for.

Survey participants agreed that, in a society increasingly concerned about the sneaking spread of sexual texts and images that it named "pornography," the newspaper was problematic. It was unbelievably affordable and reached a widely literate audience across the country. Censorship, which had been concerned with politics for most of the nineteenth century, began, under the Third Republic, to take immoral sexuality as its primary target.[29] Likewise, the coded, often literary or humorous language—a hallmark of French journalism—that had allowed newspapers to avoid the heavy tax on political newspapers under less democratic regimes was reworked for this new situation in which the press was free except where sexual morality was concerned.[30] In the classifieds, however, more than ideological and discursive dangers to the social body lurked. The presence of coded ads for sexual objects, sexual images, and sexual services led to an embodied, as well as discursive, association between print and sexual immorality. Censors and moralists could not stop this, however loudly they might cry "pornography" or "prostitution," because newspaper administrators were willing to accept advertisements with little regard for their provenance. Many advertising directors did not care whether ad revenue came from old family wealth, speculation on the stock market, factory wages, or prostitution—in their opinion, "money has no smell."[31] If the ad was written in code, how could the transaction hurt a reader, anyway? How could anyone say that there was anything *immoral* in the text of an ad placed by a matrimonial agency, a massage parlor, or a woman in dire need of a loan?

As the knowledge spread that code was used in the classifieds, that there *was* something potentially immoral about these ads, the average reader became adept at code breaking. For the millions of people that frequently perused these marketplaces while reading their daily papers, the classifieds inspired a new, widely disseminated form of reading—a suspicious one. When readers (browsers, clients, and censors alike) confronted classified pages in their daily paper, they asked themselves whether any ad could be taken at face value. Suspicious readers of all kinds worked to determine the existence of hidden meanings to such an extent that a surface reading was often assumed to be an incorrect one. In the eyes and imaginations of newspaper readers, the "underworld" and its "immoral" and "informal" labor left the margins to hide itself very much in plain sight, marking popular understandings of the classified marketplace and what could be found there. In the next section, we will see the mechanisms by which this took place.

Working Women, Back-Page Trade, and the Construction of Sexual Space

In the early twentieth century, the well-worn critique equating the press with prostitution developed into a critique of the press as literal pimp/madame, as a purveyor of female flesh. In a 1903 article entitled "The White Slave Trade" in *Le Matin*, the feminist journalist Séverine strongly condemned "the Press, procuress" for the complicit role it played in the prostitution of women, sacrificing its honor for questionable advertising revenue (and lots of it). In this article, she described how the advertising pages of mass-circulation Parisian newspapers were, contrary to the earlier dreams of *Le Petit Parisien*, a crucial technology for the "white slave trade." They allowed (or, more accurately, were imagined to allow) traffickers to lure poor, honest women into prostitution with promises of well-paying jobs abroad.[32] Séverine reported that Avril de Sainte-Croix, a feminist and prominent leader in the campaign against regulated prostitution, had told her that many of the women she had saved from this "abyss" had, "in the pocket of their short dress, the advertisement that is a trap. They believe it: it's in print!"[33] For Séverine and Avril de Sainte-Croix, the worst part of all this was that it was women in financial trouble, trying to support themselves through honest labor, who were being preyed on. Or, in the words of another contemporary critic, the ads were used to "speculate on the misery of women who had been skillfully deceived."[34]

How *were* women to tell the difference between a legitimate job opportunity and a "trap"? In a variety of sources, women were warned against ads that promised well-paying jobs, often in foreign places, including those "seeking governesses, servants, shop girls, instructors."[35] At a meeting held by various performance artists' unions at the Labor Exchange in Paris on November 18, 1903, a representative for the union of lyric artists signaled the prevalence of ads for jobs in brothels mixed in undercover with theatrical jobs.[36] Other critics underlined the danger of matrimonial ads.[37] Most troublingly, one author emphasized that, while some ads made their authors' goals rather clear, the majority of "traffickers" prefer to use "either *neutral* or even *serious* advertisements" in order to "attract their victims."[38] In a society gripped by fear of the supposed sexual trafficking of "honest" white women, looking for lucrative work was starting to seem like a dangerous business, at least where one's morality was concerned.

This was, scholars have argued, by design. Narratives of trafficking in white women served to curtail women's increased economic and sexual independence, freedom of movement, and access to public space.[39] Independence broadly conceived was thus next door to harlotry in the imaginary of the "white slave trade."[40] Warning women away from the classifieds rather than calling for their reform, however, had unintended consequences. Those who, like Séverine, advocated for the rights of women workers while railing against the sexual dangers lurking in the classifieds perversely helped discredit one of the few avenues available to women in the early twentieth century that offered them the chance to work for themselves, set their own hours, and earn a living wage. Frollo's dream of the classifieds as a safe, nonsexual space for honest women to find work had been turned completely on its head.

Despite this, not all women were (or could afford to be) put off by the sexualization of the classifieds. In many cases, they were conscious actors in the encoding and decoding of advertising, and their advertisements for sexual services—like the want ads decried above—likewise ranged from the "rather clear" to the seemingly "neutral or even serious." The intentional, encrypted presence of sex in classified ads written by women was illustrated vividly in a series by the Veber brothers (text by the novelist Pierre and drawings by the satirical illustrator Jean). In this illustration (see Figure 6.3), the Vebers produced an image of a "more attractive, explicit, and sincere" classified page by inserting, literally between the lines of classified ads, illustrations of what ads for jobs, loans, marriages, or recommended businesses—the vast majority of which were placed by women—were *really* advertising.[41] In many of the cases, these "more sincere" images depicted prostitution or sexual deviance (especially flagellation). This satirical cartoon, published on the front page of the literary (and sometimes salacious) daily newspaper *Gil Blas*, performed

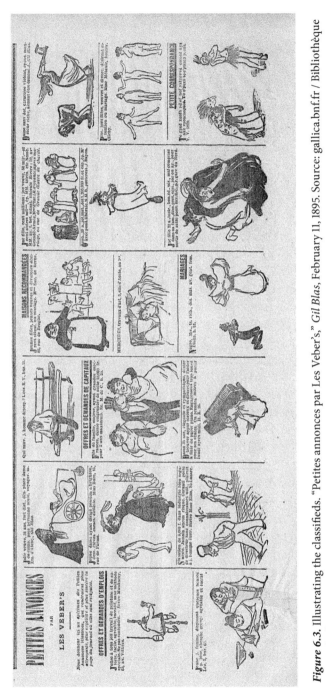

Figure 6.3. Illustrating the classifieds. "Petites annonces par Les Veber's," *Gil Blas*, February 11, 1895. Source: gallica.bnf.fr / Bibliothèque nationale de France.

a visual pastiche of the "real" classifieds on the back page, undoubtedly making the unillustrated, seemingly tame version much more stimulating reading.[42] Was the back-page ad looking for trustworthy men and women to engage in charity work really what it seemed? What about the "stylish [*coquet*]" apartment for rent? Read alone, these ads seem straightforward, unobjectionable, but the Vebers' cartoon made it difficult not to wonder if one advertiser's looking for people of both sexes was a code and if the opaque and gratuitous "etc., etc." that makes up the bulk of the description of the stylish apartment was as well.

The hidden sexual reality of the classifieds was also illuminated by the symbolist writer and journalist Maurice Schwob, who used real ads to make his point. He told his readers that the morality present on the first page of a newspaper (he obviously was not thinking of *Gil Blas*), in the form, for example, of a screed against the white slave trade, was totally absent—to the profit of its owners—on the last page. Its disappearance, however, had to be discreet so as not to shock prudish readers. To this end, easy-to-decode cryptograms were one way in which advertisers and newspapers managed to compromise. Schwob gives an example of an ad that ran in the extensive classifieds of *Le Journal*[43] on December 6, 1902, which read, seemingly nonsensically: "BÉBÉ. Xjfot xjuf nfodvmfs. Bj tpjg ef upo gpvufs. Ub rvfvf ebot nb cpvdif. Ub mboh. fo npo dvm."[44] In order to protest the immorality of such an ad, Schwob points out, its readers would have to know what sexually explicit content this gibberish had the power to communicate. To do this, the reader would first have to take "the trouble to satisfy his curiosity in going back a letter in the alphabet."[45] Meaningless text also turned out to have meaning, if only suspicious readers could break the code, and to break the code was to be drawn into the sexual economy of the classifieds and the newspapers that housed them.[46]

How, though, did readers know how to decode encrypted ads in papers like *Gil Blas* and *Le Journal* in the absence of the help of a Séverine, Veber, or Schwob? How, in other words, did knowledge of the hidden sexual market in the classifieds become widespread? One writer insisted that, even if this advertising was discreet, "smiles, kisses, and the rest have need of advertising just as much as comestibles, typewriters, and tailors," and "initiates understand all of the double-entendres."[47] Who were the initiates? At first, the number of those able to successfully decode the ads was likely quite small, greatly restricting the efficacy of these ads for "smiles, kisses, and the rest." Over time, however, this number grew exponentially, thanks to information provided by the newspapers, which profited directly from this advertising, as well as indirectly from advertisers' ability to successfully communicate the existence of hidden sexual commerce to readers.

From the 1890s to the eve of World War I, the newspaper-reading public repeatedly learned from sensational reporting on a number of criminal cases what the Vebers' series made so perfectly clear and visible: ads were sometimes not what they seemed. Let's look at a couple of examples. As early as 1892, readers learned that those who went to the address given by ads printed in *Gil Blas* that read "Mme Denize, *Massage with students*, 9, rue Léonie, 3rd [floor] on the left" or simply "Mme Denize and Co., *Massage*" would find "Mme Paganelli and a few young students of the female sex [including Paganelli's underage daughter] who had instructions to *please the clients*."[48] *Gil Blas* took some heat for its complicit role in this case, which was made public after a police officer had gone to the address out of uniform and been offered much more than massage. Just a few years later, however, the heat seemed to be gone. On November 3, 1900, *Gil Blas* printed a humorous short story called "La Masseuse" by the widely published popular novelist Guy de Téramond, in which a provincial man who goes up to Paris for a few days reads an ad for "Indian massage," goes in search of an arm massage, and is laughed at for his naiveté by the woman who placed the ad.[49] As was the case with the Vebers' cartoon, anyone who read this story would find themselves reading the ads for massage in *Gil Blas*'s classifieds, printed a few pages later, with suspicion. But it was not just massage. In 1904, for example, the column Offers and Requests for Capital was also called into question when it was found that an ad requesting a loan had been used by two mothers to prostitute their daughters.[50]

Over time, readers could not help but imagine sexual commerce everywhere in the back-page marketplace. In 1911, following an incredibly high-profile case involving ads for prostitution,[51] an article in *Le Rire* humorously informed its readers: "Professors of languages, Swedish gymnastics, mandolin, bridge, . . . ; sellers of art objects and curiosities, etc., etc., all of this is the same commerce, the same stuff. . . . The clients enter here as if into a department store:—I would like a little blond woman, rather plump, wearing a suit."[52] While *Le Rire* traded in comic exaggeration, the news had shown that this was not all that far from the truth. The classified marketplace was increasingly associated with the kind of business one might expect to find in an illicit underworld rather than in the parlor of a bourgeois home, even as it continued to travel unhindered into this space.

In response to these spectacular stories in the mass press, which made clear that ads for marriage, language lessons, massage, and even furnished apartments could all mask various forms of sexual commerce, moralists raised their voices in concern. In the short term, this did more to render this market decodable and thus visible than to stop this commerce. In some cases, this was arguably intentional. For example, in 1911, the Classes and Lessons column in the classifieds of the literary journal *Le Supplément* proclaimed: "We remind [our readers] that the administration of the SUPPLEMENT refuses any ad of an equivocal nature. Do not simply give a first name to indicate the professor." Many ads in this column, however, did just this, which inevitably raised questions about the lessons given by Daisy, Mary, and Sarita.[53] Thanks to the paratext provided by *Le Supplément* (not to mention the years of informative reporting on criminal cases regarding the classifieds), many readers had the information needed to successfully decode this textual interplay or at least to understand that these were indeed "equivocal" ads. In other words, the newspaper itself, under the guise of a moralizing gesture, played a role in raising the suspicion necessary to their advertisers' business ventures, reinforcing the sexual nature of the classified genre in the process.[54] It makes sense that it would have an interest in doing so— prostitution was more likely to produce the money required to advertise frequently than hygienic massage ever could.

As we have seen, in a world in which the number of newspapers was growing exponentially and commercial advertisers were hard to come by, newspaper directors were loath to pass up any source of revenue. Code provided plausible deniability in most cases, and the revenue was more than enough to make up for occasional fines. The self-referentiality of newspapers' reports on criminal cases involving the classifieds, the way in which they brought attention to the classifieds as a spectacular site of intrigue and interest, was not so bad for business either—editors knew that the frisson of "real" sex could only help sales. Each new scandal further fed the will to decode and left every ad potentially pregnant with sexual meaning. Sex and classified advertising had come to seem as inseparable as salt and pepper.

Capitalist Morality

If many newspaper administrators were happy to cash in on advertising revenues without looking too hard at where the money was coming from, not everyone was happy to see this reader-driven, person-to-person marketplace transform into a spectacularly ambivalent one, in which sex lurked everywhere, enticing and endangering the defenseless—young women in particular.[55] Certain newspapers chose to fight back, for real this time. Around the turn of the twentieth century, the Catholic fashion journal *Le Petit Écho de la Mode* proclaimed its refusal to print any advertisements that it considered as "immoral or dangerous for its young female readers."[56] The Catholic daily *La Croix* also rejected any ads it saw as questionable, making it very popular with advertisers: its self-proclaimed morality removed some of the taint associated with the print marketplace more generally.[57] The Catholic press pioneered an effective way to moralize the back pages.[58]

They were not alone in this fight. In the 1920s and 1930s, the police became much more interventionist. Antivice officers combed through newspapers' back pages in search of "licentious" ads.[59] Their attention was trained especially on illustrated weeklies, such as *Le Rire, Le Sourire,* and *La Vie Parisienne.* These illustrated journals, euphemistically described as "gallant," were filled with risqué humor and, according to the police, completely unveiled ads for all kinds of sexual commerce, which openly called attention to services ranging from flagellation and pederasty to group sex. If the ads drew interested clients (and they did: certain of these clandestine prostitution agencies had sumptuously furnished branch locations and extensive advertising budgets), they also made the work of the police that much easier. Raids were frequent for ads placed by women for "matrimonial agencies," "massage parlors," and "pieds-à-terre." The revenue from these same ads lined the pockets of the newspaper owners. The police frequently warned newspaper directors to cease and desist, and the newspapers grudgingly obliged, but only for a little while, before picking right back up where they left off—with their openly "licentious, provocative character."[60] Police just could not keep up. Even judicial decisions that found that thinly veiled sexual advertising was immoral in legal terms (and not just social ones) failed to stop the proliferation of these advertisements in the illustrated press.[61]

While it is clear that *Le Rire* and *Le Sourire* were not the "serious" journals that had so concerned Séverine and others (as their names, "The Laugh" and "The Smile," imply), their advertising nonetheless tainted the name of classifieds everywhere. As owners of illustrated newspapers flaunted police directives, taking money from clandestine prostitutes in order to pay their artists and keep their presses running, the mainstream media joined the fight against suspicious sexual advertising. This development is clearest in the rise of *Paris-Soir* to the position of most important daily paper in France in the

1930s (replacing the four giants of the pre-World War I Belle Époque). Its director, the businessman Jean Prouvost, was determined to reform advertising and recode it in the mind of the French people by policing it and detaching it from its associations with immorality—to finally give it, in the telling words of a historian of advertising, Marc Martin, "the face of an honest girl [*le visage d'une fille honnête*]" rather than, this formulation implies, the face of a prostitute (*fille publique*). In other words, Prouvost wanted to scrub newspaper advertising of its associations with illustrated journals, which consciously proliferated the association between the classifieds and illicit sex.[62]

The fight to legitimate newspaper advertising by promising "truth in advertising" was led in the name of a morality that encompassed both ethical business practices and sexual purity and whose goal was to chase hidden meaning (both sexual and fraudulent) from the classifieds. Following Prouvost's innovation, a corporation of admen put into place an Office for the Control of Advertising (l'Office de contrôle des annonces), which began its work in 1935. Slowly but surely, this new bureau contributed to the creation of a climate in which advertising was not a shameful profession, precisely because advertisements had been purged, purified, and decontaminated.[63]

In the classifieds, during the golden age of the press, anonymity and accessibility meant that the boundaries between trained and untrained, men and women, moral and immoral all but dissolved. It was never clear who was writing or who was telling the truth. The response, even by free market proponents, was to advocate for the reinstantiation of boundaries that would reform this heterogeneous, nearly lawless bazaar into a hierarchized, moralized market. The argument went that, to be free, the press (and its marketplace) had to be "responsible," or rather, either had to do the work of determining boundaries between formal and informal, legitimate and illegitimate, or stand the legal and social consequences of disseminating corruption and crime.

In the history of the business of French advertising as it has been written, this moralization is a story of triumph. In it, French advertising crawls out of the economic backwaters, inhabited by charlatans, crooks, pornographers, and pimps, toward specifically French forms of advertising exemplified by the artist-designed poster, which have been exported around the world. This narrative makes sense for a field that has struggled for decades for recognition as a serious object of historical study, fighting against the aftereffects of French suspicion and derision of advertising and advertisers. To allow this to be the only way the story is told, to render this period solely as something less than or outside of economic "progress," however, is to efface the history of the decades in which the mass press supported the mass classifieds (and vice versa). It renders invisible the making and unmaking of the sexual classifieds.

In this essay, I have read these processes closely, drawing them out to show how gender and sexuality have determined what is in/visible, in/formal, and im/moral so that we might better account for how these terms have shaped our understandings of what and where the market is and how it works. Acknowledging that what we see as illicit activity contributed to the licit business of running a newspaper is only part of the story. I also want to emphasize that this categorization is not innocent: it was used to contain, restrain, and stymie just as much as it was played against itself to become a source of commercial innovation and opportunities (coded as immoral or not). To take the invisibility, unimportance, or illicitness of the classifieds at face value is to reproduce the discourses of domination that have grown out of the twinned structures of capitalism and patriarchy, which continue to make it difficult for women to take part in the market on an equal footing. Today, sex work still offers lower- and middle-class women relatively high pay in a market where ill-paid part-time or service work constitute the bulk of women's employment opportunities.[64] And today, sex workers, faced with societal stigma and the dangerous effects of criminalization, remain, by necessity, innovators of advertising and business practices in an ever-changing politico-technological landscape. But only scholars of women, gender, or sexuality would tell you so.

The U.S. historian Amy Dru Stanley has forcefully critiqued the way in which the "new" history of capitalism has failed to grapple with important feminist work that argued that any narrative of economic transformation must account for sex difference or risk obscuring the gendered nature of capitalist development, its "logic of sex."[65] I add my voice to Stanley's to call for a reconsideration of capitalism's history with the tools forged by feminist historians, tools that the discipline has, prematurely if perhaps inadvertently, turned the page on in subsequent "turns" away from first social and then cultural history.[66] My analysis of the sexual classifieds reveals (and reminds us) that understanding the history of capitalism will require us to consider the methods at our disposal that allow us to question our analytic vocabulary, to think critically about how it has forged our past and our present, and to find more finely tuned instruments that will elucidate *all* the processes of the market, not just those that have been rendered visible, licit, formal, and desirable. Writing the history of the sexual classifieds as a history of capitalism thus pushes us to write histories of hidden capitalism that are at once also hidden histories of capitalism—to explore, in other words, both why and how certain markets have been hidden from our view and how confronting this concealment will lead us to write (new) new histories of capitalism, histories in which morality is no longer an invisible yet determinant factor for inclusion.

Chapter 7

Capitalism's Black Heart in Wartime France

Kenneth Mouré

Black markets thrive in times of war. Material shortages and state regulations that gear production to meet war needs increase the demand for goods and the opportunities for profit. In war zones the destruction of goods, productive capacity, and transport infrastructure increases shortages. States impose price controls and allocate war materials to maximize the war effort without setting off an inflationary rush to bid up prices for scarce goods. The circumstances provide great opportunities for exceptional profit. Black markets in World War II have attracted attention in recent years, not just for the economies crippled by war and foreign occupation but for the varieties of black market experience under differing political regimes and material circumstances. Totalitarian states can impose tighter economic controls, with less concern than democracies for whether there is popular support, but coercive systems still face resistance from producers and consumers whose interests are abused. As open defiance becomes less possible, resistance takes new, less-visible forms.

Black market activity flourished in Europe, not just in the occupied and economically deprived countries (France, Belgium, postwar Germany, Italy from summer 1943, and all of Eastern Europe) but also in Nazi Germany, where adequate rations were maintained and black market penalties severe.[1] Black markets also thrived, on a lesser scale, in Britain and the United States, countries with strong economies geared to maximize war production.[2] Black markets served not just desperate consumers but also the wealthy acting in defiance of wartime shared sacrifice, producers needing raw materials, suppliers seeking scarce goods, and conquering armies hunting hoarded stock.[3] The proliferation of black markets in wartime poses an interesting challenge to understand not just the exceptional opportunities for profit and the sometimes perverse effects of state controls but also the nature of illicit commerce and what that commerce "hides."

France during and after World War II offers an opportunity to evaluate how black markets can reassert "capitalist" principles against market restrictions. Unlike the economies crushed by Nazi exploitation in Eastern Europe, occupied France remained a productive economy and contributed more wealth than any other nation to the Nazi looting of Europe.[4] In Western Europe, France was the only country to sign an armistice and form a government to protect national interests by working with the Nazis. The result was a situation in which economic need, private greed, and patriotic resistance all contributed to channel entrepreneurial effort and social solidarities into illicit activities. Analyzing the dynamic of black market growth and the logic of what black market activity kept "hidden" can demonstrate the power of market forces to organize in opposition to inept regulation.

In France, black market activity drew an increasing share of French economic effort and gained steadily in determining how and to whom goods were distributed. The U.S. Army's Psychological Warfare Division described the black market in France in June 1944 as "a national institution, highly organized, and supported by the very large majority of the population who look to it, rather than its official counterpart, to maintain food supplies above starvation level."[5] The French control administration admitted by 1944 that black markets did better than official markets in supplying consumers with essentials, especially food.[6] After liberation in 1944, French governments kept economic controls in place to manage postwar shortages. French controllers fought a demoralizing battle against the resurgence of black market activity from autumn 1944 to mid-1947. Even if government controls were not consciously "anticapitalist," was there a fundamentally capitalist character to this resistance to market controls?

In this chapter, after providing contextual background on the shortages, the wartime control regime, and the growth of black market activity in France, I will assess what the high level of illicit traffic tells us about controls and markets in a capitalist economy. The title, "Capitalism's Black Heart," evokes the importance of market innovation to solve challenges of production and distribution as the "heart" of market forces and their potential. But the distributional and moral results of unregulated traffic and profit seeking have adverse consequences as well: the market was "black" not only in promoting illicit commerce but also in its lack of restraint on the dark impulses for economic action. The state classed all rule violations as "black market." Producers and consumers who rapidly lost faith in the equity and efficacy of state controls found ways to circumvent economic regulations, some legal, many of them stretching legal boundaries, and many more deliberately crossing clear lines into illicit commerce. In 1942, the state accepted gray areas for lighter enforcement to allow families leeway for their food needs not met by the inadequate ration system. But this state concession opened new avenues to exploit the demand for goods and seek greater profit at the expense of families in need.

The Black Market in Occupied France

The French defeat in June 1940 opened a period of severe economic contraction. The conversion of industry to focus on war goods had reduced civilian supplies in 1939. The defeat in 1940 stopped Atlantic trade and disrupted the supply and transport of goods within France. Between 1938 and 1944 industrial and agricultural output fell, by more than 25 percent for agriculture and by more than 50 percent for industry. Manpower losses (particularly the more than 1.5 million French prisoners of war); reduced imports of food and raw materials; shortages of transport equipment, fuel, and energy sources for industrial production; and a lack of fertilizers and pesticides for agriculture all contributed to declining productivity and output. German occupation policies subjected the reduced supply to brutal exploitation. The Germans levied "occupation costs" far in excess of their occupation expenditure, securing "a massive and, perhaps, unparalleled transfer of resources from France." These costs came to more than 36 percent of French GDP in 1941 and 1942, and 55.5 percent in 1943.[7] The Germans used these funds to purchase French goods. Supply for both the military and private purchases drew from the dwindling supplies of food and consumer goods for French civilians.

German authorities insisted on strict price controls and the tight rationing of food and industrial raw materials. France had adopted price controls in September 1939 and begun to ration some foods in early 1940 but did not develop rigid controls until the German authorities required them to do so, with rationing of food in September 1940 and a new price administration in October. The French head of state Philippe Pétain told the nation in October 1940 that rationing was "a painful necessity . . . imposed by the severity of the defeat and the will of the victor." In place of the failed liberal economy of the 1930s, his government claimed it would construct a New Order in France. The economy would be "organized and controlled" by controls on international trade to assure that it served national purposes and controls on domestic consumption (prices and rationing) to protect purchasing power and provide a more just distribution of goods.[8]

Controls there were, but they failed to establish a just distribution. Black market activity developed across France to serve the real needs of everyday consumption, German excess demand, and the appetites of privileged elites.[9] The real needs included finding sufficient food for survival. The ration levels dictated by German authorities in September 1940 allowed a starvation diet. At times, even the starvation rations were unavailable.[10] French industry suffered major shortfalls in the supply of raw materials. In both industry and agriculture, official prices were not always sufficient to cover production costs. Businesses shifted their efforts to produce goods that would earn profit. Foods with official prices fixed below production cost were either abandoned or grown mainly for on-farm consumption and black market sale. For fruit and vegetables, harder to price because of seasonal and regional variations, official prices had to be set according to availability. Department prefects frequently called attention to how new produce disappeared from markets as soon as official prices were set below market prices. This was a widespread and recurrent complaint in the first years of occupation: for farm produce in the Meurthe-et-Moselle,[11] for fruit and vegetables in Rennes,[12] for poultry and eggs in the Landes,[13] for farm produce in the Seine-et-Marne.[14]

More visible for the rapid growth of black market purchasing were the appetites for scarce goods on the part of those with the financial resources, the administrative privileges, and/or the political power to disregard licit prices and quantities. Privileged access to scarce food supplies was often highly visible, displaying injustices in a rationing system that, in the name of "shared sacrifice," seemed to serve the wealthy and foster abuses of power by those in charge. Paris police reported regularly on the discontent of shoppers, queuing long hours for rations and complaining that shopkeepers kept their best goods for their preferred clients, who paid extra to buy goods hidden under the counter, retrieved at the shop's back door, or delivered to their homes.[15]

Authorities at all levels, from municipalities distributing ration cards to national ministries in Vichy, exploited their privileges in office. Municipal officers distributing ration cards and tickets often trafficked in ration documents. Controllers, particularly in the food supply system, were widely suspected of profiting from the supplies they handled. In 1941 and 1942, government ministries relocated in the spa town of Vichy bought food for ministerial canteens direct from nearby farms in the department of the Allier at high prices. The Contrôle des Prix claimed that they could no longer enforce prices in the Allier, because "all the illicit traffic is for the benefit of administrative *popotes* [messes] for the Admiralty and government ministries." In the Paris press, collaborationists eager to win favor with the Germans gave front-page coverage to Vichy administrative malfeasance.[16]

Black market restaurants were one of the most visible and rumor-prone targets for public attention. They were reputed to pride themselves on serving "prewar" menus at high cost for those who could afford them. In addition to their customary wealthy clientele, these restaurants served the nouveaux riches profiting from the occupation and their German buyers and protectors. The restaurant categories created in 1941 to regulate the content and price of meals included from the outset an "exceptional category" that allowed more expensive meals. For almost a year, German and Vichy officials maintained a short list of luxury Paris restaurants *hors catégorie* ("outside the category system"), with no rules for meal content and no limit on prices. These restaurants served the German elite, their French collaborators, and an array of "people who seem to belong to the world of business born of the current economic circumstances" (i.e., commerce with the Germans and black market).[17] Prime Minister Pierre Laval, yielding to German demands for tighter restaurant controls to suppress abuses they had often themselves created, explained in 1943: "These abuses are among those that contribute the most to demoralize opinion and keep the public from bending to an economic discipline that is indispensable."[18]

Visible injustice in food access and the declining supply in official markets discredited state authority and encouraged the use of alternative markets.[19] Public confidence in the Vichy regime and its ability to protect consumers declined rapidly in 1941. The decline is evident in reports from the Paris police, from the gendarmerie (military police) who enforced economic rules outside the major cities, from department prefects' monthly reports on political opinion and economic conditions, and from the Contrôle Technique, the state service eavesdropping on phone conversations and checking postal traffic to monitor public opinion. The state was well aware that its credibility to set and enforce economic rules was crumbling. "The material difficulties for the families of workers, employees and civil servants to obtain an indispensable minimum of food supplies has created a malaise that is most evident in their bitter words with regard to the government and the German occupation authorities," Paris police reported in June 1941. "The head of state's words, claiming that all are affected equally by the restrictions, are bitterly underlined."[20] There was malaise and growing anger at the state for the injustices and corrupt administration.

In a widespread wave of protests in early 1942, housewives demanded more food when official markets failed to provide even the meager legal rations. They called on the state to fulfill its responsibility to provide sufficient food for their families, especially for their malnourished children. The most notable protest, in Sète on January 20, 1942, mobilized more than a thousand women exasperated by shortages and low rations. In previous days there had been only carrots and turnips. They demanded "Bread for our children" outside the town's city hall. When they received no response, they threw rocks and chanted, "À bas Pétain, à bas Pétain." A few demonstrators were arrested, but the municipality responded the next day by distributing dried vegetables.[21] Food protests were the main reason for public demonstrations in the first two years of the occupation.[22]

Consumers improvised various means to supplement the insufficient rations. The state encouraged growing gardens in private and public spaces and raising poultry and rabbits. But for most urban consumers, the main options were to appeal to family relations in rural areas, to buy direct from farmers, or to find intermediaries who could bring food to the city. Vichy allowed families to send food by post and by rail as "family parcels." In practice this slid easily from legal parcels to exceeding weight and quantity limits, sending foods not allowed (especially butter), and using "family parcels" to supply black market restaurants and suppliers. Raymond Ruffin's family shared a train compartment in 1942 with a woman who traveled once a week to the countryside, buying food direct from farms for one-third more than the official price and selling it in Paris at twice the price. She proudly explained that the train personnel knew her well and reserved a place for her; she paid the railway staff and Contrôle Économique inspectors with a pound of butter each.[23] Selling to the Germans offered greater profit, as well as protection from the French police. One dairy wholesaler in the Somme avoided prosecution by supplying butter to the Germans, as well as to the directors of departmental agencies who managed food supply and price controls, and even to the department's prefect.[24]

The illicit market for butter illustrates the blending of licit, borderline, and black market traffic at the expense of supply to official markets. Alfred Sauvy noted in 1942 the strong inverse correlation between the rising number of "family parcels" arriving in Paris and the steep decline in the quantity of butter delivered to officials in Normandy. From July 1941 to March 1942 the number of parcels to Paris more than doubled, while official collection of butter fell by half.[25] Milk deliveries declined steeply: the black market for butter was more lucrative, and butter was easier to conserve and transport. Most parcels sent to Paris went to affluent neighborhoods. A post office history of its functions during the occupation notes that in the transport of parcels containing butter, meat, and lard, "it is not immodest to affirm that the post office, in assuring the illicit transport of these food supplies, contributed more than any other state administration to maintain the physical and moral health of populations in the large cities."[26]

Farmers who sold directly to the Germans could earn substantial profit. The Wehrmacht collected butter and meat with their own trucks and operated beyond the authority of French controllers. Some farmers bought butter and produce from neighbors to resell to the Germans at great profit.[27] Prefects noted this as a recurrent problem in areas of troop concentration, as German troop rotations brought in new contingents seeking direct purchase. Even workers in the Organization Todt, the German organization building the Atlantic Wall, used their trucks to purchase butter, meat, milk, and eggs for their own consumption and to sell in cities, including Paris.[28] But most of the traffic in butter served French purchasers, buying direct from the farms or arranging for supply by parcels. Families with relatives in the countryside could visit, send their children on country holidays, and arrange to have parcels mailed to them. Buying direct, for those with the time and money to travel, produced a bourgeoning *tourisme alimentaire* in 1941 and 1942. In the north and west of France, the most productive and varied-crop agricultural regions, buying food became a determining factor in choosing tourist destinations. The prefect of Deux-Sèvres remarked in 1942 on "a veritable fever of purchasing essential foodstuffs as provisions for the winter" with no regard for rationing rules or prices.[29]

The flow of *colis familiaux* to meet family needs became a conduit for rationed goods not permitted in parcels (including butter, forbidden in parcels from October 1941), and for sending supplies of all sorts to friends, to acquaintances willing to pay cash, and to Paris restaurants. The prefect of Mayenne commented in late summer 1942 that he heard of Paris restaurants receiving fifteen to twenty "so-called family parcels" daily, parcels "certainly not destined for family consumption."[30] The Contrôle Économique found groups mailing twenty to fifty parcels in a period of days, food bought from farms and mailed from several rural post offices in order to disguise the traffic.[31] This commercialization of "family" traffic was all but impossible to control because of the volume of small-package traffic and the interference that control would require.[32] In a conference of regional prefects in May 1942, the minister for food supply claimed that the parcel traffic to Paris carried nearly double the amount of butter needed to fill all Paris rations. When the prefect for the Paris region claimed that this traffic helped to feed seven million Parisians, including poor families with parents in the countryside, the minister replied that the district receiving the most butter was the 8th arrondissement, one of the wealthiest districts with many restaurants.[33]

The shortages of dairy products and meat generated widespread black market activity. In 1940, initial meat rations allowed adults 360 grams per week. This fell to 250 grams in April 1941 and 120 grams in March 1943. Production declined and German requisitions took a significant share of the lower output. The loss from official markets left ordinary French citizens in some cities without meat for weeks at a time, while black market restaurants remained well supplied. "Illicit slaughter" for friends and black market sales took a growing proportion of French livestock. In 1943 and 1944, meat products constituted the largest number (31.2 percent) and the greatest value (43 percent) of black market goods seized by the Contrôle Économique.[34] Meat violations were the most frequent infractions punished in state crackdowns on restaurant offenses.[35] Postwar accounting to determine the effects of German purchasing found that meat production fell by 50 percent from 1938 to 1943 and that the Germans took 31 percent of the reduced output in 1943.[36] The rest was about equally shared between the black market and official markets.

Although the Vichy government managed the system, German officials had ultimate authority over prices. When official prices did not allow them to recover costs, farmers sold to alternative markets to recoup costs and earn profit. In September 1941, prefects in several departments reported that farmers who normally bought lean cattle as the pasture season ended to fatten for sale were not doing so. The fixed prices for fattened cattle were lower than the unregulated market price for lean; farmers stood to lose two thousand francs per head plus the cost of feed.[37] When food supply officials required that farmers provide a specific number of animals, farmers gave their leanest animals. When shortages raised prices for winter fodder, farmers slaughtered their cattle in autumn, most often for black market sale.

Clandestine slaughter became one of the most widespread black market offenses. Meat from illicit slaughter went to feed farm families (whose consumption increased during the war), relatives and neighbors, and a range of German and French black market customers. The best quality meat, and by 1943 probably the greatest quantity, went to the black market. Farmers delivered their least healthy animals to official markets, and *trafiquants* supplied farmers with *vaches maigres* ("scrawny cattle") for official requisitions in order to keep the best cattle for the black market. "The superior quality of meat furnished by black market traffickers and restaurants, without ration coupons," was readily evident.[38]

State controls needed greater legibility in transactions to facilitate enforcement by controllers, many of whom had little training. Stores were required to have price tags on all items and issue receipts recording the price and quantity for all purchases. Restaurants, though more difficult to regulate because the food purchased by diners was consumed on site, were subject to strict requirements. Menus were to be clearly visible, posted inside and outside. Menus were strictly regulated as to content and price. Tickets were required for rationed goods, and scarce foods could not be served on some days (*jours sans* for meat and alcohol) or only during restricted hours (no coffee after 3 P.M.). Receipts had to list all foods consumed and prices charged. Owners had to keep records of their menus for the previous two weeks and have correct receipts for all food on the premises. In theory this greater legibility would make it easy to identify price, quantity, and service violations. In practice, controllers often reported and fined sellers for their incomplete records. Accounting infractions were easier to detect than unrecorded transaction details. Shopkeepers kept false books; restaurants issued bills with official prices and added extras on a separate bill or charged for alcohol to include any off-menu foods. Purchasers of goods at all levels of commerce from producers to final consumers paid *soultes*—a payment on the side—to obtain goods billed at their official price.[39] The requirement for legibility prompted fraudulent practices to provide visible compliance with controls, as a cover for illicit practices that adjusted prices and quantities to reconcile the ubiquitous shortages with high levels of demand.

Frustrations

Initially, many producers turned to black markets to continue in business and employ their workers. The occupation had radically reduced supplies and access to raw materials, energy, transport, and labor. Working for the Germans offered the surest path to obtain scarce goods and secure lucrative contracts. Many industrialists rushed to make deals with the Germans in the summer of 1940.[40] Producers who used the black market to obtain raw materials engaged in a chain of transactions that generally required the use of illicit transport and energy and then sale on the black market to recoup costs. Official prices and rations paid insufficient attention to costs of production and excess demand. The price mechanism to bring supply and demand into equilibrium was banished from official markets and reasserted its power in the black market. In official markets with fixed prices, markets adjusted by reducing quantity. The production of underpriced goods shifted to the black market where higher prices would cover costs, including "insurance" costs for the risk of state confiscations and fines. The black market offered the prospect of extraordinary profits, and these incentives spurred innovation and increased the output of scarce goods to compensate for the low official prices in licit markets.

Had black market transactions resulted from French controls alone, the solutions would have been obvious. French authorities at the department level advocated increased prices and increased rations to bring goods and consumers back to official markets. But German authorities wanted low prices and routinely refused proposals to raise key market prices. German purchasing agencies benefited, as did the German soldiers sending goods home to family, and their businesses profited from access to cheap French resources. German purchasers used the black market to buy up French goods that had been hoarded or produced for illicit sale. Their purchases ranged from raw materials for war production to champagnes and fine wines, carpets, women's shoes, lingerie and cosmetics, and works of fine art. To facilitate this black market purchasing, German authorities provided French intermediaries and producers with funds, transportation, and military protection from French police.[41]

The shortages dramatically changed how consumers accessed food, which now required ration tickets and potentially lengthy waiting times in queues for uncertain results.[42] Rations provided less than 1,300 calories per day at the outset (September 1940) and declined during the occupation. Consumers in need, even when black market prices were beyond their budget, tried any means available to acquire essential goods. Their frustrations with shortages and with the proliferation of official market rules rapidly delegitimized state controls and valorized improvisation to work around obtuse and ineffective rules.

This was known as *le système D*, for *débrouillardise*, "resourcefulness" (the verb *se débrouiller*). The term had its origins in the French army in North Africa in the 1850s and became widely known for the soldiers' tactics to survive in the trenches in World War I.[43] During the occupation, it became a general term for civilian improvisation to deal with material hardship. It entailed a disregard for the law in the interest of survival. The increasingly obvious failure of state controls and the ineffectiveness of state controllers undermined the legitimacy of state efforts and encouraged black market activity. State eavesdropping on phone conversations and postal correspondence found increasing consumer tolerance for black market dealing as necessary to obtain essential foods.[44] Reliance on official rations doomed malnourished citizens to near starvation.[45] The French economist Louis Baudin wrote in 1946 of the uncertainty as to where legal limits were crossed. "The worst is that one can no longer tell where fraud begins," he explained, and observed that "the hero who refuses to use the black market and has no parents in the countryside can be distinguished by his emaciation and pallor."[46]

Liberation in 1944–1945 did little to ameliorate the shortages from declining output and damaged transport infrastructure. The German drain on French resources ended, but domestic output had fallen, and essential aid to provide for French citizens and industry was strictly limited while the Allied priority was to defeat Germany. The Vichy regime's economic controls continued, unavoidably, but now fostered greater hostility from consumers expecting improvement. Black market activities revived after areas were liberated, as expectations of improvement were confronted with increasing penury. The winter of 1944–1945 proved to be the worst of the war for many essential goods, including food and coal. A Czech diplomat who had spent the war in London, visiting Paris in January 1945, was struck by the visibility and the necessity of the black market: "Everybody needs the black market inevitably to keep alive; but in fact it is not a black market at all, because it goes on quite openly, I should almost say supervised by state authorities. It is in fact the real source from which the French draw life and most of the goods they need in order to maintain their normal living standards."[47] At a discussion in February 1945 on renewed black market activity, a ministry of justice representative stated: "It is certain that at the base of the black market lies the need of each individual to procure, illegitimately, the food supplies essential to survival that the legal food supply does not provide."[48] Public demonstrations demanding increased rations drew hundreds of thousands of protesters in March 1945. The end of the war in Europe in May offered renewed hope for a return to normalcy and further frustration as material conditions did not improve.

Consumer frustrations took many forms, including an increased willingness to use "alternative" means of supply and a general willingness to pay higher prices for needed goods that were otherwise unobtainable. The control system, created by Vichy and serving German needs, was believed to be unnecessary and run by a core of Vichy sympathizers trying to sabotage the provisional government and the restoration of liberty. Open defiance of state controls brought violent confrontations. The violence was most frequent over meat supplies in regions producing livestock. In late July 1945, in a town near Rennes, when officials closed butchers' shops for selling illicitly slaughtered meat and exceeding ration limits, a crowd of residents attacked four inspectors, who were rescued by local gendarmes.[49] In mid-August, four agents checking prices in butcher shops in Rouen were assaulted. Forty residents, alerted by the ringing of the town church bells, threatened the controllers. The gendarmerie intervened to protect them, but the crowd set their car on fire.[50] In Montendre, near Poitiers, controllers closing butcher shops for ration infractions faced a massive mobilization of townspeople. A crowd of one thousand manhandled the controllers, slashed their car tires, and threatened Contrôle Économique agents who arrived later by train.[51] According to one report, the gendarmerie saved the controllers from being lynched.[52] In Saint-Sever, the crowd roughed up a Contrôle Économique inspector investigating the clandestine slaughter of livestock. They overturned his car, smashed its windshield, and slashed the tires, stripped him of his trousers, and crowned him with butter. One newspaper account referred to the farmers as "the best boys in the world" and asked the minister of food supply, "How can they be blamed for wanting to return to a free economy after their experiences with economic controls?"[53]

In 1947, a state initiative to reduce all prices by 5 percent on January 1 and a further 5 percent on March 1 brought simmering resentments to a boil. The Contrôle Économique increased its surveillance of markets in order to enforce the lower prices. Controllers encountered hostility from shopkeepers and consumers, "hostility that a campaign has fostered across the entire country, with considerable success." Violent incidents multiplied in April,

May, and June 1947.[54] Bank of France regional directors noted "extremely violent" critiques of state *dirigisme* in April: "Everywhere people are calling for the suppression of parasitic organizations and regulations of all sorts that serve as a yoke that is choking economic activity." Producers, sellers, and consumers of all political stripes, they reported, were nearly unanimous in protesting against excessive state controls.[55]

The most dramatic confrontation took place in Dijon on May 20. Posters rallied demonstrators against the Vichy-era economic controls the organizers found intolerable in France since liberation: "We can no longer produce, manufacture, sell, or transport our goods without endless formalities required by BUREAUCRATS WHO GROW IN NUMBER EVERY DAY." French people must be permitted to work, produce, and reconstruct their country without bureaucratic obstruction.[56] Several thousand demonstrators gathered to deliver their complaints to the department prefect. Several hundred invaded state offices, breaking furniture and setting fire to all the files they could lay hands on in the offices of the Contrôle Économique and the Committee for the Confiscation of Illicit Profits.[57] In response to the rising tide of protest and the violence in Dijon, the government relaxed enforcement of controls.[58] One controller observed, "Discreet inquiries have shown that in some regions the mere presence of an agent is enough to provoke serious trouble. We hope that by appropriate measures the government can create a more favorable environment that will allow agents to accomplish their assigned duties."[59] The Contrôle Économique believed it was "the target of a particular hatred, and the actions of the service were rendered nearly impossible in many departments."[60] They retreated from tight control; the number of *procès-verbaux* completed by Contrôle personnel dropped dramatically. In the first half of the year, Contrôle officials filed 129,324 cases; in the second half, the number fell to 62,567.[61]

Hidden Capitalism

Even if outside observers found the black market remarkably visible in Paris compared to London, much remained "hidden" from state controllers. The visibility and the public clashes with state authorities give reason to consider the motives and the logic underlying the black market activity and what was "hidden" in transactions. Visibility had been critical for how the state tried to identify and punish black market activity during the war. This had new significance as black market activity surged and the new governments, de

Gaulle's provisional government and the early Fourth Republic, grappled with the punishment of wartime economic collaborators and profiteers. The Free French in Algiers planned to punish black market profiteers in 1943 and the Conseil National de la Résistance called in March 1944 for the confiscation of the property of traitors and those who profited from the black market. A decree of October 18, 1944, created department-level committees (Comités de confiscation des profits illicites, CCPI hereafter) to confiscate "illicit profits" and punish unpatriotic economic behavior—that is, actions to profit from commerce with the Germans and to exploit vulnerable French consumers.[62] A closer look at CCPI activity shows more of what consumers tried to keep hidden in black market transactions and what the state wanted to make visible. The state's inability to enforce the "legibility" of market transactions undermined the economy and the legitimacy of state controls. Consumers relied on concealment and deception, supporting illicit transactions at the "black heart" of market activity in the wartime French economy.

In addition to fixing prices and ration quantities, state controls imposed an array of measures to render market transactions more visible and thus to facilitate state monitoring. Business practices that had been legal in 1938 now had to be altered to follow new rules for legibility. All items for sale had to have price tags, even sundry items sold by street peddlers. The punishments for violations of price controls publicly displayed the state's enforcement of controls to deter new violations and increase public confidence in state control. The press reported successful actions against black market activity; officials closed businesses for control infractions and posted their violations on storefronts; municipal officials posted the names of those punished in city halls. Because continuing black market activity depended on concealment, the Contrôle Économique regularly punished sellers for failing to display prices and document sales. The frequency of these offenses attests to the state's investment in legibility to ensure rules were followed and consumers' frequent refusal to comply with either legibility or legality.

The growing shortages in official markets, the rising consumer frustration with long waits in market queues and insufficient rations, and the increasingly visible traffic in black market commerce delegitimized state control efforts. Official markets lost both goods and customers to illicit trade. After liberation in 1944, the continuing shortages and the absence of the German military force as a threat of violence and harsh punishment for offenders encouraged black market activity and pushed consumers to demand more from state food management.

The question of legibility in market activity takes on particular importance in the difficulty state officials encountered in trying to punish individuals and businesses that profited from illicit transactions. Legislation in October 1944 created the CCPI to confiscate the "illicit profits" earned in commerce with the Germans and in black market traffic with French consumers. The confiscation committees borrowed personnel and drew on the records of the Contrôle Économique for wartime infractions to identify targets for investigation, particularly for offenses they had been unable to punish because of German protection of their suppliers. Because *trafiquants* rarely kept honest accounts of black market activity and profits, the confiscation committees often had no accurate accounts of business transactions. They relied in part on "public notoriety" in their investigations and calculated changes in the individual's *train de vie* and their record of accumulated wealth to estimate the profits subject to confiscation. In egregious cases, they could impose fines of up to three times their calculation of illicit profits.

It was then up to the defendant to appeal their decision to the Conseil supérieur de confiscation des profits illicites in the ministry of finance and to provide the missing documentary evidence of activity and profits that would prove the committee estimates wrong. Investigations uncovered a variety of fraudulent measures to conceal illicit profits: cooked books to conform with the regulations rather than record actual purchase and sale prices, receipts made out to invented clients, transactions with individuals rendered untraceable by use of common surnames (Dupont, Dubois, Durand, Duval). The German purchasing offices often worked on a first-name basis, buying from French intermediaries named Pierre, Paul, Jacques.[63] The "illicit profits" were so widespread in the economy of penury that the CCPI had to limit their attention to cases of confiscations greater than 100,000 francs in most of France. In Paris, this floor level was raised to 500,000 francs, and the two confiscation committees created for Paris in 1944 had to be increased to six and then twelve in order to deal with the glut of cases.[64]

The CCPI mainly targeted commerce with the Germans. German military purchasers had massive funding thanks to the occupation cost payments and access to vehicles, fuel, and transit permits, and they routinely obstructed or terminated French interference with their traffic. French businesses that profited from this commerce disguised the traffic and invested profits in other businesses and real estate. Michel Szkolnikoff, the black market "billionaire" who made a fortune selling textiles to German military authorities, told his staff in December 1940 that with the Kriegsmarine as his main client, they no longer needed to keep accounts: "we are totally covered by the Germans."[65] For his rival black market billionaire, Joseph Joinovici, a postwar investigator found his illicit profits unquantifiable: "given the complete absence of bookkeeping, purchase receipts and any trace of payments, all operations by *trafiquants* were effected under conditions forbidden by law, but in full accord with the Occupation authorities."[66]

Although less profitable, the most widespread black market traffic was the commerce between French producers, consumers, and the intermediaries who brought them together. The transfer of activity away from official markets increased the importance of the intermediaries who could connect needy consumers with producers and supplies. They profited from the risks involved in transport and transactions for illicit commerce and served as screens for the producers whose goods they sold. Reports by controllers consistently recorded that the individuals they caught, whether consumers, retailers, or intermediaries transporting goods, claimed not to know the person from whom they had purchased goods.

The French economist Charles Rist observed in December 1943 that France was undergoing a material and moral regression that gave power to "morally unscrupulous middlemen."[67] Hubert Poissonard, the proprietor of the dairy shop in Jean Dutourd's *Au bon beurre*, the most famous fictional depiction of black market traffic, makes his fortune buying food supplies in Normandy and transporting them to a growing network of retailers in Paris.[68] His wife reigns as a queen behind her cash register, to whom customers pay daily tribute.[69] In an economy of penury, possession of or access to goods gave power in transactions. The consumer, no longer king, had become a valet.[70] Controls in official markets pushed producers seeking raw materials to maintain their business by drawing on black market opportunities for material and sales; consumers desperate for essential goods and shopkeepers needing goods to serve their client's needs and survive in business likewise found ways to get around the controls. The *système D* became not only a means of survival but also a source of pride. For some it became a form of resistance, depriving Vichy and thus the Germans of French goods.[71] For others it was a source of great profit, particularly in selling directly to the Germans. In both cases, transactions outside the law were prompted by opportunity and incentives fundamental to capitalist market activity. Profit was a key incentive but not the only one. Problem solving, serving family and community needs, and frustrating adversaries, whether German or French, could all play a part.

Black markets supplied goods for several reasons but always to meet unsatisfied demand in official markets, usually at higher prices to encourage new supply and creative effort to circumvent controls.

Significant black market activity sought to avoid losses where official prices would not cover costs. Another motivation was to acquire essential goods that were unobtainable other than through illicit transactions, whether for producers needing raw materials or for final consumers. At the local level and within families, economic regulations were violated frequently in the interest of maintaining adequate supplies of essentials, especially food. The state recognized this need and allowed low-level contraventions by individuals trying to provide for their families. Employers and owners went outside the law to maintain their businesses and their labor force. In all such examples, once the line between licit and illicit commerce had been crossed (the location of the line was often unclear), there were no clear markers to separate "gray" from "black" markets, survival from profiteering, serving family and community needs from maximizing one's own personal advantage.

So the dark side of the black market remains. Consumers relying on black market meat and dairy products for their family could also protest the failures of the postwar purge of black market profiteers. The exploitation of basic needs in the economy of penury could bring extraordinary profit to those able to access needed goods. Famished urban populations showed increasing animosity toward farmers believed to be eating well and amassing vast wealth from their black market sales.[72] The greatest profits lay in selling to the Germans, but the keenest resentments often came from the profits and the market power of local producers and retailers who visibly profited from their trade in scarce goods.

The most renowned depictions of wartime black markets in the 1950s appealed to a public angry at wartime profiteering and convinced that postwar prosecutions had failed to bring the guilty to justice.[73] The irregularity of supplies and the lack of information about goods and prices put consumers at a consistent disadvantage, often faced with a fleeting choice between paying dearly for goods they needed or having nothing. The potential for exploitation was great, and the extent of profit and the volume of commerce, unrecorded by the profit takers, remain unknown. Rumor, rancor, and resentment would all exaggerate estimates based on guesswork. Except in the very rare cases where records were found or commerce with the Germans was accurately recorded, we do not know how "black" the black market really was.

But the market dynamic for solving supply problems and meeting community needs was the same as that for seeking profit. Beyond the limits established by legal practice, the main boundaries were those set as moral standards by the communities being served. Among families and friends, those standards were often clear. Beyond those communities, particularly in dealing with the Germans, almost anything was possible.

C h a p t e r   8

The Emergence of the Offshore Economy, 1914–1939

James Hollis and Christopher McKenna

Modern commentators use the expression *offshore economy* to denote a group of complementary institutions and practices, the most important of which are tax havens, flags of convenience, and special economic zones. The word *offshore* may evoke images of islands or oil platforms, but, as the political scientist Ronen Palan argues, in contemporary usage "offshore refers not to the geographical location of economic activities, but to their juridical status."[1] The offshore economy is intermingled with the "underground economy," which the economist Ingo Walter defines as "transactions that create value but are intended to escape something (taxes, revelation of bribes, bureaucratic red tape, exchange controls, criminal prosecution, etc.)."[2] The distinguishing feature of "offshore" transactions is cross-border regulatory arbitrage, or "the creative exploitation of disjunctures in the international state system," as the legal scholar Sol Picciotto has described it.[3] Businesses engage in regulatory arbitrage to reduce or eliminate what the economist Anthony Johns terms "frictions" in transnational trade and investment; and they do so surreptitiously, as well as openly: hence, the offshore economy straddles both the legitimate and illegitimate markets.[4]

By the early twenty-first century, half of all financial transactions in the world reportedly took place "offshore."[5] The Cayman Islands, with a population of 50,000, boasted the world's fifth-largest banking center; while the shipping register of the Marshall Islands (which also has about 50,000 people) accounted for six times more merchant tonnage than that of the United States.[6] No longer "a kind of anti-system," as the eminent French journalist Alain Vernay referred to it in 1968, the offshore economy has become the default mode of global business.[7] Critics like Nicholas Shaxson argue that financial capital is in thrall to an "offshore mindset," which has normalized a pathological aversion to regulation.[8] It is something of a paradox that the offshore economic boom of the last fifty years coincided with falling barriers to global trade and the hegemony of supply-side economics, because offshore practices initially emerged as a reaction against what Vanessa Ogle calls the "long mid-century exception," lasting from the 1920s through the 1970s, which encompassed the advance and retreat of managed capitalism.[9] The work of Eric Helleiner and Gary Burn has helped cement a consensus among historians that the growth of the offshore "Euromarkets," commencing in the 1950s, was a crucial factor in the subsequent transition from a managed to a "re-marketized" capitalist model.[10]

In contrast, the Swiss historian Christophe Farquet has recently complained of the "historiographical desert" that confronts researchers investigating the offshore economy's deeper roots, in the decades before World War II.[11] "Desert" is possibly too strong, but the comparative scarcity of analysis covering the 1920s and 1930s is certainly surprising, when one considers that the conditions that stimulated offshore development after 1945—including inflation, devaluation, high rates of taxes and tariffs, quantitative trade restrictions, and controls on foreign investment—already existed in the interwar period.[12] From World War I onward, national governments greatly expanded their activities in the realm of taxing, regulating, and controlling the private sector, making the relationship between capital and the state more codependent but also more antagonistic. Figure 8.1, which depicts the top marginal income tax rates in Britain, France, Germany, and the United States from 1900 to 2000, illustrates this trend unambiguously.[13] All four countries experienced dramatic tax increases after 1914; in none of them did rates ever return to prewar levels.

The abrupt reversal of the cosmopolitan commercialism which had characterized the belle epoque meant that political risk—that is, the prospect of a contract or investment being materially affected by changes in government policy—assumed unprecedented significance for businesses everywhere, creating particular difficulties for firms involved in international trade.[14] The

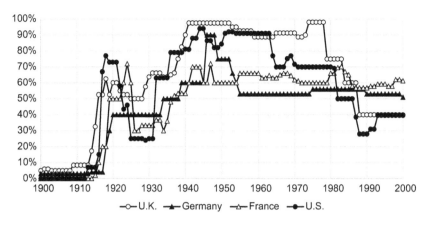

Figure 8.1. Top marginal income tax rates, 1900–2000.

growth of the administrative state, compounded by a turn to economic nationalism in the 1930s, gave rise to powerful incentives for commercial concealment and diversion.

It was predictable that capitalists would respond strategically to regulatory change by seeking out more favorable regulatory regimes. The pattern
had been apparent as far back as the Progressive Era. Until the Supreme Court
clarified the law in 1904, U.S. lawyers believed that tight combinations controlled through "holding companies" were intrinsically immune from the
1890 Sherman Antitrust Act, and several states, notably Delaware and New
Jersey, amended their statutes to encourage holding companies to register
there.[15] Similarly, after the UK government doubled their stamp duty on public share offers in 1899, corporations promoted to British investors were increasingly registered in other parts of the British Empire, instead of in Britain
itself, to avoid the stamp duty.[16] In the same period, French and German firms
were using Swiss holding companies to set up joint ventures; here, the attractions were partly regulatory and partly political: "national partnerships,
which would have been inconceivable elsewhere . . . were feasible in Switzerland."[17] The "Muscat dhows" dispute which came to a head in 1905, concerning Omani slavers who flew the French flag to evade British antislavery
patrols, provided a further contemporary example of regulatory arbitrage.
In that year, the Permanent Court of Arbitration ruled that France had
breached certain specific treaty obligations to the United Kingdom, but the
court also reaffirmed that, "generally speaking, it belongs to every sovereign

to decide to whom he will accord the right to fly his flag," a principle fundamental to the later proliferation of so-called open shipping registries.[18]

This chapter charts the development of the offshore economy from the
outbreak of World War I to the beginning of World War II and comprises
four principal sections arranged in roughly chronological order. Section one
argues that World War I was the vital catalyst for the emergence of the
offshore institutions and practices that are so prominent today. The war was
significant not only because of the way it forced international trade underground but also because the seizure of "enemy property" engendered a lasting nervousness about visible foreign investment. Section two deals with the
aftermath of World War I, when the French and German governments were
preoccupied with the extent of capital flight and tax evasion. The main beneficiaries of the offshore financial sector, namely, the United Kingdom and
Switzerland, successfully resisted French attempts to internationalize tax enforcement under the aegis of the League of Nations. In section three, we
explain that the overriding concern for treasury officials in Britain and the
United States was legal tax avoidance rather than illegal tax evasion; we discuss the technical features of British and U.S. tax law that made offshore holding companies so popular in the interwar period. The fourth section
examines how, during the 1930s, offshore practices began to spread around
the globe, through the agency of various commercial interests, including German chemical firms, Hong Kong textile manufacturers, and white-collar
criminals. In conclusion, we posit that although the interwar offshore economy was smaller than the one that developed after World War II, nevertheless it was just as diverse and is easily recognizable to our modern eyes.

Hyphenated Germans and Pseudo-Americans

Even compared with the present day, the international economy was already
highly integrated on the eve of World War I. During the first age of globalization, between 1870 and 1914, there was a remarkable rise in cross-border
trade and investment.[19] When the European powers went to war, they did so
against their biggest trading partners, which inevitably resulted in a profound
disruption of global markets. The warring states suspended the convertibil-
ity of their currencies into gold, thus paralyzing the international financial
system; and all of the belligerents engaged in economic warfare, embargo-
ing trade with enemy states and expropriating the assets of enemy nation-
als.[20] There was a sharp decline in world trade, which had barely recovered

to the prewar level before it crashed again during the Great Depression.[21] The international economy had entered a long phase of "deglobalization."

For logistical reasons, the Central powers were more vulnerable to a strategy of attrition than the Allies. After the United States entered the war in April 1917, the Allied economic blockade became increasingly effective: by 1918, Germany's imports had shrunk by 60 percent, and German exports had fallen by 75 percent, compared with 1914 levels.[22] Yet blockading the Central powers' trade and finance was an extremely complex undertaking, which raised innumerable diplomatic, operational, and commercial issues and took several years to enforce efficiently.[23] The price of goods in Germany soared to many multiples of equivalent British prices, which meant that huge profits were available to merchants who were prepared to break the law. At the outbreak of the war, the technology was simply not available for tracing the "beneficial ownership" of millions of items of cargo, which were often bought and sold in transit.[24] British officials were taken aback by the speed at which Germany rerouted its commerce via neighboring neutral states, with the aid of straw men, "cutouts," and stooges. Indeed, enforcement was perceived to be so lax in 1915 that a public scandal erupted, with the British press accusing the Foreign Office of behaving like "hyphenated Germans."[25]

Reports of a tremendous increase in British exports to Denmark, Holland, Sweden, and Norway only worsened the uproar, since those countries were known for being "an open sluice gate" to the German economy.[26] British exporters were in a quandary, since on the one hand, they were prohibited from trading with the enemy, while on the other, the government was encouraging British business to enter aggressively into new markets where German firms had traditionally been dominant.[27] Although the authorities implicated "dozens" of major British corporations in supplying goods illegally transshipped to Germany, none were prosecuted, perhaps because the scale of blockade evasion was simply too large.[28] The City of London's position as the global center for commercial credit should also have been a powerful weapon for throttling German business, but the government allowed the City to police itself, such that in 1916 "the bulk" of Germany's external trade was reportedly still being financed indirectly from London.[29]

Equally worrisome for British policy makers was the disguised trade between Germany and the United States; an $85 million drop in U.S. exports to Germany in 1914 and 1915 "was almost exactly matched by the increase in exports to Denmark, Norway and Sweden."[30] Notwithstanding the 1909 Declaration of London—which authorized the seizure of "contraband" destined for an enemy—the British authorities were reluctant to use force against neutral trade, preferring such indirect methods as pressuring neutral countries to restrict reexports and organizing a state-sponsored cartel among Dutch shipping agents.[31] To target blockade enforcement effectively and preserve diplomatic goodwill, the British had to assemble a formidable bureaucratic and intelligence apparatus, whose goal was "to monitor and regulate the flow of trade between continental Europe and the rest of the world at the micro level."[32] Cities like Rotterdam and Bern became hotbeds of espionage, aimed at uncovering who was supplying whom; one field agent in Copenhagen complained of the numerous "pseudo-American exporters" based there.[33] Swiss banks, which provided clearing facilities for trafficking across the battle line, were valued for their assistance in selecting suitable intermediaries.[34] The historian Adam Hochschild alleges that the British War Office even used a Swiss back channel, in 1915, to procure binoculars for the Allied armies from the German manufacturer Carl Zeiss.[35]

The essence of blockade running lay in concealing the ownership of consignments, which was often achieved by trading through shell corporations with misleading names, whose true affiliations were not immediately obvious. The German technique of registering "hundreds of dummy companies . . . giving a legal front to the receipt of contraband goods through neutrals" laid an oil slick for British investigators, who found themselves constantly updating the blacklist of suspect firms.[36] One examiner, tasked with stemming the leakage of contraband via Sweden, "admitted he had no reliable way of telling if the consignee named on a manifest was a consumer, a broker, a forwarding agent, or simply fictitious."[37] Dutch bankers grew rich standing in for their German clients, "using codes when transmitting orders by way of the British-operated cables, founding camouflage companies, and using middlemen to send documents and papers to the United States."[38] As the war continued, offshore companies were also employed in an effort to evade draconian laws mandating the sequestration and ultimately in many cases the confiscation of property owned by "enemy aliens."[39]

The most notorious such case involved the American Metal Company (AMC), the U.S. arm of the Frankfurt giant Metallgesellschaft, whose stock was requisitioned by the Alien Property Custodian in 1917 and later sold to AMC's local management. In 1921, a Swiss company called Société Suisse pour Valeurs de Métaux (SSM), which was in fact a vehicle for Richard Merton, the German founder of Metallgesellschaft, filed a claim with the custodian for restitution of the sale proceeds, arguing that, as a Swiss corporation, SSM was not an enemy national and claiming (falsely) that it had acquired the controlling interest in AMC before the United States entered the war. Although SSM's case was shaky, the custodian, Thomas Miller, nevertheless paid out on the claim in full and was later jailed when it emerged that Merton had bribed individuals close to President Warren Harding to the tune of $450,000.[40]

"Flagging out"—that is, reregistering enemy ships in neutral states—was another common method both of running the blockade and of attempting to escape sequestration. Shipowners transferred hundreds of German vessels to neutral registries, notably the U.S. registry, after the U.S. Congress lifted the preexisting ban on foreign-built ships.[41] Standard Oil of New Jersey, for instance, took over and reflagged some two dozen tankers belonging to its German affiliate, Deutsch-Amerikanische Petroleum Gesellschaft (DAPG).[42] Even after these transactions, DAPG still had eight vessels registered in Germany, where it was also building four new ships. Following the armistice, the Reparations Commission ruled that, despite their ultimate U.S. ownership, DAPG's operational tankers were liable to seizure. Standard's lawyers, Sullivan & Cromwell, then devised a clever scheme to make sure that the same fate did not befall the vessels still being constructed. Under the Treaty of Versailles, the territory of Danzig was to be severed from Germany and turned into a "free city." Before the treaty came into force, Standard Oil relocated the incomplete hulls to Danzig and transferred their ownership to a separate company registered there. On the treaty's operative date (January 10, 1920), the partially built ships thus automatically ceased to be "German," neatly resolving Standard's reparations problem.[43]

The restoration of peace in 1918 did not curtail the practice of flagging out, thanks in large part to the advent of Prohibition in the United States. The Bahamas, at that time a United Kingdom colony, was the foremost hub for smuggling liquor into the United States by sea, ensuring that the most fashionable flag of convenience, throughout the 1920s, was the British red ensign.[44] The Bahamas thrived under Prohibition not merely due to its geographical location but also because of the relaxed attitude of the colonial administration in Nassau and the emergence of a nascent offshore banking center there.[45] In 1920 and 1921, there was a tenfold increase in the tonnage admitted to the Bahamian shipping register, with most of the new ships owned by front men for U.S. bootleggers.[46] Britain reluctantly signed a treaty with the United States in 1924, authorizing the seizure of rum-running vessels outside U.S. territorial waters, but British statesmen had little sympathy for the U.S. predicament, dismissing Prohibition as "Puritanism run mad" and "an affront to the whole history of mankind."[47] When the Bahamian authorities tried to increase their share of the profits from bootlegging by raising the colony's customs duties, the smugglers engaged in a further piece of regulatory arbitrage, by moving their business to the minuscule French dependency of Saint-Pierre and Miquelon, where the duties were lower.[48]

In 1925, Panama entered the open registry market when it rewrote its shipping laws to make registration there easier for foreign vessels. This measure was of somewhat dubious benefit to bootleggers, because the U.S. government succeeded in coercing the Panamanian authorities into removing rum-running boats from their register.[49] The first significant growth of Panama's registry occurred in the 1930s, attributable to various factors, including the desire of U.S. shipping companies to circumvent the 1915 La Follette Act, which had improved working conditions for U.S. seafarers.[50] The naval historian Rodney Carlisle argues that, following the outbreak of World War II, the Panamanian flag became an instrument of U.S. foreign policy, with the administration of President Franklin D. Roosevelt actively encouraging U.S. firms to reregister there in order to skirt congressional legislation imposing neutrality.[51]

A Dictatorship of Snitching

The dislocation of global trade that resulted from World War I was accompanied by depression and distortion in national markets. Between 1913 and 1918, Germany suffered a 20 percent fall in output and living standards, and the decline was even worse in France, where real GDP shrank by nearly 40 percent over the same period.[52] In both countries, inflation accelerated markedly after the war. During the period of floating exchange rates in the early 1920s, the German mark ceased to have any international purchasing power whatsoever, while the French franc lost 80 percent of its value against the U.S. dollar.[53] Across continental Europe, the economic disruption of the interwar years led to huge clandestine movements of capital, generally out of currencies experiencing weakness and into more dependable ones such as the pound sterling, the U.S. dollar, and the Swiss franc.[54] This trend accelerated as European political conditions deteriorated following the 1929 Wall Street crash.

The flight of capital was not a new phenomenon: the economist Larry Neal argues, for example, that "capital flight from the Continent, induced by the

French Revolution . . . played an important, if largely concealed, role in the transformation of the British economy we now call the Industrial Revolution."[55] The international capital flows of the interwar years were unprecedented, however, both in their scale and in the degree to which they were institutionalized. Harold James observes that "tax evasion and capital flight came to be built into the Weimar system," with billions of marks being moved out of Germany annually by the late 1920s; while Eleanor Dulles estimated that in 1926 alone, deposits of "anywhere between five and thirty billion paper francs . . . were built up by the French in Amsterdam, Switzerland, London and New York."[56] Postrevolutionary Russia was another significant source of capital flight: the legendary swindler Serge Rubinstein got his first big break in 1930, when he successfully reunited one family of Russian émigrés with assets of theirs that were stranded in Switzerland, earning himself a hefty finder's fee.[57]

While the hot money of the interwar years did not always flow in one direction, there were two compelling reasons why funds extracted from the major continental European countries generally remained offshore. First, governments increasingly resorted to "exchange controls" (i.e., legal constraints on the ownership of gold and foreign currency), ever more so in the aftermath of the financial crisis that hit Europe in 1931.[58] The paradigm case was that of Nazi Germany, where exchange control evolved from an emergency measure into a permanent tool of economic management, with draconian sanctions, including the death penalty, imposed on those found guilty of violations.[59] In other European countries, as well as in Latin America, the export of capital also became an inherently transgressive activity. Ironically, although legislators imposed exchange controls with the express intention of deterring capital flight, in practice such measures tended to make it even worse, because they often locked in an artificially high exchange rate. The invariable by-products of exchange control legislation were thus black foreign exchange markets and a lively trade in smuggling gold and paper currency over national borders.[60] Yet the illicit transportation of trunk loads of banknotes across the Rhine represented the more down-market end of the industry. For the most part, monetary evasion was a genteel affair, conducted in the back offices of banks and by corporate attorneys. Structured transactions were devised to exploit loopholes in national currency regimes, while fraudulent practices were rife, including the systematic overpricing of imports and underpricing of exports.[61] Numerous offshore companies came into existence, whether as receptacles for undeclared overseas income or to obtain inflated allocations of hard currency by issuing false invoices.[62]

The second disincentive to repatriate funds was that money secretly kept offshore would (illegally) escape income and inheritance taxes, which had increased significantly since the war. The top marginal rate of income tax in France, for example, was 2 percent in 1914 but 72 percent by 1925.[63] In 1932, a scandal broke out in Paris when it became known that without the permission of the French regulator, one of Switzerland's largest banks, the Basler Handelsbank, had secretly been operating out of an apartment at the Hôtel de la Trémoille, which was raided by police following a tip-off from a whistle-blower.[64] It transpired that the unlicensed bank had more than a thousand clients, "most of whom were members of the dominant classes," including senators, deputies, bishops, and judges.[65] The government instituted criminal proceedings, but, following a backlash in the right-wing press—which complained of "a dictatorship of snitching"—they withdrew the charges and allowed the incident to fizzle out.[66] It is clear, however, that the *affaire Trémoille* revealed only the tip of a much more extensive iceberg. Christophe Farquet estimates that, taking the interwar period as a whole, "at least one half" of the investment income earned by French residents went undeclared to the tax authority; the corresponding figure for Belgium was 66 percent.[67] According to the economist Gabriel Zucman, foreign funds held in Switzerland grew from 10 billion Swiss francs in 1920 to 125 billion francs in 1938, by which point "5 per cent of all the financial wealth of French residents was deposited in Switzerland."[68] Throughout Europe, the illicit holdings of foreign exchange that would supply the initial capital stock for the Euromarkets after World War II were already beginning to accumulate during the interwar period.[69]

While domestic politics muted the effects of the *affaire Trémoille* in France, the opposite was true in Switzerland, where the federal assembly immediately acted to forestall any recurrence of the leak from the Basler Handelsbank. Controversy surrounds the "banking secrecy" provisions of the 1934 Swiss Federal Law on Banks, which for the first time criminalized the disclosure of client information to any state or private agency (including the Swiss Treasury). On one view, the legislature was concerned above all to protect the assets of German Jews against the depredations of the Gestapo, but historians now generally reject that argument, emphasizing instead a fear among the Swiss banking community that whistle-blowing could undermine their whole business model.[70] At a time when the French authorities were pressuring the Swiss to agree to mutual tax enforcement, the 1934 law signaled a clear intention on the part of landlocked Switzerland to defend its unrivaled status as an offshore financial center. It would later serve as the template for similar legislation in other tax havens.[71]

Transferring assets to "one-man companies"—thereby formally separating them from their owner, even though that individual continued to control or benefit from them—provided additional layers of privacy. The individual cantons of the Swiss confederation competed with one another in the 1920s by lowering the charges they levied on "domiciliary" (i.e., brass plate) companies.[72] Both the Liechtenstein Anstalt, introduced in 1926, and the Luxembourg "1929 holding company" were deliberately designed to cater to the requirements of foreign capital, combining effective immunity from tax with minimal disclosure requirements.[73] Luxembourg's currency union with Belgium, which meant there was no central bank in the grand duchy, made it a popular tax haven for the proverbial "Belgian dentist" and was later exploited by bankers from other countries to sidestep the minimum reserve requirements imposed by their own regulators.[74]

In 1922, the League of Nations appointed a committee of experts to consider the issue of international tax evasion. Primarily in response to French concerns, the League adopted a model convention in 1927 that recommended the reciprocal exchange of tax information in respect (inter alia) of "transferable securities, claims, deposits and current accounts."[75] This was not welcomed by many other members of the League, and the question of international cooperation in tax matters remained essentially dormant until 1939, when a handful of countries negotiated tax treaties providing for a limited exchange of data.[76] While the Swiss were the most implacable rejectionists on the expert committee, they were supported implicitly by the British, who also opposed information sharing.[77] A direct French request, in 1935, for the United Kingdom to provide a list of French citizens holding securities in London was rebuffed, after British officials had consulted the Bank of England and received the following response:

The Governor's reaction when this question was put to him was instant and emphatic . . . He said our constant policy for 70 years had been to encourage foreign capitalists to keep money here and that policy had been of great advantage to this country. The people concerned are shy birds and if they believed that the tax authorities of the two countries were co-operating would transfer their funds to some third market. That would be a grave inconvenience to us, especially at this juncture. . . . Nor could we refute his suggestion that the profits of British branches of French banks would be communicated to Paris to the immense disgust of those banks which no doubt expect to defraud the French Revenue as a matter of ordinary business.[78]

The same indifference toward the problems faced by her neighbors informed the United Kingdom's attitude to offshore financial activity in Jersey and Guernsey, two British possessions that were not subject to UK tax law and became significant havens between the wars. One British official noted in 1929 that, even if "wholesale use of the Channel Islands in this way would be rather embarrassing to our representative on the League of Nations," Britain was generally relaxed about the islands being "misused by foreigners to escape taxation," not least because most of their clients were presumed to be French.[79] Thus did a kind of fiscal mercantilism crowd out the pretensions of international solidarity.

All to the Advantage of This Country

Fraudulent tax evasion had been endemic in Victorian Britain. Then, income tax was charged at a single-digit flat rate (3 percent, on average, from 1842 to 1908), the top rate of estate duty was 10 percent, and the United Kingdom was broadly committed to free trade. Even so, an Inland Revenue study from 1870 estimated that 40 percent of traders knowingly understated their income for tax purposes.[80] During the interwar period, when the top rate of income tax averaged 56 percent, estate duty was levied at 50 percent, and tariffs resumed a central role in foreign economic policy, it would have been surprising if false accounting, concealment of assets, or smuggling had somehow disappeared. In contrast with France, however, where there was a history of resistance to direct taxation (only in 1914 did the French authorities succeed in imposing a comprehensive tax on income), by the 1920s Britain had more than a century's experience in plucking the income tax goose and had developed a reasonably subtle and effective approach to enforcement.[81] To be suspected of illegal tax evasion increasingly carried a social stigma in the United Kingdom, at least among the governing class.[82]

The same stigma did not attach to what we now call "tax avoidance" or "tax planning" (but which was usually referred to at the time as "tax dodging" or "legal evasion"). Legal tax avoidance had a long pedigree in Britain, notably where death duties were concerned, and the 1920s and 1930s witnessed a significant boom in the tax avoidance industry.[83] Although tax avoidance led to periodic outbursts of indignation in Parliament and the press, neither the judiciary nor prevailing ruling-class sentiment regarded the practice as immoral or disreputable.[84] Early legislative attempts to counteract it were piecemeal and ineffectual, making the interwar period one of "halcyon days for the tax avoider."[85] Moreover, when Parliament did pass legislation to remedy perceived abuses, the drafters failed to deal adequately with cross-border transactions, thus unintentionally boosting the attractiveness of offshore tax avoidance over and above that of the "domestic" variety.

Three structural alterations to UK income tax between 1909 and 1922 created and reinforced the incentive for capitalists to internationalize their business arrangements. Until 1909, the taxation of corporations was essentially integrated with that of individuals: both were liable for income tax at the same flat rate (5 percent), and, where a company paid a dividend, there was no additional tax on the shareholder because full credit was given for the tax paid at the corporate level. From 1909 onward, however, an additional charge, known as "super-tax," was imposed on high-income individuals, which companies did not have to pay. Even though the rate of super-tax was only 2.5 percent at the start, that was enough to encourage companies to retain earnings rather than pay dividends that would trigger a super-tax liability for shareholders. Corporate lawyers came up with ingenious ways of paying these retained earnings to shareholders as nontaxable "returns of capital," making the super-tax effectively voluntary, at least where small private companies were concerned.[86] With the onset of war, which pushed the top rate of tax from 7.5 percent to 60 percent—30 percent income tax plus 30 percent super-tax—individuals found it increasingly difficult to ignore the fact that you could instantly halve your tax bill simply by forming a company to take over your business or to hold your investments.

The second structural reform in UK taxes came in 1922, when the authorities tried to curb the proliferation of holding companies by enacting what became known as the "close company" rule.[87] This rule was supposed to tax profits "unreasonably" retained by private companies as if they had been paid to the shareholders as dividends. Some legislators objected because the rule only applied to companies registered in the United Kingdom, thereby leaving the door open to offshore avoidance. The British finance minister dismissed their concerns, reassuring them that there was "a natural disinclination even on the part of people who wish to evade their tax to set up companies abroad."[88] Yet the minister's statement was immediately belied by a rush to form companies in the Channel Islands and other tax havens, a problem that became so serious in the mid-1920s that the British government made a tentative effort to stop Jersey and Guernsey from issuing any more company licenses.[89] They aborted this initiative after the Channel Islanders successfully argued that the companies in question "would move to other places, such as Cyprus, as soon as they were threatened."[90] The British government seems to have decided that it was actually better for companies to be registered in the Channel Islands, whose administrators they could occasionally pressure into divulging information, than in jurisdictions like Switzerland or Monaco, which were resolutely uncooperative.

The final relevant structural change involved a substantive widening of the British tax base in respect of overseas investment income. Historically, passive income with a UK source, such as a dividend on British company shares, was taxable whenever it "arose" (meaning, in this example, as soon as the company declared the dividend). Conversely, the equivalent income from foreign sources was not taxed unless it was "remitted" to the United Kingdom. (In other words, dividends from overseas companies were only taxed if they were paid into a British bank account.)[91] Well before World War I, the Inland Revenue had identified this as a problem area, with more and more British taxpayers opening offshore bank accounts that they used to accumulate foreign income without paying tax.[92] In 1914, therefore, Parliament tightened the law by aligning the tax treatment of overseas investment income with that from UK sources.[93]

This legislative change had an unintended knock-on effect, since it further incentivized the formation of offshore holding companies. The taxpayer would register a company in, say, Guernsey, and then transfer their overseas investments to this new company. The Guernsey company did not pay any dividends but instead made regular payments of "capital" to the taxpayer. To ensure that the company was nonresident and thus exempt from British tax, the taxpayer would appoint Guernsey natives as directors, who notionally controlled the company but in practice did nothing apart from cash the underlying dividend warrants. This structure enabled British taxpayers to bypass the 1914 law change entirely and was implemented widely, alongside an alternative setup that utilized an offshore discretionary trust. By 1933, the Inland Revenue estimated that the British exchequer was losing one and a half million pounds annually (approximately one hundred million in today's money) just to these two schemes, and in 1936 they passed a new law whereby income diverted to offshore holding companies and trusts was treated as if it still belonged to the taxpayer.[94] This antiavoidance measure certainly looked fearsome on paper, even if it subsequently turned out to be full of loopholes.

The 1936 law change only applied to private clients, but British companies were equally interested in tax planning, and multinationals even more so, because taxes had risen throughout the world, not just in Britain. The problem of "double taxation" (tax on the same profits in two or more countries) began to affect the structure of international business for the first time.[95] A British company with a branch office abroad would be taxed in that country on the profits the branch made and then taxed again in the United Kingdom, since Britain asserted its right to tax the company's worldwide profit. If the other country was also in the British Empire, there was a partial credit for the foreign tax, but no credit was available otherwise.[96] The obvious solution was for the British company to turn its foreign branch into a wholly owned subsidiary, appointing local directors to exercise nominal "control." The nonresident subsidiary was not subject to British tax, and the UK parent company would only be taxed on the subsidiary's profits if it received them as a dividend. It was easy to extract the profits without paying dividends, for example by having the subsidiary make soft loans to the parent company.

Alternatively, the parent company could set up an intermediate holding company in a tax haven, pay the dividends there, and reallocate the cash around the group without giving rise to a tax charge: British firms became adept at using offshore jurisdictions in this way.[97] The UK government was extremely reluctant to interfere with management prerogatives concerning taxation. In fact, at the height of World War I, British officials tacitly encouraged some businesses to remove their corporate "control" from the United Kingdom, in order to mitigate wartime taxation.[98] The Union Cold Storage Company, for instance, moved its international management to Argentina, a step the government judged was "all to the advantage of this country," because it allowed the company to compete more keenly with its U.S. rivals, preventing the latter from cornering the market in frozen beef, of which the British army was the world's biggest purchaser.[99] It was not until after World War II that the British began to get nervous about companies "emigrating," at which point Parliament passed a law forcing the directors of UK-resident multinationals to obtain official permission before shifting control away from the country or face up to two years in prison.[100]

While there were differences between the British and U.S. tax systems, both countries witnessed similar developments in the interwar period. In the United States, there were even stronger reasons for retaining earnings in companies rather than paying them out as dividends, because U.S. tax law did not give shareholders full credit for corporate income tax paid.[101] It was also easier to set up offshore holding companies, because the United States treated all foreign corporations as nonresident; it did not apply the British "control test." Newfoundland, the Bahamas, and Panama were all popular jurisdictions where wealthy Americans formed shell companies to keep their assets out of reach of the Internal Revenue Service.[102] U.S. Secretary of the Treasury Henry Morgenthau reported to President Franklin D. Roosevelt in 1937 that U.S. taxpayers had "resorted to all manner of devices to prevent the acquisition of information" regarding these companies.[103] That same year, the U.S. Congress legislated against "foreign personal holding companies," but, like the British law of 1936, this provision only struck at individuals, leaving U.S. multinationals free to use tax haven subsidiaries to accumulate offshore income.[104]

An Agreement Between Gentlemen that Vaults over Frontiers

To be sure, a fair proportion of the tax planning discussed in the preceding section was implemented perfectly openly; after all, since these techniques were legal, it was hardly necessary to conceal the fact you were using them. In practice, however, even taxpayers who took care to stay on the right side of the law found it advantageous to muddy the waters, not least because it reduced the likelihood of the law being changed against them. There was no obligation on taxpayers to disclose tax avoidance schemes, and because accounting standards were in their infancy, you could present your financial statements almost any way you liked.[105] This meant it sometimes took years for the government to get a full grasp of the facts. Offshore holding companies were a convenient way to keep the authorities guessing because of the ease with which they could be incorporated and wound up, leaving virtually no documentary trace. These features naturally laid them open to abuse by people with purposes a good deal more nefarious than fiddling their taxes.

Between 1922 and 1931, for example, the Swedish industrialist Ivar Krueger raised nearly a quarter of a billion dollars in the United States, promising investors double-digit returns based on loans to foreign governments that were tied to monopolies on the manufacture and sale of matches.[106] Krueger funneled his investors' money into secret subsidiaries in Liechtenstein and the Netherlands, using the funds for a variety of clandestine transactions, including bribes to government officials, paying dividends out of capital, supporting his own stock price, and acquiring a minority stake in his principal U.S. competitor in breach of U.S. antitrust law.[107] When Krueger's financial empire collapsed, in 1932, his securities became practically worthless. Irving Trust Company, the trustee for the duped investors, knew the bonds would rebound in value once Krueger's estate was liquidated; the market had overestimated the extent of his failure. The problem was, in the process of realizing this value, there would be a capital gains tax hit on the U.S. bondholders. To avoid this, in 1936 Irving established one of the first "exempted companies" in the British colony of Bermuda, where a special law had to be passed for the purpose, to buy up the bonds.[108] The Krueger scandal was thus unusual, because the offshore system played a role not only in Krueger's dissipation of his investors' money but also the subsequent attempts to recover it. Normally you got the former without the latter, as in the case of the Wall Street "pump and dump" operator Wallace Groves, who was jailed in 1941 for using two Bahamian corporations to defraud the U.S. public of $750,000.[109]

While some capitalists prized offshore companies for their invisibility, others found them invaluable as a form of false labeling. One area where this was useful was in overcoming the commercial chauvinism of the interwar period, a difficulty that afflicted German firms more than most, since "the First World War had caused pronounced anti-German feelings in important world markets," notably the United States.[110] To disguise their identity, German multinationals engaged in a practice known as "cloaking," which had two mutually reinforcing aspects. First, German companies dressed their U.S. subsidiaries to look as all-American as possible, with English names, managing boards composed of U.S. citizens, and, at least on paper, U.S. shareholders (who in substance were mere nominees for the German parent). Second, and with increasing urgency as the international political horizon darkened in the 1930s, they transferred the control of their subsidiaries to friendly third parties in neutral countries, usually banks, creating a further layer of camouflage.[111] These cloaking arrangements had several collateral advantages, permitting German firms to evade the more onerous features of Nazi currency control, to avoid taxes and tariffs, and to get around U.S. antidumping rules, which applied more stringently to foreign-owned corporations than to domestic ones.[112]

In the case of the German chemicals giant IG Farben, the memory of World War I was institutionalized in the person of managing director Hermann Schmitz, who, as a junior executive for Metallgesellschaft, had been responsible for the transactions involving the American Metal Company outlined above. IG Farben had a Swiss holding company called IG Chemie, which, via a chain of nominees, owned the controlling interest in General Aniline & Film Corporation, one of the largest producers of dyestuffs in the United States. All through the 1930s, the board of General Aniline—which included such titans of U.S. business as Walter Teagle (of Standard Oil) and Edsel Ford—persistently denied any link to IG, asserting that they did not know who, if anyone, ultimately controlled their company.[113] Dissatisfied with this explanation, in 1942 the Alien Property Custodian seized General Aniline and other suspected IG affiliates in the United States. After World War II, with the backing of the Swiss government, IG Chemie (which had meanwhile been renamed Interhandel) sued the custodian for return of the seized assets. It took almost two decades to resolve this dispute, but Interhandel ultimately received compensation of more than $120 million in 1965.[114]

Offshore companies were also important in the context of the wave of cartelization that rippled around the globe during the "golden age" of international monopolies in the 1920s and 1930s.[115] While antitrust enforcement was becoming an increasingly fractious issue in the United States, elsewhere, cartels were almost universally regarded as legitimate business practice.[116] U.S. officials looked on in horror as industry after industry fell prey to what they quaintly dubbed "an agreement between gentlemen which vaults over frontiers."[117] Typically, as in the case of the aluminum and the electric light bulb cartels, offshore companies were used to monitor output ratios and fine any members who exceeded their quotas.[118] Jurisdictions such as Belgium and Switzerland were favored for this role on account of their "liberal regulations."[119] Sometimes (as the example of IG Chemie demonstrates) the offshore company would own some of the cartel's assets, in addition to performing the aforementioned policing function.

The rise of protectionism in the 1930s, which saw the establishment of competing trade and monetary blocs, created incentives to reorganize chains of production. Under the system of "imperial preference" inaugurated in 1932, for example, countries in the British orbit applied tariff schedules that discriminated between imports originating within and outside of the empire. The legislation initially laid down that, in order to obtain preferential treatment, no more than 25 percent of the cost of production needed to represent value added inside the empire.[120] This definition opened the way for Hong Kong manufacturers to import raw materials and semifinished items from China and Japan for final assembly, whereupon, "while only minimal parts of the production process were conducted in Hong Kong, these products nonetheless qualified for certification as Empire products."[121] So successfully did Hong Kong clothing manufacturers expand into the British market that, in 1937, the British government bowed to pressure from domestic producers and raised the relevant empire content requirement to 100 percent. "This was an impossible standard that most Chinese manufacturers in Hong Kong could not meet," but responsibility for certifying the origin of the raw materials was effectively delegated to the private sector.[122] When Commonwealth preference resumed after World War II, abuse of the certification procedure was an open secret: Hong Kong firms were known to charge higher prices for the same (nonqualifying) goods accompanied by preference certificates, reflecting a division of the benefit of evading British tariffs between the supplier and the customer.[123]

Another corollary of protectionism was the spread of tariff suspension regimes, such as the foreign trade zones (FTZs) introduced in the United States in 1934.[124] Designed to promote the U.S. entrepôt trade, technically FTZs did not allow manufacturing, but the definition of "manufacturing" was narrow enough to permit heavy industrial processes like tungsten refining to take place inside the zone. Moreover, the facility to store products duty-free enabled the development of structured financial transactions circumventing foreign exchange control laws. A 1936 article in the *New York Times* revealed, for instance, that U.S. investors were using blocked Brazilian milreis to buy cargoes of nuts—which they shipped from Brazil to the FTZ on Staten Island, where they were left in bond—and then borrowing against the nuts in dollars.[125]

The short-lived and ineffectual sanctions imposed by the League of Nations in 1935 to protest Italy's war in Ethiopia provide a final illustration of the diffusion of "offshore" practices in the decade before World War II. Although a "post mortem" the League conducted in 1936 concluded that, as far as they went, sanctions were administered fairly by the participating countries, considerable evidence of malpractice reached the ear of the British authorities. There were reports of "the establishment of new commercial houses in Switzerland to undertake entrepôt trade between Italy and sanctionist countries"; of prohibited goods leaving Singapore "ex consignor's order" (i.e., destination undisclosed) to be carried to Italy in Japanese ships; of governments "conniving at irregular practices" in connection with certificates of origin; and of British banks financing sanctions-busting transactions through their affiliates in the Tangier International Zone.[126] Similar patterns of behavior would be observed from the 1960s through to the 1980s, when the United Nations implemented sanctions first against the white minority regime in Southern Rhodesia and later apartheid South Africa.[127]

Conclusion

As Kenneth Mouré's essay in this volume confirms, the scale of black market activity during World War II outstripped anything seen during World War I, and so did the scope and sophistication of economic warfare.[128] In the decade after World War II, the phenomenon of clandestine capital movement assumed "notoriously large and disturbing" proportions, despite the systematic application of exchange controls.[129] Yet the offshore economy of the Bretton Woods era represented less an innovation than a reanimation of techniques that first saw widespread use during World War I. Secret bank accounts, offshore holding companies, and flagging out were not invented in 1914, but it was the exigencies of World War I that made them commonplace. Moreover, as the historical criminologist Tom Naylor observes, economic warfare invariably has an enduring impact, in that it leaves behind "talent and infrastructure" that are "easily adapted to peacetime pursuits."[130] Relationships and know-how accumulated during World War I were kept alive during the interwar period, when "economic warfare was never quite off the agenda of national policy makers."[131] As international trade and investment became increasingly politicized, one way capitalists responded to deglobalization was by becoming differently globalized, moving assets to more convenient jurisdictions, and using new corporate forms of ownership, to minimize the incidence of tax or evade regulations.

When frictions increased, financial capital became more slippery. Regulatory arbitrage figured in numerous types of interwar business activity, from rum running to cartelization. Contemporaries were conscious of a moral dimension to these chameleonic tendencies. Part of the British public decried those who went offshore as "miserable, unpatriotic scoundrels," while the economist Victor Tranter went as far as to suggest that "incurable evasion" should be treated as "a certifiable form of insanity."[132] Novelists articulated a certain societal paranoia concerning secretive, unaccountable capital.[133] The historian John McDermott argues that "business ethics themselves were significantly eroded by the advent of total war."[134] Unquestionably, there was a faction of the interwar ruling class, in all industrialized states, that had not reconciled itself to permanent increases in tax and regulation and consequently had little compunction about giving the authorities the runaround. Tax havens supplied an opt-out from national fiscal and monetary regimes for people who were willing to assume the necessary risks, and some offshore centers were already providing a full-spectrum service, competing with one another to legislate for low-tax, low-scrutiny environments.

At the same time, even if states did not have the administrative resources to eliminate offshore activity, they often lacked the political will as well. There were already evident, during the interwar years, what the financial journalist Alain Vernay would later characterize as "ambiguous liaisons" between onshore and offshore jurisdictions.[135] In France, tax evasion went unpunished because it implicated half of the establishment, while Britain refused to assist because London and the Channel Islands benefited from handling this illicit French money. British and U.S. tax law positively incentivized the establishment of offshore holding companies. The Nazi regime turned a blind eye to "cloaking" by German firms, even though they knew that the same devices were also used to evade German regulations. Administrators in Britain, France, Germany, and the United States all selectively tolerated offshore activity insofar as they believed it contributed to national competitiveness. Their attitude of fiscal and regulatory pragmatism is remarkably reminiscent of the philosophy that pervades our own "reglobalized" world in the twenty-first century.

PART IV

Hidden Market Spaces in Planned Economies

Chapter 9

Comrades In-Between: Transforming Commercial Practice in the People's Republic of China, 1949–1962

Philip Scranton

> Although the relative share of the private sector in total economic activity decreased from 1949 to 1953, there was a substantial increase in the absolute volume of private . . . retail trade. It may be argued that a large part of this . . . was the result of recovery from the war. Nevertheless, the fact that the Communists permitted the value of . . . private retail trade to increase by 40 percent reveals to some extent their high dependence on the private sector.[1]

> It was estimated that in eleven large cities in 1957, some 130,000 unlicensed traders were active; 20,000 were to be found in Beijing alone. In one part of Hebei, . . . unlicensed traders were twice as numerous as private traders had been before the "socialist transformation." . . . Only through frequent evasion has the [commercial] system been rendered viable.[2]

What does commerce do? From a "red" viewpoint, really nothing very interesting, just moving goods and funds around the economic chessboard through exchanges remote from adding value and building socialism. What

Table 9.1. Private Enterprise Shares of Wholesale and Retail Trade, PRC, 1950–1953

Year	1950	1952	1953
Private wholesale trade (billion ¥)	8.0	6.9	8.0
Total wholesale trade (billion ¥)	10.5	19.1	26.8
Pvt. share of Total (%)	76	36	30
Private retail trade (billion ¥)	10.1	12.1	14.1
Total retail trade (billion ¥)	12.1	20.9	28.2
Pvt. share of total (%)	83	58	50

Adapted from Table 1 in Ecklund, "Protracted Expropriation," 242.

does commerce do? From an "expert" perspective, something that's critical to any functioning economy—executing transactional flows—without which enterprises and families would wither in isolation. Yet following the values and priorities of those they studied, most researchers analyzing actually existing socialisms have emphasized manufacturing and agriculture: paying some attention to transport and communications, taking note of construction, echoing consumer complaints about shortages and poor-quality goods, and largely ignoring the structure, institutions, and processes of socialist commerce. A half century ago, the economist Audrey Donnithorne systematically and successfully departed from this pattern, so this review of commercial practices in the early People's Republic of China (PRC) follows her lead.[3]

As in other domains, the PRC's commercial system relied initially on transformation and centralization. During reconstruction, the state campaigned with rising urgency for merchants' participation in "joint public-private enterprises," in which they would work as salaried managers compensated through profit sharing and by 5 percent interest on any capital contributed. By 1954, however, just one thousand such firms had been established; whereas operationally, private wholesale and retail dealers had remained axial to commercial activity, as Table 9.1 suggests.

Moving from reconstruction into the first Five Year Plan, commercial activity had made rapid gains, more than doubling in three years as private enterprises' market shares fell steadily. However, gross turnover figures for "national capitalists" in trade remained stable in wholesaling and rose sharply in retailing. Merchants were hardly fading away; instead, in the mid-1950s, the Ministry of Commerce aggressively pushed them into public-private consolidations just as the rush to create peoples' communes surged. If peasants' private plots presented a path to "spontaneous capitalism" (and were erased, though temporarily), so too did small merchants, stall or street sellers, and peddlers exemplify backward-looking "capitalist roadism." Starting in January 1956, the state began to move all elements of the economy under its control, sending cadres "deep into market towns and rural zones to assist in the transformation of private merchants." In Guiyang (the capital of Guizhou Province) "gongs and drums" shook the city, celebrating the transformation of "35 private commercial trades."[4]

By late 1957 the journal *Industrial and Commercial Circles* calculated that nearly two million households "have been transferred from participation in private commerce to participation in public-private, jointly-operated shops, cooperative shops, cooperative brigades or State-operated shops," perhaps 85 percent of onetime merchant families.[5] The agency directing this program descended from the PRC's inaugural Ministry of Trade, which divided in 1952 into agencies for commerce, foreign trade, and food. These spawned further spin-offs through reorganizations, most significantly creating the "specialized," or national, corporations whose operations accounted for much of the early 1950s commercial expansion.[6] Focused on commodity classes, they bought, sold, and transferred great volumes of grain, cotton, coal, salt, building materials, and more, through regional, provincial, and county subsidiaries and ground-level supply and marketing cooperatives (SMCs), which also ran most rural retailing. Producer co-ops and the SMCs "opened more than 200,000 retail outlets and purchasing points" by 1955. State wholesalers distributed materials purchased by the national corporations and operated through a scaled series of depots, graded 1, 2, and 3, for provincial capitals, districts, and *xian*, covering territories defined by administrative structures. This scheme short-circuited earlier spatial trading patterns and would generate long-term problems.[7]

Meanwhile, a 1957 Soviet delegation touring China's cities was amazed at the vitality of entrepreneurs, the absence of queues, and the diversity of the goods and services available. They reported that in Beijing there were small trading firms, dining rooms, eating establishments, and shops for general services. These enterprises held an impressive array of goods: 1,500 varieties of silk fabrics and 1,000 of cotton. Similarly impressive were the more than 6,000 eateries. It seemed to the delegation that "literally in every house there is an enterprise participating in serving the population—be it a store, shop or lunch room."[8]

Mobile, pop-up restaurants were ubiquitous as well, competing with the established restaurants. They might be as small as a buffet bar mounted on a bicycle or propped against a wall.[9] Tiny shops offering specific kinds of goods could be found on hundreds of commercial streets. In Shanghai, there were many shoe stores, with leather footwear abundant and woolen and cotton fabrics and garments of all types; "clothes, dresses, trousers" were sold in abundance. By one estimate Shanghai had an enterprise for every forty-five inhabitants.[10]

Beyond shops and stalls, urban peddlers glued together elements of the commercial system that planning could not encompass. "The services rendered by them are so diverse and universal that even many of the large stores do not offer them," the Soviets reported. These particularly included repairs to furniture by strolling artisans "holding high a transparency bearing a picture of a divan." Some repaired bicycles, shoes, rubber boots, or even fountain pens. Others sported "a wooden box to which copper plates are attached, which chime when struck." These craftsmen renewed metal objects of all sorts, even replacing lost keys by disassembling locks. The delegation remarked, "The technical skill of such masters is extremely high."[11]

Recycling, essential to conserving resources, led urban hawkers to engage in the practice of buying up old and unusable articles to supply industry with raw materials. Shanghai had some 10,000 hawkers and Beijing some 2,000. The report noted, "[They] walk along the streets with their yokes, attracting attention by shouting, and collecting worthless copper utensils, rusted iron, torn linen, old books, broken glass . . . and other things from the people," either exchanging them for goods needed in the home or paying cash.[12] As might be expected, by 1957, city peddlers had been persuaded to join "cooperatives, cooperative shops, or cooperating groups," gaining access to "social funds" and preferential tax treatment, alongside handicraftsmen "and other persons who display private-enterprise initiative." Performing valuable work within socialist commerce, their provision of "direct services" represented "a useful inheritance from the old society."

In rural districts, commerce became more diversified during the 1956 decentralization phase, with the reopening of periodic market fairs for vending agricultural surpluses or handicrafts and with the reconstitution of thousands of trade or "brokerage" warehouses. A generation earlier, nearly 30,000 of these facilities clustered in urban, coastal, and dense agricultural areas, each a "focal point for transshipping and concentrating commodities and acting as a channel for the interflow of commodities between urban and rural areas." Given their plainly capitalist nature and widespread complaints that they served as "instruments for speculation and fleecing the peasants," they gradually closed shop, until the PRC reactivated them in 1957. As before, they handled the wholesale trade in agricultural and subsidiary products. The trade was organized into three basic lines: agents buying and selling, transactions between buyers and sellers, and buying and selling on their own account. Merchants also performed services, ranging from inspecting commodities to bargaining over prices to appraising and billing. One contemporary report noted, "Some also pay taxes for customers, provide overnight lodging, stables, storage and safekeeping facilities, and act as agents in transport and processing."[13]

Located in "large or medium-sized cities or in centers for scattered markets" (hence the provision of lodgings), and crucial to information flows, the warehouses connected peasants and co-ops with "state-operated commerce units," SMCs, private-public shops, and even peddlers, but they barred consumer purchases and were not supposed to sell goods on their own account. Retailing was designed to flow through shops, department stores, and market exchanges, such as rural fairs and urban food marts or street stalls. "Control commissions" governed exchange sites, "regulating the market and balancing production and consumption on the basis of consultation with concerned offices."[14] Yet the formal management of socialist commerce, with its perennial concern with surveillance and control, thinly veiled the market centrality of these institutions inside an ostensibly planned economy.

Consider price-setting guidelines. Prices in trade warehouses, the guidelines stated, "should generally accord with the market," being settled "according to quality grades. . . . The voluntary agreement of buyers and sellers should be obtained. The brokerage warehouse must not use compulsion in price matters." Similarly, at retail food marts, the procedures were expected to work as follows:

Early in the morning, exchange officials should hold an informal meeting and decide on the price range (highest and lowest price) for each minor native product. The determined price will be made on the basis of the market supply and demand situation, the procurement prices paid by State-operated commerce and the SMCs, and recent price movements on the market. The prices decided upon must meet the approval of buyers and sellers, but if prices are far too high or too low, the exchange officials can urge buyers and sellers to conclude bargains at reasonable prices.[15]

Here we encounter market socialism in action, with little theorizing yet imbued with the deep pragmatism that informed PRC economic practice, outside periods of ideological overload. Officials were to mediate and supervise market activity, to prevent speculation and gluts that would depress prices and discourage sellers from bringing in goods, but they could only "urge" the actors toward moderation and had to seek traders' approval of, rather than dictate, prices. It may seem ironic that commerce trended toward pushing responsibility downward in the system at the same time that the tide of communalization was consolidating Chinese agriculture. Of course, ideology drove the latter, especially the search for scale returns, whereas the former acknowledged the specificities and locality of trading relations and market exchange, a situation that hymns to the progress of "socialist commerce" poorly concealed. The two dynamics stood in contradiction, in a system Donnithorne aptly termed "cellular"; neither effort proved internally consistent.[16] Substantial problems arose, demanding urgent fixes that at times bypassed the PRC's reliable practices of prototyping and experimentation.[17]

Given unreliable roads and an insufficient supply of trucks, rail transport was the essential commercial link between city and countryside, particularly because "suburban" farming of "locally produced vegetables" outside Beijing, Tianjin, Shanghai, Mukden (Shenyang), Baotou, Chengdu, and Guangdong could provide only 70 percent of urban requirements in 1956–1957. The rest had to be shipped long distances, as for example 35,000 tons of cabbage hauled 1,800 kilometers from Shandong north to Harbin, costing ¥50/ton [$21US] for produce worth just ¥100/ton [$42], with spoilage in transit of nearly 40 percent. Shipping expenses could not be recovered through the market price, and "the State took a loss" of ¥24/ton [$10]on the cabbages successfully delivered (21,000 tons → ¥500,000 loss [$208K]), plus another ¥1.4 million [$580K] for cabbage that rotted in transit.[18] On long journeys, commercial freight trains halted many times, slowing progress. For the 1,000-kilometer trip from Wuhan to Guangzhou, "a freight train operated directly . . . took four to five days, while a train with stops for wagons to be taken off or added at intermediate stations to from seven to eight days."[19] Figure nearly two weeks for Harbin's cabbages. Little wonder that in 1957, Beijing's government initiated "a policy of attempting self-sufficiency in vegetable supply" through expanding "crops in nearby areas," which also makes the Ministry of Railways' late-1950s emphasis on building short-haul lines sensible.

Meanwhile, the restoration of open markets was becoming, if anything, too successful. At Lanzhou, the provincial capital of Gansu, three city markets drew over 18,000 sellers, January to June 1957, half of them "merchants with proper documentation" or representatives of advanced producer cooperatives (APCs) and handicraft groups. A third were peasant vendors, three-fifths of whom "had abandoned agriculture and were dealing in commerce [while] the remainder were Tibetan merchants," far from home. Reported six-month sales reached ¥2.4 million [$1M], a 250 percent increase over the same period in 1956. However, agents from "state-operated and jointly-operated enterprises in Beijing, Shandong, Inner Mongolia and other areas" were breaking the rules. They had commissioned local shop personnel "to purchase skins and fur clothing, all without the approval of local industry and commerce administrative agencies and at prices one-third higher than the official prices." Such maneuvers wrongly encouraged peasants to think "that they can enrich themselves by dealing in commerce," a surely correct point.[20] Similarly in Hunan, "outside purchasing agents" were disrupting the crucial bicycle trade by going directly to a provincial company's receiving depot and contracting for large quantities, undercutting allocations aimed to ease factory workers' journeys to their jobs.[21]

In Fujian, a party committee investigating "black market households" running shops and stalls without permits found that "ninety percent or more of them were members of APCs, but had abandoned agriculture to devote themselves to trade after the opening of the free market." They handled materials supposed to be channeled to unified purchasing and procurement and, worse, illegally bought citizens' ration coupons for grain, vegetable oils, and meat, which they acquired from state enterprises and then shipped to the provincial capital for sale at higher prices. Party leaders understood that those who suffered from the 1956 drought had turned to commerce "temporarily . . . to solve their livelihood problems," but they showed no signs of returning to farming, which was worrisome.[22]

Shanghai administrators sought to put a stop to the practice of "agencies, units, schools, factories, enterprises, merchants and peddlers" going to the countryside to "buy live hogs and pork directly from the peasants." This irregular purchasing encouraged "unlicensed hawkers and cut into the business of permanently licensed vendors," so new controls on pork flows came into force on September 10, 1957.[23] As in Lanzhou, given market opportunities, organizations became entrepreneurial, or at least opportunistic—the problem did not simply involve a handful of reckless traders. Beijing had moved already in May, shutting down its "state-guided free vegetable market" so as to restore proper controls. Late in 1956, because fall yields were low, large onions in the market sold for ¥0.48/kg[20¢], more than double the official price (¥0.22 [9¢]). The same was true for cabbages, but a broader issue loomed. As a contemporary report noted, "high free-market prices resulted in the failure of vegetable producing co-ops to turn over vegetables to the State-operated corporations. Instead they sold vegetables at high prices to unlicensed peddlers and outside peasants. Some co-op members requested vegetables at official prices from the co-operative, then took them to the free market for sale."[24]

In January 1957, city authorities had tried to tighten price management, decreeing that only for produce of higher than usual quality could market prices exceed official settings. This proved insufficient; for after the first spring harvest, the Municipal Vegetable Corporation (MVC) could secure only one-third as much spinach as in 1956. The rest "went mostly to the free market, where prices were generally twice" official levels. Hence, in a May attempt at recentralization, the authorities "abolished" the free market. In its place, the MVC ruled that regional produce could be sold only to its agents. In the city, it "set up 159 permanent vegetable retail outlets and 512 traveling vendors. In addition, 227 households in the beef, mutton and pork business [were] organized to sell vegetables. [Still, by fall 1957] the traffic in vegetables [had] not yet been completely stopped. The Beijing Market Control Commission still [had] about *a hundred cases daily* [involving] illegal vegetable sales."[25]

A hundred cases daily, thousands every month in the capital—how could this happen? As specialists have noted, in China's cellular society, "outward compliance" with official rules was readily offered but was "apt to remain superficial." Cadres and citizens appreciated "the limits to which both can go"; hence, public conformity could contrast sharply with private behavior. Donnithorne noted, "Sabotage need be none the less effective for being done in silence. Indeed, the more contrary to central orders that local cadres may be acting, the more loudly they may give verbal support to those orders."[26] As with cadres, so with peasants, co-op members, and peddlers—though officially forbidden, illicit vegetable commerce proceeded apace and persisted quietly. In this context, conventional Cold War images of a thought-controlled, totalitarian China are incomplete politically and wholly inadequate for understanding business practice. Beijing's policy lurches could indeed have dramatic and drastic effects but chiefly when provincials and locals *actually followed* urgent central directives or had no options to subvert outward enthusiasm with covert evasion, as during the spasms yielding the peoples' communes, the Great Leap Forward and the Cultural Revolution.[27]

Between enthusiastic periods, pragmatism and opportunism seem to have been quite common, even dominant.

Amid these crosscurrents, the Ministry of Commerce announced a comprehensive reorganization to take effect on January 1, 1958, a "structural simplification" pushing authority and responsibility downward in the business system.[28] In a series of fall 1957 planning sessions, ministry officials replaced the "national corporations" with a set of "trade bureaus" to monitor activity in textiles or construction materials but no longer directly supervising "commercial agencies on the provincial, municipal or autonomous regional level." Instead, managing such operations devolved to lower-level authorities, who also would "develop plans . . . for business operations, fiscal provisions and statistics," with the latitude to create distinctive, nonstandardized programs that, though reported to the ministries, did not need their approval.[29] Provincial agencies would provide the center with "overall figures on profit and loss" in commerce but not details on enterprise "profit and loss for each class of commodity." Moreover, inventories would no longer be fixed by rules based on outlet size but could fluctuate within upper and lower limits based on "historical data" documenting supply and demand. These moves reduced the ministries' need for control personnel, whose numbers dropped by 50 percent in Beijing, cuts made possible in part "because the [quality] of work of basic-level cadres [had] risen in recent years."[30]

Commercial reform in Jilin Province addressed a number of nagging but largely invisible problems. Five (or more) stages had been necessary to move rural goods to cities or factories, from purchasing sites to market towns to *xian* centers to urban state wholesalers and lastly to the retailer or industrial user. As each administrative unit added its "costs" to every shipment, "passing along the discounted expense, level-by-level," in a context of fixed end-use prices, acquisition payments to rural producers were depressed. It seemed that "even goods sent directly [to users] were formally entered in meaningless bookkeeping entries of the wholesale links, where 'expenses' were discounted and added to [their] profits." Leather might be sent from the provinces to the industrial departments, but the billing went through to city, *xian*, and cooperative so that these units could get their (9.75 percent) profit. Artificial links and billing practices such as these meant goods sat piled up in warehouses, often ruined by the time they reached the consumer.[31]

This complex of rules and regulations—created "to restrict capitalist speculative activity"—had become "a hindrance to commerce" and had to be simplified. Just moving goods from an urban wholesale depot to a retailer involved twelve procedures among six agencies, taking "five to seven days." After consolidation, warehouse-based personnel completed a shorter list of steps, taking a day and a half. A contemporary article noted that "retail stores . . . also reduced the former four-stage procedure a customer had to go through to a one-stage system of 'money in one hand and goods in the other.'" As a result, eggs from rural Jilin, which took twenty days (and over 350 kilometers) to travel among agencies before reaching urban buyers, now shipped directly from co-op to retailer in seven days (covering 60 kilometers). This lowered expenses by more than 40 percent "and reduced losses and damage."[32]

Shanxi reformers admitted that the prior structure "put too much emphasis on vertical lines of command [which] lessened local incentives." In truth, "state-operated corporations had a big head but a small body; that is, many of the *hsiang* and the villages had no [sales and purchasing] agencies." Decentralization led to broader market coverage while sharply reducing paper flows to the center, the scope of detail they contained, and the personnel necessary to generate them. Shanxi's You-Tz'u special district, comprising 730 townships, submitted numerous plans and statistical reports covering various corporations and commodities. Eventually these reports were substantially reduced in number.[33] Thereby, one district alone released nearly nine hundred county-level commercial officials from bloated staff rosters, saving an estimated ¥460,000 [$190K]annually, while improving coordination and shrinking waste, duplication, and competition over resources. Two consequences were plain: the Ministry of Commerce experienced "a great loss of authority," and commercial practices developed "very considerable divergences" geographically. Each offered ammunition to later recentralization advocates.[34] A third consequence lingered: displaced and reassigned cadres, not least those shipped out to agricultural posts, became ineffectual and disillusioned managers, having been shunted aside. Their resentments and others' resentments against them would deepen.

The Great Leap Forward disrupted transportation and thus the commercial reforms as well. Stressing rapid industrialization through both vast and tiny construction projects, Beijing prioritized the rail shipment of coal, iron, steel, and equipment, pulling thousands of freight cars out of local/regional rural-urban food and goods exchanges. Broader managerial issues were also involved. A 1958 transport crisis reflected the large quantities of goods needing transport, as well as inefficiency stemming from a lack of counterflow goods and "unnecessarily long hauls." These problems reflected "the weaknesses in planning and organization of production, supply and transport, together with continuing deficiencies in the allocation of raw materials, imperfections and instabilities in the distributive system and dislocations between production, supply, transport, and sales."[35]

Party journals claimed that, in order to handle "steel and iron transportation," both the military and millions of peasants pitched in using "modern airplanes, steamers and motor vehicles [as well as] sampans, carts drawn by horses or mules and carts pushed by hand [and] tractors and bicycles."[36] Known as *shock transport*, this technique proved crucial to sustaining urban populations. For example, trouble was brewing in Tianjin, where the population "[depended] mainly on outside shipments for foodstuffs," including vegetables, pork, beef, mutton and lamb, etc. In October 1958, both transportation capacity and the rural labor force were being strained and squeezed owing to the great leap forward. "As a result, agricultural products could not be concentrated in time and transported into the city and supplies of subsidiary foodstuffs on the Tianjin market were reduced."[37] Acknowledging the crisis, an emergency effort in December 1958 moved 200,000 tons of stranded goods, including "over 1300 cars of cotton, grain, vegetables and meat for Beijing, Tianjin, Shanghai, Wuhan, Shenyang, Anshan and other large cities. . . . The Shenyang Railway Bureau utilized passenger cars, baggage cars, maintenance cars, and trains from nearby suburbs to load up and transport daily necessities."[38]

Further stress on commerce derived from the commune-formation drive, one impetus for which was to assure state capture of agricultural and subsidiary products. Two practices followed from this: closing thousands of rural markets where co-op and household surpluses had been sold and eliminating families' private plots so their yields could be integrated into communal totals. These constraints further undermined the remaining village merchants, as virtually all commercial transactions were to flow through communes into state channels. Whether this actually happened is doubtful, as "from the early days of the communes this was felt too cumbersome." Production teams were dealing directly with the state commercial organization, even though they were meant to get supplies from the commune. These practices were redundant, and "it was considered superfluous for the state commercial organization to maintain its own machinery inside the communes."[39]

By extension, wholesaling relations "atrophied," trade warehouses closed, and open markets in midsize and major cities stopped functioning. Mikhail

Klochko, a Soviet chemist sent to the PRC in 1958, discovered on arriving in Beijing "hundreds of little shops and boutiques, [including] special tea shops where one could find a staggering variety of different teas at various prices. There were other specialty shops—greengrocers, butchers, poultry shops." Nothing like this existed in Moscow. Returning to China three years later, he noticed "the disappearance of the fruit and vegetable stalls in the streets," even as urban trade was steadily reviving from the Great Leap's crash. Given central policy reversals, agencies and cadres set about restoring rural markets (40,000 in 1961), reopening wholesale trading warehouses (approximately 12,000 initially), reestablishing millions of private plots, revitalizing urban trade, and reinvigorating SMCs' purchasing and supply mechanisms, particularly for subsidiary goods and handicrafts.[40] A U.S. contemporary explained:

> Supplies of subsidiary foods and other consumer products had fallen so low by November 1960 that peasants were once again permitted to cultivate small private plots, were encouraged to engage in household subsidiary production [e.g., bamboo mats, baskets, ceramics, embroideries], and were allowed to sell their extra produce at rural trade fairs. These three elements of private initiative in a socialist state the Communists referred to as "the small freedom under the big collective."[41]

Despite their capitalist aura, rural fairs and "sideline" production were again legitimized, even celebrated, as providing a "supporting role in socialist commodity exchange." Still, the "overwhelming majority" of fairs reportedly were "scattered on the plains and the mountains" far from the industrial north and the densely settled, highly visible eastern and southeastern provinces. Though co-ops and SMCs did operate stalls, "individual commune members" accounted for two-thirds of all fair sales, concentrating on meat, eggs, vegetables, and "complicated varieties" of handicrafts. This increased members' income, yet closely supervising vendors and enforcing spatial restrictions on their travel affirmed the principle that "nobody is permitted to give up farming in favor of trading," evidently a lesson from mid-1950s practice.[42]

Echoing complaints launched (and then stifled) during the short-lived Hundred Flowers campaign, in the early 1960s Beijing's economic newspaper, *Ta Kung Pao*, began publishing articles critiquing commercial management. One writer accused SMC cadres "in all parts of the country" of "aimless purchases, the misappropriation of capital, and extensive waste." In Henan, the native products office had bought and shipped 36,000 cement bags (¥28,800) "for which there was no demand on the market" and which "must be considered as overstocked inventory." Comparably, Hunan SMC business agents had purchased 16,000 kilograms of "orchid-grass seeds" (¥27,200 [$11.3K]) now lying uselessly in storage. In Jiangsu, SMC and co-op representatives had held a five-day conference, spending three times the funds normally allocated for such functions in consuming "a total of 8 hogs, 20 ducks, 100 *chin* [50 kg] of beef, 195 *chin* [98 kg] of fresh fish, and 61 *chin* [30 kg] of samshu [a rice liquor]. In addition, ¥42.80 was spent for cigarettes and tea, ¥32.40 went for firecrackers, and 1406 theater tickets were purchased for ¥459 [$190]."[43] Nice for party planning but hardly exemplary administration.

Meanwhile, responding to Zhou Enlai's call at the Second National People's Congress to "take stock of inventories," the commercial cadre Zhang Gao-feng, while in Heilongjiang Province for purchasing, investigated local "conditions concerning the supply of industrial products." At Shao-tung *xian*, the state's wholesale department supplied 64,000 people in four communes through forty-eight SMC stores. Zhang learned that 35 percent of its on-hand stock was dead inventory (approximately ¥311,000 [$130K]), chiefly "commodities that could not find buyers, had deteriorated in quality or were poor in quality but high in prices, large in quantities but limited in outlets. Among them were tape recorders, gramophones, records, accordions and other things, totaling 100 different kinds, which could not be sold locally." Acquired without considering demand and often "not properly looked after," thus reflecting badly on local managers, they had to be moved on and out to clear floor space and to recover the funds sunk into them. This could be done by soliciting buyers from other regional units, altering goods to improve salability, reducing prices, or, as a last resort, treating them "as waste, with the approval of higher authorities." However, Zhang discovered that department workers had "no legs" for making "arrangements with units in other localities," no facilities for altering goods, and no consent from higher up either to cut prices or discard anything. County and provincial officials declined to address the problem (likely seeking to avoid accepting account losses), whereas the wholesale unit's "monthly gross profit" had cratered, such that its interest payment to the state bank, ¥7100 [$3K] per month on a ¥1.18 million [$490K] loan, could no longer be paid.[44] As the Great Leap unwound, socialist commerce's contradictions became more evident—featuring tensions between serving the people and serving careers, between close supervision to prevent capitalist backsliding and constraints that prevented staff initiatives, between pressure from above to follow plans and programs and silence from above when things went wrong. These troubles resonate with deficiencies in central European socialisms and surely echo organizational miseries encountered in the West. Beijing's nagging problem was that none of this was supposed to happen in the PRC.

Certain bright spots helped offset such disappointments, some reflecting learning from the Great Leap's failures. Reacting to costly food losses due to slow transport, in 1962 the Wuhan Railway Bureau inaugurated a fast freight service to Guangzhou, regularly hauling "fresh, live, and easily perishable items." Cutting a five-day trip to just fifty-two hours assured the reliable delivery of pork, fish, "eggs, poultry, melons and fruits, vegetables, seeds, and saplings." The railway designated three wagons on each train for receiving "scattered small lots" from rural production brigades, while tanks holding "fish fry and live fish" always occupied "the eleventh car behind the locomotive, to facilitate opening the doors" to add fresh water.[45] In mountainous Yunnan Province, where pack animals and human bearers tripled the freight volume hauled by motor vehicles, regional authorities undertook to establish "through traffic." They created three classes of lines: the province's twelve main roads being the first class, some three hundred highway branches and wagon trails constituting the second, and "numerous mountain post roads and walk trails" grouped as the third. Within this structure, "pack animal traffic [was] to go on post roads, wagon traffic on highway branches and motor traffic on highway trunk lines. Trucking lines operated by provincial authorities [were] to operate on the first line, taking over freight from the second and third lines. Trucks and wagons operated by special districts [went] in the second line and pack animals and men carrying loads [were] the third line of transportation."[46]

Replacing earlier unorganized haulers were about 1,500 "subsidiary transportation groups" and 140 "civil transportation cooperatives," running some 44,000 pack horses and "pack cows," as well as 13,000 "man-pulling and animal-pulling carts." In tandem, "various related agencies . . . established 970 stables and boarding stations along post roads and walk trails to take care of pack animals and drivers." In consequence, the system handled roughly 80,000 tons of material monthly, one-quarter of its third-line goods delivered to second-line intercepts for forwarding. Meanwhile, deaths of pack animals had fallen by half, between 1960 and 1961.[47] Here again PRC officials relied on organizational strategies rather than technological investments to husband capital and resources when strengthening socialist enterprise. Building truck-worthy roads and populating them with vehicles would have demanded billions of yuan, sums far more needed for industrial and military uses.

In wholesaling, the reopened trade warehouses rapidly gained traction, as reports from Tinajin and Chongqing document. Jiang Feng reported that transactions were made in honey from Ch'in-huang-do, straw and rattan articles from Tianjin and other districts, ginger and fur from Shandong, and melon and fruits from Hebei, Shandong, and Tangshan. The warehouse was a cart depot serving peasants in the region, with space for "50 or 60 big carts," as well as stables and accommodations. Peasants arrived with wares, such as straw mats, which were examined so that prices could be set based on quality and condition. Once the inspection was finished, payment was made, in all a process that took little over an hour.[48]

Warehousemen strove to find outlets for goods that production teams had made without considering users' needs, as with laundry baskets from Yong-ch'ing and An-t'zu *xian*, rejected by bathhouses as too large. To reduce mismatches, they informed makers of market standards and specifications (e.g., fifty of them defined for rattan articles). To project cordiality, they served tea to arriving vendors and provided them with "petty cash" advances against anticipated sales. Yet behind apparently simple transactions lay "complex questions" that informed pricing in socialist commerce. The complex process of transacting was described as follows:

The comrade of the cooperative warehouse marketing section . . . gave me a price [calculating] list for the "bramble bee honey" of Ch'in-huang-dao. On this list are ten items: purchase price at producing area, packaging expenses, commissions at the warehouse of the producing area, damage, loss [in transit], interest, administrative expenses, profit, tax, and selling price [to retailers]. First is the price at the producing area. Whether this price is rational or not will directly affect the reproduction of agricultural and subsidiary products. If it is unreasonable, the peasants won't accept it. Next comes the transaction price at the Tianjin warehouse. If it is too high, it won't be accepted by the consumers, thus causing a stockpiling of the product. The third consists of the expenses between these two prices, and they may be affected by such departments as railway, shipping, banking, and taxation.[49]

These details are immensely valuable, as they confirm the intricacy of price making in a voluntarist market environment far from the corridors of centrally administered pricing (cotton, wheat, rice), as well as wholesalers' sensitivity to what levels would (1) stimulate producers to continue making and selling and (2) entice retailers to keep buying. To be sure, these practices only affected surplus-to-quota second-category goods and third-category products from private plots and household fabrication, yet they framed a vivid contrast with the leading ideologies of party and state administration. Perhaps more than that, they provided a reminder that market and plan could be (must be?) symbiotic, that dealing with planning's limits could imply *either* accepting/denouncing shortages and illicit dealing *or* managing regulated, profitable exchanges that offered material incentives to rural households and work teams. As the latter option gained momentum, as "socialist profit" was defined and defended in academic journals and the press, leading Maoists envisioned an austere, egalitarian society withering. The Cultural Revolution would serve as their counterattack, with vaporizing markets one of its priorities.

In the meantime, as "peasants sell in order to buy," Chiang Feng also sketched warehouses offering manufactured goods for co-op agents' return trips. At Tianjin's Xin-zheng wholesaler, July 1962 sales to 170 rural "units" totaled ¥1.5 million [$625K], with ¥1 million [$400K] more added on August 1–15. As a contemporary article noted, "for instance, the Ba-xian cooperative of Hebei sold its baskets, mats, etc. and bought tooth powder, hair oil, toys and pencils. The An-t'zu coop . . . bought iron hoes, cotton gloves, and machines for making ice sticks [i.e., popsicle sticks]."[50] Managers at Chonqing's Liang-lou-gou warehouse sponsored a broader venture, reorganizing the region's carting system to match merchandise purchases with delivery services. They first sponsored research that documented "the historical basis of dual routes of sources of goods and product exchange," disrupted in recent decades. The key was to coordinate incoming carts consigning and unloading rural merchandise with urban goods' purchases (for reloading the same carts), a process critically mediated by prestocking warehouses with items most commonly required in the countryside. This in turn necessitated arranging for production (and delivery to warehouses) both of key goods production teams sought and of "daily necessities" and "kitchen utensils" for households. Wholesalers discovered some supplies as inventory surpluses at area industrial concerns; others had to be commissioned. As a result, commune teams stocked up on "barrows, shovels, tools, and electrical equipment, hardware and chemical items, including dyestuffs and calcium sulfide [for fertilizing]," whereas SMC buyers gathered "hair pins, thimbles, oil cloths, shoe polishes, and stationery [along with] soup ladles, spatulas, fire-tongs, kitchen choppers and iron pots" for households.[51]

Working through the old vertical routines was "cumbersome"; now, direct links governed supply transactions, and quality standards could be enforced. For example, "when Tangshan *xian* warehouse requested 3,000 pear crates to transport 200,000 *chin* [100,000 kg] of salted vegetables to Chonqing, Liang-lou-gou warehouse negotiated with Hong-yan Bamboo Articles Factory . . . to satisfy the demand." Management tried to promote a "spirit of responsibility on the part of both the purchasing and sales sides."[52] Partners failing to meet contractual terms found their goods returned, as with two hundred low-quality kitchen choppers refused in 1961 and three thousand defective soup ladles rejected that March, with the order rerouted to another factory. Were such practices to generalize, not least dealing directly across province borders, decentralization could undermine party control, especially control by provincial authorities, as autonomous commercial enterprises commenced serving scattered users and makers, coordinating transportation and negotiating prices, much as in the West and much different from central European and Soviet commerce.

Similar effective and unsettling achievements also materialized in retailing.

Approaching trade from the production side, Chonqing's Hardware, Communications and Electrical Materials Company began "holding circuit fairs in rural areas and setting up stalls to supply small hardware commodities," a move that "effectively reduced the stagnation of commodities and accelerated capital turnover." One staffer judged that area townships needed "15 tons of nails for the repair of 19,500 sets of water wheels and 15,000 winnowers," opening a market for nails idling in Chonqing's storehouses, tying up capital, and restricting "improvement of the company's operation and management." Rural SMC buyers routinely made block, "blind purchases," ignoring local conditions, slowing their stock turnover, and annoying peasants. The hardware fairs bypassed these stagnant retailers, displaying the company's "nails, wire, axes for carpenters, drills, files, chains, wooden screws, electricians' knives, cooking utensils and wooden scales." Sales above ¥8,000 [$3.3K] were swiftly accomplished, "equivalent to 112% of the total hardware business in January–May this year in these localities." Field representatives also fielded complaints about ineffective products (files that overheated in use, shoddy plastic plates for wooden scales) and pledged improvements. Word of mouth drew buyers from distant villages and brought requests "for the setting up of stalls" in their areas, too. Local cadres were embarrassed: "Living in rural areas, we are ignorant of their conditions, and being near to peasants, we do not understand their requirements, which shows that we have not done our part."[53] Here, a corporate initiative that ignored administrative structures revealed both latent local demand and ineffectual local retailing. What next?

Henan's Changzhou Department Store had responded briskly to the "three clearances" campaign in 1961 by critically evaluating its inventories but found that "over 50% of its commodities in stock were questionable products of low quality, which were bogged down and hard to sell."[54] Though getting rid of them posed a serious problem, plans for reorganizing purchasing were being implemented.[55] Worse, according to K'ang P'ing, in resisting decentralization, Beijing's municipal "commercial departments" had "inappropriately placed special and unique enterprises under the leadership of basic control stores" (which failed to sustain policies of "good quality and favorable prices"), foolishly merged specialized shops, and ended "the necessary seasonal mark-downs . . . resulting in irrational prices, the deterioration of quality and decline of output [i.e., turnover]." If authorities resisted stock-clearing price cuts, dead inventory would continue to balloon. Sadly, if the capital's renowned specialty retailers (many of whom made hats, shoes, medicines, or clothing on-site) were "squeezed out," a terrible loss of traditional skills and products would be sustained. These specialists, admired by Klochko, had long been prized by their customers and should be defended.

Consider the Nei-lian-shang Shoe Store and its renowned "1,000-layer-sole" footwear, "skillfully made by hand, with 81-110 stitches on each square ts'un of each sole [11 sq. cm, or 1.7 sq. inches] . . . guaranteed to be neat, soft, good looking and respectable, and not to get hairy, twist their corners, or fade in color." Or perhaps treasure the Rui-fu-xiang Silk Fabrics Store's elevated standards of service: helping every client "solve his clothing problem, from the selection of fabrics to tailoring," taking "orders by telephone and cash on delivery," and facilitating "off-hour sales" for overscheduled customers. Many specialist shops, now surely jointly owned by the state and onetime proprietors, employed veteran salesmen, technicians, and master craftsmen and artists, whose "rich operational experiences . . . constitute a most precious heritage." Their capabilities were ideal for "train[ing] new apprentices . . . so as to augment gradually the professional and technical ranks of specialized enterprises."[56] Yet in defending them, K'ang P'ing surely highlights another fracture point in socialist commerce, as the enterprises he cherishes serviced the Beijing elite (and doubtless visiting worthies) with luxury goods rather than advancing egalitarianism or serving the masses. We might think of them as following a precapitalist road, which radical cadres soon would seek to pave over.

Other retailers, such as Yenkuhui Supplementary Foodstuffs Store, interacted more directly and perhaps more progressively with "the people." This Tianjin grocery had since 1960 not only sponsored vegetable-selling carts in its neighborhoods; it also provided delivery services in each district for goods only sold at the store "for sanitation purposes" (fish, soy sauce). However, in fall 1961, it sold area residents 5,000 kilograms of carrots without applying a 30 percent discount "stipulated by the upper-level organization." Though some clerks thought the sum was trivial (¥.04/kg [1.6¢], or in total ¥200 [$83]), with prodding from party cadres they consulted the "registry" of household purchases and processed refunds to all carrot buyers. Yenkuhui then over-contracted for spinach in spring 1962, with deliveries amounting to 1.5 kg/day/person for the district's entire population. Some staff proposed making scarce leeks and green onions available only to customers who bought several kilos of spinach; others proposed selling it "by piles to dispose of it." Instead managers "called a conference of customers to bring the problem to their attention." There, a "consumer representative" suggested that spinach blanched in boiling water could be dried "and would then last for a long time without losing much of its taste."[57] This information being shared among residents, the surplus of spinach "was thus quickly sold," and waste was avoided. Detailed record keeping facilitated the carrot refunds, whereas drawing on Ministry of Food expertise likely saved the spinach.

Department stores in Tianjin and Beijing also faced record-keeping challenges. Before 1957, Wei Fu-k'ai explained, state-operated retailers and SMCs "kept a record of commodities sold and balanced their accounts day by day." During the Great Leap, many stores shifted to monthly inventory checks, accepting clerks' claims that daily accounts were too much work and "did little to improve operations and management." The result was, as might have been expected, a rising flood of errors, with shrinkage amounting to 1 percent of turnover, double the pre-1958 rate. Moreover, in the absence of daily sales records, balancing the monthly inventory account could become a nightmare. It was hoped that "with proper organization of work, all the [daily accounts] tasks to be done after the close of business [could] be completed within a period of 30 minutes to an hour" and thus also reduce the time needed for monthly account balances, which had taken two or three days (and in an extreme case more than twenty days) to complete.[58] Yet resuming daily accounting was problematic, as it provided, in addition to guiding purchasing, surveillance and evaluation data that enabled "the leadership of an enterprise to know which of the comrades were conscientiously responsible, were apathetic in work, were proficient . . . and making rapid progress, or were not making enough efforts," thereby informing the managers so they could "[treat] these comrades accordingly."[59] The question remained: how to resolve the tensions between responsibility and hierarchy in a socialist manner?

In the early 1960s, state actors promoted organization, responsibility, and order in other commercial domains as well. In Nanjing, Jiangsu Province, ostensibly at their request, the party committee fashioned an association for the municipality's 33,000 street vendors, many of whom sold home-made goods. Plainly, its mission was to "educate and supervise the venders to follow government regulations and policies," like making popular pastries and cakes properly, schooling less-skilled providers, facilitating "inspections," preventing short-weighting in transactions, and paying taxes. Conserving resources was also a theme. Sellers in the Mu-re Lane Vegetable Market were spending too much on motor vehicle transportation of rural produce. The association thus counseled them "to use carts instead of trucks." The result: "the expense has been reduced and the profit has been increased."[60]

Indeed, the Beijing vegetable markets had also resumed but with improvements sponsored by "market functionaries." Across three earlier years (1959–1961), the once-huge Zhao-nei market had sold just 200,000 kilograms of vegetables, generating only ¥26,600 [$10,8K] in toto. By summer 1962, its monthly sales topped 700,000 kilograms, yielding ¥100,000 [$42K] to the market's 100–140 sellers. What had changed? Vendors had "hooked up with 15 production teams of the Huang-t'u-gong, Nan-yuan, and Seu-ji-ch'ing communes in the suburbs," from which came over 90 percent of the market supply. Three designated buyers regularly visited the communes to assess the variety and quality of vegetables nearing ripeness, conveying vendors' "comments" about prior deliveries to the teams. Price setting followed formal quality reviews, not piecemeal negotiations with random providers, and vendors understood there could be "no sale of aging vegetables."[61] Instead of featuring diverse peasants and others arriving in carts layered with produce and illegalities, Beijing's "Largest Vegetable Market" had become systematized, bureaucratized, perhaps more efficient, and certainly more hierarchical. Such was progress thus far in socialist commerce, gradually moving closer to the state and farther from unmanaged entrepreneurship. Yet there would be further surges and slippages during the 1960s, as entrepreneurial farmers and traders increasingly evaded administrative and party controls during the "adjustment period" that emerged after the Great Leap's collapse. The ready reception of these minimal steps onto the "capitalist road" appalled radicals at the center and contributed to a severe curtailment of commercial independence during the Cultural Revolution. But this too passed. With Mao's death and the displacement of the Gang of Four and its minions, commercial life again blossomed in late-1970s China, building on practices established in the first decades of socialist construction.

So what did it mean to have active and expanding market practices and institutions within the dynamics of "building socialism"? Three things, I'd suggest at this juncture. First, in the Chinese case, this phenomenon reinforces the larger scholarly consensus that Chinese party and administrative leaders sought a gradual socialization of the economy, in parallel with stepwise advances in literacy and health care and the modernization of military forces. As my work on central European communist enterprises and Anna Kushkova's chapter in this volume both suggest, Soviet-style destruction of commercial and handicraft enterprises created long-term deficiencies, which the USSR's "artel" shops grudgingly (and temporarily) sought to remedy.[62] Second, despite militants' fears, market activity did not indicate that a "back to capitalism" countermovement was surging upward through rural markets and city department stores. The state held sway over the "commanding heights" of the economy, in financial allocations, in agricultural purchasing, and in huge industrial, construction, and transportation enterprises where trial-and-error experimentation brought sustained growth that surprised and confused Western observers. Still, lively markets did suggest the incompleteness of mass socialist education, citizens' ongoing prioritizing of family over nation building, and the attractions consumer goods, bicycles, and quality agricultural tools continued to hold. These were political issues that demanded attention. Third, the creativity and flexibility of "socialist commerce" showed that there were "holes in the plan"; indeed, there are oversights in and limits to *any* planning process. Rejecting Stalinist absolutism, which triggered resentment and stimulated the illegal "second economy," PRC officials acted pragmatically, managing and regulating market behavior where possible, stepping aside elsewhere, to permit flows of goods and services that fueled expanded production and exchange.[63] While ideologically uncomfortable, commercial market relations proved practical and essential to creating "socialism with Chinese characteristics" in the PRC's first decades.

Hidden Realms of Private Entrepreneurship: Soviet Jews and Post–World War II Artels in the USSR

Anna Kushkova

This chapter presents a case study of the Jewish ethnic economy in the postwar decades within the "planned" or "command" economy of the Stalinist Soviet Union. I argue that the formation of ethnic economic niches resulted from the state prohibition of private economic agency, which foregrounded the principles of shared ethnicity and trust for the purposes of clandestine production. The chapter explores issues related to the formation of Jewish ethnic communities under the Soviet regime: their internal solidarity based on kinship, common origin, and shared collective memory, as well as the tacit and overt antisemitic pressures of the state. It also examines how ethnic traditions of entrepreneurship—reconfigured under the new political, ideological, and economic circumstances of the immediate postwar decades— enabled Jewish private economic pursuits to thrive in remarkably close proximity to a major center of Communist Party control.

In the first part of the twentieth century, Moscow's suburbs became a destination for several successive waves of Jewish internal migration from the western regions of the Russian Empire known as the Pale of Settlement. Since the late eighteenth century, Russian authorities had forbidden most Jews to live and work outside the Pale. Many Russian Jews had immigrated to the

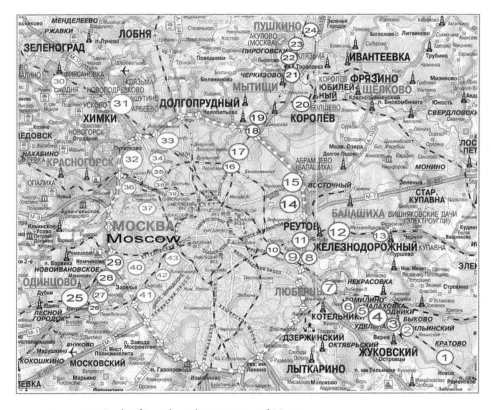

Figure 10.1. Circle of Jewish settlements around Moscow.

United States between 1881 and 1914 to escape the harsh conditions of shtetl life, and still more migrated to Russia's interior during World War I to escape the invading German army. This initial wave of Jewish migrants to Moscow's suburbs turned into a massive influx during the 1920s and 1930s and was followed by a smaller and final inflow after World War II. These waves of migration created such a dense pattern of Jewish residence in the suburbs surrounding the country's capital that even today these areas are sometimes referred to as the Soviet Jewish Pale. Even though this was a largely metaphorical "pale," it does indicate a distinctive Jewish sociocultural environment characteristic to these settlements—not fully coinciding with that of the shtetl yet still different from that of a large urban setting.

The Jewish settlements, denoted on the map above by the numbered white circles, clustered in the northern, eastern, and western areas surrounding Moscow (see Figure 10.1). Over time, Moscow incorporated several Jewish suburbs into the city premises, but some settlements have retained their suburban status and their distinctively Jewish social and cultural milieu to this day.

The major factors that contributed to this specific "not fully urban" Jewish suburban identity included more compact habitation, the closer network of communication within the Jewish milieu, the presence of the local community's religious core, and the specific occupational profile of Jewish residents. This chapter, based on interviews I recorded in the settlements of Malakhovka and Saltykovka (nos. 4 and 12 on the map), focuses on one distinct economic niche occupied by suburban Jews in the first decades after World War II: artels, or small producer cooperatives. While officially a legal sector in the state economy, artels turned into sites of clandestine production that contradicted the core ideological premises of the socialist order.

Artels as a Way of Transition to Socialist Production

Historically, an artel was a small or medium-sized producer unit engaged in either permanent or seasonal types of work, such as construction, fishing, mining of precious metals, or production of art objects. By the prerevolutionary period artels constituted a viable and widespread type of economic organization throughout Russia.[1] The early Soviet authorities saw artels as a useful link in facilitating the transition from "capitalist" to "socialist" ways of production. Determined to eradicate private economic initiative yet hoping that cooperation would rescue the country from the economic quagmire of the early 1920s, Vladimir I. Lenin promulgated his famous "cooperative plan."[2] Soon after, a large cooperative movement started in the country, fueled by preferential state legislation that lowered taxes on cooperatives and provided them "with monetary and material resources."[3] The names of many prewar artels—"Lenin's Way,"[4] "Hammer of October,"[5] "Red Nail-Maker"[6]—clearly show that they were conceived as an element of the socialist modernization project.

The preferential treatment given to early Soviet producer artels was particularly important for the Jewish shtetl population, which included a large number of private artisans and craftsmen. While Soviet officials prohibited large-scale private production, some individual private producers could still qualify for the position of the "shtetl proletariat" even though officials did not recognize the private nature of their economic pursuits as "ideologically correct." The Bolshevik "productivization" of the Russian Jewish population implied, among other things, that individual artisans would be organized into state-run artels. As Gennady Estraikh, a Jewish historian and writer, explains, "the Soviet authorities saw these [artels] as a rather progressive mode of production, an intermediate stage on the way to mechanized manufacturing."[7] Given the virtual economic catastrophe that befell the shtetl in the first decade of Soviet rule, for the majority of shtetl artisans the possibility of joining artels and gaining access to the material support provided there was tantamount to staying physically alive.[8]

Joining artels was an important survival strategy for *lishentsy,* people deprived of voting and other political and social rights based on their "non-toiler" background.[9] A higher percentage of Jews were branded as *lishentsy* than any other ethnic group in the Soviet Union.[10] In some shtetls their number was as high as 40 to 60 percent.[11] Although early Soviet artels were never officially established as ethnically specific (Jewish) units, within the former tsarist Pale of Settlement the number of Jewish artisans in small-scale producer cooperatives reached up to 70 to 75 percent in the Ukraine and 80 to 90 percent in Belorussia. Yiddish, not surprisingly, served as the "main working language."[12] While the less rigid organization of artels allowed artisans to abstain from work on Sabbaths, many Jews used artel affiliation as a form of disguise that allowed them to continue their religious observance. Such practices would have been impossible in the deeply politicized and rigid Soviet production regime of the first industrial sector.[13] By and large, one may hypothesize that the artels strengthened the connection between economy and ethnicity (Jewishness) during the first two decades of Soviet rule.

Postwar Artels in the Soviet Union

During the initial period of Soviet rule, artels were seen as a progressive type of economic organization due to their role in reorienting the national economy to the socialist track. After World War II, however, attitudes toward artels changed. On the one hand, officials still saw them as an intermediary stage of "small-scale commodity production" that would eventually evolve into a "communal socialist economy" and foster the development of "collectivist mentality."[14] Yet the presence of such "small-scale" production units became problematic for the centralized economic regime. Soviet officials' teleological rhetoric of progress placed artels in the "archaic" economic slot, viewing them as economic laggards compared to enterprises in the industrial sphere. As the Russian historian A. A. Nikolaev explains, "each economic formation is defined by specific forms of cooperative formations. Artels emerged in under-developed economic systems, with the dominance of the natural economy and primitive forms of trade."[15] Such attitudes were a logical continuation of the interwar perception of artisans that Sheila Fitzpatrick described as a "not-fully-proletariat," "petty-bourgeois," and "backward" group lacking "modernity."[16]

The dismal postwar economy made Soviet officials reluctant to abandon the artels. The devastated economic infrastructure, the large number of war invalids, the reduced number of working-age men, and the calamitous shortage of consumer goods resembled the dire situation of the early 1920s, immediately following the civil war and the policy of "war communism." One of my informants described the postwar experience as "living beyond the pale of poverty" and hoping merely "to eat enough."[17] According to the historian D. Filtzer, "in 1946 the Soviet clothing industry produced one-quarter of a piece of underwear, less than one pair of socks, and half a pair of shoes for each of its citizens. Soap was almost impossible to acquire."[18]

It would only seem natural and expedient in a situation like this to make all the best efforts to fill the multiple gaping holes in national consumer demand—and some such attempts were indeed undertaken. Julie Hessler has characterized the first postwar years in the Soviet Union as a "perestroika" of sorts, when small-scale private entrepreneurship and trade had a chance to be revived. At this time some top-level politicians attempted, in conjunction with local party leaders, to legalize—or, rather, decriminalize—certain types of private entrepreneurship while simultaneously making it profitable for the state.[19] As the Russian historian Elena Zubkova argues, this, in fact, would have been similar to reinstating some elements of the New Economic Policy for the sake of resolving the country's economic problems, first and foremost its food-related problems.[20] However, attempts to negotiate a certain allowance for private agency in the economic sphere failed because of the ideological consequences of such initiatives.[21]

For the party authorities, loosening the state's grip on the economy would entail the loss of political control. Instead of legalizing small-scale private economic initiative, as officials had done in the 1920s, the postwar government followed a different path: it granted more leeway in production and marketing to small producer units within the Soviet cooperative sector. On August 22, 1945, the USSR Council of People's Commissars adopted a decree titled "On the measures to increase mass consumption goods and foodstuffs by enterprises of the local industry, producer cooperation and cooperation of invalids." The decree stipulated that half of the production generated by local enterprises may remain at the disposal of local party executive bodies (rather than be shipped away to meet state production targets). It also exempted certain types of artel-manufactured commodities (such as furniture, barrels, bricks, chalk, and shingles) from centralized distribution and permitted the artels to sell them. Finally, the decree allowed artels to collect and use scrap materials for their production and required larger state industries to render technological assistance to artels.[22] A year later, on November 9, 1946, the Council of People's Commissars issued further regulations on cooperative production and trade, allowing the organization of "tailor, shoe-maker and repair workshops, as well as hair-dresser saloons and workshops for the production of mass-consumption goods." The regulations also granted a number of taxation benefits to cooperative production units and allowed these units to purchase surplus local agricultural produce "on the basis of prices formed at the market."[23]

Cooperation, even if this sector of state economy was viewed as a "second-class industry,"[24] thus received a certain "carte blanche" to organize production and distribution along less rigid lines than the first sector of the Soviet economy. Yet they still operated under close oversight of the authorities. As one informant effectively summarized, "the state granted the system of cooperation the right to feed people, to sustain them. . . . We give you resources, we allow you to organize production, yet all of this under the 'roof of the state.'[25] . . . Cooperation was a state within the state. It was the strongest link in the Soviet system; it presented a closed cycle from procuring raw materials to production and marketing."[26] The state permitted these private initiatives in the hope that the system of cooperation would decrease the pervasive shortage of consumer goods and foodstuffs, alleviate some of the production burden in the industrial sphere, and take some employment pressure off the first sector of economy, especially by providing employment for war invalids. I also argue that until their abolition in the early 1960s, artels became a niche where private economic agency found its temporary abode.

Artels as "Not Fully Socialist" Production Units?

Alain Besançon, a French historian of Russia, has argued that the cooperative sector in general and producer artels in particular lay "outside of the sphere of socialism" and thus did "not comply with the principle of the con-

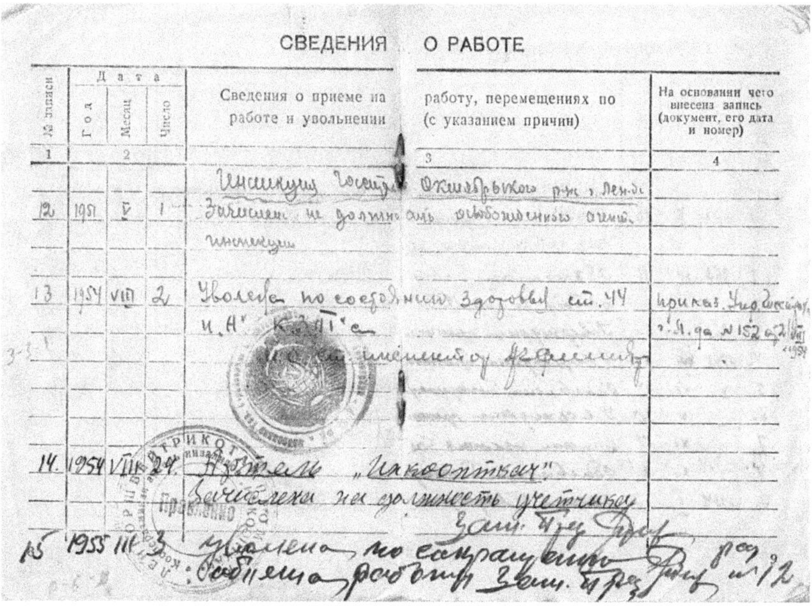
СВЕДЕНИЯ О РАБОТЕ

№ записи	Дата			Сведения о приеме на работу, перемещениях по работе и увольнении (с указанием причин)	На основании чего внесена запись (документ, его дата и номер)
	Год	Месяц	Число		
1	2			3	4

Figure 10.2. Page from the official labor book (Russ.: *trudovaya knizhka*) of Batsheva Aronovna Belyat, indicating that from August 1954 to March 1955 she was employed as an accountant in the "*Inkooptkach*" artel in Leningrad (second entry from the bottom). Courtesy of B. A. Belyat's daughter.

struction of socialism."[27] This view, however, does not accurately reflect the formal regulations that governed the daily operations of artels. According to their statute, artels were cooperative organizations that established their production on the basis of "communal socialist property" and had to meet certain production targets to fulfill their "state [production] obligations."[28] Artels paid state taxes and functioned as state-appointed workshops controlled by state financial organs. They were required to produce annual reports that supplied data on the number of workers they employed, the salaries they paid, and the volume of production they generated. The *Producer Cooperation*, the main journal of the cooperative production sector, praised the efforts of artels to "fulfill and over-fulfill" state production plans and touted the achievements of artel "shock-workers." The journal also published pictures of artels' "red corners" with universal Soviet paraphernalia (red banners, V. I. Lenin portraits, and the like), and described social benefits allocated to artel employees, such as food rationing coupons and official "labor books" (see Figure 10.2).

Despite such evidence of the artels' ties to the Soviet state, today people often describe artels as "not (fully) Soviet" production units or "not (fully) socialist" niches in the Soviet economy. As one informant said, "this was private production . . . under the jurisdiction of the state."[29] Another observed, "Artels were functioning virtually as private [units]."[30] My informants often drew analogies and even constructed a direct continuity between postwar artels and the production units of the 1920s, when the New Economic Policy temporarily decriminalized private economic initiative.[31] These analogies seem to hinge on three major ideas: the "primitive" nature of artel production, the possibility of illegal enrichment they provided, and the image of artels as "Jewish places."

Artels as a "Primitive" Production Unit

The Soviet economy presented a perfect example of the simultaneous existence of two distinct economic "orders" (*uklad* in Russian): the highly industrial technological sector (heavy industry) and the consumer goods and services sector. More often than not, the latter was financed according to the "residual principle." The lengthy "mobilization" periods of rapid prewar industrialization and postwar economic restoration both happened at the expense of consumer goods production. Postwar artels were fully compatible with the economic devastation left in the wake of the war: they produced "rudimentary" supply to meet "rudimentary" consumer demand. My informants consistently spoke of artels as a "primitive" or "premodern" production unit—both in terms of how their production process was organized and the goods they manufactured. In a situation where "everything was missing,"[32] artels produced "mass consumption goods necessary for all, like pots, spoons, ladles"[33] or "plastic buttons, gowns, shirts . . . everyday things."[34] There were special artels that darned old socks[35] or dyed old shoes to prolong their service life.[36]

Another important feature of artel production was their low degree of specialization. Many artels produced a large variety of small and not necessarily related goods, no matter what the official production profile of the artel mandated. Consider, for instance, the range of objects produced by a Saltykovka artel "Sport and Hunting" in 1950: "nets, coils, men's and women's shoes on a rubber soil, slippers, straps for men's watches, nail files, combs, whistles, dog collars, dog muzzles, canvass gun cases, gun waddings, caps for pens, butter dishes, children's toy guns, shooting targets."[37] This assemblage emphasizes an important principle in the operation of artels: the larger the scope of items produced, the higher the chance to fulfill or exceed state targets.

While the quality of goods produced in the first sector often left much to be desired, the quality of artel goods was usually much lower. As one informant observed, "I remember that their knitwear was trashy . . . well, their whole production, their equipment. . . . It was like do-it-yourself stuff."[38] Some descriptions of artel production in the official reports to the Council of Ministers of the Russian Soviet Federative Socialist Republic bear a nearly satirical character. The reports mentioned "mineral soap that doesn't lather" and "buttons that have different number of holes—two, three, five, or none at all." Worse still was the "dark grey tooth powder that causes tooth enamel to fall off" and was only "sold to passengers on the railway stations because the local population, knowing its quality, doesn't buy it."[39] Despite the low quality of products, artels aimed to satisfy the growing demand for consumer goods. In the absence of alternatives, customers could not be particularly choosy about the quality of merchandise.

Artels and the Second Economy

Virtually all oral descriptions of artels stress their double positioning between the official and the clandestine spheres of production. One informant noted, "They [artels] were making money on the goods in short supply. Something is missing in the stores . . . and handymen would immediately emerge in an artel and start solving the problem."[40] Another admitted, "One had to know how to organize production in artels. Half for the state, half for oneself [*laughs*]."[41] Yet another confided that "[artels were doing] *geshefts*,[42] money making . . . lots of things were produced parallel to the state plan."[43]

In a "resource-constrained economy,"[44] where production materials simultaneously constituted the major asset and the major "shortage,"[45] the socialist state attempted to maintain strict control over the centralized allocation of resources to various production units. The only way to obtain production materials for on-the-side production was to "divert" them from the state. According to one informant, "shadow entrepreneurs were stealing raw materials from the state. At that time the state possessed everything. They would join the cooperation structure . . . and organize their own production."[46] Another informant expressed a common opinion that to "get rich in a planned economy . . . one has to 'go to the left.'"[47]

To obtain production materials for clandestine production, artels had to acquire information about where to find the desired materials, who could be relied upon to make the deal, how much money would be expected, and how many additional benefits might the seller require. This information was hard to get in the Soviet economic structure, where "horizontal" exchange among economic agents was essentially censured, except for cases controlled by the state. Because officials granted the cooperative sector some leeway in obtaining production materials and selling merchandise, artels became a fertile ground for the emergence of "information experts" who engaged in various forms of horizontal economic exchange. These experts, the Soviet version of what Clifford Geertz called "bazaari," established and maintained connections with the "proper people," both locally and cross-territorially, often creating extensive networks of economic exchange.[48] One informant recalled traveling eight hundred miles to get yarn from Astrakhan. "Nahum Davydovich [the head of the artel] trusted me, a young guy then, with money, and I would go there with one hundred thousand [rubles] on me." When asked why he traveled so far for yarn, he explained, "Well, ours was an 'invalid artel,' and we were allegedly buying low-quality tangled yarn at a low price—but indeed it was arranged so that we were bringing them the money and getting good yarn. . . . There were *geshefts* like this."[49]

The materials required for production often necessitated cross-territorial ties. "Furriers sometimes had their own agents go to Siberia, to the special farms, for silver fox pelts," an informant recalled.[50] Such ties were also essential for marketing clandestinely produced merchandise. To sell them locally would be tantamount to "suicide" since it would be much easier to discover the producers.[51] Among the destinations of Moscow suburban artel products were, for instance, Mordovia and Chuvashia, republics in the Volga region of Russia[52] and Ukraine.[53]

Apart from horizontal ties, networking for the sake of clandestine production and distribution necessarily possessed a vertical dimension. Artels paid in cash or in kind for the protection of local Soviet authorities, who were usually well aware of what was going on. Illegal producers, one informant explained, "had hard life, and they paid their 'dues' to the cops. There was no racket at that time—the only racket was the state racket."[54] Another informant noted, "Each head of the artel had connections. He certainly paid somebody in order to keep it afloat . . . Inspection organs were naturally having their share of this all, and when it would come to a critical point, they would close [the business] and opened something new."[55]

A range of local officials—state financial agents, militiamen, and members of the regional party committees—benefited from illegal production conducted on their territory. The side payments to local officials followed a recognizable historical pattern described by that historian Tamara Kondratjeva as *korlmenie* (literally "feeding" or "nourishing"): an alternative remuneration whereby appointed officials were allowed to "feed" off the lands they were tasked with administering.[56] As the historian Stefan Hedlund argues, a number of old "Muscovite" patterns of social relations were "reconstituted" in the context of the "planned economy." In the case of *kormlenie* these social relations undermined the idea of "contractual relations" with the state, encouraged local officials to squeeze resources out of their administered territory, and created a hierarchy of more or less "lucrative" positions.[57] Eventually this led to what Soviets called a "merger" (*srashchivanie* in Russian) of private entrepreneurship structures and political power at various levels.[58] *Korlmenie* fostered the "development of ingrown ties of small-scale artisanal production with personal material interests of state officials and planning organs."[59] Artels found it easier to establish and maintain close relations with state officials in smaller places than in a large city, where officials were more numerous and often competed among themselves for the "feeding" benefits. In terms of size, suburban settlements were the most favorable setting in this respect.

In the situation when consumer demand far exceeded the existing state supply, artisanal production could become a lucrative occupation, even without major infringement on the legal code. As one informant explained, "people who worked in state organizations, they didn't earn much. Let's say, an engineer—a hundred to a hundred twenty rubles [a month]. A person working in an artel could get two to two and a half thousand."[60] Another informant concurred: "In the artel one could *fardinen*."[61]

This was particularly true of the so-called invalid artels, created for people with limited capacities; such artels could negotiate lower production targets in advance and then exceed the state-appointed targets. This provoked the indignation of the state controlling organs, who complained that "with some [artel] workers the salary reaches three hundred to four hundred percent of the existing tariff rates. In June, the average salary in the 'Kommutator' artel (Moscow) amounted to twelve hundred fifty rubles, with the tariff rate being four hundred eighty-five rubles."[62] In addition, many artels often used a "putting-out system," whereby "at-home workers" (*nadomnik*) produced goods at home to boost their pay. By involving other family members, including children and the elderly in the process of production, at-home workers increased their output and hence their salaries, since people were usually paid by how much they produced.[63] While the use of the "family labor force" essentially infringed upon the socialist production ideology, in some cases it enabled artel members to surpass the productivity of industrial workers.[64]

While the outsourcing of work to family members boosted artel workers' salaries, such activity did not yet constitute a "second economy" in the proper sense of the word. The foundation of the second economy instead rested on private production within the official artel structures. While private entrepreneurial activity could not be fully eliminated in the first, more strictly supervised sphere of the Soviet economy, many viewed the cooperative sector with suspicion precisely because officials granted the sector more latitude in obtaining production resources and selling its finished merchandise. In the words of the Soviet lawyer and dissident Konstantin Simis, "underground private enterprise gets its strongest foothold in the smaller factories, [particularly in] those parts of the promkooperatsiya (producer cooperation) system, known officially as cooperative artels."[65]

The Russian expression for the second economy, "shadow economy," seems to be particularly instrumental in that it emphasizes the interdependence between the "first" (official) and the "second" (clandestine) economies. Katherine Verdery has described this interdependence through the metaphor of "host and parasite."[66] Similarly, Konstantin Simis has described this interdependence as a "symbiotic" relationship.[67] In the Soviet planned economy these two spheres drew upon the same state production resources and operated within the official production structures. In many cases clandestine economic agents were regular Soviet employees engaged in socialist production like other citizens of the country. Expressions such as "private trader" or "private entrepreneur" (*chastnik*), commonly used in various governmental regulations or court protocols, should not thus create an impression that these people operated completely outside of the state production-and-distribution structures.

These "private producers" had to navigate the multiple formal requirements and constraints of the Soviet production system and at the same time exploit the possibilities it provided for extracting additional private gain. Descriptions of clandestine economic pursuits conducted within the postwar cooperative production network leave no doubt that artels turned into spaces of economic invention on virtually every level of their activity. Artels found ways to extract profit from the acquisition of materials necessary for the "left" production. They contrived ways of manufacturing goods off the books and misrepresented the monetary sums earned by or paid to artel members. They used fictitious purchase invoices and changed assigned production technologies to get "surplus" materials for nonreported goods. One informant described how Nahum Davydovich, the head of the artel, devised a trick to exploit the popularity of German tablecloths and Polish coverlets. "Our artel produced cheap Jacquard coverlets, nine, twelve, fourteen rubles each—whereas the German ones cost twenty-eight, thirty-two rubles. So, what did we do? We selected yarn of the right colors and did a pattern on our coverlets similar to that on the German ones, and then sold them as German. The price difference was ours."[68] Another informant recalled an invalid artel that "started producing plastic napkins, which were considered pretty at the time. They were getting material somewhere, and then . . . adjusted [the] artel's sewing machines . . . inserted a knife instead of the needle, put three layers of this plastic beneath, and cut them according to a predesigned pattern. And then sold these napkins on a flea market and made good money on them."[69] If what Elizabeth Dunn called an "ingenuity to improvise solutions" was to some degree a common "survival kit" of all socialist subjects, clandestine producers had to be much more inventive and resourceful than the rest of the Soviet people.[70] One person even suggested that "freedom of creativity" was a major reason why certain people would choose to work in artels rather than in industrial enterprises.[71]

One should not get the impression that all artels engaged in "on-the-side" production—or that all artel employees would necessarily become "rich." As a number of my informants emphasized, many people were pushed into illegal activities for the sake of mere survival: "They contrived to earn some 'left' money because the 'right' money was so meager."[72] It is hard to say whether sensationalistic stories about "crystal vases full of diamonds"[73] or "hidden milk-cans filled with gold"[74] represented folk images of "uncountable wealth" or corresponded to actual realities. Irrespective of the extent of extralegal profit, the Soviet criminal code designated such profits as "nonlabor income" (netrudovye dokhody). This phrase sounds paradoxical against the fact that producers were investing their personal labor and time into making goods that exceeded the state production targets and that would be sold to people who would otherwise be unable to buy them. In the socialist state where, in the words of Hedlund, "the line between power and property is erased,"[75] Soviet officials saw independent economic agency as a violation of political allegiance, and "entrepreneurial money . . . whether large or small" as evidence "of disloyalty to the Soviet regime."[76]

Artels as a "Jewish Business"

Although I was unable to track down official statistics on the ethnic composition of artel employees in Moscow's suburbs, my interviewees consistently described artel-based economic activity as "Jewish."[77] Some claimed that Jews "invented this business."[78] Most people explained that Jews are "naturally" "entrepreneurial," "resourceful," "industrious,"[79] and capable of finding "vulnerable points in the [state] industry."[80] These explanations, however, do not identify which factors, both historical and contemporaneous, shaped the postwar Jewish economic behavior in the Soviet Union. In my view, three major factors explain why Jews joined artels in Moscow's suburbs: (1) the age and the time of migration from the Pale, (2) the effect of World War II on generational life trajectories, and (3) the intensification of state antisemitism after the war.

The most numerous cohort involved in postwar artel production was born at the tail end of the nineteenth century or first decade of the twentieth. Most were raised in the shtetl, where they acquired a variety of artisanal skills as tailors, shoemakers, furriers, watchmakers, glaziers, cabmen, bakers, or producers of carbonized water. This cohort likely participated in various entrepreneurial activities during the New Economic Policy of the 1920s—or at least remembered this time well enough.[81] At the same time, this cohort bore the major brunt of adaptation in the new environment after they came to Moscow's suburbs in the first decade of the Soviet regime. As a result, few attained substantial Soviet schooling or formal diplomas that would allow them to seek employment as engineers, physicians, or teachers, and many turned to the Soviet cooperative sphere for employment. The cooperative sector, as one informant recalled, drew "people who were formed before the revolution, who in the 1940s were fifty, sixty years old, who received this entrepreneurial drive from their parents and preserved it. . . . So, when the state slightly opened the possibility of private or semiprivate, or disguised private entrepreneurship, these people started using their talents, ties, skills."[82] Another informant noted that "only elderly people, with no education, were involved in this . . . business, shadowy or semishadowy."[83]

People born in the 1920s, whether still in the shtetls or already in large Russian cities, were the first fully Soviet Jewish generation who did not remember either any "traditional" Jewish entrepreneurship or the temporary revival of business activities in 1920s. They had been socialized in Soviet society and had a chance to get higher education and become specialists in various walks of life. World War II interrupted their educational trajectories, however. Most of these people served at the front, and those who returned home had to face a dire economy. Often they became the principal breadwinners for their families, which sometimes included survivor relatives from Belorussia or Ukraine. These breadwinning responsibilities made it difficult to get an education or acquire a profession, and many turned to the cooperative sector, which did not require a formal diploma or too many skills and would bring money right away. One informant explained that his father chose to work in an artel because "it was difficult to find a job" after the war. "He had to feed five people and [had] no real education except for the secondary school."[84] While demobilization, as the historian Zubkova noted, "turned out to be a serious problem for many, first of all for the youngest ones, born between 1923 and 1927 . . . who left for war from school, not having received any profession or a stable social status," this factor was not entirely ethnically neutral.[85] One may suppose that the collective trauma of the Holocaust particularly foregrounded the necessity of physical survival in the Jewish milieu.

Postwar antisemitic campaigns in the Soviet Union also increased the presence of Jews in the cooperative sphere. Most of the literature on this topic focuses on the political opponents and elites targeted by the campaign, such as members of the Jewish Anti-Fascist Committee, writers, or top medical professionals.[86] Few address what happened to ordinary Jews who lost their jobs or were turned down from educational institutions. The evidence suggests that many found employment in the cooperative sector. Evgenija Evelson, a Soviet lawyer who took part in four hundred trials for the illegal production and distribution of goods, stresses that many of her Jewish defendants were forced to leave their chosen occupational sphere and seek "shelter" in trade and cooperative production units.[87] My interviews likewise show that the cooperative sector was less affected by state antisemitic campaigns due to its special status in the structure of socialist production and its lower "visibility." Many Jews came to work in artels for the sake of physical survival. One informant noted that "in [19]49, after the extermination of the Anti-Fascist Committee, a massive purge of Jews from the 'middle layer' was launched, so they started coming to artels."[88] Another recalled that "a horrendous antisemitic campaign" in the 1950s made it "virtually impossible" to land "a job with a last name like Katzman . . . or Shmulevich." Much as Jews had done "in the time of the Pale of Settlement, people would become artisans, would go to artels."[89] Many Soviets regarded working in artels as a nonprestigious and undignified occupation. As one informant recalled, "To work in artel was as shameful as to stand in the market and sell things . . . [People said:] 'Speculator! Huckster!'"[90] Postwar state antisemitism thus limited Jewish economic choices, even though not necessarily through overt "laws and regulations."[91]

It is important to emphasize that artels existed throughout the country and employed other groups besides Jews. Moreover, Moscow's suburban Jewish population included teachers, physicians, and engineers. The formation of the "interlayer of 'shadow Jews'" in Moscow's suburbs, however, was not accidental.[92] Several factors contributed to what may be called the "social embeddedness" of postwar Jewish entrepreneurship.[93] These factors included the compactness of Jewish residence; the multiple ties based on the shared place of origin, affinities of neighborhood, and possibly kinship; the Jewish tradition of mutual self-help; and the value Jews put on maintaining a distinct linguistic and religious milieu and a "semipatriarchal" way of suburban Jewish life.[94] One can also speak about the "cultural embeddedness" of Jewish entrepreneurship. Jewish collective memory and the Jewish experience in Russia deepened Jewish beliefs in the special Jewish "entrepreneurial spirit" and linked Jewishness to a set of economic practices, which included conducting economic transactions with other Jews and non-Jews, interacting with authorities around economic matters, and engaging in artisanal and middlemen activities.

The substantivist approach in economic anthropology, which inaugurated the concept of "embeddedness," states, in the words of Karl Polanyi, that human economy is "embedded and enmeshed in institutions, economic and noneconomic."[95] This approach foregrounds the role of kinship, religion, and ethnicity in shaping people's economic behavior. As the historian Mark Edele has argued, the socialist political and economic order could not wipe out "continuous ('traditional') social forms [that] included the family, religious groups, and nationalities."[96] One path of Jewish integration into this new order utilized precisely these social forms and the types of agency they facilitated.

This theoretical perspective raises the question of whether the planned economy inadvertently created the conditions for a higher degree of economic embeddedness in certain sectors of production. In my view, the Soviet case suggests that the state-imposed prohibition of private entrepreneurship, largely ideological rather than economic by nature, provoked a likewise not strictly economic response "from below." In other words, the sacrosanct Soviet principle of "no exploitation of one man by another" was in itself the aim of the socialist regime. That it brought about persistent economic shortages, the precipitous decrease of the population's well-being, and at times hunger and death was less important for the regime than keeping this principle intact. The consolidation of economic actors along ethnic lines thus presented one response to this prohibition. Since any private entrepreneurship, if it were to emerge at all, had to be clandestine, such categories as "trust" and "common origin" turned out to be more important than one's experience and skill in production per se. Moscow's suburban Jews were inclined to involve "their own" in their not fully legal economic schemes, even at the expense of production quality and size of output.

The culturally pervasive notion that "a Jew cannot betray another Jew" (even though it was not always fully supported by the actual realities) often determined which workers were brought into clandestine entrepreneurial network. Because trust was essential, "only one's own people were taken there," one informant recalled.[97] Put differently, the "second" economy tended to be ethnic in proportion to the degree of its official prohibition. As a result, the supply, production, and distribution networks of small-scale artels in Moscow's suburbs emerged and were sustained as Jewish ethnic networks. To use the expression of Marilyn Strathern, "kinship" and "economy" turned into two principles each "bearing on the other."[98] Jewishness in this context became an asset, enabling economic activities that would otherwise be highly problematic.

The principle of "accepting only one's own" did not completely exclude non-Jewish actors from clandestine entrepreneurial networks. Even if suburban Jews exhibited what S. Baron and A. Kahan called "economic tribalism," they were also part of the common Soviet Russian-Jewish milieu and had multiple ties across ethnic lines.[99] "Trust" could be based on alternative grounds to "common ethnic origin."[100] While clandestine production in the suburbs "sharpened ethnic boundaries"[101] between Jewish and non-Jewish residents, it paradoxically could also strengthen (economic) ties across ethnic borders.[102]

Several characteristic features of Soviet clandestine economic practices are perfectly compatible with the essential elements of a market economy. Clandestine entrepreneurs adapted their production to satisfy actual consumer demand; they developed extensive "horizontal" networking with other producers and sellers; and they calculated the optimal prices that the market could bear and still benefit producers. Not surprisingly, many present-day informants came to view Soviet underground economic practices as the "sprouts" of the market system that emerged in the 1990s. One informant claimed that the artels "tried to live by the market laws."[103] Another described them as "crops of the market economy in the Soviet Union."[104]

The notion that the artels were "harbingers of new economic relations" highlights two paradoxes.[105] First, the Jewish economic role in modern European history has been viewed through the lens of modern economic practices in finance, technology, and industrial development.[106] In the Soviet planned economy Jews (and other clandestine entrepreneurs) put advanced (market) principles into practice in the spheres that were the least "modern" or "developed," such as small-scale production and distribution. Paradoxically, in the Soviet case modernization was "taking place alongside the shift to traditional and even archaic forms in the political sphere and monetary relations," creating "spaces of backwardness, sometimes spatially non-distinguishable from the 'advanced' sectors."[107] In a way, Soviet economic organization inadvertently supported clandestine entrepreneurship, as well as the continuity of traditional Jewish production and distribution practices, because it heavily relied on such "spaces of backwardness" to meet basic consumer needs.[108] Jewish small-scale entrepreneurs carried the "spirit of the market" while remaining in the "preindustrial" economic niche.

The second paradox relates to the popular assumption that those who were "schooled" in the socialist planned economy, particularly in its clandestine sphere, will succeed in the Western-type market economy. As the economist Marshall Goldman has argued, "despite—or maybe because of—the state monopoly and its central planning format, the Soviet economy provided an unintended training ground for many of those who ultimately emerged as the country's leading business oligarchs." Soviet wheeler-dealers, Goldman continued, "had to operate with a level of ingenuity" that provided clandestine entrepreneurs with the "perfect preparation for a transition to the marker economy."[109] Several of my informants, especially those who continued business pursuits in the postsocialist period, supported this idea. As one explained, "this was a school in its own right. . . . Having gone through this school, one could go anywhere with no problems—America, Canada—and get on their feet."[110] This principle did not always prove true, especially if people moved to capitalist countries. Consider the case of a former clandestine entrepreneur who opened a store when he immigrated to Israel. He soon discovered that "the whole street was filled with stores selling exactly the same goods. And people would go to the stores they were already used to." His new business venture and the bank loan he took against his house "all proved to be worthless."[111]

This example of failure highlights how crucial local networks and ethnic connections were to the success of clandestine business in the Soviet Union. The artels may have drawn upon free market principles in their operations, but these principles also hinged upon the existence of ethnicity-based "grooved channels [of] clientilization."[112] Besides, the official prohibition of private entrepreneurship reduced much of the competition in the market for everyday consumer goods, thus creating a less competitive environment than would exist in a more typical market economy. In other words, skills of survival and success in the socialist planned economy, however ingenuous and creative, were not automatically transferable to a different economic and sociocultural context.

The lack of scholarly attention to the postwar private economy in the USSR has contributed to a perception that the "only historical precedent" to "perestroika in the late 1980s . . . was Lenin's New Economic Policy six decades before."[113] The economic pursuits discussed here suggest a good candidate to fill this void.

The End of Artels

Soviet authorities kept a watchful eye on the cooperative sector, at times waging true wars against clandestine producers. As time went on, artel affiliation became increasingly dangerous. Stories of persecution are very common in almost every narrative about people who worked in Moscow's suburban artels. One informant relayed that "militia were after them all the time, especially in 1950s. . . . People would hush any conversation about artels."[114] Another noted that artel workers "would be put to prison quite often—half of Saltykovka who was in this business served their terms."[115] Most of those who worked in artels made every effort to ensure that their children received a decent Soviet education and stayed far away from their business. As one informant said, "no mother wanted her child to work in the artel. Because this would most certainly entail prison. By one hundred percent."[116] One informant's grandfather did not want to pass his clandestine business to his son because he "understood it was dangerous, and . . . nobody knew that the Soviet regime will once be over [laughs]. . . . Nobody here inherited anything."[117]

Artel-based entrepreneurship was thus a short-lived phenomenon, involving one or at most two generations of Soviet Jews. Children of clandestine artel producers typically became Soviet professionals of all kinds.

The Soviet regime could not long tolerate the existence of virtually semi-autonomous and not fully controllable production units such as artels. As the state prepared to appropriate the cooperative production sector, official rhetoric started emphasizing the increased mechanization, modernization, and output of artel production and the resulting "parallelism" between the cooperative and the first, industrial production spheres. On April 14, 1956, the Central Committee of the Communist Party of the Soviet Union and the USSR Council of Ministers decreed that "presently many enterprises of producer cooperation ceased to bear artisanal character and do not essentially differ from enterprises in the state industrial sphere."[118]

Following the 1956 decree, the state abolished producer cooperation and merged former artels into larger state-supervised factories, securing its control in the sphere of production and its ideological grip on cooperation. Common people, especially those whose families were involved in artel production, saw the decree as a closure of entrepreneurial possibilities. The artels, one respondent recalled, were "a wonderful thing, but they were difficult of watch over. And since our state certainly has to control everything, they were closed."[119] Between 1956 and 1960 around 1.9 million artel employees became workers of the main state production system.[120] A. Besançon described the artels as a "life buoy" that made it "possible to cross the turbulent waters of the socialism under construction and not to perish in the process."[121] After 1960 producer artels ceased to exist. Soviet private entrepreneurship would have to reconfigure itself in new circumstances.

Notes

Introduction

1. Kathleen Murray, "Underground Economy," *Business Researcher*, April 3, 2017, http://businessresearcher.sagepub.com/sbr-1863-102479-2775997/20170403/underground-economy (accessed January 27, 2019); Benjamin Bridgman, Andrew Dugan, Mikhael Lal, Matthew Osborne, and Shaunda Villones, "Accounting for Household Production in the National Accounts, 1965–2010," *Bureau of Economic Analysis*, May 2012, https://apps.bea.gov/scb/pdf/2012/05%20May/0512_household.pdf (accessed January 27, 2019). Nils Gilman, Jesse Goldhammer, and Steve Weber, eds., *Deviant Globalization: Black Market Economy in the 21st Century* (New York: Continuum, 2011).

2. Susan Douglas, *Inventing American Broadcasting, 1899–1922* (Baltimore: Johns Hopkins University Press, 1989); Fred Turner, *From Counterculture to Cyberculture: Stewart Brand, the Whole Earth Network, and the Rise of Digital Utopianism* (Chicago: University of Chicago Press, 2006).

3. Jeanne Boydston, *Home and Work: Housework, Wages and the Ideology of Labor in the Early Republic* (New York: Oxford University Press, 1994); Eileen Boris, *Home to Work: Motherhood and the Politics of Industrial Homework in the United States* (New York: Cambridge University Press, 1994); Martha May, "The Historical Problem of the Family Wage: The Ford Motor Company and the Five-Dollar Day," *Feminist Studies* 8 (Summer 1982): 399–424.

4. Edward Balleisen, *Fraud: An American History from Barnum to Madoff* (Princeton, NJ: Princeton University Press, 2017); Alan Karras, *Smuggling: Contraband and Corruption in World History* (Lanham, MD: Rowman and Littlefield, 2009); Alejandro Portes, "The Informal Economy and Its Paradoxes," in *The Handbook of Economic Sociology*, ed. Neil J. Smelser and Richard Swedberg, 426–449 (Princeton, NJ: Princeton University Press, 1994).

5. Larry Neal, ed., *The Cambridge History Capitalism*, vol. 1 (Cambridge: Cambridge University Press, 2014).

6. Marx did identify one important hidden dimension of markets and capitalism: commodity fetishism, or the way that markets obscured relations between people by substituting relations among things.

7. In the neoclassical theory of mainstream economics, competition is the driving force that keeps prices down and productivity up and delivers goods into the hands of consumers. Marxists do not deny these "progressive" features of capitalism, which, as a mode of production, is far better than the feudal, Asiatic, or ancient ones based on political coercion. Marxists, however,

also see competition as capitalism's fatal flaw, as it forces misery on the majority until they finally rise up and institute socialism.

8. Ellen Meiskins Wood, *The Origins of Capitalism* (London: Verso, 2017).

9. Karl Polanyi, *The Great Transformation: The Political and Economic Origins of Our Time* (Boston: Beacon Press, 2007); Joyce Appleby, *The Relentless Revolution: A History of Capitalism* (New York: W. W. Norton, 2010), 4, 12, 118–119.

10. Douglass North, *Institutions, Institutional Change and Economic Performance* (Cambridge: Cambridge University Press, 2011); *Understanding the Process of Economic Change* (Princeton, NJ: Princeton University Press, 2005). Mark Granovetter, "Economic Action and Social Structure: The Problem of Embeddedness," *American Journal of Sociology* 91, no. 3 (1985): 481–510. While liberal (or today, neoliberal) ideology may try to performatively make the world conform to the theories and mechanics of pure economics, the on-the-ground reality is that this sort of transformation is never realized in practice.

11. Bas van Bavel, *The Invisible Hand? How Market Economies Have Emerged and Declined since AD 500* (Oxford: Oxford University Press, 2016). On the multiple possibilities for measuring the ends of economic life, see Martha Nussbaum and Amartya Sen, eds., *The Quality of Life* (Oxford: Clarendon Press, 2010).

12. Michael Zakim and Gary Kornblith, eds., *Capitalism Takes Command: The Social Transformation of Nineteenth-Century America* (Chicago: University of Chicago Press, 2012); William Sewell, "A Strange Career: The Historical Study of Economic Life," *History and Theory* 49, no. 4 (2010): 146–166; Jeffrey Sklansky, "The Elusive Sovereign: New Intellectual and Social Histories of Capitalism," *Modern Intellectual History* 9, no. 1 (2012): 233–248. For more, see Kenneth Lipartito, "Reassembling the Economic: New Departures in Historical Materialism," *American Historical Review* 11, no. 1 (February 2016): 101–139. Abandoning the earlier emphasis on how capitalism emerged and how free markets displaced an earlier embedded market society, the new history of capitalism threatens, as Jeffrey Sklansky has noted, to return to a consensus view of history marked by little conflict.

13. Sven Beckert, *Empire of Cotton: A Global History* (New York: Knopf, 2014). Immanuel Wallerstein, *The Modern World-System: Capitalist Agriculture and the Origins of the European World Economy in the Sixteenth Century* (New York: Academic Press, 1974). See also Immanuel Wallerstein, "The Rise and Future Demise of the World Capitalist System: Concepts for Comparative Analysis," *Comparative Studies in Society and History* 16, no. 4 (1974): 387–415. Evolving out of an earlier "dependency school" theory that sought to explain why some parts of the world were wealthy and economically developed and others remained poor, rural, and economically underdeveloped, Wallerstein's world systems theory argued that capitalism had a global division of labor, with the core areas keeping the less developed periphery as underdeveloped supply regions. See also Andre Gunter Frank, *Capitalism and Underdevelopment in Latin America* (New York: Monthly Review, 1967). For a critique of world-systems theory from a more traditional Marxist perspective, see Robert Brenner, "The Origins of Capitalist Development: A Critique of Neo-Smithian Marxism," *New Left Review* I/104 (July–August 1977): 25–92.

14. Trevor Burnard, "Slavery and British Industrialisation: The 'New History of Capitalism' and Eric Williams' *Capitalism and Slavery*," unpublished paper, January 2017.

15. Edward Baptist, *The Half Has Never Been Told: Slavery and the Making of American Capitalism* (New York: Basic, 2014); Walter Johnson, *River of Dark Dreams: Slavery and Empire in the Cotton Kingdom* (Cambridge, MA: Harvard University Press, 2013); Caitlin Rosenthal, *Ac-*

counting for Slavery: Masters and Management (Cambridge, MA: Harvard University Press, 2018). Cf. Sidney Mintz, *Sweetness and Power: The Place of Sugar in Modern History* (New York: Viking, 1985); Mintz did not believe that slavery was a capitalist mode of production.

16. The most obvious difference between slavery and wage labor is that the means of profit rested on ownership of bodies rather than employment of workers. On profit and history, see Mary O'Sullivan, "The Intelligent Woman's Guide to Capitalism," *Enterprise & Society* 19, no. 4 (December 2018): 751–802.

17. Slavery's brutal exploitation of labor and rabid pursuit of profits did not itself make it capitalist. As Mary O'Sullivan has argued, exploitation alone does not guarantee profit, not when every other slave owner has recourse to the same tools of exploitation. O'Sullivan notes that profitability is an exceedingly slippery concept, even in mainstream economics. O'Sullivan, "Intelligent Woman's Guide to Capitalism."

18. As other economic historians have also argued, the ability to exploit labor by coercive means led parts of the New World that practiced slavery to these same deficits. John Majewski, *A House Dividing: Economic Development in Pennsylvania and Virginia before the Civil War* (New York: Cambridge University Press, 2000); Stanley Engerman and Kenneth Sokoloff, *Economic Development in the Americas since 1500* (New York: Cambridge University Press, 2012); Louis Galambos and Franco Amatori, "The Entrepreneurial Multiplier," *Enterprise & Society* 17, no. 4 (December 2016): 763–808.

19. The new history of capitalism in the U.S. case does not always argue from a world-systems perspective, though it does focus on the interaction of the slave South and the nonslave North—in terms of production, finance, and consumption—making the same argument within one nation. Seth Rockman, "Negro Cloth: Mastering the Market for Slave Clothing in Antebellum America," in *American Capitalism: New Histories*, ed. Sven Beckert and Christine Desan, 170–194 (New York: Columbia University Press, 2018). Likewise, it looks at the relations in the United States between eastern capital and western development in a manner similar to the relations between the advanced capitalist world and the underdeveloped world. Noam Maggor, "To Coddle and Caress These Great Capitalists: Eastern Money, Frontier Populism, and the Politics of Market-Making in the American West," *American Historical Review* 122, no. 1 (February 2017): 55–84.

20. Recent writing on the new history of capitalism has taken a somewhat more flexible and constructivist view of markets, though mainly from the perspective of political economy and still with a strong focus on the dominance of what we call mainstream capitalism rather than its alternatives. See Sven Beckert and Christine Desan, eds., *American Capitalism: New Histories* (New York: Columbia University Press, 2018), esp. 1–34.

21. Brian P. Luskey and Wendy A. Woloson, "Introduction," in *Capitalism by Gaslight: Illuminating the Economy of Nineteenth-Century America*, ed. Brian P. Luskey and Wendy A. Woloson (Philadelphia: University of Pennsylvania Press, 2015), 2–4.

22. There is a long history of studying the oppositional forces of capitalism, but this literature frequently references a precapitalist past or makes somewhat romantic suggestions about alternatives rooted in a noncapitalist communal world that tries to keep itself together despite the relentless push of commodification and markets.

23. Amy Dru Stanley presents a trenchant critique of the inattention to women and gender by the new historians of capitalism in "Histories of Capitalism and Sex Difference," *Journal of the Early Republic* 36 (Summer 2016): 343–350.

24. Luskey and Woloson, *Capitalism by Gaslight*, 9.

25. Our work is sympathetic to the "varieties of capitalism" literature, but we find it too structural and rigid, mainly focusing on the relationship between state structures and political organization and business structures and financial systems. This volume takes a more open-ended and fluid view of how capitalism can vary, emphasizing conflicts within the system and subnational, regional alternatives, as well as complex mixtures that may occur at the national level. Peter Hall and David Soskice, *Varieties of Capitalism: The Institutional Foundations of Comparative Advantage* (Oxford: Oxford University Press, 2013). For an approach closer to what we are advocating, see Charles F. Sabel and Jonathan Zeitlin, "Stories, Strategies, Structures: Rethinking Historical Alternatives to Mass Production," in *Worlds of Possibility: Flexibility and Mass Production in Western Industrialization*, ed. Charles F. Sabel and Jonathan Zeitlin, 1–36 (Cambridge: Cambridge University Press, 1997).

26. To the extent commodification means a relentless advance that draws all into the market, it is not terribly different from the nominalist position of neoclassical economics, where there are always markets that operate much the same way in any place and time.

27. Marx sent Darwin a copy of *Capital*, and some have argued he even intended to dedicate volume 2 to the English naturalist, but this turns out to be a myth. Margaret Fay, "Did Marx Offer to Dedicate Capital to Darwin? A Reassessment of the Evidence," *Journal of the History of Ideas* 39, no. 1 (1978): 133–146.

28. This concept is used by Steven Johnson, *Where Good Ideas Come From: The Natural History of Innovation* (New York: Riverhead, 2010).

29. Dave Elder-Vass, *Profit and Gift in the Digital Economy* (Cambridge: Cambridge University Press, 2016).

30. Reciprocal exchanges and free exchanges of knowledge need not be seen as purely beneficent or charitable. The uncompensated information that users of websites and apps give up is also a form of appropriation used to benefit the companies that run these software products.

31. Jennifer Le Zotte, *From Goodwill to Grunge: A History of Secondhand Styles and Alternative Economies* (Chapel Hill: University of North Carolina Press, 2015), 101, 104.

32. Charles Duhigg, *The Power of Habit: Why We Do What We Do in Life and Business* (New York: Random House, 2014), 182–212.

33. Andrew Konove, *Black Market Capital: Urban Politics and the Shadow Economy in Mexico City* (Berkeley: University of California Press, 2018); Mark H. Haller, "Policy Gambling, Entertainment, and the Emergence of Black Politics: Chicago from 1900 to 1940," *Journal of Social History* 24 (Summer 1991): 719–739; Aaron Ahuvia, Giacomo Gistri, Simona Romani, and Stefano Pace, "What Is the Harm in Fake Luxury Brands? Moving Beyond the Conventional Wisdom," in *Luxury Marketing: A Challenge for Theory and Practice*, ed. Klaus-Peter Wiedmann and Nadine Hennings, 279–293 (Wiesbaden: Springer Gabler, 2013).

34. Jamie Pietruska, *Looking Forward: Prediction and Uncertainty in Modern America* (Chicago: University of Chicago, 2017).

35. Dara Orenstein, "Foreign-Trade Zones and the Cultural Logic of Frictionless Production," *Radical History Review* 109 (Winter 2011): 36–61.

36. Bertell Ollman, ed., *Market Socialism: The Debate Among Socialists* (New York: Routledge, 1998).

37. Hernando de Soto, *The Mystery of Capital: Why Capitalism Triumphs in the West and Fails Everywhere Else* (New York: Basic, 2000); Muhammad Yunus, *Banker to the Poor: Micro-Lending and the Battle Against World Poverty* (New York: Public Affairs, 1999).

Chapter 1. Lifting the Veil of Money

1. "Stern Review: The Economics of Climate Change," executive summary, https://webarchive .nationalarchives.gov.uk/+/http://www.hm-treasury.gov.uk/sternreview_index.htm (accessed February 13, 2019). On GDP, see Dirk Philipsen, *The Little Big Number: How GDP Came to Rule the World and What to Do About It* (Princeton, NJ: Princeton University Press, 2015); Andrew Yarrow, *Measuring America: How Economic Growth Came to Define American Greatness in the Late Twentieth Century* (Amherst: University of Massachusetts Press, 2011). On the construction of the concepts "developed nation" and "developing nation," see James Ferguson, *The Anti-Politics Machine: "Development," Depoliticization, and Bureaucratic Power in Lesotho* (Cambridge: Cambridge University Press, 1990). On the Chinese government's use of GDP for provincial promotions, see Li Hongbon and Li-An Zhou, "Political Turnover and Economic Performance: The Incentive Role of Personnel Control in China," *Journal of Public Economics* 89 (September 2005): 1743–1762.

2. "Most Important Problem," Gallup Poll, http://www.gallup.com/poll/1675/most-important -problem.aspx (accessed April 8, 2013). On the birth of "the economy," see Timothy Mitchell, "Fixing the Economy," *Cultural Studies* 12, no. 1 (1998): 82–101; Timothy Shenk, "Inventing the American Economy," PhD diss., Columbia University, 2016.

3. Michael Norton and Dan Ariely, "Building a Better America—One Wealth Quintile at a Time," *Perspectives of Psychological Science*, 6 (January 2011): 9–12. For the *New York Times*, see http://markets.on.nytimes.com/research/economy/indicators/indicators.asp (accessed February 13, 2019).

4. "Trump Welcomes Stock Market Surge, Consumer Confidence on Twitter," Reuters, March 2, 2017, https://www.reuters.com/article/us-usa-trump-idUSKBN1691EJ (accessed February 13, 2019). See also Glenn Kessler and Meg Kelly, "Trump Keeps Celebrating Stock Market Highs, *Washington Post*, August 2, 2017.

5. "U.S. Economy Grew 3% in 2nd Quarter, Fastest Pace in 2 Years," *New York Times*, August 30, 2017.

6. Sarah Igo, *The Averaged American: Surveys, Citizens and the Making of a Mass Public* (Cambridge, MA: Harvard University Press, 2008).

7. E. P. Thompson, "The Moral Economy of the English Crowd," *Past and Present*, 50 (1971): 115.

8. Eli Cook, *The Pricing of Progress: Economic Indicators and the Capitalization of American Life* (Cambridge, MA: Harvard University Press, 2017).

9. Mary Poovey, *A History of the Modern Fact* (Chicago: Chicago University Press, 1998); Ted Porter, *Trust in Numbers: The Pursuit of Objectivity in Science and Public Life* (Princeton, NJ: Princeton University Press, 1995); Alain Desrosieres, *The Politics of Large Numbers: A History of Statistical Reasoning* (Cambridge, MA: Harvard University Press, 2002); Paul Starr, "The Sociology of Official Statistics," in *The Politics of Numbers*, ed. William Alonso and Paul Starr, **7–61** (New York: Russel Sage Foundation, 1987).

10. On slavery and economic indicators, see Cook, *Pricing of Progress*, chaps. 2–3, 6.

11. Patricia Cline Cohen, *A Calculating People: The Spread of Numeracy in Early America* (Chicago: University of Chicago Press, 1982), 175–205; Nikolas Rose, "Calculable Minds and Manageable Individuals," *History of Human Sciences* 1 (October 1988): 179–200. The term "moral statistics" came from Europe. See Michael J. Cullen, *The Statistical Movement in Early Victorian*

Britain: The Foundations of Empirical Social Research (New York: Barnes and Noble, 1975); Frank Hamilton Hankins, *Adolphe Quetelet as Statistician* (New York: AMS, 1908), chap. 4.

12. Joseph Worcester, *The American Almanac of Useful Knowledge* (Boston: Bowen, 1838), 189; *The Man*, November 27, 1834; Cong. Globe, 25th Cong., 3d Sess. 209 (1839).

13. New York secretary of state report cited in *Yazoo City Whig*, May 23, 1845; Lemuel Shattuck, *Report to the Committee of the City Council Appointed to Obtain the Census of Boston for the Year 1845* (Boston, 1846), 107, 125–126; Nahum Capen and Jesse Chickering, *Letters Addressed to the Hon. John Davis, Concerning the Census of 1849* (Washington, DC: T. Ritchie, 1849).

14. *McDowall's Journal*, February–May 1834; *Annual Report of the New York Magdalen Society*, 1830; "Report by the New York Female Reform Society," in Butt Ender, *Prostitution Exposed; or, A Moral Reform Directory* (New York, 1839); *Licentiousness, Its Effects and Causes* (Boston, 1846). For Cincinnati's "census of prostitutes," see *Cincinnati Daily Gazette*, December 13 and 15, 1858. See also Timothy J. Gilfoyle, *City of Eros: New York City, Prostitution, and the Commercialization of Sex, 1790–1920* (New York: Norton, 1994), 57–59.

15. William Sanger, *History of Prostitution* (New York, 1858), 458; Michael Zakim, *Readymade Democracy: A History of Men's Dress in the American Republic 1760–1860* (Chicago: Chicago University Press, 2003), chap. 6.

16. For the scandal surrounding insanity statistics, see Cohen, *Calculating People*, 175–205; Edward Jarvis, "Statistics of Insanity in the United States," *Boston Medical and Surgical Journal* 27, no. 7 (September 21, 1842): 116–121. On the rise of the asylum, see David Rothman, *Discovery of the Asylum: Social Order and Disorder in the New Republic* (Boston: Little, Brown, 1971).

17. Samuel Woodward, *Tenth Annual Report of the Trustees of the State Lunatic Asylum at Worcester, Massachusetts* (Boston, 1842); *Phrenological Journal and Magazine of Moral Science* 17 (1843): 31. Jarvis quoted in Rothman, *Discovery of the Asylum*, 115–116.

18. Robert Dalzell, *Enterprising Elite: The Boston Associates and the World They Made* (Cambridge, MA: Harvard University Press, 1987), Appleton quote on 12. Joseph Sturge, *A Visit to the United States in 1841* (London, 1842), 143–145. Moral statistics also cropped up in the local newspaper. See, for instance, *Lowell Offering*, December 1843, 47.

19. *The Madisonian*, September 8, 1838. For databases, see Corpus of Historical American English, corpus.byu.edu/coha/ (accessed February 13, 2019); Google Ngram; Newsbank's American Historical Newspapers. For other typical uses of the term *priceless* in the era, see *Illinois Free Trader and LaSalle County Commercial Advertiser*, June 24, 1842; *Rutland Herald*, June 13, 1837, and April 19, 1842; *American Sentinel*, February 10, 1830; *Carroll Free Press*, August 5, 1836; *The Emancipator*, November 15, 1838, July 19, 1838, and March 29, 1838; *Philadelphia Inquirer*, May 5, 1830; *Southern Argus*, November 14, 1837.

20. Hinton Rowan Helper, *The Impending Crisis in the South: How to Meet It* (New York, 1857), v, 35, 39, 54, 64–66, 71, 283, 286; On Helper and his book, see David Brown, *Southern Outcast: Hinton Rowan Helper and the Impending Crisis of the South* (Baton Rouge: Louisiana State University Press, 2006).

21. Ezra Seaman, *Essays on the Progress of Nations* (New York, 1846), 127, 302–305; T. S. Lambert, "The Money or Commercial Value of Man," *Hunt's Merchants' Magazine* 35 (July 1856): 34–37.

22. "Freeman Hunt on the Science of Business," *Business History Review* 18 (1944): 9–10; Freeman Hunt, "The Moral End of Business," *Hunt's Merchants' Magazine* 1 (1839): 390; Freeman Hunt, *Worth and Wealth: A Collection of Maxims, Morals, and Miscellanies for Merchants and Men of Business* (New York, 1856), 106. For Hunt, see Cook, *Pricing of Progress*, chap. 5.

23. Matthew Hale Smith, *Twenty Years Among the Bulls and Bears of Wall Street* (New York, 1896), 523; Thomas Prentice Kettell, *Southern Wealth and Northern Profits* (New York, 1860); "Influence of Railroads," *De Bow's Review* 10 (1852). For other examples of Kettell's financial journalism, see "Progressive Wealth and Commerce of Boston," *Hunt's Merchants' Magazine* 15 (1846): 34; "The Commercial Growth and Greatness of New York," *Hunt's Merchants' Magazine* 5 (1841): 30–44; " "Progress of American Commerce, Agriculture and Manufacture," *De Bow's Review* 4 (1847): 85–95.

24. William Cronon, *Nature's Metropolis: Chicago and the Great West*, (New York: WW Norton, 1991) 81; Alfred Chandler, *Henry Varnum Poor: Business Editor, Analyst and Reformer* (Cambridge, MA: Harvard University Press, 1956).

25. Henry Varnum Poor, *American Railroad Journal* 25 (1852).

26. Massachusetts Bureau of Labor Statistics, *First Annual Report*, 18–23, 25–31, 134.

27. "Origin of the Society," *Bulletin of the American Geographical and Statistical Society* 1, no. 1 (August 1852): 3–14; updated member lists appear in each bulletin.

28. "Transactions of the Society," *Bulletin of the American Geographical and Statistical Society* 1, no. 1 (August 1852): 13, 61, 105; "Transactions of the Society," *Bulletin of the American Geographical and Statistical Society* 11 (January 1857): 23, 33, 39, 47; E. C. Strazinsky, *Catalogue of the Library of the American Geographical and Statistical Society* (New York, 1857); "Transactions of the Society," *Bulletin of the American Geographical and Statistical Society* 11 (January 1857): 6–11; "Memorial," *Bulletin of the American Geographical and Statistical Society* 11 (January 1857): 16–18. For lobbying efforts, see *Report of the Joint Special Committee of the Chamber of Commerce and American Geographical Statistical Society on the Extension of the Decimal System to Weights and Measures of the United States* (New York, 1857); John Jay, *A Statistical View of American Agriculture . . . with Suggestions for the Schedules of the Federal Census in 1860* (New York, 1859).

29. Charles Spahr, *An Essay on the Present Distribution of Wealth in the United States* (Boston, 1896), 69.

30. For the little we know of Spahr's life, see the pamphlet *In Memory of Charles B. Spahr* (New York: Social Reform Club, 1905).

31. Richmond Mayo-Smith, "Review," *Political Science Quarterly* 12 (1897): 346–348; Richmond Mayo-Smith, *Statistics and Economics* (Baltimore, 1888).

32. U.S. Senate Committee on Finance, *Wholesale Prices, Wages, and Transportation: Report by Mr. Aldrich from the Committee on Finance, Part 1* (Washington, DC, 1893). For the politics behind the Aldrich report, see Thomas Stapleford, *The Cost of Living in America: A Political History of Economic Statistics* (New York: Cambridge University Press, 2009), 41–50.

33. Committee on Finance, *Wholesale Prices*, 6–7. On the consumerist turn and the labor question, see Lawrence Glickman, *A Living Wage: American Workers and the Making of a Consumer Society* (Ithaca, NY: Cornell University Press, 1997); Roseanne Currarino, *The Labor Question in America: Economic Democracy in the Gilded Age* (Champaign: University of Illinois Press, 2011).

34. Massachusetts Bureau of Labor Statistics, *Third Annual Report* (Boston, 1871/1872), 293–335; Massachusetts Bureau of Labor Statistics, *Fourth Annual Report*, 172, 228. On Carroll Wright's career as a labor statistician, see James Leiby, *Carroll Wright and Labor Reform: The Origins of Labor Statistics* (Cambridge, MA: Harvard University Press, 1960).

35. National Woman Suffrage Association, *Report of the Industrial Council of Women* (Washington, DC, 1888), 155; Knights of Labor, *Proceedings of the General Assembly*, 1886 report (Minneapolis, 1887), 952. For Barry, see Eleanor Flexner, *Century of Struggle: The Woman's Rights*

Movement in the United States (Cambridge, MA: Harvard University Press, 1959), 177, 190–193; Philip S. Foner, *Women and the American Labor Movement: From the First Trade Unions to the Present* (New York: Free Press, 1979), 205–206.

36. "A Demand to Have the Next U.S. Census Show the Mortgage Indebtedness," *Aberdeen (SD) Daily News*, November 27, 1889.

37. German Lopez, "2017 Was the Worst Year Ever for Drug Overdose Deaths in America," August 16, 2018, https://www.vox.com/science-and-health/2018/8/16/17698204/opioid-epidemic-overdose-deaths-2017 (accessed February 13, 2019); Richard Luscombe, "Life Expectancy Gap Between Rich and Poor US Regions Is 'More than 20 Years,'" *The Guardian*, May 8, 2017; Melanie Lockhart, "Average U.S. Household Debt Continues to Rise," *Credit Karma*, September 13, 2018.

38. On the twentieth century, the National Bureau of Economic Research, and the invention of GDP, see Shenk, "Inventing the American Economy"; Cook, *Pricing of Progress*, epilogue.

Chapter 2. Accounting for Reproductive Labor

Acknowledgments: I would like to thank the editors of this collection, as well as Jill Jensen, Howard Brick, Dorothy Sue Cobble, and Dorothea Hoehtker, for comments on versions of this piece and the ILO archives for their aid in my research. Funding was possible through the Hull Chair in Women and Social Justice, which I hold.

1. ILO, *Women at Work: Trends 2016* (Geneva: ILO, 2016), 19–20.

2. Programme on Rural Women, "Medium Term Plan," 2, WEP 10-4-04-01, Jacket 11, International Labour Organization Archives, Geneva. Unless otherwise specified, all archival material comes from this location.

3. On the ILO, see Gerry Rodgers, Eddy Lee, Lee Sweptson, and Jasmien Van Daele, eds., *The ILO and the Quest for Social Justice, 1919–2009* (Ithaca, NY: Cornell University Press, 2009). Formed in the cauldron of worker unrest following World War I, the ILO had a unique tripartite organization of government, employer, and worker representatives from member states. It consisted of an International Labour Conference, International Labour Office, and Governing Body.

4. Devaki Jain, *Women, Development, and the UN: A Sixty-Year Quest for Equality and Justice* (Bloomington: Indiana University Press, 2005), 53–54; Nyket Kardam, *Bringing Women In: Women's Issues in International Development Programs* (Boulder, CO: Lynne Rienner, 1991).

5. See the contribution herein: Eli Cook, "Lifting the Veil of Money: What Economic Indicators Hide," in *Capitalism's Hidden Worlds*, ed. Kenneth Lipartito and Lisa Jacobson, 25–43 (Philadelphia: University of Pennsylvania Press, 2019); Alessandra Pescarolo, "Productive and Reproductive Work: Uses and Abuses of the Old Dichotomy," in *What Is Work? Gender at the Crossroads of Home, Gamily, and Business from the early Modern Era to the Present*, ed. Raffaella Sarti, Anna Bellavitis, and Manuela Martini, 114–138 (New York: Berghahn, 2018).

6. Anne Winslow, "Specialized Agencies and the World Bank," in *Women, Politics, and the United Nations*, ed. Anne Winslow, 155–175 (Westport, CT: Greenwood, 1995).

7. Maria Mies, *The Village and the World: My Life, Our Times* (North Melbourne: Spinifex, 2008); Mies, *The Lace Makers of Narsapur* (North Melbourne: Spinifex, 2012), originally published by Zed Books in 1982 based on Mies, *Housewives Produce for the World Market: The Lace Makers of Narsapur*, World Employment Programme Research Working Paper, December 1980 (Geneva: ILO, 1980). All quotes from the 2012 Spinifex edition.

8. United Nations, *Report of the World Conference of the International Women's Year* (New York: United Nations, 1976), 22–24.

9. "Programme of Action," in International Labour Conference, 61st Session, 1976; and Tripartite World Conference on Employment, Income Distribution and Social Progress and the International Division of Labour, June 1976, *Australian Delegation Report* (Canberra, 1977), 90.

10. Zubeida Ahmad, "The ILO Programme on Rural Women: Action Oriented Research—a Preview of the Findings," 32, January 18, 1979, WEP 10-4-04, Jacket 6.

11. Zubeida Ahmad to Maria Mies, November 9, 1979, WEP 10-4-04-33-1, Jacket 1.

12. Zubeida Ahmad, "Meeting of ILO Office Directors and CTAs of Regional Teams—Bangkok," 11, January 6, 1982, WEP 10-4-04, Jacket 12.

13. Not all of these women used the term *feminist*, but they all defended women and the budget and portfolio of their program. Benería certainly defined herself as such, and Ahmad went on to be a founder of DAWN. "Lourdes Benería," in *Engendering Economics: Conversations with Women Economists in the United States*, ed. Paulette I. Olson and Zohreh Emami, 227–248 (New York: Routledge, 2002); Zubeida Ahmad, "Mission to New Delhi and Bangalore August 18 to 29 1984," WEP 10-4-04, Jacket 21.

14. Nancy Folbre, *Greed, Lust and Gender: A History of Economic Ideas* (New York: Oxford University Press, 2009).

15. Lourdes Benería and Gita Sen, "Class and Gender: Inequalities and Women's Role in Economic Development—Theoretical and Practical Implications," *Feminist Studies*, 8, no. 1 (Spring 1982): 158–161 especially.

16. Ester Boserup, *Woman's Role in Economic Development* (New York: St. Martin's, 1970).

17. Lourdes Benería and Gita Sen, "Accumulation, Reproduction, and 'Women's Role in Economic Development': Boserup Revisited," *Signs: A Journal of Women in Culture and Society*, 7, no. 2 (Winter 1981): 279–281.

18. Arvonne S. Fraser, "Preface," in *Developing Power: How Women Transformed International Development*, ed. Arvonne S. Fraser and Irene Tinker, ix (New York: The Feminist Press, 2004).

19. Frances Vavrus and Lisa Ann Richey, "Editorial: Women and Development; Rethinking Policy and Reconceptualizing Practice," *Women's Studies Quarterly*, 31, nos. 3/4 (Fall–Winter 2003): 6–18.

20. Jocelyn Olcott, *International Women's Year: The Greatest Consciousness-Raising Event in History* (New York: Oxford University Press, 2017).

21. Irene Tinker, "Challenging Wisdom, Challenging Policies: The Women in Development Movement," in Fraser and Irene Tinker, *Developing Power*, 67–70.

22. Elisabeth Prügl, "Home-Based Producers in Development Discourse," in *Homeworkers in Global Perspective: Invisible No More*, ed. Eileen Boris and Elisabeth Prügl (New York: Routledge, 1996), 39–40; Naila Kabeer, *Reversed Realities: Gender Hierarchies in Development Thought* (London: Verso, 1994).

23. Kate Young, Carol Wolkowitz, and Roslyn McCullagh, *Of Marriage and the Market: Women's Subordination in International Perspective* (London: CSE, 1981), vii–xi, quote at viii.

24. Eileen Boris, "Subsistence Production and Household Labour," in *Handbook of Global History of Work*, ed. Karin Hofmeester and Marcel van der Linden (Munich: De Gruyder Oldenbourg), 342.

25. Benería and Sen, "Boserup Revisited," 287.

26. Ibid., 288.

27. Ibid., 286.

28. Ibid., 290; Edward Shorter, *The Making of the Modern Family* (New York: Basic, 1975); Thomas Dublin, *Women at Work* (New York: Columbia University Press, 1975); Louise A. Tilly, Joan W. Scott, and Miriam Cohen, "Women's Work and European Fertility Patterns," *Journal of Interdisciplinary History* 6, no. 3 (Winter 1976): 447–476.

29. Benería and Sen, "Boserup Revisited," 291.

30. For the debates at this time, see Ellen Malos, ed., *The Politics of Housework* (London: Allison & Busby, 1980).

31. Lydia Sargent, ed., *Women and Revolution: A Discussion of the Unhappy Marriage of Marxism and Feminism* (Boston: South End, 1981).

32. Lourdes Benería, "Future Directions of Research on Rural Women: A Summary," 6, WEP 10-4-04-0-100, Jacket 1.

33. Lourdes Benería, "Introduction," in *Women and Development: the Sexual Division of Labor in Rural Societies*, ed. Lourdes Benería (New York: Praeger, 1982), xii.

34. Benería and Sen, "Boserup Revisited," 296–297.

35. Ibid., 298.

36. K. Griffin, Minutes, January 7, 1975, WEP 10-4-04, Jacket 1, proposes her hiring to organize research on women and work on human nutrition. See also J. Sykes to Mr. Emmerij, September 5, 1975, Minutes, WEP 10-4-04, Jacket 1.

37. Author biography, back cover, Ingrid Palmer, *The Impact of Agrarian Reform on Women* (West Hartford, CT: Kumarian, 1985); A. G. Kenwood and A. L. Lougheed, *Economics at the University of Queensland, 1912–1997* (Brisbane, Australia: University of Queensland, 1997), 12; Palmer to Barbara Harriss, September 1, 1975, WEP 10-4-04, Jacket 1.

38. Ingrid Palmer, "Rural Women and the Basic-Needs Approach to Development," *International Labour Review* 115, no. 1 (January–February 1977): 104.

39. Ingrid Palmer, ILO Activities on Women to Program (Mr. Martin), copies to Mr. Emmerij, Mme. Béguin, Mr. Griffin, Mrs. Janjic, September 30, 1975, WEP 10-4-04, Jacket 1.

40. Martha Nussbaum, "The Professor of Parody: The Hip Defeatism of Judith Butler," *New Republic* 22 (February 1999): 37–45.

41. Palmer, ILO Activities on Women to Program (Mr. Martin).

42. Ibid.

43. Ingrid Palmer, "Women in Rural Development," 3–5, concept paper, WEP 10-4-04, Jacket 1.

44. Ingrid Palmer to Mr. Aboughanen (COORD), January 30, 1976, WEP 10-4-04, Jacket 1.

45. Ingrid Palmer to Sylvia Golanos, September 16, 1975, WEP 10-4-04, Jacket 1.

46. Palmer, "Rural Women and the Basic-Needs Approach," 105.

47. Ingrid Palmer, "Letters: Women's Future Role," *New York Herald Tribune*, July 16, 1976.

48. Ingrid Palmer, ILO Activities on Women to Program (Mr. Martin).

49. Ingrid Palmer to Adrienne Germain, Ford Foundation, February 8, 1976, WEP 10-4-04, Jacket 1. See also Mary Racelis Hollnsteiner to Palmer, September 12, 1975; I. Z. Bhatty to Palmer, September 27, 1975; Palmer to National Council on Women and Development, Accra, November 21, 1975; Palmer to Achola Pala, December 9, 1975; Palmer to Jette Bukin, January 27, 1976, all in WEP 10-4-04, Jacket 1.

50. Kelly Coogan-Gehr, "The Politics of Race in U.S. Feminist Scholarship: An Archaeology," *Signs*, 37 (Autumn 2011): 83–107.

51. See budget proposal attached to "Women in Development" conveyed by Antoinette Béguin, November 25, 1975, WEP 10-4-04, Jacket 1, including Palmer's analysis and proposals.

52. Louis Emmerij to Griffin, February 20, 1976, WEP 10-4-04, Jacket 1. These became Tahrunnessa Abdullah and Sondra Zeidenstein, *Village Women of Bangladesh: Prospects for Change* (Oxford: Pergamon, 1982); Richard Longhurst, *Rural Development Planning and the Sexual Division of Labour: A Case Study of a Moslem Hausa Village in Northern Nigeria*, Working Paper (Geneva: ILO, 1982).

53. Ingrid Palmer to Abe Weisblatt, November 27, 1975, WEP 10-4-04, Jacket 1.

54. Ingrid Palmer to Sylvia Golanos, September 16, 1975, WEP 10-4-04, Jacket 1.

55. Ingrid Palmer to Ros Morpeth, October 28, 1975, WEP 10-4-04, Jacket 1.

56. Palmer, "Rural Women and the Basic-Needs Approach," 106.

57. "Lourdes Benería," 237–238, 245.

58. Lourdes Benería, *Gender, Development, and Globalization: Economics as if All People Mattered* (New York: Routledge, 2003), ix–xi.

59. She repeated this reasoning in concept papers and memos. See Lourdes Benería to Mrs. Ahmad, Mrs. Korchounova (Femmes), "Comments des Progres Intervenus dans l'Application du Principe de l'Egalite de Chances et de Traitement pour les Travailleuses Inventaire des Donnees a Rassembler," Minutes Sheet, June 6, 1977, WN-1-1-02-1000, Jacket 1.

60. Proposal for Advisory Informal Consultants Meeting, n.d., WEP 10-4-04-0-100, Jacket 1.

61. Margalit Fox, "Fatema Mernissi, a Founder of Islamic Feminism, Dies at 75," *New York Times*, December 9, 2015.

62. Lourdes Benería, *Women and Development*; On Savané, see Valentine M. Moghadam, *Globalizing Women: Transnational Feminist Networks* (Baltimore: Johns Hopkins University Press, 2005), 87–88.

63. "Curriculum Vita: Filomina C. Steady," available at https://www.wellesley.edu/sites /default/files/steadyf-cv-2011_7.pdf (accessed February 14, 2019).

64. CODESRIA Web2, "Mrs Zenebeworke Tadesse (2003–2005)," Council for the Development of Social Science Research in Africa (website), About Us, The Executive Committee, June 1, 2011, http://www.codesria.org/spip.php?article1483&lang=en (accessed February 14, 2019).

65. See http://nekrologi.wyborcza.pl/0,11,,158873,Barbara-Tryfan-kondolencje.html (in Polish; accessed February 14, 2019); https://opendocs.ids.ac.uk/opendocs/bitstream/handle /123456789/10814/IDSB_10_3_10.1111-j.1759-5436.1979.mp10003014.x.pdf;jsessionid=B0119448B 8A3B63A79585810ADC86CBF?sequence=1 (accessed February 14, 2019).

66. Zahrah Nesbitt-Ahmed and Jenny Edwards, "Gender, Sexuality and Development: Revisiting and Reflecting," *IDS Bulletin* 47, no. 2 (2016), http://bulletin.ids.ac.uk/idsbo/article/view /2721/html (accessed February 14, 2019).

67. "Elisabeth Croll," *The Guardian*, October 9, 2007.

68. Lya Yaneth Fuentes Vásquez, "Magdalena León Gómez: A Life Consecrated to Building Bridges Between Women, Knowledge and Action," *Nómadas* 18 (2003): 165–179, https://dialnet .unirioja.es/descarga/articulo/3991835.pdf (accessed February 14, 2019).

69. Draft, "Women and Rural Development: A Report of an Informal Consultants' Meeting" (Geneva, May 22–23, 1978), 1–6, WEP 10-4-04-0-100, Jacket 1; ILO, *Women in Rural Development: Critical Issues* (Geneva: ILO, 1980).

70. Gita Sen, "Women Workers and the Green Revolution," in *Women and Development*, ed. Benería, 54–55.

71. Draft, "Women and Rural Development: A Report of an Informal Consultants' Meeting (Geneva, May 22–23, 1978), WEP 10-4-04-0-100, Jacket 1; ILO, *Women in Rural Development*.

72. Lourdes Beneria to Mr. Ghai, November 11, 1977; Ingrid to Dharam, February 10, 1977, WEP 10-4-04, Jacket 2.

73. Lourdes Benería, Mission Report, Accra, December 12–17, 1977 and Dakar, December 12–17 1977, December 22, 1977, WEP 10-4-04, Jacket 3.

74. Zubeida Ahmad and Martha Loutfi, *Women Workers in Rural Development* (Geneva: ILO, 1985), 43–47.

75. Benería to Mies, July 22, 1977, Lourdes to Maria, October 19, 1977, WEP 10-4-04-33-1, Jacket 1.

76. Ahmad to Ghai, November 15, 1977, WEP 10-4-04-33-1, Jacket 1.

77. Maria Mies, "Interim Report on Project, 'Impact of Market Economy on Women's Productive and Reproductive Work in the Rural Subsistence Economy of India,'" November 1978, 1, WEP 10-4-04-33-1, Jacket 1.

78. Mies, *Lace Makers*, xii–xiii, xx–xxi.

79. Ibid., xx–xxi.

80. Mies, "Interim Report," 5.

81. Mies, *Lace Makers*, 9, 51, 81.

82. Ibid., 201–202.

83. Maria de los Angeles Crummett, *Rural Women and Industrial Home Work in Latin America: Research Review and Agenda*, WEP Working Paper 46 (Geneva: ILO, June 1988), 29.

84. Mies, *Lace Makers*, xx; Ahmad and Loutfi, *Women Workers in Rural Development*, 14.

85. Zubeida Ahmad to Ms. Ebeid, March 11, 1983; Ebeid to Dr. Ahmad, April 2, 1983; Ebeid to Mr. Ghai, February 23, 1983, WEP 10-4-04-33-1, Jacket 1; Ahmad to Ghai, April 6, 1982, WEP 10-4-04, Jacket 13.

86. Ahmad to Lourdes, October 11, 1982, WEP 10-4-04, Jacket 14.

87. Ahmad, "Mission to New Delhi and Bangalore August 18 to 29 1984," WEP 10-4-04, Jacket 21.

88. Peggy Antrobus, "Development," draft paper for discussion, August 1984, 10, WEP 10-4-04, Jacket 21.

Chapter 3. The Loose Cotton Economy of the New Orleans Waterfront in the Late Nineteenth Century

1. "Actual Stock of Cotton," *Daily Picayune* (New Orleans), July 3, 1873, 6. The term *city crop* first appears in the columns of the *New-Orleans Times* in the summer of 1866.

2. "On 'Change,'" *New-Orleans Times*, July 28, 1866, 15; "The Waste Of Cotton," *Daily Picayune*, June 10, 1874, 3.

3. "Country Whiskey Shops," *Daily News* (Charleston, SC), December 5, 1868, 2; "Stealing," *Daily News*, September 20, 1865, 2. On the theft of seed cotton, see, for instance, Charles L. Flynn Jr., *White Land, Black Labor: Caste and Class in Late Nineteenth-Century Georgia* (Baton Rouge: Louisiana State University Press, 1983), 95–96; Jeff Forret, *Race Relations at the Margins: Slaves and Poor Whites in the Antebellum Southern Countryside* (Baton Rouge: Louisiana State University Press, 2006), 82.

4. Harold D. Woodman, *King Cotton and His Retainers: Financing and Marketing the Cotton Crop of the South, 1800–1925* (Columbia: University of South Carolina Press, 1990 [1968]).

5. Giorgio Riello, *Cotton: The Fabric That Made the Modern World* (Cambridge: Cambridge University Press, 2013); Sven Beckert, *Empire of Cotton: A Global History* (New York: Vintage, 2015); Robert Bouilly, "The Development of American Cotton Exchanges, 1870–1916" (PhD diss.,

University of Missouri, 1975); John R. Killick, "The Cotton Operations of Alexander Brown and Sons in the Deep South, 1820–1880," *Journal of Southern History* 43 (May 1977): 169–194; John R. Killick, "The Transformation of Cotton Marketing in the Late Nineteenth Century: Alexander Sprunt and Son in Wilmington, N.C., 1884–1956," *Business History Review* 55 (Summer 1981): 143–169; John R. Killick, "Risk, Specialization and Profit in the Mercantile Sector of the Nineteenth Century Cotton Trade: Alexander Brown & Sons, 1820–1880," *Business History* 16 (January 1974): 1–16; L. Tuffly Ellis, "The Texas Cotton Compress Industry: A History" (PhD diss., University of Texas, 1964); L. Tuffly Ellis, "The Round Bale Cotton Controversy," *Southwestern Historical Quarterly* 71, no. 2 (October 1967): 194–225; L. Tuffly Ellis, "The Revolutionizing of the Texas Cotton Trade, 1865–1885," *Southwestern Historical Quarterly* 73, no. 4 (April 1970): 478–508; L. Tuffly Ellis, "The New Orleans Cotton Exchange: The Formative Years, 1871–1880," *Journal of Southern History* 39, no. 4 (November 1973): 545–564; Kenneth J. Lipartito, "The New York Cotton Exchange and the Development of the Cotton Futures Market," *Business History Review* 57, no. 1 (Spring 1983): 50–72; Bruce E. Baker and Barbara Hahn, *The Cotton Kings: Capitalism and Corruption in Turn-of-the-Century New York and New Orleans* (New York: Oxford University Press, 2015).

6. The archival resources to support such work exist and are, if anything, more readily accessible than they were three or four decades ago. In the past few years, the records of the Liverpool Cotton Association, the Memphis Cotton Exchange, and the New York Cotton Exchange have all been made available in archives.

7. Peter Linebaugh, *The London Hanged: Crime and Civil Society in the Eighteenth Century*, 2nd ed. (London: Verso, 2003), xxiii.

8. This is part of a trend in business history to consider not just abstractions but materiality. For a discussion, see Kenneth J. Lipartito, "Connecting the Cultural and the Material in Business History," *Enterprise and Society* 14, no. 4 (December 2013): 696–702.

9. Eric Arnesen, "Race and Labour in a Southern US Port: New Orleans, 1860–1930," in *Dock Workers: International Explorations in Comparative Labour History, 1790–1970*, vol. 1, ed. Sam Davies, Colin J. Davis, David de Vries, Lex Heerma van Voss, Lidewij Hesselink, and Klaus Weinhauer (Aldershot, UK: Ashgate, 2000), 41.

10. "Covering the Cotton," *Anderson (SC) Intelligencer*, September 27, 1888, 2.

11. Thanks to Emily Moffat for drawing my attention to this image.

12. Thomas C. Holt, "Slave and Citizen in the Modern World: Rethinking Emancipation in the Twenty-First Century," in *After Slavery: Race, Labor, and Citizenship in the Reconstruction South*, ed. Bruce E. Baker and Brian Kelly (Gainesville: University Press of Florida, 2013), 25.

13. Linebaugh, *London Hanged*, 371–401.

14. "On 'Change,'" 15, 17.

15. Clarence Major, *Juba to Jive: A Dictionary of African-American Slang* (New York: Penguin, 1994), 112. The term *cooning* often seems to denote an unauthorized acquisition of something of negligible value that would not be missed by its owner. It seems to have most often been used in reference to watermelons. See Alex Haley, *The Autobiography of Malcolm X* (London: Penguin, 1968), 95; Donald Kranendonk, *Oostburg Rides Again* (n.p.: Xlibris, 2009), 76. In his memoir, the Civil War historian Bruce Catton describes picking up windfall apples in neighborhood orchards (which was acceptable) as compared to picking apples from the trees (which was wrong) before describing "older boys" going out "cooning" watermelons, which "did not seem like stealing." Bruce Catton, *Waiting for the Morning Train: An American Boyhood* (Detroit: Wayne State University Press, 1987), 57.

16. "Topic: Honesty and Dishonesty," *Dictionary of American Regional English*, http://dare .wisc.edu/survey-results/1965-1970/honesty-and-dishonesty/v5a (accessed September 21, 2017).

17. "Great Race," *Daily Picayune*, February 15, 1839, 2.

18. "Stolen Cotton," *Daily Picayune*, December 29, 1870, 2. Pilferage has long been a standard feature of waterfronts. For a detailed discussion of pilferage in antebellum Charleston, see Michael D. Thompson, *Working on the Dock of the Bay: Labor and Enterprise in an Antebellum Southern Port* (Columbia: University of South Carolina Press, 2015), 84–93. Other studies of waterfront pilferage include Michael Grüttner, "Working-Class Crime and the Labour Movement: Pilfering in the Hamburg Docks, 1888–1923," in *The German Working Class, 1888–1933: The Politics of Everyday Life*, ed. Richard J. Evans, 54–79 (London: Croom Helm, 1982); Gerald Mars, "Dock Pilferage," in *Deviance and Social Control*, ed. Paul Rock and Mary McIntosh, 209–228 (London: Tavistock, 1974).

19. "Cotton Thieves," *Daily Picayune*, June 27, 1879, 2.

20. "Levee Thieves," *Daily Picayune*, January 17, 1874, 1.

21. "Cotton Thief," *Daily Picayune*, December 12, 1873, 8; "Stealing Cotton," *Daily Picayune*, November 21, 1874, 8; "Stealing Cotton," *Daily Picayune*, January 30, 1875, 8; "Cotton Stealing," *Daily Picayune*, March 5, 1875, 8; "Cotton Thief," *Daily Picayune*, February 24, 1876, 2; "Larceny," *Daily Picayune*, November 14, 1877, 14. Obviously, it is also possible that more than one person named "Mary Sullivan" stole cotton.

22. "Levee Thieves," *Daily Picayune*, December 31, 1874, 8.

23. "Lower Recorder's Court," *New-Orleans Times*, June 10, 1864, 5; "The Courts," *New-Orleans Times*, April 26, 1866, 10; "Third District," *Daily Picayune*, December 22, 1866, 4; "Miscellaneous," *Daily Picayune*, July 26, 1873, 8; "More Dryades Street Robberies," *Daily Picayune*, March 9, 1872, 8; [untitled], *New Orleans Republican*, March 26, 1872, 5; "Robbery," *Daily Picayune*, December 2, 1872, 14; "Larceny on Burgundy Street," *Daily Picayune*, August 21, 1873, 8; "Larceny," *Daily Picayune*, November 9, 1873, 4; "The Latest Victim," *Daily Picayune*, January 25, 1874, 8.

24. "St. Louis Cotton Tactics," *Daily Picayune*, August 20, 1874, 3; "Actual Stock of Cotton," *Daily Picayune*, July 3, 1873, 6.

25. "St. Louis Cotton Tactics," 3; "Actual Stock of Cotton," 6; "Loose Cotton and Its Correction," *Daily Picayune*, October 11, 1874, 3; "The Waste of Cotton," *Daily Picayune*, June 10, 1874, 3; "Commerce and Finance," *Daily Picayune*, October 26, 1873, 10; "Cotton-Sampling," *Daily Appeal* (Memphis), February 4, 1880, 4.

26. "Cotton Stealing," *Daily News* (Charleston, SC), January 17, 1868, 3; [untitled], *Daily News* (Charleston, SC), December 23, 1872, 4.

27. "Two Bales of Cotton Stolen," *Morning Star* (Wilmington, NC), December 11, 1869, 1; "More of the Stolen Cotton Found," *Morning Star* (Wilmington, NC), December 12, 1869, 1.

28. "Our Fayetteville Correspondence," *Wilmington Herald*, October 10, 1865, 1; "Locals in Brief," *Public Ledger* (Memphis), March 24, 1868, 3.

29. R. H. Law, "Cotton Waste—Its Uses and Abuses," *Journal of the Textile Institute* 43, no. 7 (July 1952): 303–308; Eli Sowerbutts, *The Cotton Waste Dealers' Directory; being a complete list of waste dealers, and of all other trades connected therewith* (Manchester: Heywood and Son, 1883); "Cotton Waste: Note on Cotton Waste Trade with Particular Reference to the Making of Engine Cleaning Waste," LAB 11/628, National Archives, Kew, England.

30. A. Wilmore, *South Lancashire*, Cambridge County Geographies (Cambridge: Cambridge University Press, 1928), 84–86.

31. Andrew Morrison, *The Industries of New Orleans, Her Rank, Resources, Advantages, Trade, Commerce and Manufactures* (New Orleans, 1885), 63, 70, 104, 125; Wilmore, *South Lancashire*, 86.

32. Morrison, *Industries of New Orleans*, 63, 70, 104, 125.

33. Peter Walter, *The Felt Industry* (Oxford: Shire Publications, 2010), 13–17.

34. "Carbonic Acid Gas Ship Fire Annihilator," *Daily Picayune*, March 18, 1877, 6.

35. Advertisement, *New-Orleans Times*, March 6, 1886, 12; Morrison, *Industries of New Orleans*, 164. For details on mattress manufacture using cotton, with illustrations, see Virgil W. Dean and Ramon Powers, "'In No Way a Relief Set Up': The County Cotton Mattress Program in Kansas, 1940–1941," *Kansas History* 37, no. 4 (Winter 2014–2015): 243–255.

36. Dard Hunter, *Papermaking: The History and Technique of an Ancient Craft* (New York: Alfred A. Knopf, 1947), 529.

37. Edward Chauncey Worden, *Nitrocellulose Industry: A Compendium of the History, Chemistry, Manufacture, Commercial Application, and Analysis of Nitrates, Acetates, and Xanthates of Cellulose as Applied to the Peaceful Arts; with a Chapter on Gun-Cotton, Smokeless Powder, and Explosive Cellulose Nitrates*, vol. 1 (London: Constable, 1911), 11–16; J. B. Littlewood, "Nitro-Cellulose," *Scientific American* 65, no. 7 (August 15, 1891), 97; "Compressed Gun Cotton," *Scientific American* 27, no. 6 (August 10, 1872), 80; "Uses Of Gun-Cotton," *Scientific American* 23, no. 23 (December 3, 1870), 361.

38. *Soards' New Orleans City Directory* (New Orleans, 1879), 771.

39. "In the Byways," *Daily Picayune*, June 1, 1873, 6.

40. "Home Industries," *Daily Picayune*, August 19, 1873, 3.

41. *Soards' New Orleans City Directory*, 821.

42. "Home Industries," *Daily Picayune*, August 19, 1873, 3.

43. Zsuzsa Gille, "Actor Networks, Modes of Production, and Waste Regimes: Reassembling the Macro-Social," *Environment and Planning* 42 (2010): 1049–1050.

44. Susan Strasser, *Waste and Want: A Social History of Trash* (New York: Henry Holt, 1999); Wendy A. Woloson, "'Fence-ing Lessons': Child Junkers and the Commodification of Scrap in the Long Nineteenth Century," *Business History*, March 2017, 1–35.

45. D. A. Tompkins, *Cotton Mill, Commercial Features: A Textbook for the Use of Textile Schools and Investors* (Charlotte, NC: D. A. Tompkins, 1899), 54.

46. *Soards' New Orleans City Directory*, 752; "Home Industries," *New-Orleans Times*, August 19, 1873, 3.

47. This description is tentative and based on a number of fragmentary accounts of pickeries in New Orleans, including "By C. E. Girardey & Co.," *Daily Picayune*, December 3, 1865, 6; advertisement, *Daily Picayune*, August 29, 1868, 5; "City Council," *New Orleans Crescent*, August 27, 1868, 4; "Sunstroke," *New-Orleans Times*, June 30, 1871, 6. The most detailed description, and the source of the quotation, is "Home Industries," *New-Orleans Times*, August 19, 1873, 3.

48. "Home Industries," 3.

49. Morrison, *Industries of New Orleans*, 105, 126.

50. "Home Industries," 3. See also the listings for each year in *Soards' New Orleans City Directory*. The number and location of pickeries varied somewhat over this period, but in general they remained concentrated in what is now considered the Lower Garden District, with a few outliers elsewhere.

51. Advertisement, *Public Ledger* (Memphis), December 7, 1871; [untitled], *Greenville (MS) Times*, August 6, 1887, 3.

52. "The New Orleans Cotton Exchange: Sixth Annual Meeting," *Daily Picayune*, November 30, 1876, 2.

53. Ibid.

54. See, for instance, "Country Damage to Cotton," *Daily Picayune*, August 6, 1874, 3; "Country Damage to Cotton," *Daily Picayune*, August 19, 1874, 3.

55. "'Country Damaged' Cotton," *Daily Picayune*, October 19, 1874, 8.

56. "Cotton, the New Orleans Exchange and the Liverpool Brokers," *Daily Picayune*, June 18, 1875, 3; "The Cotton Exchange," *Daily Picayune*, December 2, 1875, 2.

57. "The New Orleans Cotton Exchange: Sixth Annual Meeting," 2.

58. "Pilfering Loose Cotton," *Daily Picayune*, February 11, 1875, 3; "The Loose Cotton Question," *Daily Picayune*, February 14, 1875, 7.

59. "The New Orleans Cotton Exchange: Sixth Annual Meeting," 2.

60. *Soards' New Orleans City Directory.*

61. Naturally, the newspaper itself is not extant for this period, but much of the substance of the criticism can be gleaned from other newspapers' responses.

62. [untitled], *Atlanta Constitution*, July 23, 1885, 4.

63. "Cotton Prospects of New Orleans," *Daily Picayune*, August 9, 1885, 3.

64. "Cotton Abuses," *Daily Picayune*, August 14, 1885, 2.

65. Scott P. Marler, *The Merchants' Capital: New Orleans and the Political Economy of the Nineteenth-Century South* (New York: Cambridge University Press, 2013), 206–230.

66. Woodman, *King Cotton and His Retainers*, xvi.

67. Ibid., xvii; Baker and Hahn, *Cotton Kings*.

Chapter 4. Jim Crow's Cut

1. "An Outrage," *Daily Picayune* (New Orleans), September 13, 1874. The paper called the waterway Bayou Bonticau, which does not exist. Bayou Bonfouca does and lies within the area described in the article. The *Daily Picayune* identified the man as "S. Poitevent," which was certainly a reference to Samuel Poitevent. Samuel was the son of Poitevent and Favre president W. J. Poitevent and was listed as living in St. Tammany's Ward 3 in the 1900 census, an area that also included individuals who appeared in the Bonfouca census tract in the 1870 census. See 1900 US Federal Census [database] (Provo, UT: Ancestry.com Operations, 2004), Police Jury Ward 3, Saint Tammany, Louisiana; Roll: 583; Page: 1B; Enumeration District: 008, Family History Library microfilm: 1240583.

2. While this map represents the state of the New Orleans Great Northern Railroad in 1910, it includes details of most of the waterways and railroads mentioned in this essay. The old route of Poitevent and Favre's East Louisiana Railroad appears as the line from Bonfouca to Mandeville in St. Tammany Parish. The Kentwood and Eastern Railroad appears between Kentwood and Hackley in Washington Parish. Bayou Bonfouca is not depicted. It flows into Lake Pontchartrain from the north near the Bonfouca rail stop.

3. On Poitevent and Favre's shipments abroad, see "The Pearl River Country," *The (Jackson, MS) Comet*, April 5, 1879; and "Resources of the Pine Woods," *Daily Picayune*, February 27, 1876. On the skilled population of African American sailors and ship carpenters on the coast, see Etienne William Maxson, *The Progress of the Races* (Nashville, TN: McQuiddy Printing, 1955), 10–12, 16–20.

4. The Piney Woods is a belt of longleaf, loblolly, and slash pine that stretches along the southern coastal plain of Texas to Virginia, including the forests surrounding Bayou Bonfouca. Law-

rence S. Early, *Looking for Longleaf: The Fall and Rise of an American Forest* (Chapel Hill: University of North Carolina Press, 2004), 1–2, 79–83; Bill Finch, Beth Maynor Young, Rhett Johnson, and John C. Hall, *Longleaf, Far as the Eye Can See: A New Vision of America's Richest Forest* (Chapel Hill: University of North Carolina Press, 2012), 69–77; Albert G. Way, *Conserving Southern Longleaf: Herbert Stoddard and the Rise of Ecological Land Management* (Athens: University of Georgia Press, 2011), 60–62, 81–142.

5. On the "cut out and get out" narrative, see William Boyd, *The Slain Wood: Papermaking and Its Environmental Consequences in the American South* (Baltimore: Johns Hopkins University Press, 2015), 3–6, 20–23; James E. Fickle, *Mississippi Forests and Forestry* (Jackson: University Press of Mississippi, 2001), 92–119.

6. William Cronon, *Nature's Metropolis: Chicago and the Great West* (New York: W. W. Norton, 1991), 85 (quote), 224. For a critique of the "logic of capital" concept, particularly its tendency to obscure "economic, social, and cultural diversity," see Paul S. Sutter, "The World with Us: The State of American Environmental History," *Journal of American History* 100, no. 1 (June 2013): 114–115.

7. On the transformative power of contracts, mortgages, and record keeping, see Cronon, *Nature's Metropolis*; Michael Zakim and Gary J. Kornblith, eds., *Capitalism Takes Command: The Social Transformation of Nineteenth-Century America* (Chicago: University of Chicago Press, 2010); Edward E. Baptist, *The Half Has Never Been Told: Slavery and the Making of American Capitalism* (New York: Basic, 2014); Caitlin Rosenthal, *Accounting for Slavery: Masters and Management* (Cambridge, MA: Harvard University Press, 2018).

8. This essay responds to Kenneth Lipartito's call to reintegrate "mentality and materiality" in business history by moving beyond the field's tendency to focus on corporate strategy and corporate structure; see Kenneth Lipartito, "Connecting the Cultural and the Material in Business History," *Enterprise and Society* 14, no. 4 (December 2013): 686.

9. On New Deal scholarship and Piney Woods agriculture, see Rupert B. Vance, *Human Geography of the South: A Study in Regional Resources and Human Adequacy* (Chapel Hill: University of North Carolina Press, 1922), 109–144; Howard W. Odum, *Southern Regions of the United States* (Chapel Hill: University of North Carolina Press, 1936), 80–83, 575–576. On the relationship between agriculture, clear-cutting, and reforestation, see Edward L. Ayers, *The Promise of the New South: Life After Reconstruction* (New York: Oxford University Press, 1992), 123–130; Thomas D. Clark, *The Greening of the South: The Recovery of Land and Forest* (Lexington: University Press of Kentucky, 1984), 54–72; Boyd, *Slain Wood*, 1–6.

10. Samuel C. Hyde Jr., *Pistols and Politics: The Dilemma of Democracy in Louisiana's Florida Parishes, 1810–1899* (Baton Rouge: Louisiana State University Press, 1996), 17–45; Claire Strom, *Making Catfish Bait out of Government Boys: The Fight Against Cattle Ticks and the Transformation of the Yeoman South* (Athens: University of Georgia Press, 2009), 43–75.

11. For classic takes on southern herding practices that emphasize British upland and Scots-Irish "Cracker Culture," see Frank Lawrence Owsley, *Plain Folk of the Old South* (Baton Rouge: Louisiana State University Press, 1949), 90–132; Grady McWhiney, *Cracker Culture: Celtic Folkways in the Old South* (Tuscaloosa: University of Alabama Press, 1988), 51–79; David Hackett Fischer, *Albion's Seed: Four British Folkways in America* (New York: Oxford University Press, 1989), 757–783. For an overview of white herdsmen in southeast Louisiana that has greatly influenced this study, see Hyde, *Pistols and Politics*, 17–45. For a very different view that places African herding traditions at the heart of Louisiana's open range herding culture, see Andrew Sluyter,

Black Ranching Frontiers: African Cattle Herders of the Atlantic World, 1500–1900 (New Haven, CT: Yale University Press, 2012), 61–95.

12. John C. Willis, *Forgotten Time: The Yazoo-Mississippi Delta After the Civil War* (Charlottesville: University Press of Virginia, 2000), 41 (quote), 41–75.

13. Mark Schultz, *The Rural Face of White Supremacy: Beyond Jim Crow* (Urbana: University of Illinois Press, 2005), 49–56; Adrien Montieth Petty, *Standing Their Ground: Small Farmers in North Carolina Since the Civil War* (Chapel Hill: University of North Carolina Press, 2013), 44–54.

14. "St. Tammany," *New Orleans Republican*, July 14, 1875.

15. Ibid.

16. Nollie Wade Hickman, *Mississippi Harvest: Lumbering in the Longleaf Pine Belt, 1840–1915* (Jackson: University Press of Mississippi, 1962), 52; 42 Cong. Rec., 2162 (1875) (quote). President Grant reaffirmed this authority by executive order on July 27, 1875. See "Contractor Eads Regulated by the President," *New Orleans Republican*, July 29, 1875.

17. "Cutting Timber for the Jetties," *New Orleans Republican*, July 17, 1875.

18. "The Timber Cutting at Bonfouca," *New Orleans Republican*, July 21, 1875.

19. "St. Tammany," *New Orleans Republican*, July 14, 1875 (quote). For examples of the real estate held by the "mulatto" households of sailors, see "United States to Raymond Carriere," June 1, 1858, in US Bureau of Land Management, General Land Office Records, https://glorecords.blm .gov/details/patent/default.aspx?accession=LA0020___.446&docClass=STA&sid=fw1ncnlw .ui5#patentDetailsTabIndex=0; 1870 US Federal Census [database] (Provo, UT: Ancestry.com Operations, Inc., 2009), Ward 3, St Tammany, Louisiana; Roll: M593_532; Page: 22A; Family History Library Film: 55203. Carriere is one of several residents listed as white with a mulatto family in the 1870 census and as mulatto in the 1880 census. For an example of one of the laborers who took up homesteads in the 1870s, see "United States to Henry Beals," July 23, 1880, in US Bureau of Land Management, General Land Office Records, https://glorecords.blm.gov/details/patent /default.aspx?accession=LA0330___.275&docClass=STA&sid=po3lmljx.rac.

20. Eric Arnesen, *Waterfront Workers of New Orleans: Race, Class, and Politics, 1863–1923* (New York: Oxford University Press, 1991), 21–25, 94–95.

21. Michael Williams, *Americans and Their Forests: A Historical Geography* (Cambridge: Cambridge University Press, 1989), 240 (quote).

22. Hickman, *Mississippi Harvest*, 53; "St. Tammany," *Daily Picayune*, February 13, 1888 (quote).

23. On the etymology of wilderness, see William Cronon, "The Trouble with Wilderness; or, Getting back to the Wrong Nature," in *Uncommon Ground: Rethinking the Human Place in Nature* (New York: W. W. Norton, 1996), 70–71, 80–81.

24. On conflicts over fencing between planters and small farmers in the old South, see Jack Temple Kirby, *Mockingbird Song: Ecological Landscapes of the South* (Chapel Hill: University of North Carolina Press, 2006), 129–131.

25. Petty, *Standing Their Ground*, 54–74; Steven Hahn, "Hunting, Fishing, and Foraging: Common Rights and Class Relations in the Postbellum South," *Radical History Review* 26, no. 37 (October 1982): 37–64. Van Woodward, *The Origins of the New South, 1877–1913* (Baton Rouge: Louisiana State University Press, 1951), 85; Ayers, *Promise of the New South*, 189–190.

26. Poitevent & Favre Lbr. Co. to Great Southern Lumber Co., March 6, 1906, Conveyance Book 10, Washington Parish Clerk of Court, Franklinton, Louisiana (hereinafter cited as

WPCOC), 660–662 (quotes); Poitevent & Favre Lbr. Co. to New Orleans G.N.R.R. Co., March 6, 1906, Conveyance Book 10, WPCOC, 662–663.

27. "Notes About the Wilson and Magee Families," Horace Mann Bond Papers, Part 2: Subject Files, 1926–1971 (microfilm), frame 9, in Bostock Library, Duke University, Durham, North Carolina (hereinafter cited as Bond Papers); Horace Mann Bond, "Forty Acres and A Mule," in *The Star Creek Papers: Washington Parish and the Lynching of Jerome Wilson*, ed. Adam Fairclough (Athens: University of Georgia Press, 1997), 98–99; Fleet Magee to Green Magee, January 10, 1880, Conveyance Book 1, 457–458, WPCOC; J. W. Magee to Green Magee, December 16, 1899, Conveyance Book 3, 476–477, WPCOC. "The First Lynching of 1935," Bond Papers, Part 2, reel 29, frame 1316.

28. "Notes About the Wilson and Magee Families," Bond Papers, Part 2, reel 30, frame 9. On the upland soils between the Bogue Chitto River's tributaries, see A. C. Anderson, C. B. Manifold, J. Ambrose Elwell, F. A. Hayes, Robert Wildermuth, and E. W. Knobel, "Soil Survey of Washington Parish, Louisiana" in *Field Operations of the Bureau of Soils, 1922* (Washington, DC: U.S. Department of Agriculture, 1928), 356, 361.

29. "Notes about the Wilson and Magee Families," Bond Papers, Part 2, reel 30, frame 9; United States to James Hart, June 23, 1896, US General Land Office Records, 1796–1907 [database] (Provo, UT: Ancestry.com Operations, 2008), frame 1052; United States to George Magee, October 22, 1896, US General Land Office Records, 1796–1907, frame 1073.

30. Wilson's knowledge of his neighbors was remarkable, although he did tend to round up homestead acreages to multiples of eighty. Hart's and Magee's claims thus appear in Bond's notes as 160 acres apiece. "Notes About the Wilson and Magee Families," Bond Papers, Part 2, reel 30, frame 9. On the methodological problems associated with determining exactly when landowners filed homestead claims, see Claude F. Oubre, *Forty Acres and a Mule* (Baton Rouge: Louisiana State University Press, 1978), 135–136.

31. Oubre, *Forty Acres and a Mule*, 135–136; "Notes About the Wilson and Magee Families," Bond Papers, Part 2, reel 30, frame 8.

32. "Notes About the Wilson and Magee Families," Bond Papers, Part 2, reel 30, frame 8.

33. "Notes About the Wilson and Magee Families," Bond Papers, Part 2, reel 30, frames 14 and 29 (quotes). On changing logging techniques, see Williams, *Americans and Their Forests*, 244–285.

34. Roy V. Scott, *Eugene Beverly Ferris and Agricultural Science in the Lower South* (Oxford, MS: Center for the Study of Southern Culture, 1991), 52–109; E. B. Ferris, *Clearing Pine Lands*, Mississippi Agricultural Experiment Station Bulletin No. 118 (Starkville: Mississippi Agricultural Experiment Station, 1909), 3–11.

35. "Notes About the Wilson and Magee Families," Bond Papers, Part 2, reel 30, frame 14 (first quote); "Mr. John Wilson's Account of What Happened, July 21, 1934," Bond Papers, Part 2, reel 29, frames 1289–1290 (quote).

36. E. B. Ferris, *Sugar Cane for Syrup Making*, Mississippi Agricultural Experiment Station Bulletin No. 199 (Starkville: Mississippi Agricultural Experiment Station, 1921), 3–20 (quotes).

37. Courtenay De Kalb, *Bogalusa: Perpetual Timber Supply Through Reforestation as Basis for Industrial Permanency of Bogalusa*, (Baltimore, MD: Manufacturers Record, 1921), 2. "Abita Springs," *St. Tammany (LA) Farmer*, February 23, 1907; "Farmers Organize," *Franklinton (LA) Era-Leader*, May 5, 1921 (quote).

38. On "neighbor-to-neighbor capitalism" in the antebellum period, see Bonnie Martin, "Neighbor-to-Neighbor Capitalism: Local Credit Networks and the Mortgaging of Slaves," in

Slavery's Capitalism: A New History of American Economic Development, ed. Sven Beckert and Seth Rockman, 107–121 (Philadelphia: University of Pennsylvania Press, 2016).

39. "Q: Beginning of the Wilson Family," Bond Papers, Part 2, reel 29, frame 1305 (first quote); "Notes About Wilson and Magee Families," Bond Papers, Part 2, reel 30, frame 8 (second quote).

40. "Notes About Wilson and Magee Families," Bond Papers, Part 2, reel 30, frame 8.

41. United States to Jacob Elzey, January 28, 1890, US General Land Office Records, 1796–1907, frame 799; "Notes about Wilson and Magee Families," Bond Papers, Part 2, reel 30, frame 8 (first and second quotes) and frame 9 (third quote). On the Banner Lumber Company and Kentwood and Eastern Railroad agreements, see WCPCOC, book 3, 320–343, 372–395.

42. United States to Jacob Elzey, January 28, 1890, US General Land Office Records, 1796–1907, frame 799 (first three quotes); Jacob Ellzy to Banner Lumber Co. Ltd., WCPCOC, book 3, 379–380 (last two quotes).

43. "Notes About Wilson and Magee Families," Bond Papers, Part 2, reel 30, frame 8.

44. United States to William J. Alford, January 20, 1883, US General Land Office Records, 1796–1907, frame 738. Petition for Plaintiff, *William J. Alford* v. *Kentwood and Eastern Railway Company*, no. 1504, WPCOC (quotes); Judgment, *William J. Alford* v. *Brooks Scanlon Co., et al*, no. 1874, WPCOC.

45. Michael Zakim and Gary J. Kornblith, "Introduction: An American Revolutionary Tradition," in Zakim and Kornblith, *Capitalism Takes Command*, 5.

46. "1931 Annual Narrative: Washington Parish, Franklinton, Louisiana—Myrtis A. Magee, Local Agent," in Agricultural Extension Service Records: Narrative and Statistical Reports of Administrative and Supervisory Work with Negroes/Assistant County and Home Agents for Work with Negroes (hereinafter cited as Extension Service Records), box 66, folder 23, LSU Special Collections, Louisiana State University, Baton Rouge. "Annual Report of County Extension Workers for the State of Louisiana: Report of T. J. Jordan, Assistant State Agent in Negro Work, December 1, 1930–December 1, 1931," Extension Service Records, box 60, folder 385.

47. Petty, *Standing Their Ground*, 54.

Chapter 5. In the Shadow of Incorporation

1. W. E. Gortner to Hon. T. B. Catron, January 28, 1905, Series 103, Box 22, Folder 1, Thomas B. Catron Papers (CP), Center for Southwest Research, University Libraries, University of New Mexico.

2. This history of hidden capitalism builds upon decades of New Mexico land-grant scholarship, including but not limited to Charles L. Briggs and John R. Van Ness, eds., *Land, Water, and Culture: New Perspectives on Hispanic Land Grants*, New Mexico Land Grant Series (Albuquerque: University of New Mexico, 1987); David Benavides, "Lawyer-Induced Partitioning of New Mexican Land Grants: An Ethical Travesty" (master's thesis, Department of History, University of New Mexico, 1990); Malcolm Ebright, *The Tierra Amarilla Grant: A History of Chicanery* (Santa Fe, NM: Center for Land Grant Studies, 1993); Malcolm Ebright, *Land Grants and Lawsuits in Northern New Mexico*, ed. John Van Ness, New Mexico Land Grant Series (Albuquerque: University of New Mexico Press, 1994); Roxanne Amanda Dunbar, *Land Tenure in Northern New Mexico: An Historical Perspective* (PhD diss., UCLA, 1974); Phillip B. Gonzales, "Struggle for Survival: The Hispanic Land Grants of New Mexico, 1848–2001," *Agricultural History* 77 (Spring 2003): 293–324; Maria Montoya, *Translating Property: The Maxwell Land Grant and the Conflict over Land in the American West, 1840–1900* (Lawrence: University of Kansas Press, 2002); Manuel Garcia Y Griego, "Persistence and Disintegration: New Mexico's Community Land Grants

in Historical Perspective," *Natural Resource Journal* 48 (Fall 2008): 847–856; David Correia, *Properties of Violence: Law and Land Grant Struggle in Northern New Mexico*, Geographies of Justice and Social Transformation (Athens: University of Georgia Press, 2013).

3. W. E. Gortner to Hon. T. B. Catron, January 28, 1905, Series 103, Box 22, Folder 1, CP.

4. W. E. Gortner to TBC, October 13, 1902, Series 103, Box 16, Folder 1, CP; A. A. Jones to TBC, February 7, 1903, Series 103, Box 16, Folder 5, CP; A. A. Jones to TBC, March 18, 1903, Series 103, Box 17, Folder 1, CP; William Gortner to Bob Gortner, October 15, 1904, Series 103, Box 21, Folder 3, CP; William Gortner to TBC, October 21, 1904, Series 103, Box 21, Folder 3, CP.

5. For the evolution of capitalism in New Mexico, see Herbert O. Brayer, *William Blackmore: The Spanish-Mexican Land Grants of New Mexico and Colorado, 1863–1878, Volume 1: A Case Study in the Economic Development of the West* (Denver: Bradford Robinson, 1948); Scott Fritz, "Merchants and Modernity: Market Transformation in New Mexico and the Southwest, 1865–1929" (PhD diss., University of Northern Arizona, 2004).

6. For consideration of a group's "legibility" within the eyes of the state, see James C. Scott, *Seeing Like a State: How Certain Schemes to Improve the Human Condition Have Failed* (New Haven, CT: Yale University Press, 1998), 2.

7. Clark S. Knowlton, "Violence in New Mexico: A Sociological Perspective," *California Law Review* 58, no. 5 (October 1970): 1054–1084.

8. Sarah Deutsch, *No Separate Refuge: Culture, Class, and Gender on an Anglo-Hispanic Frontier in the American Southwest, 1880–1940* (New York: Oxford University Press, 1987), 24. As argued by Deutsch, "Socially as well as economically marginalized by the new order, the economic and social foundations of their culture threatened by new Anglo institutions of industry, government, and education, many Hispanics organized along ethnic lines to resist the onslaught, control it, or even turn it back."

9. Rosemary E. Ommer and Nancy J. Turner. "Informal Rural Economies in History," *Labour / Le Travail* 53 (Spring 2004): 127–157.

10. Marshall Sahlins, "Cosmologies of Capitalism: The Trans-Pacific Sector of 'The World System,'" *Proceedings of the British Academy*, 74 (1988): 1–51.

11. Leonard J. Arrington, *The Changing Economic Structure of the Mountain West, 1850–1950* (Logan: Utah State University Press, 1963).

12. Max L. Moorhead, *New Mexico's Royal Road: Trade and Travel on the Chihuahua Trail* (Norman: University of Oklahoma Press, 1958); Susan Calafate Boyle, *Los Capitalistas: Hispano Merchants and the Santa Fe Trade* (Albuquerque: University of New Mexico Press, 1997); William Patrick O'Brien, *Merchants of Independence: International Trade on the Santa Fe Trail, 1827–1860* (Kirksville, MO: Truman State University Press, 2014); Samuel Truett and Elliot Young, eds., *Continental Crossroads: Remapping U.S.-Mexico Borderlands History* (Durham, NC: Duke University Press, 2004).

13. Natale A. Zappia, "Indigenous Borderlands: Livestock, Captivity, and Power in the Far West," *Pacific Historical Review* 81, no. 2 (May 2012): 193–220; Pekka Hämäläinen, *The Comanche Empire*, Lamar Series in Western History (New Haven, CT: Yale University Press, 2007); Montoya, *Translating Property*; Charles L. Kenner, *The Comanchero Frontier: A History of New Mexican-Plains Indians Relations* (Norman: University of Oklahoma Press, 1994); Frances Leon Swadesh, *Los Primeros Pobladores: Hispanic Americans of the Ute Frontier* (Notre Dame, IN: University of Notre Dame Press, 1974). Regarding the use of the term *Nuevomexicano,* consider the following for differing uses of terminology: Phillip B. Gonzales, *Política: Nuevomexicanos and American Political Incorporation, 1821–1910* (Lincoln: Nebraska University Press, 2016); Erlinda

Gonzales-Berry and David R. Maciel, eds., *The Contested Homeland: A Chicano History of New Mexico* (Albuquerque: University of New Mexico Press, 2000); Doris Meyer, *Speaking for Themselves: Neomexicano Cultural Identity and the Spanish-Language Press, 1880–1920* (Albuquerque: University of New Mexico Press, 1996); Deutsch, *No Separate Refuge.*

14. Ommer and Turner, "Informal Rural Economies," 129–130.

15. Two exemplary discussions of the mixed results of state and market attempts at incorporation include Steven Stoll, *Ramp Hollow: The Ordeal of Appalachia* (New York: Hill and Wang, 2017); and James C. Scott, *The Art of Not Being Governed: An Anarchist History of Upland Southeast Asia* (New Haven, CT: Yale University Press, 2009).

16. Deutsch, *No Separate Refuge*; Suzanne Forrest, *The Preservation of the Village: New Mexico's Hispanics and the New Deal*, ed. John R. Van Ness, New Mexico Land Grant Series (Albuquerque: University of New Mexico Press, 1989).

17. Victor Westphall, *Mercedes Reales: Hispanic Land Grants of the Upper Rio Grande Region* (Albuquerque: University of New Mexico Press, 1983).

18. See David Benavides and Ryan Golten, "Righting the Record: A Response to the GAO's 2004 Report Treaty of Guadalupe Hidalgo: Findings and Possible Options Regarding Longstanding Community Land Grant Claims in New Mexico," *Natural Resources Journal* 48, no. 4 (2008): 857–926.

19. William DeBuys, *Enchantment and Exploitation: The Life and Hard Times of a New Mexico Mountain Range* (Albuquerque: University of New Mexico Press, 1985), 256–257.

20. Pedro Perea, from Washington, D.C., to Hon. T. B. Catron, January 9, 1900, and December 7, 1900, Series 103, Box 9, Folder 4 CP; and Box 11, Folder 5, CP, respectively.

21. For examples of the transformations in land-grant ownership and the framing of Nuevomexicano residents as squatters, see Montoya, *Translating Property*; W. Turrentine Jackson, "The Chavez Land Grant: A Scottish Investment in New Mexico, 1881–1940," *Pacific Historical Review* 21, no. 4 (November 1952): 349–366; William DeBuys, "Fractions of Justice: A Legal and Social History of the Las Trampas Land Grant, New Mexico" *New Mexico Historial Review* 56 (January 1981): 71–97, 89.

22. Frank Clark to T. B. Catron, March 15, 1907, Series 103, Box 28, Folder 2, CP; William E. Gortner to Robert, August 18, 1902, Series 103, Box 15, Folder 4, CP.

23. William E. Gortner to T. B. Catron, October 13, 1902, Series 103, Box 16, Folder 1, CP.

24. DeBuys, *Enchantment and Exploitation*, 11–12.

25. Forrest, *Preservation of the Village*, 21. Suzanne Forrest argues that "the loss of so much range land, along with the rapid expansion of the commercial livestock business, had the effect of imprisoning both the Hispanic and Indian populations of New Mexico upon a land base entirely inadequate to their needs." It should be no surprise then to consider the numerous ways that Nuevomexicanos and Native Americans resisted the economic and cultural encroachment. Also see Clark S. Knowlton, "The Mora Land Grant: A New Mexican Tragedy," in *Spanish and Mexican Land Grants and the Law*, ed. Malcolm Ebright, 59–73 (Manhattan, KS: Sunflower University Press, in cooperation with the Center for Land Grants Studies, 1989).

26. On the importance of the forest ecology for rural subsistence households, see Stoll, *Ramp Hollow*, 106.

27. David Corriea, "Taking Timber, Earth, and Water: The Denver and Rio Grande Railroad and the Struggle for New Mexico's Land Grants," *Natural Resource Journal* 48 (Fall 2008): 949–962.

28. See the contribution herein: Owen Hyman, "Jim Crow's Cut: White Supremacy and the Destruction of Black Capital in the Forests of the Deep South," in *Capitalism's Hidden Worlds*, ed. Kenneth Lipartito and Lisa Jacobson, 81–98 (Philadelphia: University of Pennsylvania Press, 2019).

29. Richard Dunn, Mgr, Mora Timber Co., to Thomas B. Catron, December 30, 1902, Series 103, Box 16, Folder 3, CP.

30. Richard Dunn, Mgr, Mora Timber Co., to Thomas B. Catron, February 10, 1903, Series 103, Box 16, Folder 5, CP.

31. Ommer and Turner, "Informal Rural Economies," 128.

32. Historians of New Mexico, as well as those of cohesive rural communities, have directed our attention to the importance of social networks as stabilizing and even empowering agents for otherwise marginal populations. See Deutsch, *No Separate Refuge*; Forrest, *Preservation of the Village*; Swadesh, *Los Primeros Pobladores*; Ommer and Turner, "Informal Rural Economies."

33. On New Mexico's long struggle for statehood, see David V. Holtby, *Forty-Seventh Star: New Mexico's Struggle for Statehood* (Norman: University of Oklahoma Press, 2012); Robert Larson, *New Mexico's Quest for Statehood, 1846–1912* (Albuquerque: University of New Mexico Press, 1968).

34. J. A. Carruth, *Business Directory of Arizona and New Mexico, for 1897* (Las Vegas, NM: Daily Examiner Printing and Binding Establishment, 1897), Henry Huntington Library, San Marino, CA. For regional afflictions of national depression, see Lance E. Davis, "The Investment Market, 1870–1914: The Evolution of a National Market," *Journal of Economic History* 25 (September 1965): 355–399.

35. More than sufficient evidence detailing the intense difficulties of the debt market for New Mexico after the Panic of 1893 can be found in the bank records and correspondence of the William Parish Papers, 1700–1964, Center for Southwest Research, University Libraries, University of New Mexico.

36. For history of Nuevomexicano resistance, including the activities of Las Gorras Blancas, see David Correia, "Retribution Will Be Their Reward: New Mexico's Las Gorras Blancas and the Fight for the Las Vegas Commons," *Radical History Review* 108 (Fall 2010): 49–72; Robert J. Rosenbaum, *Mexicano Resistance in the Southwest: "The Sacred Right of Self Preservation"* (Dallas: Southern Methodist University Press, 1998).

37. Richard Wells Bradfute, *The Court of Private Land Claims: The Adjudication of Spanish and Mexican Land Grant Titles, 1891–1904* (Albuquerque: University of New Mexico Press, 1975).

38. Approximately the size of the state of Alabama in rejected acreage.

39. Benavides, "Righting the Record."

40. Ebright, *Land Grants and Lawsuits*, 45–46.

41. Knowlton, "Violence in New Mexico," 1070.

42. The listed national forests are found in Box 57, Folders 1–7; and the acreage in "Address of Governor O.A. Larrazolo of New Mexico Before the Joint Senate and House Committees on Public Lands," September 1919, Box 25, Folder 2, Papers of Albert B. Fall (FP), 1887–1941, Henry Huntington Library, San Marino, CA.

43. William G. Ritch, *A Complete Business Directory of New Mexico, and Gazetteer of the Territory for 1882* (Santa Fe: New Mexican Printing and Publishing Company, 1882), 214–218.

44. Charles F. Kanen, *Kanen's New Mexico Corporation Laws: Containing the Compiled Laws of 1897 and All Subsequent Session laws, Including 1909, with Amendments and Repeals* (Albuquerque: Press of the Morning Journal, 1910), 747.

45. Kanen, *Kanen's New Mexico Corporation Laws*, 698.

46. William G. Ritch, *New Mexico Blue Book, 1882* (Santa Fe: New Mexico Printing, 1882); Kanen, *Kanen's New Mexico Corporation Laws*.

47. Holtby, *Forty-Seventh Star*, 245–246.

48. David V. Holtby, "Historical Reflections on New Mexico Statehood: New Mexico's Economy; A Case Study of Mining to 1940," *New Mexico Historical Review* 88, no. 1 (Winter 2013): 65–94, 65, 68.

49. State of New Mexico, *First Annual Report of the State Corporation Commission for the Period Commencing January 16, 1912 and Ending December 31, 1912* (Albuquerque: Albright & Anderson, 1913).

50. Larry Schweikart, "Early Banking in New Mexico from the Civil War to the Roaring Twenties," *New Mexico Historical Review* 63 (January 1988): 1–24, 17; Larry S. López, "The Rio Puerco Irrigation Company," *New Mexico Historical Review* 57, no. 1 (January 1982): 63–79.

51. Marc Simmons, *Albuquerque: A Narrative History* (Albuquerque: University of New Mexico Press, 1982). As mentioned in the introduction, William E. Gortner's law office in East Las Vegas presents an example of this trend.

52. *Polk's Arizona and New Mexico Pictorial State Gazetteer and Business Directory: First Statehood Edition, 1912–1913* (St. Paul, MN: R. L. Polk, 1912); Bryan W. Turo, "Politics, Identity, and Statehood at the New Mexico Territorial Fair, 1881–1912," *New Mexico Historical Review* 87 (Fall 2012): 391–421.

53. *Polk's Arizona*, 586. The list included Alamogordo, Albuquerque, Artesia, Aztec, Carlsbad, Deming, East Las Vegas, Farmington, Gallup, Las Cruces, Mora, Raton, San Marcial, Santa Fe, Silver City, and Tucumcari.

54. Ralph Emerson Twitchell, *New Mexico.: Some Reasons and a Plea for Statehood* (Santa Fe, NM: New Mexican Printing, 1900).

55. Acting Secretary of the Interior to the Governor of New Mexico, June 29, 1907, Annual Reports, Territories, New Mexico, Department of the Interior, Office of the Secretary, Record Group 126, Office of Territories Classified Files, 1907–1951, NARA II.

56. Twitchell, *Some Reasons*, 2, 8.

57. Address of Governor O. A. Larrazolo of New Mexico Before the Joint Senate and House Committees on Public Lands, c. September 1919, Box 25, Folder 2, FP.

58. In their characterization of the informal economy, Alejandro Portes and William Haller represent one of its core paradoxes in similar terms, arguing that "the more credible the state enforcement apparatus is, the more likely its record-keeping mechanism will miss the actual extent of the informal economy and, hence, the feebler the basis for developing policies to address it." This certainly resonates in terms of New Mexico, especially during the early decades of the twentieth century. Alejandro Portes and William Haller, "The Informal Economy," in *The Handbook of Economic Sociology*, 2nd ed., ed. Neil J. Smelser and Richard Swedberg, (Princeton, NJ: Princeton University Press, 2005), 418.

59. Suzanne Forrest, "A Trail of Tangled Titles: Mining, Land Speculation, and the Dismemberment of the San Antonio de las Huerta Land Grant," *New Mexico Historical Review* 71, no. 4 (Fall 1996): 361–393; Corriea, "Taking Timber"; Stephen Bogener, "Land, Speculation, and Manipulation on the Pecos," *Great Plains Quarterly*, 28, no. 3 (Summer 2008): 209–229.

60. Hugh C. Calkins, "Village Dependence on Migratory Labor in the Upper Rio Grande Area," United States Department of Agriculture Soil Conservation Services, Conservation Economic Series, no. 20, Region Bulletin 47 (1937); Deutsch, *No Separate Refuge*, 10.

61. Charles Montgomery, *The Spanish Redemption: Heritage, Power, and Loss on New Mexico's Upper Rio Grande* (Berkeley: University of California Press, 2002); Hal Rothman, *The Culture of Tourism, the Tourism of Culture: Selling the Past to the Present in the American Southwest* (Albuquerque: University of New Mexico Press, 2003).

62. John Nieto-Phillips, *The Language of Blood: The Making of Spanish American Identity in New Mexico, 1880s–1930s* (Albuquerque: University of New Mexico Press, 2004).

63. Leah Dilworth, *Imagining Indians in the Southwest: Persistent Visions of a Primitive Past* (Washington, DC: Smithsonian Institution Press, 1996); Sylvia Rodríguez, "Fiesta Time and Plaza Space: Resistance and Accommodation in a Tourist Town," *Journal of American Folklore* 111 (Winter 1998): 39–56; Nieto-Phillips, *Language of Blood*.

64. Chris Wilson, *The Myth of Santa Fe: Creating a Modern Regional Tradition* (Albuquerque: University of New Mexico Press, 1997), 72–73.

65. George Pierre Castile, "The Commodification of Indian Identity," *American Anthropologist* 98, no. 4 (December 1996): 743–749.

66. Barbara A. Babcock and Marta Weigle, eds., *The Great Southwest of the Fred Harvey Company and the Santa Fe Railway* (Tucson: University of Arizona Press, 1996); Scott Norris, ed., *Discovered Country: Tourism and Survival in the American West* (Albuquerque: Stone Ladder, 1994); D. H. Thomas, *The Southwestern Indian Detours: The Story of the Fred Harvey / Santa Fe Railway Experiment in "Detourism"* (Phoenix: Hunter, 1978).

67. Joe C. Williams Jr., "A Study of the Economy: City of Santa Fe, New Mexico," prepared for the City Council and the City Planning Commission, City of Santa Fe, New Mexico, (Santa Fe, NM: Harman, O'Donnell & Henninger Associates, 1961).

68. Patricia Nelson Limerick, *The Legacy of Conquest: The Unbroken Past of the American West* (New York: W. W. Norton, 1987); William G. Robbins, *Colony and Empire: The Capitalist Transformation of the American West* (Lawrence: University Press of Kansas, 1994); Samuel Truett, *Fugitive Landscapes: The Forgotten History of the U.S.-Mexico Borderlands* (New Haven, CT: Yale University Press, 2006).

69. Memorial of the Senate and House of Representatives of the State of New Mexico, to the Secretary of Agriculture and the Chief Forester of the National Forest Service, with reference to Grazing Fees in National Forests, February 28, 1919, Box 50, Folder 11, FP.

70. Holtby, "Historical Reflections," 87. In 1926 these standings were out of forty-eight states.

71. Forrest, *Preservation of the Village*, 11.

72. Evidenced by the tax sale of large-acreage land grants in the 1910s and 1920s, this trend proved true for the largest landowners as well as the smallest. For an example, see Robert D. Shadow and María Rodríguez-Shadow, "From *Repartición* to Partition: A History of the Mora Land Grant, 1835–1916," *New Mexico Historical Review* 70 (July 1995): 257–298.

73. Forrest, *Preservation of the Village*, 30.

74. "The New Map of Economic Growth and Recovery," Economic Innovation Group (Washington, DC: May 2016).

75. Richard Baldwin, *The Great Convergence: Information Technology and the New Globalization* (Cambridge, MA: Belknap Press of Harvard University Press, 2016), 10–14.

Chapter 6. Capitalism's Back Pages

1. There has been more interest in the earlier history of classified advertising, when a small, text-based ad was not yet a sign of backwardness (and, perhaps, before this advertising was linked to illicit sex). See Gilles Feyel, *L'annonce et la nouvelle: La presse d'information en France sous*

l'ancien régime (1630–1788) (Oxford: Voltaire Foundation, 2000). In the modern period, the classifieds are more often referred to as a footnote in histories about other things or explored through the prism of a single type of ad, especially personal or matrimonial ads. For example, see Morag Martin, *Selling Beauty: Cosmetics, Commerce, and French Society, 1750–1830* (Baltimore: Johns Hopkins University Press, 2009); Pamela Epstein, "Selling Love: The Commercialization of Intimacy in America, 1860s–1900s," (PhD diss., Rutgers University, 2010); H. G. Cocks, "Peril in the Personals: The Dangers and Pleasures of Classified Advertising in Early Twentieth-Century Britain," *Media History* 10, no. 1 (April 2004): 3–16; Marc Martin, "Images du mari et de la femme au XXe siècle, les annonces de mariage du 'Chasseur Français,'" *Revue d'histoire moderne et contemporaine* 27, no. 2 (June 1980): 295–311. Even Philippe Artières, who asks us to pay close attention to classified advertising, does so precisely *because* he sees it as banal. Philippe Artières, *Miettes: éléments pour une histoire infra-ordinaire de l'année 1980* (Paris: Verticales, 2016).

2. Popular interest in classified advertising as a diverting window onto past (proto-online) dating practices may also have rendered the subject less than proper. This interest is itself likely an offshoot of the discursive sexualization I trace in this chapter. For examples of popular studies of the classifieds, see Marc Schlicklin, *Les petites annonces du Chasseur Français* (Paris: Solar, 2014); *Les perles des petites annonces* (Paris: Larousse, 2014).

3. Global capitalism has been constructed through a multiplication of local processes combining marginalization and legitimization. For another example of this process, see Johan Mathew's analysis of the relationship between trafficking and free trade (the market and its so-called margins) in the Arabian Sea. Johan Mathew, *Margins of the Market: Trafficking and Capitalism Across the Arabian Sea* (Berkeley: University of California Press, 2016).

4. In *La civilisation du journal*, a recent literary and cultural history of the French press in the nineteenth century, contributors argue that the newspaper transformed French society into a "civilization of the newspaper." The classifieds, however, barely cause a ripple in the volume's 1,600-page analysis of the world the press made, despite the fact that small ads often covered anywhere from a sixth to a third (or more!) of a newspaper's surface at regularly determined intervals by the early twentieth century. The newspaper marketplace, with its apartments for rent, used furniture for sale, marriage agencies, massage parlors, and personal exchanges—each one licit or illicit, depending on how you look at it—is nowhere to be found. While Arina Makarova, a specialist on death notices in the press, discusses the classifieds in her brief contribution to the volume, "Le carnet et les petites annonces," she minimizes their status as a print marketplace by bundling them with gossip columns and notices of death, birth, engagements, and marriage. In this entry, and in Marc Martin's on advertising, the commercial nature of the classifieds is minimized. Dominique Kalifa, Philippe Régnier, Marie-Ève Thérenty, and Alain Vaillant, eds., *La civilisation du journal : une histoire culturelle et littéraire de la presse française au XIXe siècle* (Paris: Nouveau Monde éditions, 2011), 1041–1058.

5. Jean Frollo was a collective pseudonym used to sign *Le Petit Parisien*'s lead articles.

6. Jean Frollo, "Les colonnes du travail," *Le Petit Parisien*, September 30, 1880.

7. "Les petites annonces," *Le Petit Parisien*, November 25, 1883.

8. A note on terminology: In this chapter, I translate *petites annonces*, literally "small ads," as "classifieds." In the interwar period, it became common to refer to them as *petites annonces classées*, thereby integrating the idea of classification into their name, which had previously referred solely to their size.

9. "Avis, offres et demandes," *La Presse*, October 14, 1889.

10. Newspaper advertising, invented in the seventeenth century, had been an important source of income for the press since the late 1820s. Advertising revenues rose from this moment through the Second Empire (1852–1870) before falling drastically during the early Third Republic to take up three times less place in 1885 than in 1865. As the number of newspaper titles proliferated following the liberalization (1868) and subsequent freedom of the press (1881), the commercial advertising pie was continually being divided into ever smaller pieces. In 1867, there were twenty-one daily newspapers printed in Paris, in 1880 there were sixty, and in 1914, fifty-seven. Marc Martin, *Trois siècles de publicité en France* (Paris: Éditions Odile Jacob, 1992), 90–92. For circulation figures, see Kalifa et al., *La civilisation du journal*, 264.

11. To take a particularly successful example, in 1900, the Saturday edition of *Le Journal* ran on six pages instead of the more traditional four, making space for between one, two, and sometimes nearly three pages of classified advertising.

12. Eugène Veuillot, "Paris, 24 Mars 1875," *L'Univers*, March 25, 1875.

13. *Figaro* published cryptic ads such as "M. oe. de Paq. en témoin de m.e.attach.à qd.16.G.E." or "A+B=X-Z=23." "Petite correspondance," *Le Figaro*, April 13, 1879.

14. This relationship was also made clear when Senate debates on the inclusion of sexual classified advertising within the law on immorality in the press descended into uncontrollable laughter. Moral concern and erotic fantasy were intimately connected where sexuality in the classifieds was concerned. *Journal Officiel de la République Française : Débats parlementaires, Sénat*, April 8, 1897, 786–787.

15. *Paris-Soir*, February 3, 1924.

16. Ibid.

17. "Nos petites annonces," *Paris-Soir*, December 3, 1924.

18. On the mid-nineteenth-century debate about "women's work," see Joan W. Scott, "'L'ouvrière! Mot impie, sordide . . .': Women Workers in the Discourse of French Political Economy, 1840–1860," chap. 7 in *Gender and the Politics of History* (New York: Columbia University Press, 1988). For a longer frame analysis of the problem of "women's work," see Judith Coffin, *The Politics of Women's Work: The Paris Garment Trades, 1750–1915* (Princeton, NJ: Princeton University Press, 1996).

19. Sylvia Schafer has shown how the idea of the "woman worker" was so thoroughly considered to be immoral that the state itself was seen as morally compromised by its implementation, in the late nineteenth century, of a vocational program to train female wards of the state to be skilled needleworkers. See Sylvia Schafer, "When the Child Is the Father of the Man: Work, Sexual Difference and the Guardian-State in Third Republic France," *History and Theory* 31, no. 4 (December 1992): 98–115.

20. On the fin-de-siècle association of women with interior designing and tasteful consumption, see Debora L. Silverman, *Art Nouveau in Fin-de-Siècle France: Politics, Psychology, and Style* (Berkeley: University of California Press, 1989); Lisa Tiersten, *Marianne in the Market: Envisioning Consumer Society in Fin-de-Siècle France* (Berkeley: University of California Press, 2001).

21. Victoria E. Thompson has analyzed the meanings and effects of the use of a discourse of sex and prostitution in the expulsion of women from market spaces across central Paris in the middle third of the nineteenth century in *The Virtuous Marketplace: Women and Men, Money and Politics in Paris, 1830–1870* (Baltimore: Johns Hopkins University Press, 2000).

22. See Jürgen Habermas, *The Structural Transformation of the Public Sphere: An Inquiry into a Category of Bourgeois Society*, trans. Thomas Burger (Cambridge, MA: MIT Press, 1989), esp. chap. 20 on the "public sphere as a platform for advertising."

23. Gustave Le Poittevin, *La liberté de la presse depuis la révolution, 1789–1815* (Paris: Arthur Rousseau, 1901), 2. For a study of advertising that sees it as a "structural subversion of a democratic press," see C. Edwin Baker, *Advertising and a Democratic Press* (Princeton, NJ: Princeton University Press, 1994), esp. chap. 1.

24. Henry Bérenger, "Les responsabilités de la presse," *Revue bleue*, December 4, 1897, 706–710.

25. "Lettre de M. Maurice Talmeyr," *Revue bleue*, December 4, 1897, 717.

26. "Lettre de M. Jean Jaurès," *Revue bleue*, December 4, 1897, 713.

27. This charge had already been made earlier in the century, for example in Honoré de Balzac's novel about Parisian newspapers, *Illusions perdues* (1837–1843). It took on new importance, however, due to the imbrication between the press and the republic.

28. Beginning in the seventeenth century, newspaper advertising, especially for medical services and goods, was seen as the domain of charlatans. See chap. 10 of Laurence Brockliss and Colin Jones, *The Medical World of Early Modern France* (Oxford: Oxford University Press, 1997).

29. On the democratization of pornography as a threat to the social body, see Carolyn J. Dean, *The Frail Social Body: Pornography, Homosexuality, and Other Fantasies in Interwar France* (Berkeley: University of California Press, 2000). On antipornography campaigns, see Annie Stora-Lamarre, *L'enfer de la IIIe République: censeurs et pornographes, 1881–1914* (Paris: Imago, 1990).

30. On earlier uses of coded language to get around political censorship, see Kalifa et al., *La civilisation du journal*, 301, 326.

31. Henri Vathelet, *La publicité dans le journalisme* (Paris: Albin Michel, n.d. [1911]), 160.

32. While references to classified advertising abound in the archive of the "white slave trade," there has been, to my knowledge, no sustained analysis of the place of advertising as a site of danger within this transnational myth. Outside of academic literature, nonprofit organizations have reinvigorated fears about the use of fraudulent classified advertising in contemporary transnational human trafficking cases. See Rochelle Keyhan, *Human Trafficking in Illicit Massage Businesses* (Washington, DC: Polaris, 2017), 22–26. Contemporary sex trafficking legislation has also targeted classified advertising. For example, see Niraj Chokshi, "Craigslist Drops Personal Ads After Passage of Sex Trafficking Bill," *New York Times*, March 23, 2018. See also Hannah Frydman, "Policing Backpage and the Backpages," *Public Books*, April 19, 2018, http://www.publicbooks.org/policing-backpage-and-the-backpages/ (accessed February 21, 2019).

33. Séverine, "La traite des blanches: la presse entremetteuse," *Le Matin*, April 14, 1903. On Sainte-Croix's crusade against prostitution and fight for equal pay for equal work, see Karen Offen, "Intrepid Crusader: Ghénia Avril de Sainte-Croix Takes on the Prostitution Issue," *Journal of the Western Society for French History* 33 (2005): 352–374.

34. Paul Appleton, *La traite des blanches: thèse pour le doctorat (Université de Lyon, faculté de droit)*, (Paris: Arthur Rousseau, 1903), 26.

35. Appleton, *La traite des blanches*, 27. Séverine discusses the following ad: "In a hurry. Seek. yng. girls for *tableaux vivants. Office central Concerts*, 55, Fbg-St-Martin, 10 to 12." Séverine, "La traite des blanches."

36. "Bureaux de placement," Archives Nationales, Pierrefitte-sur-Seine (AN), BB/18/6806.

37. The highly mediatized trial of the serial killer Landru, who found many of his victims through the personals, likely intensified this fear after World War I.

38. Raymond de Ryckère, *La servante criminelle: étude de criminologie professionnelle* (Paris: Maloine, 1908), 305.

39. Judith R. Walkowitz, *City of Dreadful Delight: Narratives of Sexual Danger in Late-Victorian London* (Chicago: University of Chicago Press, 1992); Elisa Camiscioli, *Reproducing the French Race: Immigration, Intimacy, and Embodiment in the Early Twentieth Century* (Durham, NC: Duke University Press, 2009), 99–113.

40. On the construction of the discourse of the "white slave trade" and the social, political, and cultural uses to which it was put in early twentieth-century France, see Molly McGregor Watson, "The Trade in Women: 'White Slavery' and the French Nation, 1899–1939" (PhD diss., Stanford University, 2000).

41. "Petites annonces par Les Veber's," *Gil Blas*, February 11, 1895. For the full series, see Pierre Veber, *Les Veber's. Les Veber's. Les Veber's* (Paris: E. Testard, 1895), 40.

42. It is hard to know how many people would have seen this cartoon in 1895. *Gil Blas*, known for its publication of work by such literary icons as Emile Zola and Guy de Maupassant, had a circulation of around 27,000 in late 1883. By 1911, circulation had fallen to 5,000 copies. Claude Bellanger, Jacques Godechot, Pierre Guiral, Fernand Terrou, eds., *Histoire générale de la presse française, Tome III* (Paris: Presse Universitaires de France, 1972).

43. *Le Journal* had a circulation of 300,000 in 1894 and 600,000 in 1904. Michael Stephen Smith, *The Emergence of Modern Business Enterprise in France, 1800–1930* (Cambridge, MA: Harvard University Press, 2006), 364.

44. Schwob does not decode this sexually explicit ad for his reader. He instead provides them with the key to decrypt it themselves, thereby inciting them to undertake the same process as readers of *Le Journal*. The ad decodes to read: "Wiens wite menculer. Ai soif de ton foutre. Ta queue dans ma bouche. Ta lang. en mon cul." This ad and the subsequent announcement that *Le Journal* would no longer print ads "made up of words with no apparent meaning or combinations of inverted letters" did in fact run on the dates Schwob indicates.

45. Loyson-Bridet [Marcel Schwob], *Mœurs de diurnales: traité de journalisme* (Paris: Société du mercure de France, 1903), 157–158.

46. The police were among those who knew how to crack the code. The prosecutor general at the court of appeals in Paris ordered an investigation into the ad analyzed by Schwob. Letter from the Prosecutor General to the Minister of Justice, December 27, 1902, AN BB 18 6167, 44 BL 21.

47. La Mésangère [Henri Boutet], *Les petits mémoires de Paris: les coulisses de l'amour* (Paris: Dorbon l'aîné, 1908), 27–28. Boutet was an artist best known for his depictions of La Parisienne.

48. "La traite des blanches—Le salon de massage de la rue Léonie," *Le Matin*, February 9, 1892.

49. Guy de Téramond, "La masseuse," *Gil Blas*, November 3, 1900.

50. "Nouvelles diverses à Paris: une affaire de mœurs," *Le Figaro*, June 10, 1904.

51. Victor Flachon, the erstwhile director of *La Lanterne*, was found guilty of frequenting underage prostitutes who were trafficked by a ring of women that drummed up business through advertisements for many different things in a variety of columns in the classifieds of *Le Supplément*. Rumor had it that the prime minister, who was a friend of Flachon's, was also somehow involved in the affair, but no proof ever came to light.

52. Pick-Me-Up, "Le Rire de la semaine," *Le Rire*, December 2, 1911.

53. "Petites annonces: cours et leçons," *Le Supplément*, May 23, 1911, 3.

54. This pseudomoralizing stance was a productive one. It is reminiscent of tactics used in New York in the 1840s by "flash" papers that posed as moral-reform organs while providing their readers with insider information about brothels. On the flash press, see Patricia Cline Cohen, Timothy J. Gilfoyle, and Helen Lefkowitz Horowitz, *The Flash Press: Sporting Male Weeklies in 1840s New York* (Chicago: University of Chicago Press, 2008). The journalist Georges-Anquetil also used a similar tactic in 1925 when he published a scathing denunciation of the presence of hundreds of ads in newspapers placed by prostitutes who "solicit[ed] publicly and officially," followed by nine pages of reproductions of advertisements for sex workers and other sexual goods. Georges-Anquetil, "C'en est trop!: la publicité des masseurs et des masseuses devient un scandale et un danger," *Grand Guignol*, March 1925. An article in a more sexually explicit magazine—which also printed such advertising—described Anquetil's article as a very complete "brothel guide" and argued that it was "one of the biggest advertising stunts of 1925." "A Grand Guignol Comedy," *Jazz*, March 15, 1925, 8.

55. *Le Supplément*, well known for the sexual nature of its classifieds, was a big hit with young women in French cities. For one characterization of the reader of *Le Supplément* as a young milliner or needleworker, see André Hofgaard, "Le journal et le journalisme," *Recueil des publications de la Société havraise d'études diverses* (Le Havre: H. Micaux, 1901), 335. Another source stated that, in an unnamed French industrial city, a newspaper salesman was said to have sold three-fourths of his copies of *Le Supplément*, described as a "broker of unnamable industries," to young women workers. Tommy Fallot, *Communication sur l'organisation de la lutte contre la pornographie faite au Congrès de l'association protestante pour l'Etude pratique des questions sociales, Marseille, 28 et 29 Octobre 1891* (Nice: V.-Eug. Gauthier, 1891), 13, 20.

56. Martin, *Trois siècles de publicité*, 97.

57. Ibid., 173.

58. Other Catholic figures would pioneer more spectacular forms of protest. On December 27, 1929, the priest Louis Bethléem publicly ripped up a copy of the illustrated *Journal amusant* on the Boulevard Bonne-Nouvelle to protest the fact that the journal contained ads for prostitutes. "Le 'Journal amusant' a été condamné et flétri par les tribunaux, il faut qu'il disparaisse," *Revue des lectures*, January 15, 1930, 145–146.

59. The police commissioner Albert Priolet, head of the infamous antivice Brigade Mondaine, mentions the "advertising branch of his department" in a letter to the director of the Police Judiciaire (in charge of criminal investigation), dated December 12, 1929. Archives de la Préfecture de Police de Paris (APP), BA 1690.

60. Report, Priolet to public prosecutor [*Procureur de la République*], October 28, 1931. APP BA 2243.

61. For one particularly important decision that, contrary to moralists' high hopes, did very little to stem the tide of immoral advertising during the interwar period, see "Cour de cassation: CRIM. 23 juin et 21 juill. 1928," *Dalloz: Recueil périodique et critique*, 1928, Part 1: Cour de cassation, 161–163.

62. Martin, *Trois siècles de publicité*, 232.

63. Martin, *Histoire de la publicité*, 141–147. In the 1940s, Prouvost and *Paris-Soir* were purged for collaborating with the Vichy regime, but the mark Prouvost had on advertising was long lasting. A sanitized and "legitimate" form of advertising (sexual in form but not in content) would take off in France in the postwar decades. Article 120 of the 1939 Code de la famille would also aid in this postwar moralization, as it rendered illegal any advertisement that "publicly attracts attention to an opportunity for debauchery."

64. The economic reasons for the participation of middle-class women in indoor prostitution in postindustrial societies are explored in Elizabeth Bernstein, *Temporarily Yours: Intimacy, Authenticity, and the Commerce of Sex* (Chicago: University Of Chicago Press, 2007), 80–81.

65. Amy Dru Stanley, "Histories of Capitalism and Sex Difference," *Journal of the Early Republic* 36, no. 2 (Summer 2016): 343–350.

66. Judith Surkis explains how the metadisciplinary language of "turns" and the narrative of "turning" away from the linguistic turn have "consign[ed] the critical resources of feminism to a chronologically and politically exhausted moment." See Judith Surkis, "When Was the Linguistic Turn? A Genealogy," *American Historical Review* 117, no. 3 (June 2012): 700–722, 721 (quote).

Chapter 7. Capitalism's Black Heart in Wartime France

Acknowledgments: Professor Mouré gratefully acknowledges financial support for this research from the Social Sciences and Humanities Research Council of Canada, grant IG 435-2013-1219.

1. On France, see Fabrice Grenard, *La France du marché noir (1940–1949)* (Paris: Payot, 2008); Paul Sanders, *Histoire du marché noir, 1940–1946* (Paris: Perrin, 2001). Regrettably, Belgium has received little attention in recent literature; see John Gillingham, *Belgian Business in the Nazi New Order* (Ghent, Belgium: Fondation Jan Dhondt, 1977); Jean Colard, *L'alimentation de la Belgique sous l'Occupation allemande 1940–1944* (Louvain, Belgium: Nouvelles Publications Universitaires, 1945). For postwar Germany, see Paul Steege, *Black Market, Cold War: Everyday Life in Berlin, 1946–1949* (Cambridge: Cambridge University Press, 2007); Willi A. Boelcke, *Der Schwarzmarkt 1945–1948: Vom Überleben nach dem Krieg* (Braunschweig, Germany: Westermann, 1986). For an overview of the effect of wartime priorities on civilian consumption, see Kenneth Mouré, "Les canons avant le beurre: consommation et marchés civils en temps de guerre," in *1937–1947: La guerre-monde*, vol. 2, ed. by Alya Aglan and Robert Frank, 1972–2001 (Paris: Gallimard, 2015). For Germany, see Malte Zierenberg, *Berlin's Black Market 1939–1950* (Houndsmill, UK: Palgrave Macmillan, 2015); Jill Stephenson, "War and Society in Wurttemberg, 1939–1945: Beating the System," *German Studies Review* 8, no. 1 (1985): 89–105.

2. Mark Roodhouse, *Black Market Britain 1939–1955* (Oxford: Oxford University Press, 2013); Ina Zweiniger-Bargielowska, *Austerity in Britain: Rationing, Controls, and Consumption 1939–1955* (Oxford: Oxford University Press, 2000), chap. 4; Marshall B. Clinard, *The Black Market: A Study of White Collar Crime* (New York: Holt, Rhinehart and Winston, 1952); Hugh Rockoff, *Drastic Measures: A History of Wage and Price Controls in the United States* (Cambridge: Cambridge University Press, 1984).

3. Sanders, *Histoire du marché noir*.

4. Alan S. Milward, *War, Economy and Society 1939–1945* (Berkeley: University of California Press, 1977), 135–49; Peter Liberman, *Does Conquest Pay? The Exploitation of Occupied Industrial Societies* (Princeton, NJ: Princeton University Press, 1996), 36–68; Hein Klemann and Sergei Kudryashov, *Occupied Economies: An Economic History of Nazi-Occupied Europe, 1939–1945* (London: Berg, 2012), 99.

5. National Archives and Records Administration, College Park, MD [NARA], RG 331 Box 26, Psychological Warfare Division, "Preliminary Report on the Black Market in France," June 30, 1944.

6. Service des archives économiques et financières, Savigny-le-Temple [SAEF] B 49516, "Rapport mensuel du mois de décembre 1943," on Contrôle Économique activity in the Department

of the Seine (Paris), which found that clandestine traffic, with activity increasingly in the hands of professionals, operated in a more organized manner than the regular market.

7. Filippo Occhino, Kim Oosterlinck, and Eugene N. White, "How Much Can a Victor Force the Vanquished to Pay? France Under the Nazi Boot," *Journal of Economic History* 68, no. 1 (2008): 1–45, 2 (quote), figures from Table 1, p. 7.

8. Philippe Pétain, *Discours aux Français, 17 juin 1940–20 août 1944*, ed. Jean-Claude Barbas (Paris: Albin Michel, 1989), 84, 88–93.

9. The term *"marché noir"* came to be used, initially in quotes, for all transactions that violated price and ration controls. For the adoption of the term in 1940, see Grenard, *La France du marché noir*, 19–21.

10. Kenneth Mouré, "Food Rationing and the Black Market in France (1940–1944)," *French History* 24, no. 2 (2010): 262–282.

11. Archives Nationales, Paris [AN] AJ 41 378, prefect report of January 1, 1941.

12. AN AJ 41 373, prefect report of July 3, 1941.

13. Archives Départementales [AD], Pyrénées-Atlantiques, Secretary-General of Landes to Prefect of Basses-Pyrénées, November 3, 1941.

14. AN AJ 41 391, prefect report for the Seine-et-Marne in April 1942, May 5, 1942.

15. Such complaints became more frequent in 1942; Archives de la Préfecture de Police, Paris [APP] 220W 10, "Situation de Paris au 14 décembre 1942," for complaints that reduced supplies in stores were because shopkeepers sold goods from the back of the store or reserved them for "clients intéressants."

16. AN F 60 291, Garde des Sceaux to Vice-Président du Conseil, March 3, 1942; Fabrice Grenard, *Les scandales du ravitaillement: Détournements, corruption, affaires étouffées en France, de l'Occupation à la guerre froide* (Paris: Payot, 2012), 99–113.

17. Kenneth Mouré, *"La Capitale de la Faim*: Black Market Restaurants in Paris, 1940–1944," *French Historical Studies* 38, no. 2 (2015): 311–341; 338 (quote), police report of October 30, 1942, in APP, BA 1808.

18. AD Seine-Maritime 40W 125, Chef du gouvernement (Laval) to Préfet de Police et MM. les Préfets Régionaux et Départementaux, May 31, 1943.

19. In the United Kingdom and United States, having sufficient supplies to guarantee the provision of rations as a base level for consumption was seen as essential to the success of the system. John Kenneth Galbraith, *A Life in Our Times: Memoirs* (New York: Ballantine, 1982), 156; Frederick James Marquis, *The Memoirs of the Rt. Hon. Earl of Woolton* (London: Cassell, 1959), 191–192.

20. APP 220W 4, "Situation à Paris au 16 juin 1941."

21. AN AJ 41 24, Gendarmerie summary for January 1942, and the account of the demonstration given later, "La révolte des ménagères à Sète," *France*, August 19, 1942, in AN F 60 1697. For the growing support for popular protests during the occupation, see the analysis by Megan Barber, "Popular Street Protest in Vichy France," (PhD diss., UC Santa Barbara, 2012).

22. Jean-Marie Guillon, "Le retour des 'émotions populaires': manifestations de ménagères en 1942," in *Mélanges Michel Vovelle, volume aixois. Sociétés, mentalités, cultures France (XVe-XXe siècles)*, ed. Bernard Cousin, 267–276 (Aix-en-Provence: Publications de l'Université de Provence, 1997); Danielle Tartakovsky, "Manifester pour le pain, novembre 1940–octobre 1947," in *Le temps des restrictions en France (1939–1949)*, special issue of *Les cahiers de l'IHTP* nos. 32–33 (1996): 465–478.

23. Raymond Ruffin, *Journal d'un J3* (Paris: Presses de la Cité, 1979), 141.

24. AN F 23 408, "Affaire Lemaire," "Note (M. Julienne) pour M. l'inspecteur général Jeannin, February 21, 1944.

25. Institut de Conjoncture, *Situation économique au début du mois de Juillet 1942*, Rapport no. 11. Sauvy repeats these statistics in *La vie économique des Français de 1939 à 1945* (Paris: Flammarion, 1978), 134.

26. André Paul, "Histoire des PTT pendant la deuxième guerre mondiale (1939–1945)," unpublished manuscript at the Bibliothèque historique des postes et télécommunications, Paris, 288.

27. AD Seine-Maritime 40 W 126; one farm couple doing this for several months paid from 70 to 140 francs per kilogram for butter they resold at an unspecified price. They were interned by administrative decree for four months.

28. AD Ille-et-Vilaine 43 W 4, prefect of Morbihan monthly report, July 31, 1942.

29. AN AJ 41 392; monthly report for September and October 1942, November 3, 1942. Prefects reported this *tourisme alimentaire*, buying butter, eggs, and meat, in Ille-et-Vilaine, Finistère, Côtes-du-Nord, and Morbihan.

30. AN F 1a CIII 1168; prefect monthly report for July–August 1942, dated September 1, 1942.

31. SAEF B 49511, several cases from 1942 and 1943, but post office reporting of persons sending numerous packages, upon investigation, often proved to be families sending food all for their own consumption.

32. AN AJ 41 24, "Synthèse des rapports mensuels des Commandants des Légions de Gendarmerie de la Zone libre (Août 1942)," for Gendarmerie comment on the impossibility of suppressing "l'envoi abusive des colis familiaux."

33. AD Rhône 182W 6, procès-verbal de la conférence des préfets régionaux du 29 mai 1942.

34. SAEF B 9860, Direction Générale du Contrôle Economique, *Rapport sur l'activité de la DGCE au cours de l'année 1944* (1945), Table 3. Butter counted for 16.7 percent of the cases and 7.7 percent of the value of goods.

35. Mouré, "La capitale de la faim," 330.

36. AN F 37 120, Commission Consultative des Dommages et des Réparations, "Prelèvement Allemands de produits agricoles, Monographie P.A. 4: Viande" (Paris: Imprimerie Nationale, 1947), 48.

37. AN AJ 41 393, rapport mensuel for September, prefect of the Vendée, October 2, 1941.

38. AN F 60 1010, Formery to Laval, July 27, 1943.

39. On types of restaurant fraud, see Mouré, "La capitale de la faim," 317–320; on the prevalence of *soultes* in commerce, see Fabrice Grenard, "La soulte, une pratique généralisée pour contourner le blocage des prix," in *Les entreprises de biens de consommation sous l'Occupation*, ed. Sabine Effosse, Marc de Ferrière le Vayer, and Hervé Joly, 29–43 (Tours, France: Presses Universitaires François-Rabelais de Tours, 2010).

40. This behavior is emphasized, too exclusively, in Annie Lacroix-Riz, *Industriels et banquiers sous l'Occupation: La collaboration économique avec le Reich et Vichy* (Paris: Armand Colin, 1999). Talbot Imlay and Martin Horn provide a fascinating case study of the complexity and the conflicting interests in industrial collaboration for Ford France in *The Politics of Industrial Collaboration During World War II: Ford France, Vichy and Nazi Germany* (Cambridge: Cambridge University Press, 2014).

41. The most notorious German purchasing group, the Bureau Otto, is described in Jacques Delarue, *Trafics et crimes sous l'Occupation*, rev. ed. (Paris: Fayard, 1993); Sanders, *Histoire du marché noir*, 175–181; Grégory Auda, *Les belles années du 'milieu' 1940–1944: Le grand banditisme dans la machine répressive allemande en France* (Paris: Éditions Michalon, 2002), 67–78; Renaud

de Rochebrune and Jean-Claude Hazera, *Les patrons sous l'Occupation*, rev. ed. (Paris: Odile Jacob, 2013), 195–202.

42. Kenneth Mouré and Paula Schwartz, "On vit mal: Food Shortages and Popular Culture in Occupied France, 1940–1944," *Food, Culture & Society* 10, no. 2 (2007), 281–284; Paul Achard, *La queue: Ce qui s'y disait, ce qu'on y pensait* (Paris: Éditions mille et une nuits, 2011; written 1940–1942, first published in 1945).

43. Libby Murphy, *The Art of Survival: France and the Great War Picaresque* (New Haven, CT: Yale University Press, 2016), 43–63.

44. AN F 7 14928 and F 7 14930 for Contrôle Technique reports on opinion in 1943 and 1944; and Grenard, *La France du marché noir*, 124–132.

45. Those who could not use *le système D*—prisoners, patients in hospitals, and patients in mental asylums who had often been abandoned by their families—suffered much more from hunger. See the contributions in Isabelle von Beultzingsloewen, ed., *"Morts d'inanition": Famine et exclusions en France sous l'Occupation* (Rennes, France: Presses universitaires de Rennes, 2005).

46. Louis Baudin, *Esquisse de l'économie française sous l'occupation allemande* (Paris: Librairie de Médicis, 1946), 154–156.

47. TNA FO 371 49096, intercepted Czech letter to "A. Hayek" (probably Friedrich Hayek), January 30, 1945.

48. AN F 1a 3250, "Note pour M. le Directeur Général" re: Conférence tenue ce jour à la Direction Générale du Contrôle Économique, February 2, 1945.

49. AN F 1a 3250, Seine-Inférieure.

50. AN F 1a 3250, Prefect of Calvados to the Commissaire régional in Rouen, August 21, 1945.

51. AN F 1a 3250, Charente-Maritime file, August 30, 1945; accounts were published in *Paris-Presse* and *France-Soir*, September 4, 1945.

52. AN 72 AJ 384; report of August 30, 1945, which claims the crowd was about three hundred.

53. The incident took place on August 28; quote from "L'affaire de Saint-Sever," *Franc-Tireur*, September 3, 1945.

54. Direction Générale du Contrôle et des Enquêtes Economique, *Rapport sur l'activité de la DGCEE au cours de l'année 1947*, 4.

55. Archives de la Banque de France, Paris; 1069201226 29, summary of directors' reports for April 1947.

56. AD Côte d'Or 40 M 278, poster, capitals in original.

57. SAEF 30 D 02, "Des manifestants mettent à sac des services du Contrôle économique du Ravitaillement et du Contrôle laitier," *Le bien public*, May 21, 1947; AD Côte d'Or, 40 M 278, prefect report of May 21, 1947.

58. SAEF B 49890; notes de services no. 931, June 21, 1947; no. 934, June 24, 1947; and no. 980, September 17, 1947.

59. SAEF B 49525; "Rapport mensuel, Résumé de l'activité de l'Echelon S.N.R.E. pendant le mois de Mai 1947," June 3, 1947.

60. Direction Général du Contrôle et des Enquêtes Economique [DGCEE], *Rapport sur l'activité de la DCEE au cours de l'année 1947* (1947), 13.

61. DGCEE, *Rapport 1947*, 11–15.

62. See AN 3AG2 419 for the development of confiscation policies; summarized in Kenneth Mouré and Fabrice Grenard, "Traitors, *Trafiquants*, and the Confiscation of 'Illicit Profits' in France, 1944–1950," *Historical Journal* 51, no. 4 (2008): 974–977.

63. Rochebrune and Hazera, *Les patrons sous l'Occupation*, 248.

64. Mouré and Grenard, "Traitors, *Trafiquants*," 979; Marc Bergère, ed., *L'épuration économique en France à la Libération* (Rennes, France: Presses Universitaires de Rennes, 2008).

65. Delarue, *Trafics et crimes*, 62–65.

66. Commissaire Petit report to the Direction générale du contrôle économique, January 25, 1946, cited in André Goldschmidt, *L'affaire Joinovici: collaborateur, résistant, et bouc-émissaire* (Toulouse: Privat, 2002), 41.

67. Charles Rist, *Season of Infamy: A Diary of War and Occupation, 1939–1945*, trans. Michele McKay Aynesworth (Bloomington: Indiana University Press, 2016), 364.

68. Jean Dutourd, *Au bon beurre: Scènes de la vie sous l'Occupation* (Paris: Galliimard, 1952; reprinted edition in Collection Folio, 1972).

69. Dutourd, *Au bon beurre*, 107.

70. Baudin, *Esquisse*, 154, his phrase to describe the change in consumer status was "ce roi devient valet." Dutourd provides very similar comment in *Au bon beurre*, 134–135.

71. Grenard, *La France du marché noir*, 260–267.

72. AN F 7 14927, 14929 and 14930, Contrôle Technique reports on public opinion in 1943 and 1944.

73. Kenneth Mouré, "Black Market Fictions: *Au bon beurre, La traversée de Paris*, and the Black Market in France," *French Politics, Culture & Society* 32, no. 1 (2014): 47–67.

Chapter 8. The Emergence of the Offshore Economy, 1914–1939

1. Ronen Palan, *The Offshore World: Sovereign Markets, Virtual Places and Nomad Millionaires* (Ithaca, NY: Cornell University Press, 2003), 2.

2. Ingo Walter, *Secret Money: The Shadowy World of Tax Evasion, Capital Flight and Fraud*, 2nd ed. (London: Unwin, 1989), 11.

3. Sol Picciotto, "Offshore: The State as Legal Fiction," in *Offshore Finance Centers and Tax Havens: The Rise of Global Capital*, ed. Mark Hampton and Jason Abbott (Basingstoke, UK: Macmillan, 1999), 48.

4. Anthony Johns, *Tax Havens and Offshore Finance: A Study of Transnational Economic Development* (London: Bloomsbury, 1983), 2–19.

5. Hilton McCann, *Offshore Finance* (Cambridge: Cambridge University Press, 2006), xi.

6. Palan, *Offshore World*, 3–4; United Nations Conference on Trade and Development, *Review of Maritime Transport* (New York: United Nations, 2009), 55.

7. Alain Vernay, *Les paradis fiscaux* (Paris: Seuil, 1968), 315.

8. Nicholas Shaxson, *Treasure Islands: Tax Havens and the Men Who Stole the World* (London: Bodley Head, 2011), 215–243.

9. Vanessa Ogle, "Archipelago Capitalism: Tax Havens, Offshore Money, and the State, 1950s–1970s," *American Historical Review* 122, no. 5 (December 2017): 1432–1433.

10. Eric Helleiner, *States and the Reemergence of Global Finance: From Bretton Woods to the 1990s* (Ithaca, NY: Cornell University Press, 1994); Gary Burn, *The Re-emergence of Global Finance* (Basingstoke, UK: Palgrave, 2006).

11. Christophe Farquet, *Histoire du paradis fiscal suisse: Expansion et relations internationales du centre "offshore" suisse au XXᵉ siècle* (Paris: Sciences Po, 2018), 7.

12. See Ronen Palan, Richard Murphy, and Christian Chavagneux, *Tax Havens: How Globalization Really Works* (Ithaca, NY: Cornell University Press, 2010), 107–133.

13. Data for Figure 8.1 sourced from http://piketty.pse.ens.fr/en/capital21c2 (France, Germany, the United States); supplemented by own research (United Kingdom).

14. Christopher Kobrak, Per Hansen, and Christopher Kopper, "Business, Political Risk, and Historians in the Twentieth Century," in *European Business, Dictatorship and Political Risk, 1920–1945*, ed. Christopher Kobrak and Per Hansen (New York: Berghahn, 2004), 10.

15. Charles Yablon, "The Historical Race: Competition for Corporate Charters and the Rise and Decline of New Jersey, 1880–1910," *Journal of Corporation Law* 32, no. 2 (Winter 2007): 323–380.

16. National Archives of the UK (TNA): IR 74/173, Memorandum by W. Adams, March 12, 1907.

17. Serge Paquier, "Swiss Holding Companies from the Mid-Nineteenth Century to the Early 1930s: The Forerunners and Subsequent Waves of Creations," *Financial History Review* 8, no. 2 (October 2001): 163–182.

18. Rodney Carlisle, *Rough Waters: Sovereignty and the American Merchant Flag* (Annapolis, MD: Naval Institute, 2017), 72–86.

19. Kevin O'Rourke and Jeffrey Williamson, *Globalization and History: The Evolution of a Nineteenth-Century Atlantic Economy* (Cambridge, MA: MIT Press, 1999), 13–14.

20. See generally Simon Mollan, Andrew Smith, and Kevin Tennent, eds., *The Impact of the First World War on International Business* (New York: Routledge, 2017).

21. Albrecht Ritschl and Tobias Straumann, "Business Cycles and Economic Policy, 1914–1945," in *The Cambridge Economic History of Modern Europe, Vol. 2: 1870 to the Present*, ed. Stephen Broadberry and Kevin O'Rourke (Cambridge: Cambridge University Press, 2010), 175.

22. Alan Kramer, "Blockade and Economic Warfare," in *The Cambridge History of the First World War, Vol. 2: The State*, ed. Jay Winter (Cambridge: Cambridge University Press, 2013), 477–478.

23. See Greg Kennedy, ed., *Britain's War at Sea, 1914–1918: The War They Thought and the War They Fought* (Abingdon, UK: Routledge, 2016), esp. chaps. 2 and 5 by Keith Neilson and John Ferris, respectively.

24. Nicholas Lambert, *Planning Armageddon: British Economic Warfare and the First World War* (Cambridge, MA: Harvard University Press, 2012), 14.

25. John McDermott, "Total War and the Merchant State: Aspects of British Economic Warfare Against Germany, 1914–16," *Canadian Journal of History* 21, no. 1 (April 1986): 69.

26. Gerd Hardach, *The First World War, 1914–1918* (Berkeley: University of California Press, 1977), 18–19.

27. John McDermott, "Trading with the Enemy: British Business and the Law During the First World War," *Canadian Journal of History* 32, no. 2 (August 1997): 202–219.

28. Lambert, *Planning Armageddon*, 354–355.

29. Ibid., 360–361.

30. Kramer, "Blockade," 469.

31. Samuel Kruizinga, "NOT Neutrality: The Dutch Government, the Netherlands Oversea Trust Company and the Entente Blockade of Germany, 1914–1918," in *Caught in the Middle: Neutrals, Neutrality and the First World War*, ed. Johan den Hertog and Samuel Kruizinga, 85–103 (Amsterdam: Aksant, 2011).

32. Lambert, *Planning Armageddon*, 14.

33. Ibid., 276.

34. Ibid., 264.

35. Adam Hochschild, *To End All Wars: How the First World War Divided Britain* (London: Macmillan, 2011), 160–162.

36. Eric Osborne, *Britain's Economic Blockade of Germany, 1914–1919* (London: Frank Cass, 2004), 70.

37. Lambert, *Planning Armageddon*, 382.

38. Marc Frey, "Trade, Ships and the Neutrality of the Netherlands in the First World War," *International History Review* 19, no. 3 (August 1997): 548.

39. See generally Daniela Caglioti, "Property Rights in Time of War: Sequestration and Liquidation of Enemy Aliens' Assets in Western Europe During the First World War," *Journal of Modern European History* 12, no. 4 (2014): 523–545.

40. Joseph Borkin, *The Crime and Punishment of IG Farben* (New York: Free Press, 1978), 211–228.

41. Lambert, *Planning Armageddon*, 240–251.

42. George Gibb and Evelyn Knowlton, *History of Standard Oil Company (New Jersey): The Resurgent Years, 1911–1927* (New York: Harper, 1956), 159.

43. Ibid., 269–271.

44. Carlisle, *Rough Waters*, 123.

45. Daniel Okrent, *Last Call: The Rise and Fall of Prohibition* (New York: Scribner, 2010), 161, 375.

46. Lawrence Spinelli, *Dry Diplomacy: The United States, Great Britain, and Prohibition* (Wilmington, DE: Scholarly Resources, 1989), 3.

47. Okrent, *Last Call*, 172.

48. Peter Andreas, *Smuggler Nation: How Illicit Trade Made America* (Oxford: Oxford University Press, 2013), 238.

49. Carlisle, *Rough Waters*, 120–129.

50. Leon Fink, *Sweatshops at Sea: Merchant Seamen in the World's First Globalized Industry, from 1812 to the Present* (Chapel Hill: University of North Carolina Press, 2011), 179.

51. Carlisle, *Rough Waters*, 133–134.

52. Stephen Broadberry and Mark Harrison, "The Economics of World War I: An Overview," in *The Economics of World War I*, ed. Stephen Broadberry and Mark Harrison (Cambridge: Cambridge University Press, 2005), 12.

53. Robert Aliber, *The New International Money Game*, 7th ed. (Basingstoke, UK: Palgrave, 2011), 70.

54. Charles Feinstein and Katherine Watson, "Private International Capital Flows in Europe in the Inter-War Period," in *Banking, Currency, and Finance in Europe Between the Wars*, ed. Charles Feinstein (Oxford: Clarendon Press, 1995), 109–113.

55. Larry Neal, "A Tale of Two Revolutions: International Capital Flows, 1789–1819," *Bureau of Economic and Business Research Faculty Working Paper*, no. 90-1663, July 1990, 2.

56. Harold James, *The German Slump: Politics and Economics, 1924–1936* (Oxford: Clarendon Press, 1986), 132; Eleanor Dulles, *The French Franc, 1914–1928: The Facts and Their Interpretation* (New York: Macmillan, 1929), 227.

57. Gene Smith, *The Life and Death of Serge Rubinstein* (Garden City, NJ: Doubleday, 1962), 49–50.

58. See generally Paul Einzig, *Exchange Control* (London: Macmillan, 1934).

59. Howard Ellis, *Exchange Control in Central Europe* (Cambridge, MA: Harvard University Press, 1941), 307–308.

60. James, *German Slump*, 298–301.

61. Ellis, *Exchange Control*, 40–44, 145.

62. Mira Wilkins, "Multinationals and Dictatorship: Europe in the 1930s and Early 1940s," in *European Business, Dictatorship and Political Risk, 1920–1945*, ed. Christopher Kobrak and Per Hansen (New York: Berghahn, 2004), 27.

63. See Thomas Piketty, *Capital in the Twenty-First Century*, trans. Arthur Goldhammer (Cambridge, MA: Harvard University Press, 2014), 499–503.

64. Nicholas Faith, *Safety in Numbers: The Mysterious World of Swiss Banking* (New York: Viking Press, 1982), 65–72.

65. Sébastien Guex, "1932: The Tax Fraud Affair and the Herriot Government," *L'Économie politique*, no. 33 (2007): 89–104.

66. Ibid.

67. Christophe Farquet, "Capital Flight and Tax Competition After the First World War: The Political Economy of French Tax Cuts, 1922–1928," *Contemporary European History* 27, no. 4 (November 2018): 541.

68. Gabriel Zucman, *The Hidden Wealth of Nations: The Scourge of Tax Havens*, trans. Teresa Lavender Fagan (Chicago: University of Chicago Press, 2015), 14–16.

69. See Catherine Schenk, "The Origins of the Eurodollar Market in London: 1955–1963," *Explorations in Economic History* 35, no. 2 (April 1998): 221.

70. See, for example, Sébastien Guex, "The Origins of the Swiss Banking Secrecy Law and its Repercussions for Swiss Federal Policy," *Business History Review* 74, no. 2 (Summer 2000): 237–266.

71. Ian Paget-Brown, "Bank Secrecy and Criminal Matters: Cayman Islands and US Cooperative Development," *Case Western Reserve Journal of International Law* 20, no. 2 (1988): 370–371.

72. Palan, Murphy, and Chavagneux, *Tax Havens*, 111–119.

73. Ibid.; George Glos, "The Analysis of a Tax Haven: The Liechtenstein Anstalt," *International Lawyer* 18, no. 4 (Fall 1984): 929–955.

74. Peter Norman, *Plumbers and Visionaries: Securities Settlement and Europe's Financial Market* (Chichester, UK: Wiley, 2007), 26.

75. See Xavier Oberson, *International Exchange of Information in Tax Matters: Towards Global Transparency* (Cheltenham, UK: Elgar, 2015), 14–15.

76. Steven Dean, "The Incomplete Global Market for Tax Information," *Boston College Law Review* 49, no. 3 (May 2008): 639–649.

77. Christophe Farquet, "Lutte contre l'évasion fiscale: l'échec de la SDN durant l'entre-deux-guerres," *L'Économie politique*, no. 44 (2009): 93–112.

78. TNA: IR 63/141, Memorandum by Richard Hopkins, October 18, 1935.

79. TNA: T 233/1579, Note by unidentified official, February 23, 1929.

80. Martin Daunton, *Trusting Leviathan: The Politics of Taxation in Britain, 1799–1914* (Cambridge: Cambridge University Press, 2001), 197–198.

81. Peter Alldridge, *Criminal Justice and Taxation* (Oxford: Oxford University Press, 2017), 7–24.

82. Randolph Paul, "The Background of the Revenue Act of 1937," *University of Chicago Law Review* 5, no. 1 (December 1937): 46.

83. Brian Simpson, *A History of the Land Law*, 2nd ed. (Oxford: Clarendon Press, 1986), 23, 173–207.

84. Assaf Likhovski, "Tax Law and Public Opinion: Explaining *IRC v Duke of Westminster*," in *Studies in the History of Tax Law, Vol. 2*, ed. John Tiley, 183–221 (Oxford: Hart, 2007).

85. David Stopforth, "1922–36: Halcyon Days for the Tax Avoider," *British Tax Review* [1992]: 88–105.

86. Oliver Stanley, *Taxology: The Perpetual Battle of Wits Between the Inland Revenue and the Taxpayer* (London: Weidenfeld & Nicolson, 1972), 70–79.

87. Finance Act 1922, section 21(6)(a).

88. HC Deb. (5th Ser.), June 20, 1922, Vol. 155, Col. 1231.

89. Johns, *Tax Havens*, 85–88.

90. TNA: T 171/265, Note of Meeting at HM Treasury, July 14, 1927.

91. John Avery-Jones, "Taxing Foreign Income from Pitt to the Tax Law Rewrite: The Decline of the Remittance Basis," in *Studies in the History of Tax Law, Vol. 1*, ed. John Tiley (Oxford: Hart, 2004), 44.

92. TNA: IR 74/42, Memorandum by Matthew Nathan, March 10, 1912.

93. Finance Act 1914, section 5.

94. TNA: IR 40/4574, Report of the Evasion Committee, February 1934; Finance Act 1936, section 18.

95. Simon Mollan and Kevin Tennent, "International Taxation and Corporate Strategy: Evidence from British Overseas Business, circa 1900–1965," *Business History* 57, no. 7 (October 2015): 1054–1081.

96. Sol Picciotto, *International Business Taxation: A Study in the Internationalization of Business Regulation* (Cambridge: Cambridge University Press, 1992), 14–25.

97. Ryo Izawa, "The Formation of Companies for Tax Avoidance: The Relationship Between UK Multinationals and International Double Taxation in the Interwar Period," *Business and Economic History On-line* 13 (2015): 1–10.

98. TNA: IR 74/61, Memorandum by Charles Spry, January 17, 1916.

99. TNA: LCO 2/2570, Memorandum by George Younger, June 27, 1922.

100. Finance Act 1951, section 36.

101. Steven Bank, *Anglo-American Corporate Taxation: Tracing the Common Roots of Divergent Approaches* (Cambridge: Cambridge University Press, 2011), 70–104.

102. Joseph Thorndike, *Their Fair Share: Taxing the Rich in the Age of FDR* (Washington, DC: Urban Institute, 2013), 177–205.

103. Franklin D. Roosevelt Library: PSF/166, Memorandum by Henry Morgenthau, May 21, 1937.

104. Keith Engel, "Tax Neutrality to the Left, International Competitiveness to the Right, Stuck in the Middle with Subpart F," *Texas Law Review* 79, no. 6 (May 2001): 1532–1534.

105. See, for example, Bank, *Corporate Taxation*, 108–112; A. V. Tranter, *Evasion in Taxation* (London: Routledge, 1929), 93.

106. Paul Clikeman, *Called to Account: Financial Frauds That Shaped the Accounting Profession*, 2nd ed. (New York: Routledge, 2013), 26.

107. Frank Partnoy, *The Match King: Ivar Krueger and the Financial Scandal of the Twentieth Century* (London: Profile, 2009), 48–49, 81, 128, 212.

108. Catherine Duffy, *Held Captive: A History of International Insurance in Bermuda* (Toronto: Oakwell, 2004), 10–11.

109. Alan Block, *Masters of Paradise: Organized Crime and the Internal Revenue Service in the Bahamas* (New Brunswick, NJ: Transaction, 1991), 27–28.

110. Gerard Aalders and Cees Wiebes, *The Art of Cloaking Ownership: The Secret Collaboration and Protection of the German War Industry by the Neutrals; The Case of Sweden* (Amsterdam: Amsterdam University Press, 1996), 9.

111. Christopher Kobrak and Jana Wüstenhagen, "International Investment and Nazi Politics: The Cloaking of German Assets Abroad, 1936–1945," *Business History* 48, no. 3 (July 2006): 399–427.

112. Christopher Kobrak, *National Cultures and International Competition: The Experience of Schering AG, 1851–1950* (Cambridge: Cambridge University Press, 2002), 147–148, 164, 282–286.

113. Borkin, *IG Farben*, 236–239.

114. Ibid., 281–282.

115. Marco Bertilorenzi, "Legitimising Cartels: The Joint Roles of the League of Nations and of the International Chamber of Commerce," in *Regulating Competition: Cartel Registers in the Twentieth-Century World*, ed. Susanna Fellman and Martin Shanahan, 30–47 (London: Routledge, 2016).

116. Wyatt Wells, *Antitrust and the Formation of the Postwar World* (New York: Columbia University Press, 2002), 72.

117. Ibid., 39.

118. Ibid., 20, 61.

119. Geoffrey Jones, *Entrepreneurship and Multinationals: Global Business and the Making of the Modern World* (Cheltenham, UK: Elgar, 2013), 199.

120. Norman Miners, "Industrial Development in the Colonial Empire and the Imperial Economic Conference at Ottawa, 1932," *Journal of Imperial and Commonwealth History* 30, no. 2 (2002): 58.

121. Ibid., 61–69; Huei-Ying Kuo, *Networks Beyond Empires: Chinese Business and Nationalism in the Hong Kong–Singapore Corridor, 1914–1941* (Leiden, Netherlands: Brill, 2014), 216.

122. Ibid., 244; TNA: CUST 49/2431, Correspondence relating to the Hong Kong rubber footwear industry, April–December 1939.

123. Lawrence Mills, *Protecting Free Trade: The Hong Kong Paradox, 1947–97* (Hong Kong: Hong Kong University Press, 2012), 39–40.

124. Dara Orenstein, "Foreign-Trade Zones and the Cultural Logic of Frictionless Production," *Radical History Review*, no. 109 (Winter 2011): 36–61.

125. Ibid., 49–51.

126. TNA: T 160/678, Sundry correspondence concerning the evasion of sanctions, 1935–1936.

127. Luise White, *Unpopular Sovereignty: Rhodesian Independence and African Decolonization* (Chicago: University of Chicago Press, 2015), 126–148.

128. See the contribution herein: Kenneth Mouré, "Capitalism's Black Heart in Wartime France," in *Capitalism's Hidden Worlds*, ed. Kenneth Lipartito and Lisa Jacobson, 139–156 (Philadelphia: University of Pennsylvania Press, 2019); see also David Gordon and Royden Dangerfield, *The Hidden Weapon: The Story of Economic Warfare* (New York: Harper, 1947).

129. Arthur Bloomfield, *Speculative and Flight Movements of Capital in Postwar International Finance* (Princeton, NJ: Princeton University Press, 1954), 2.

130. R. T. Naylor, *Patriots and Profiteers: Economic Warfare, Embargo Busting and State-Sponsored Crime*, 2nd ed. (Montreal: McGill-Queen's University Press, 2008), 33.

131. Ritschl and Straumann, "Business Cycles," 158.

132. TNA: T 161/189, Anonymous letter to Winston Churchill, January 5, 1926; Tranter, *Evasion*, 161.

133. Luc Boltanski, *Mysteries and Conspiracies: Detective Stories, Spy Novels and the Making of Modern Societies*, trans. Catherine Porter (Cambridge: Polity, 2014), 111–114, 121–169.

134. McDermott, "Trading with the Enemy," 203.

135. Vernay, *Les paradis fiscaux*, 281–310.

Chapter 9. Comrades In-Between

Note: In-text Anglicized Chinese names and places are presented in the pinyin transcription form now customary in Chinese studies. However, to preserve reference accessibility, Chinese terms in the notes retain the earlier Wade-Giles spellings, which were used by those creating the source translations cited below.

1. George Ecklund, "Protracted Expropriation of Private Business in Communist China," *Pacific Affairs* 36 (1963): 242.

2. Audrey Donnithorne, *China's Economic System* (New York: Praeger, 1967), 279–280, 317.

3. We note at the outset that, as central planning focuses primarily on material outputs, setting measurable targets, and on financial flows to fund capital investments, commercial transactions are not readily subject to comparable planning, indexing, or direction. It makes little sense to mandate X billion yuan of transactions in port Y or city Z, or in any commodity. Commerce was, however, *regulated and monitored* through rule systems that shifted with political changes and in crises. See Sun Chih-fang, "Commercial Planning Tables," in *Chinese Economic Planning*, ed. Nicholas Lardy, 149–163 (Armonk, NY: ME Sharpe, 1977); Dwight Perkins, *Market Control and Planning in Communist China* (Cambridge, MA: Harvard University Press, 1966).

4. Ibid., 243–244.

5. "Figures on the Transformation of Private Commerce," *Kung Shang Chieh* (Industrial and Commercial Circles), December 10, 1957, translated in Joint Publications Research Service [hereafter JPRS] Report 876, "Domestic Trade in Communist China," November 24, 1958, 111. From 1957 to 1995, the JPRS was a branch of the U.S. Department of Commerce, quietly funded and partly staffed by the CIA, which undertook extensive translation projects from unclassified foreign newspapers, journals, technical and trade periodicals, broadcasts, speeches, and reports, for policy use by government agencies and for research use at universities. Newsbank has placed approximately 1.7 million of these documents online for subscription access.

6. For policy debates within the ministries and implementation issues, see Dorothy Solinger, *Chinese Business Under Socialism: The Politics of Domestic Commerce, 1949–1980* (Berkeley: University of California Press, 1984). Solinger worked thematically, with a focus on the period after 1970.

7. Donnithorne, *China's Economic System*, 274–279.

8. S. A. Selivankin, *Notes on Trade in China* (Moscow: State Publishing House, 1959), JPRS Report 3524, July 8, 1960, 1. "During our two-month stay in the PRC, we did not see a single queue—neither in the large stores, nor in the small stores, nor in any of the general services shops" (2).

9. Ibid., 26.

10. Ibid. In Beijing there was one retail enterprise for every eighty-five residents; Shanghai commerce was evidently the densest in the PRC.

11. Ibid., 3.

12. Ibid.

13. "Brokerage Warehouses," *Chung-Yang Ho-tso T'ung-hsun* (Central Cooperative Journal), September 11 and November 11, 1957, JPRS Report 876, 54–58; Donnithorne, *China's Economic System*, 292.

14. "Brokerage Warehouses," 55–56. See also Solivankin, *Notes on Trade*, JPRS Report 3524, 18–20.

15. Ibid., 58.

16. Audrey Donnithorne, "Central Economic Control," *Bulletin of the Atomic Scientists* 20 (June 1966): 11–20, esp. 18–20. Into the mid-1960s, Donnithorne notes that, both spatially and sectorally, Beijing authorities' control and oversight capabilities were profoundly limited, in a nation whose twenty-one provinces averaged thirty to forty million residents, where reliable, competent administrators were scarce and where transport and communications off the main tracks was patchy and slow. Provincial (and lower) officials thus had considerable latitude to follow, adjust, or ignore central directives so long as their required transfers of grain, cotton, and so forth were fulfilled. This frustrated party militants and had no small role in their rising bitterness against regional bureaucrats, not a small element in triggering the Cultural Revolution.

17. The imputed exchange rate between the yuan and the U.S. dollar at this time was ¥2.4 = $1.00.

18. "The Economics of Long-Distance Vegetable Shipments," *Ta Kung Pao*, October 16, 1957, JPRS Report 876, 11–12.

19. "Express Freight Train on Canton-Hankow Railway," *Ta Kung Pao*, September 9, 1962, JPRS Report 15831, 47–51.

20. "Illegal Market Activity in Kansu," *Jen-min Shui-wu* [People's tax affairs], October 4, 1957, JPRS Report 876, 83. It's worth noting that monthly earnings for an APC farmworker would amount to ¥40–60 at this time. City-based workers made appreciably more. Also, 18,000 was the total number of sellers across six months, not the number present on any given market date.

21. "For example, the Feng-feng Trading Corporation of Hebei Province has bought up 720 bicycles from the Communications and Electrical Equipment Corporation in Chaozhou and from the [same] corporation in Changsha since April and May 1957, respectively. The Zheng-ding *xian* [county] SMC in Hebei Province bought 240 bicycles from these corporations in May 1957 and other non-Hunan units a further 345 bicycles. . . . The odd thing is that Hunan does not produce bicycles; they are all brought in from outside sources in the course of the nation-wide balanced allocation. The local selling units give out the bicycles because they want to 'fulfill the plan' or quota assigned to them."

"Disruption of Bicycle Allocation," *Shang-yeh Kung-tso* (Commercial Work), September 19, 1957, JPRS Report 876, 118–19. Bicycles were not cheap (estimated at three to four months of a workers' yearly earnings), and workers' ability to purchase them in a timely fashion without financing may well have threatened meeting sales quotas. See Edward Rhoads, "Cycles of Cathay: A History of the Bicycle in China," *Transfers* 2, no. 2 (2012): 95–120; "Life on Two Wheels," CCTV, 2009, http://www.bicyclekingdom.com/bicycle/Bicyclekingdom1.htm (accessed May 19, 2017).

22. "Black Market in Chang-p'u Hsien, Fukien," *Nung-ts'un Kung-tso Tung-hsun* [Rural work bulletin], August 20, 1957, JPRS Report 876, 83–85. For problems in Hunan, see "Operations of a Market Control Commission," *Ta Kung Pao*, January 19, 1958, JPRS Report 880, November 24,

1958, 34–35. For official responses, see "Notification on Permits for Peasant Marketing," *Jen-min Shui-Wu* [People's tax affairs], March 19, 1958, JPRS Report 1266-N, 24–30.

23. "Pork Control in Shanghai," *Ta Kung Pao*, September 3, 1957, JPRS Report 876, 85.

24. "Abolition of the Peiping Free Vegetable Market," *Ta Kung Pao*, September 5, 1957, JPRS Report 876, 89–91.

25. Ibid., 91 (emphasis added). Similarly, *Ta Kung Pao* reported that supplies of quilters' batting "indispensable for poor working men for cotton coats and coverlets" were not well managed, as it often "[found] its way into the black market to be used for native spinning and weaving." Given its centrality to textile industrial expansion, no cotton could be sold outside state procurement channels, but leakage plainly was happening. "Supplies of Cotton for Quilting," *Ta Kung Pao*, November 18, 1957, JPRS Report 876, 12–13.

26. Donnithorne, "Central Economic Control," 20.

27. As so often, it is the spasms that have commanded scholarly attention, but the everyday operations of households, ministries, and enterprises loomed large in cementing the PRC's durability. Cold War U.S. observers (think Joseph Alsop and the "China watchers") repeatedly anticipated China's collapse; then, when this failed to occur and economic growth gathered momentum in the 1980s, their successors turned to "the Chinese miracle" as a replacement metaphor. Neither characterization is at all adequate.

28. Franz Schurmann, *Ideology and Organization in Communist China*, 2nd ed. (Berkeley: University of California Press, 1968), 182.

29. Chao Kuo-Chun, *Economic Planning and Organization in China: A Documentary Study (1949–1957)*, vol. 2 (Cambridge, MA: Harvard East Asian Research Center, 1963), part 5, "Trade and Cooperatives," 9–10; "Ministry of Commerce Organizational Changes to Take Effect 1 January 1958," *Ta Kung Pao*, December 31, 1957; "Conference on Reform of Statistics, Planning, and Finance and Accounting Systems," *Shang-yeh Kung-tso* [Commercial work], September 26, 1957, both in JPRS Report 876, 37–43.

30. "Conference on Reform," 41–42; "Peiping Commerce Units Reorganized," *Ta Kung Pao*, November 27, 1957, JPRS 876, 45–48.

31. "Reform of Commerce in Kirin Province," *Chi-hua Ching-Chi* [Planned economy], October 17, 1958, JPRS Report 1359-N, March 16, 1959, 22–30, 23 (quote).

32. Ibid., 28, 29. See also Shen I San, "New System for Distribution of Material," *Chi-hua Ching-chi* [Planned economy], October 7, 1958, JPRS Report 1359-N, March 16, 1959, 34–43.

33. "Reform of Commercial Agencies in Shansi," *Ta Kung Pao*, December 1, 1957, JPRS 876, 48–51.

34. Donnithorne, *China's Economic System*, 288.

35. Ibid., 258, quote from Kuo Yu-Huang, "The Need for Vigorous Organization of Rational Transport in the Economic Activities of the Nation," *Jingli Yanjiu* [Economic research], July 17, 1959.

36. Wang Shou-tao, "The Entire Party and People Take Part in Transportation," *Hung Ch'i* [Red flag], January 16, 1959, JPRS Report 1629-N, May 25, 1959, 42–50.

37. "Tientsin Short of Foodstuffs," *Ta Kung Pao*, December 11, 1958, JPRS Report 880, March 16, 1959, 16.

38. "Shock Transport of Consumer and Industrial Goods," JPRS Report 880, 13.

39. Donnithorne, *China's Economic System*, 294–295.

40. Mikhail Klochko, *Soviet Scientist in Red China* (New York: Praeger, 1964), 43–45, 160; Donnithorne, *China's Economic System*, 302–307.

41. Ecklund, "Protracted Expropriation," 247.

42. Ho Cheng and Wei Wen, "On Trade in Rural Fairs," *Ching-chi Yen-chiu* [Economic research], April 17, 1962, JPRS Report 15010, August 28, 1962, 48–52.

43. "Supply and Marketing Cooperatives Misuse Capital," *Ta Kung Pao*, June 12, 1962, JPRS Report 15010, August 28, 1962, 52–54. ¥459 roughly equaled a peasant's yearly earnings at approximately ¥40/month.

44. Chang Kao-Feng, "Prompt Assistance Must Be Rendered to Commercial Basic-Level Units in Dealing with Idle Goods and Material," *Ta Kung Pao*, May 19, 1962, JPRS Report 15010, August 28, 1962, 54–56.

45. "Express Freight Train on Canton-Hangkow Railway," *Ta Kung Pao*, September 9, 1962, JPRS Report 15831, October 22, 1962, 47–51.

46. "Yunnan Province Expedites the Transportation of Agricultural Subsidiary Products from Mountain Areas," *Ta Kung Pao*, June 5, 1962, JPRS Report 14809, August 13, 1962, 7–10. This approach was to be generalized; see "Three-Line Through Traffic Transportation," *Ta Kung Pao*, June 5, 1962, JPRS Report 14809, August 13, 1962, 11–13.

47. "Yunnan Province," 7–10.

48. Chiang Feng, "Some Important Problems Faced by Warehouses," *Ta Kung Pao*, August 29, 1962, JPRS Report 15582, 5 October 1962, 4–11, 4–5 (quotes).

49. Ibid., 7.

50. Ibid., 10.

51. "Liang-liu-kou Warehouse in Chunking Organizes Return Goods for Cargo Delivery Units," *Ta Kung Pao*, July 17, 1962, JPRS Report 15196, September 10, 1962, 48–50.

52. Ibid.

53. "Rural Areas Require Small Hardware Commodities," *Ta Kung Pao*, July 5, 1962, JPRS Report 14928, August 22, 1962, 79–82.

54. Clearance of warehouses, clearance of commodities, clearance of capital funds sunk in inventory.

55. "Questionable Commodities Not Permitted in Warehouses," *Ta Kung Pao*, July 3, 1962, JPRS Report 14928, August 22, 1962, 70–73.

56. K'ang P'ing, "Some Observations on the Maintenance and Development of Certain Operational Characteristics of Retail Trade," *Ka Tung Pao*, July 2, 1962, JPRS Report 14928, August 22, 1962, 45–56.

57. For this process, see http://www.wikihow.com/Blanch-Spinach. It precedes either freezing or drying for preservation.

58. Wei Fu-k'ai, "My Views on the Adoption of the System of Keeping a Record of Commodities Sold at Sales Counters," *Ta Kung Pao*, June 19, 1962, JPRS Report 14753, August 2, 1962, 34–38.

59. Ibid., 38.

60. "The Organization of Venders' Association in Nanking," *Ta Kung Pao*, July 16, 1962, JPRS Report 15196, September 10, 1962, 51–52.

61. Yueh Wu, "Operations at Peiping's Largest Vegetable Market," *Ta Kung Pao*, April 27, 1962, JPRS Report 15010, August 28, 1962, 57.

62. Philip Scranton, "Managing Communist Enterprises: Poland, Hungary and Czechoslovakia, 1945–1970," *Enterprise and Society* 19 (2018): forthcoming; also see the contribution herein: Anna Kushkova, "Hidden Realms of Private Entrepreneurship: Soviet Jews and Post–World War

II Artels in the USSR," in *Capitalism's Hidden Worlds*, ed. Kenneth Lipartito and Lisa Jacobson, 203–222 (Philadelphia: University of Pennsylvania Press, 2019).

63. Michael Alexeev and Gregory Grossman, "Studies on the Soviet Second Economy," Berkeley-Duke Occasional Papers on the Second Economy in the USSR, No. 11, Durham, NC, 1987; Konstantin Simis, *The Second Economy and Corruption at the District Level* (Washington, DC: National Council for Soviet and East European Research, 1986).

Chapter 10. Hidden Realms of Private Entrepreneurship

1. For more on prerevolutionary artels, see Nikolai Kalachev, *Arteli v drevnei i nyneshnei Rossii* (Saint Petersburg: Tipografija V. Golovina, 1864); A. Isaev, *Arteli v Rossii* (Yaroslavl: Pechatnia Gubernskogo Pravlenija, 1881); V. V. Averjanov, V. Y. Venediktov, and A. V. Koslov, eds., *Artel' i artel'nyi chelovek* (Moscow: Institut russkoi tsivilizatsii, 2014), 213–227.

2. See V. I. Lenin, "O kooperatsii," in *Polnoe sobranie sochinenii*, vol. 45 (March 1922–March 1923), 5th ed. (Moscow: Politicheskaya literatura, 1970), 371, 373.

3. I. S. Kondurushkin, *Chastnyi capital pered Sovetskim sudom. Puti i metody nakoplenija po sudebnym i revizionnym delam 1918–1926 gg.* (Moscow: Gosudarstvennoe izdatel'stvo, 1927), 120. In 1925 there existed 8,600 artisanal cooperatives in the country, and by 1941, when the process of artisanal cooperation countrywide was "largely completed," the country had 25,600 producer cooperatives with a membership of 2.6 million people (A. I. Buzlaeva, "Promyslovaya kooperatsija," in *Economic Encyclopedia. Political Economy*, vol. 2, ed. M. Rumiantsev [Moscow: Sovetskaya Entsiklopedija, 1975], 252–253).

4. Administration of Producer Cooperation under RSFSR Council of Ministers, Planning and Economy Department, Production activity reports of producer artels, Moscow region, Vol. 2, 1946, Fund 395, Inventory 1, File 802, 167. State Archive of the Russian Federation, Building 2 [hereafter abbreviated as GARF-1 (Building 1 of the Archive) or GARF-2 (Building 2)].

5. Ibid., vol. 3, 6.

6. Ibid., 33.

7. Gennady Estraikh, "The Soviet Shtetl in the 1920's," *Polin: Studies in Polish Jewry* 17 (2004): 201.

8. See, for example, V. G. Tan, "Evreiskoe mestechko v revoljutsii," in *Evreiskoe mestechko v revoljutsii*, ed. V. G. Bogoraz-Tan, 7–27 (Moscow: Gosudarstvennoe izdatel'stvo, 1926); A. Bragin and M. Kol'tsov, *Sud'ba evresikikh mass v Sovestkom Souyze* (Moscow: Gosudarstvennoe izdatel'stvo, 1924); I. I. Veitzblit, *Derazhnia. Sovremennoe evreiskoe mestechko* (Moscow: Gosizdat, 1929).

9. See, for example, Golfo Alexopoulos, *Stalin's Outcasts: Aliens, Citizens, and the Soviet State, 1926–1936* (Ithaca, NY: Cornell University Press, 2003), 3.

10. See, for example, Estraikh, "The Soviet Shtetl," 200, 205; Oleg Budnitsky, "Evrei i VChK (1917–1921)," *Kazus. Individual'noe i unikal'noe v istorii. 2007–2009*, no. 9 (2012): 138; Arkadii Zeltser, *Evrei sovetskoi provintsii: Vitebsk i mestechki, 1917–1941* (Moscow: ROSSPEN, 2006), 6.

11. E. Shkol'nikova, "*Transformatsija evreiskogo mestechka v SSSR v 1930-e gody (po materialam Gosudarstvennogo Arkhiva Rossiiskoi Federatsii i evreiskoi pressy na idish i russkom)*" (Moscow: Obshchestvo "Evreiskoe nasledie," 1996), http://jhistory.nfurman.com/lessons9/1930.htm; Veitzblit, *Derazhnia*, 80.

12. Arkadii Zeltser, "Artels," in *YIVO Encyclopedia of Jews in Eastern Europe*, vol. 1, ed. Gershon David Hundert (New Haven, CT: Yale University Press, 2008), 74.

13. A. Kirzhnits, *Trudiashchiesia evrei v bor'be s religiei (Iz itogov 1929–1930 gg.)* (Moscow: Bezbozhnik, 1931), 65; Arcadius Kahan, *Essays in Jewish Social and Economic History*, ed. Roger Weiss, intro. Jonathan Frankel (Chicago: University of Chicago Press, 1986), 194; Zeltser, "Artels," 73.

14. "Artel," in *Bol'shaya sovietskaya entsiklopedija*, vol. 3, ed. S. I. Vavilov (Moscow: Bol'shaya Sovetskaya Entsyklopedia, 1950), 123.

15. A. A. Nikolaev, *Osnovnye vidy kooperatsii v Rossii: istoriko-teoretichesky ocherk*, ed. V. A. Ilyinykh (Novosibirsk: Institut istorii SO RAN, 2007), 28.

16. Sheila Fitzpatrick, "After NEP: The Fate of NEP Entrepreneurs, Small Traders, and Artisans in the 'Socialist Russia' of the 1930s," *Russian History / Histoire Russe* 13, nos. 2–3 (Summer–Fall 1986): 187, 210, https://doi.org/10.1163/187633186X00089.

17. JEES_083_DT_MK, b. 1943, b. 1934, F, F, November 17, 2013, Balashikha. Citations of field materials include the abbreviation of the project title (JEES, Jewish Ethnic Economy Under Socialism), the number of the interview, informant(s) initials, gender (F/M), the year(s) of informants' birth, and the date and the place of the recording. All interviews were recorded by me and are kept in my personal archive.

18. D. Filtzer, "The Standard of Living of Soviet Industrial Workers in the Immediate Postwar Period, 1945–1948," *Europe-Asia Studies* 51, no. 6 (1999): 1018, http://www.jstor.org/stable /153670.

19. Julie Hessler, "A Postwar Perestroika? Toward a History of Private Enterprise in the USSR," *Slavic Review* 57, no. 3 (Autumn 1998): 517–518, https://doi.org/10.2307/2500710.

20. Elena Zubkova, *Poslevoennoe sovetskoe obshchestvo: politika i povsednevnost', 1945–1953* (Moscow: ROSSPEN, 2000), 71.

21. Hessler, "A Postwar Perestroika," 533.

22. For more detail, see *Direktivy KPSS i Sovetskogo pravitel'stva po khoziaistvennym voprosam. 1917–1957*, vol. 2, 1929–1945, comp. by V. N. Malin i A. V. Korobov (Moscow: Politicheskaya literatura, 1957), 867–873.

23. *Direktivy KPSS i Sovetskogo pravitel'stva po khoziaistvennym voprosam. 1917–1957*, vol. 3, 1946–1952, comp. by V. N. Malin i A. V. Korobov (Moscow: Politicheskaya literatura, 1958), 110–111.

24. Frederick Leedy, "Producers' Cooperatives in the Soviet Union," *Monthly Labor Review* 80, no. 9 (1957): 1064.

25. Russian expression meaning "under the legal jurisdiction of" or "under the cover of."

26. JEES_128_SP, b. 1952, M, July 13, 2014, Malakhovka.

27. Alain Besançon, *Sovetskoe nastojashchee i russkoe proshloe: Sbornik statei* (Moscow: MIK, 1998), 281.

28. *Ustav kooperativnoi promyslovoi arteli* (Leningrad: Kooperativnoe izdatel'stvo, 1953), 1–6.

29. JEES_130_DT, b. 1941, M, July 15–16, 2014, Malakhovka.

30. JEES_105_VG, b. 1923, M, April 29, 2014, Malakhovka.

31. For example, JEES_024_IB, b. 1938, F, June 26, 2013, Saint Petersburg; JEES_051_PZ, b. 1948, M, October 3, 2013, Moscow; JEES_052_SU_GK_LL, b. 1953, b. 1956, b. 1944, M, M, M, October 6, 2013, Moscow.

32. JEES_117_YT_IT, b. 1932, b. 1931, M, F, May 30, 2014, Il'yinka.

33. JEES_068_GG, b. 1945, M, October 29, 2013, Saltykovka.

34. JEES_077_VC, b. 1930, F, November 13, 2013, Saltykovka.

35. A. Malyshkin, "Zdes' remontirujut noski," *Promyslovaya kooperatsija* 2 (January 1958): 14.

36. R. Meltser, "Okraska noshenoi obuvi," *Promyslovaya kooperatsija* 6 (June 1959): 38.

37. Council of Producer Cooperation of RSFSR, Department of accounting and reporting, Reports for the artels of the Moscow region for the year of 1950, Vol. 5, Fund 395, Inventory 1, File 1222, 128–129, GARF-2.

38. JEES_112_FK, b. 1926, M, May 10, 2014, Malakhovka. See also JEES_074_GR, b. 1936, F, November 9, 2013, Saltykovka; JEES_117_YT_IT, b. 1932, b. 1931, M, F, May 30, 2014, Il'yinka.

39. Council of Ministers of the RSFSR, On the improvement of quality of mass consumption goods produced by local industry, producer cooperation and cooperation of invalids, December 28, 1944–April 2, 1945, Fund A 259, Inventory 6, File 201, 26–26 rev., 28 rev., GARF-1.

40. JEES_105_VG, b. 1923, M, April 29, 2014, Malakhovka.

41. JEES_111_RD, b. 1934, M, May 9, 2014, Malakhovka.

42. A Yiddish word for "business," not necessarily fully legal and usually pursued for profit; borrowed by the Russian language with the same meaning.

43. JEES_097_AS, b. 1942, M, April 20, 2014, Malakhovka.

44. János Kornai, "Resource-Constrained Versus Demand-Constrained Systems," *Econometrica* 47, no. 4 (July 1979): 804, http://www.jstor.org/stable/1914132.

45. See, for instance, Katherine Verdery, *What Was Socialism and What Comes Next?* (Princeton, NJ: Princeton University Press, 1996), 20–22; Karen Dawisha, "Communism as a Lived System of Ideas in Contemporary Russia," *East European Politics and Societies* 19 (2005): 481, https://doi.org/10.1177/0888325405278105; Joseph Berliner, "Blat Is Higher than Stalin!" *Problems of Communism* 3, no. 1 (1954): 22–31.

46. JEES_128_SP, b. 1952, M, July 13, 2014, Malakhovka.

47. JEES_017_MB, b. 1923, M, June 4, 2013, Moscow. "Go to the left" means "to do things in a not fully legal—or completely illegal—way." "Left" is often used as an adjective, to signify that certain goods were not produced or sold in the legal way (as in "left goods").

48. Clifford Geertz, "The Bazaar Economy: Information and Search in Peasant Marketing," *American Economic Review* 68, no. 2 (1978): 31, http://www.jstor.org/stable/1816656.

49. JEES_078_VM, b. 1946, M, November 11, 2013, Saltykovka. On the "invalid artels," created specifically to provide job placement for people disabled as a result of the war, see M. A. Gelfer, *Sovetskoe ugolovnoe pravo. Chast' osobennaya*, no. 7 (Moscow: Vsesoyuznyi yuridicheskii zaochnyi institut, 1959), 15, 16; *Ob usilenii bor'by s zloupotreblenijami, izvrashchenijami i narushenijami Ustava artelei iz soyuzov kooperatsii invalidov. Postanovlenie Prezidiuma Ukrainskogo Soveta kooperatsii invalidov № 171 ot 29-go marta 1948 g.* (Kiev: Ukoopinsovet, 1948), 3–4.

50. JEES_015_RK_SK, b. 1938, b. 1934, F, M, May 30, 2013, Babylon, NY.

51. JEES_073_IV, b. 1946, M, November 7, 2013, Saltykovka.

52. JEES_097_AS, b. 1942, M, April 20, 2014, Malakhovka.

53. JEES_111_RD, b. 1934, M, May 9, 2014, Malakhovka.

54. JEES_119_MS_SS, b. 1943, b. 1943, M, F, June 2, 2014, Malakhovka.

55. JEES_126_VS, b. 1929, M, July 9, 2014, Saltykovka.

56. Tamara Kondratjeva, *Kormit' i pravit': o vlasti v Rossii XVI–XX v.* (Moscow: ROSSPEN, 2006). The book presents a systematic analysis of "feeding" as the major principle of Russian polity over four centuries, including during Soviet rule.

57. Stefan Hedlund, *Invisible Hands, Russian Experience, and Social Science: Approaches to Understanding Systemic Failure* (New York: Cambridge University Press, 2011), 111–120, 133.

58. Orders and decrees of the Administration Collegium of Producer Cooperation under the RSFSR Council of Ministers (originals and copies), 1948, Fund 396, Inventory 2, File 93, 129–130, GARF-2.

59. For instance, Evgenija Evelson, *Sudebnye protsessy po ekonomicheskim delam v SSSR (shestidesiatye gody)* (*"Second Economy" in the USSR [Trials of the 1960s]*) (London: Overseas Publications Interchange, 1986), 22, 71.

60. JEES_109_SG_IG, b. 1934, b. 1960, M, M, May 2, 2014, Bronnitsy.

61. Yiddish for "earn." JEES_094_MG_RG, b. 1924, b. 1939, M, F, April 16, 2014, Malakhovka.

62. Orders and decrees, 154.

63. JEES_108_AP, b. ca. 1940, F, May 1, 2014, Zhukovsky; JEES_094_MG_RG, b. 1924, b. 1939, M, F, April 16, 2014, Malakhovka.

64. Decrees, protocols and transcripts of meetings of collegium for the issues of cadres and special activities over the year of 1948 (originals), Administration of Producer Cooperation under the RSFSR Council of Ministers, Secret department, June 17–December 1, 1948, Fund 396, Inventory 2, File 95, 45, GARF-2.

65. Konstantin Simis, *USSR: The Corrupt Society; The Secret World of Soviet Capitalism,* trans. Jacqueline Edwards and Mitchell Schneider (New York: Simon and Schuster, 1982), 146.

66. Verdery, *What Was Socialism,* 27.

67. Simis, *USSR: The Corrupt Society,* 146.

68. JEES_078_VM, b. 1946, M, November 11, 2013, Saltykovka.

69. JEES_015_RK_SK, b. 1938, b. 1934, F, M, May 30, 2013, Babylon, NY.

70. Elizabeth Dunn, *Privatizing Poland: Baby Food, Big Business, and the Remaking of Labor* (Ithaca, NY: Cornell University Press, 2004), 17.

71. JEES_099_IK, b. 1931, F, April 23, 2014, Malakhovka.

72. JEES_022_LG, b. 1947, M, June 15, 2013, Saint Petersburg.

73. JEES_121_FZ, b. 1952, F, June 7, 2014, Moscow.

74. JEES_082_LV, b. 1954, M, November 16, 2013, Moscow.

75. Hedlund, *Invisible Hands,* 122.

76. Marina Hakkarainen, "'Evreiskie den'gi' v epokhu transformatsii: obshchestvo, vlast', etnichnost' v vospominaniakh o sovetskom vremeni," *Antropologichesky Forum* 18 (2013): 261, http://anthropologie.kunstkamera.ru/files/pdf/018online/hakkarainen.pdf.

77. JEES_119_MS_SS, b. 1943, b. 1943, M, F, June 2, 2014, Malakhovka.

78. JEES_099_IK, b. 1931, F, April 23, 2014, Malakhovka.

79. E.g., JEES_101_ArV_AnV, b. 1943, b. 1937, F, M, April 25, 2014, Malakhovka; JEES_078_VM, b. 1946, M, November 11, 2013, Saltykovka; JEES_074_GR, b. 1936, F, November 9, 2013, Saltykovka.

80. JEES_131_AR, b. 1964, F, July 16, 2014, Saltykovka.

81. See, for example, JEES_014_EB, b. 1933, M, May 30, 2013, New York, NY; JEES_080_EZ_AS_DS, b. 1961, b. 1961, b. 1962, F, F, M, November 15, 2013, Moscow.

82. JEES_014_EB, b. 1933, M, May 30, 2013, New York, NY.

83. JEES_020_LL, b. 1944, M, June 6, 2013, Moscow. See also JEES_100_MZ, b. 1973, M, April 23, 2014, Malakhovka; JEES_114_FK, b. 1937, F, May 15, 2014, Kraskovo.

84. JEES_123_EO, b. 1951, F, July 8, 2014, Malakhovka. See also JEES_090_IA, b. 1926, M, November 30, 2013, Saltykovka; JEES_097_AS, b. 1942, M, April 20, 2014, Malakhovka; JEES_100_MZ, b. 1973, M, April 23, 2014, Malakhovka; JEES_111_RD, b. 1934, M, May 9, 2014, Malakhovka; JEES_121_FZ, b. 1952, F, June 7, 2014, Moscow.

85. Zubkova, *Poslevoennoe*, 28.

86. Jehoshua A. Gilboa, *The Black Years of Soviet Jewry, 1939–1953* (Boston: Little, Brown, 1971), 146–352; Zvi Gitelman, *A Century of Ambivalence: The Jews of Russia and the Soviet Union, 1881 to the Present* (Bloomington: Indiana University Press, 2001), 144–174; B. Pinkus and J. Frankel, *The Soviet Government and the Jews 1948–1967: A Documented Study* (Cambridge: Cambridge University Press, 1984), 83–96, 194–201; David Brandenberger, "Stalin's Last Crime? Recent Scholarship on Postwar Soviet Antisemitism and the Doctor's Plot," *Kritika: Explorations in Russian and Eurasian History* 6, no. 1 (Winter 2005): 187–204, https://doi.org/10.1353/kri.2005.0001.

87. Evelson, *Sudebnye protsessy*, 15.

88. JEES_052_SU_GK_LL, b. 1953, b. 1956, b. 1944, M, M, M, October 6, 2013, Moscow.

89. JEES_001_ER, b. 1937, M, January 9, 2013, Grahamsville, NY.

90. JEES_068_GG, b. 1945, M, October 29, 2013, Saltykovka.

91. Adam Teller, "Economic Life," in *YIVO Encyclopedia of Jews in Eastern Europe*, vol. 1, ed. Gershon D. Hundert (New Haven, CT: Yale University Press, 2008), 443. A number of historians argued that the closure of "institutions, posts, and entire fields of professional activity" made Jews turn "to underground dealings in the economic sphere" (Yaacov Ro'i, "Economic Trials," in *YIVO Encyclopedia of Jews in Eastern Europe*, vol. 1, ed. Gershon D. Hundert [New Haven, CT: Yale University Press, 2008], 454) and that this was the major "historical reason" why "the underground business world in the large cities of Russia, the Ukraine, and the Baltic republics has been predominantly Jewish" (Simis, *USSR: The Corrupt Society*, 153). These conclusions, however, primarily refer to large-scale private entrepreneurship (something that in Russian is called *tsekhovoi biznes*) rather than to artel-type economic engagements. Even though they share a number of significant similarities, the latter deserve separate consideration.

92. JEES_128_SP, b. 1952, M, July 13, 2014, Malakhovka.

93. See a complementary discussion on the role of social networks in maintaining "economic pluralism" in the contribution herein: Bryan Turo, "In the Shadow of Incorporation: Hidden Economies of the Hispano Borderlands, 1890–1930," in *Capitalism's Hidden Worlds*, ed. Kenneth Lipartito and Lisa Jacobson, 99–116 (Philadelphia: University of Pennsylvania Press, 2019).

94. JEES_020_LL, b. 1944, M, June 6, 2013, Moscow.

95. Karl Polanyi, "The Economy as Instituted Process," in *Economic Anthropology*, ed. E. LeClair Jr. and H. Schneider (New York: Holt, Rinehart and Winston, 1968), 127.

96. Mark Edele, "Soviet Society, Social Structure, and Everyday Life: Major Frameworks Reconsidered," *Kritika: Explorations in Russian and Eurasian History* 8, no. 2 (Spring 2007): 356, https://doi.org/10.1353/kri.2007.0025.

97. JEES_099_IK, b. 1931, F, April 23, 2014, Malakhovka.

98. Marilyn Strathern, "Kinship and Economy: Constitutive Orders of a Provisional Kind," *American Ethnologist* 12, no. 2 (May 1985): 192, http://www.jstor.org/stable/644216.

99. Salo W. Baron and Arcadius Kahan, *Economic History of the Jews*, ed. Nachum Gross (New York: Schocken, 1976), xi.

100. Even matzo baking, a paradigmatic Jewish ethnic business, largely clandestine in the USSR as a money-generating enterprise, relied on non-Jewish workers—particularly in Malakhovka, where it assumed the size of a supralocal business, providing matzo to Jews in many other places (e.g., JEES_097_AS, b. 1942, M, April 20, 2014, Malakhovka; JEES_101_ArV_AnV, b. 1943, b. 1937, F, M, April 25, 2014, Malakhovka). None of those non-Jewish workers ever denounced the organizers to the authorities: monetary consideration overweighed any others, even if those existed to begin with.

101. Katherine Verdery, "Ethnic Relations, Economies of Shortage, and the Transition in Eastern Europe," in *Socialism: Ideals, Ideologies, and Local Practice*, ASA Monographs 31, ed. C. M. Hann (Taylor & Francis e-Library, 2005), 170, 172.

102. Even though, as most interviews suggest, there must have been an important ethnic divide, whereby Jews usually performed the role of the managerial "brain center," while rank-and-file workers could be of various ethnic backgrounds (e.g., JEES_119_MS_SS, b. 1943, b. 1943, M, F, June 2, 2014, Malakhovka).

103. JEES_023_AL_ET, b. 1953, b. 1937, F, F, June 26, 2013, Saint Petersburg.

104. JEES_028_NG_ES, b. 1951, b. 1954, M, F, July 4, 2013, Saint Petersburg.

105. JEES_043_GL, b. 1938, M, August 15, 2013, Saint Petersburg. See also JEES_051_PZ, b. 1948, M, October 3, 2013, Moscow; JEES_101_ArV_AnV, b. 1943, b. 1937, F, M, April 25, 2014, Malakhovka; JEES_131_AR, b. 1964, F, July 16, 2014, Saltykovka.

106. Kahan, *Essays*, 83. See also Teller, "Economic Life," 444; Jacques Attali, *The Economic History of the Jewish People* (Washington, DC: Eska, 2010), 305; Ismar Schorsch, *From Text to Context: The Turn to History in Modern Judaism*. (Boston: Brandeis University Press; Hanover, NH: University Press of New England, 1994), 123–124, 130–131.

107. A. Kimerling, "Razryvy in konventsii pozdnei stalinskoi epokhi," in *Razryvy i konventsii v otechestvennoi kul'ture*, ed. O. L. Leibovich (Perm': Permskii gosudarstvennyi institut iskusstva i kul'tury, 2011), 125.

108. See Andrew Sloin, "Speculators, Swindlers and Other Jews: Regulating Trade in Revolutionary White Russia," *East European Jewish Affairs* 40, no. 2 (2010): 103–125, https://doi.org/10.1080/13501674.2010.494042; Alan M. Ball, *Russia's Last Capitalists: The Nepmen, 1921–1929* (Berkeley: University of California Press, 1987), 85–190; Besançon, *Sovetskoe nastojashchee*, 280–281; George Dalton, "Theoretical Issues in Economic Anthropology," *Current Anthropology* 10, no. 1 (1969): 67, http://www.jstor.org/stable/2740685.

109. M. I. Goldman, "Russian Jews in Business," in *Jewish Life After the USSR*, ed. Z. Gitelman (Bloomington: Indiana University Press, 2003): 81–82.

110. JEES_109_SG_IG, b. 1934, b. 1960, M, M, May 2, 2014, Bronnitsy.

111. JEES_121_FZ, b. 1952, F, June 7, 2014, Moscow.

112. Geertz, "Bazaar Economy," 30.

113. Hessler, "Postwar Perestroika," 516.

114. JEES_099_IK, b. 1931, F, April 23, 2014, Malakhovka.

115. JEES_073_IV, b. 1946, M, November 7, 2013, Saltykovka.

116. JEES_119_MS_SS, b. 1943, b. 1943, M, F, June 2, 2014, Malakhovka.

117. JEES_131_AR, b. 1964, F, July 16, 2014, Saltykovka.

118. *Reshenija partii i pravitel'stva po khoziaistvennym voprsam: sbornik dokumentov za 50 let (1917–1967)*, vol. 4, 1953–1961, comp. by V. N. Malin i A. V. Korobov (Moscow: Politicheskaya literatura, 1968), 297.

119. JEES_022_LG, b. 1947, M, June 15, 2013, Saint Petersburg.

120. S. L. Seniavskiy and V. P. Tel'pukhovskiy, *Rabochii klass SSSR (1938–1963)* (Moscow: Mysl', 1971), 146.

121. Besançon, *Sovetskoe nastojashchee*, 281.

Contributors

Bruce E. Baker is Lecturer in American History at Newcastle University and coauthor, with Barbara Hahn, of *The Cotton Kings: Capitalism and Corruption in Turn-of-the-Century New York and New Orleans* (2016). His current book project is a study of crime in the cotton trade from the Civil War to the New Deal.

Eileen Boris is Hull Professor and Distinguished Professor of Feminist Studies at the University of California, Santa Barbara. She has forthcoming from Oxford University Press, *Making the Woman Worker: Precarious Labor and the Fight for Global Standards, 1919–2019.*

Eli Cook is Assistant Professor of History at the University of Haifa. His book, *The Pricing of Progress: Economic Indicators and the Capitalization of American Life*, received the 2017 Best Book award from the Society of U.S. Intellectual Historians, as well as the Morris D. Forkosch Book Prize from the *Journal of the History of Ideas*. He is currently working on a book on the relationship between the idea of choice and the realities of capitalism in the late twentieth century.

Hannah Frydman is a PhD candidate in history at Rutgers University–New Brunswick. She is writing a dissertation entitled "Classified Commerce: Gender, Labor, and Print Capitalism in Paris, 1881–1940." Her writing has appeared in *Public Books*, and her research has been supported by fellowships from the Social Science Research Council and the Chateaubriand Fellowship.

James Hollis is a DPhil candidate in history at Brasenose College, Oxford, where he holds the Walter Scott Studentship in the Global History of

Capitalism. His doctoral thesis is titled "Pax Pecuniaria? Offshore Finance in the Twilight of the British Empire, 1922–1984." He has a decade's practical experience as an attorney and is author of several technical articles on aspects of corporate taxation.

Owen James Hyman is Visiting Assistant Professor of History at Utah State University Eastern, where he is completing the manuscript "Cut over Color Lines: An Environmental History of Jim Crow in the Deep South's Forests." His work has been supported by the Walter S. Rosenberry Fellowship from the Forest History Society, the Reed Fink Award in Southern Labor History from the Southern Labor Archives, and the Department of Black Studies at the University of California, Santa Barbara.

Lisa Jacobson is Associate Professor of History at the University of California, Santa Barbara, and author of *Raising Consumers: Children and the American Mass Market in the Early Twentieth Century* (2004) and editor of *Children and Consumer Culture in American Society* (2008). She is currently working on a book manuscript titled "Fashioning New Cultures of Drink: Alcoholic Beverages and the Politics of Pleasure After Prohibition."

Anna Kushkova is Research Assistant Professor of Anthropology at the University of North Carolina, Chapel Hill. She received her first professional degree (equivalent of PhD) in Anthropology from the European University of Saint Petersburg and received a second PhD from UNC Chapel Hill in 2017. She is author of *Peasant Quarrel: A Study of Rural Everyday Life* (2016).

Kenneth Lipartito is Professor of History at Florida International University and past president of the Business History Conference. His most recent book, *Corporate Responsibility: The American Experience* (2012), received the 2014 Best Book Award from the Social Issues in Management Division, Academy of Management. Among his other publications are *A History of the Kennedy Space Center* (2007) and *The Bell System and Regional Business: The Telephone in the South* (1989). He is currently writing a history of surveillance and capitalism.

Christopher McKenna is University Reader in Business History and Strategy in the Said Business School, a Fellow of Brasenose College, and Co-Director of the Global History of Capitalism Project in the Oxford Centre for Global History, all within the University of Oxford. He is author of *The World's Newest Profession: Management Consulting in the Twentieth Century* (2006), and his current book project is a global history of white-collar crime from the South Sea bubble to the present, tentatively titled "Partners in Crime."

Kenneth Mouré is Professor of History at the University of Alberta. His publications include *Managing the Franc Poincaré* (1991) and *The Gold Standard Illusion* (2002). He is completing research for a book on economic controls and black market activity in France during and after World War II, with the working title "Marché Noir: Economic Strategies for Survival in Wartime France."

Philip Scranton is Board of Governors Professor Emeritus, History of Industry and Technology at Rutgers University. His most recent publications are *The Emergence of Routines* (Oxford University Press, 2017), coedited with Daniel Raff, and *Enterprise, Technology and Organization in China, 1950–1971: A Socialist Experiment* (2019).

Bryan W. Turo is Director of Operations at NextWave Safety Solutions, Inc., as well as Adjunct Professor of History at Concordia College, New York. He earned his PhD at the University of New Mexico in 2015, where he completed his dissertation, "An Empire of Dust: Thomas Benton Catron and the Rise of Capitalism in New Mexico, 1840–1921." His current research focuses on the ways disparate and overlapping economic systems interacted across the nineteenth-century American Southwest.

Index

Ahmad, Zubeida, 47, 60, 62–63
Aldrich, Nelson, Senator, and the Aldrich
    Report, 39–40
American Geographical and Statistical
    Society (AGSS). *See* Economic indicators
    in mid-nineteenth-century northern US
American Metal Company (AMC), 162, 174
Appleby, Joyce, 5
Appleton, Nathan, 33
Arnesen, Eric, 69

Bahamas, 163, 172
Baron, Salo W., 219
Barry, Leona, 41
Baudin, Louis, 149
Beckert, Sven, and *Empire of Cotton*, 6, 68, 79
Beijing. *See* People's Republic of China (PRC)
    commercial system
Belgium, 139, 166, 167, 174
Benería, Lourdes, 47, 49–52, 56–57, 60–61
Besançon, Alain, 208–209, 222
Black markets: and the Committee for the
    Confiscation of Illicit Profits (CCPI), 151,
    152–154; and Contrôle Économique agents,
    150–151; and "family parcels," 144–146; and
    food protests, 143–144, 149–151; and de
    Gaulle's response, 152; and German
    involvement in, 145–146, 148; and German
    occupation policies of price controls and
    rationing, 141–142; and illicit butter
    market, 145–146; and illicit meat slaughter,
    146–147; and luxury Paris restaurants, 143,

147; in Nazi-occupied France, 17–18,
    140–147; in World War II Europe, Nazi
    Germany, UK, US, 139–140; and privileged
    access to, 142–143; and producers' use of,
    148; and state controls vs. illicit commerce,
    140–142, 147; and *le système D* (resourceful-
    ness), 148–149, 154, 256n45; and Vichy
    regime response to, 18, 143–144, 146,
    149–151. *See also* Hidden markets
Bond, Horace Mann, 91, 94
Boserup, Ester, and *Women's Role in
    Economic Development*, 47–50, 59
Bouilly, Robert, 68
Burn, Gary, 158
Burnard, Trevor, 6

Capitalism: as a cultural system, 5; and
    environmental destruction, 16, 27, 84–85,
    88, 90, 98, 115; and gender inequalities, 14,
    41, 45, 48–50, 53, 56, 125, 137; historiogra-
    phy of, 4–9; as a hybrid system, 9; and
    racism, 16, 27, 82, 84–85, 88, 92–93, 97–98,
    105; and socialist economies and societies,
    viii, 9, 11, 19–20, 59, 181, 182, 184–186, 192,
    193, 195, 199–201, 205–206, 208–210, 211,
    214–215, 217, 218–219, 220, 221; traditional
    definition of, 1. *See also* Hidden markets;
    Informal economy; New historians of;
    Social history of
Carlisle, Rodney, 164
Carl Zeiss (German manufacturer), 162
Cayman Islands, 157

China. *See* People's Republic of China (PRC) commercial system

Classified advertising (*petites announces*) in late nineteenth- and early twentieth-century Parisian daily newspapers and weekly magazines: *Le Figaro*, 121–122, 127; *Gil Blas*, 130–132, 133, 251n42; *Le Journal*, 121, 132; *Le Matin*, 121, 129; *Paris-Soir*, 122, 124, 135–136, 252n63; *Le Petit Journal*, 121, 127; *Le Petit Parisien*, 120–121, 129; *Le Rire*, 135; *Le Sourire*, 122–123; *Le Supplément*, 134, 251n51, 252n55; *La Vie Parisienne*, 135; and Henry Bérenger's "Responsibilities of the Press," 127–128; as economic opportunities for women, 125–126, 133; and first and second French media revolutions, 126–127; and freedom of the press law (1881), 126; and Jean Frollo, 120, 121, 124, 126, 130; as intimate forms of entrepreneurship, 119–120, 125–126; and Jean Jaurès, 127–128; and opposition against, 122, 135–136; press and abortionists, 119, 125; press and pornography, 127–128; press and prostitution, 119, 121, 125, 127, 129–130; and Jean Prouvost, 136, 252n63; as revenue, 121, 127, 249n10; and Avril de Sainte-Croix, 129; and Maurice Schwob, 132; and Séverine's "The White Slave Trade," 129–130, 135; and Maurice Talmeyr, 127–128; use of coded language in, 119–120, 128–129, 130, 132, 134, 251n44; and Jean and Pierre Veber, 130–132. *See also* Hidden markets

Commodification, and Marxian models, 4, 5, 7

Conference of International Labour Statisticians (2013), definition of unpaid reproductive labor as "work," 4

Cotton: "city crop," 67; handling of cotton bales, 69–71; "junk shops" in, 74–75, 78; New Orleans and, 14, 67–68; New Orleans Stock Exchange (NOCE), new ways of understanding capitalism, 80; "pickeries" in, 75–77, 78; products made from, 74; regulation of, 14, 67, 77–78; in Southern cotton ports, 73; theft of cotton, 71–73.

See also Hidden markets; Second-hand economies

Counterfeit merchandise. *See* Hidden markets

Court of Private Land Claims (CPLC). *See* New Mexico (1890–1930)

Cronon, William, 36, 84

Darwin, Charles, 10; and the tangled bank theory, 10, 12

Deep South Piney Woods (South and Southeast Louisiana): African American landowners in, 82, 85–86, 89–90, 91; Bayou Bonfouca, 81–82, 84, 85, 86–87, 89, 91, 95, 238nn1–2; "cut out and get out" analysis framework of, 82, 84–85, 90–91, 93, 97–98; formal and informal markets in, 84; Homestead Acts and, 84–85; interracial economy in, 82, 84–86, 88, 90–91, 93–95, 97–98; Jim Crow in, 82, 88, 92, 95, 96; lumber companies activities in, 15–16, 81–83, 85, 88, 95–96, 98; St. Tammany Parish, 81–82, 89, 90, 94; sugarcane production in, 15, 93–94; Washington Parish, 91–92, 94, 95, 98; white supremacy and deforestation in, 15–16, 82, 84, 85, 97–98. *See also* Lumber; Railroad companies; US South post Civil War

De Soto, Hernando, 20

Deutsch, Sarah, 243n8

Deutsch-Amerikanische Petroleum Gesellschaft (DAPG), 163

Donnithorne, Audrey, 181–182, 186, 264n16

Dulles, Eleanor, 165

Dunn, Elizabeth, 215

Dutourd, Jean, and *Au bon buerre*, 154

Ecklund, George, 181

Economic indicators: consumer price index (CPI), 13; Dow Jones Industrial Average, 13, 26, 27, 39, 42; gross domestic product (GDP), 13–14, 42, 25–27, 29, 42, 43; unpaid reproductive labor as an, 44–45, 63. *See also* Economic indicators in mid-nineteenth-century northern US; Moral statistics, early nineteenth century

Economic indicators in mid-nineteenth-century northern US, 28–29, 33–34, 42–43; influence of the railroad revolution on, 36, 38; role of the American Geographical and Statistical Society (AGSS) on, 38. *See also* Economic indicators; Moral statistics, early nineteenth century

Edele, Mark, 218

Elder-Vass, Dave, 10–11

Ellis, Tuffly, 68

Entrepreneurs and Entrepreneurship: and China, 9, 19–20, 183, 201; and creative form of, 4; and classified advertising, 17, 119–120, 125–126; and illicit form of, 3, 8, 17; and New Mexico, 108–109; and New Orleans, 80; and women, 80, 119–120, 125–126; and World War II France, 17–18; and Soviet Union, 9, 19–20, 203, 207, 211, 213–214, 216–222

Estraikh, Gennady, 206

Evans, George H., and the Workingmen's Party, 30

Evelson, Evgenija, 217

Farquet, Christophe, 158, 166

Feminism, 49, 53, 56, 58, 63; and feminists, 47–49, 55–57, 129, 231n13; and feminist development economists, 2, 13–14, 44–47, 49, 50, 62–63; and feminist scholarship, viii, 3, 13, 49, 55–57, 58, 137; and Third World women workers, 59–62. *See also* Classified advertising; International Labour Organization (ILO)

Ferris, Eugene Beverly, 93

Filtzer, D., 207

Fitzpatrick, Sheila, 207

Ford, Edsel, 174

Foreign trade zones (FTZs). *See* Offshore economy

Forest Reserve Act (1891), 109

Forrest, Suzanne, 244n25

Foster, George G., and *New York Naked*, 31

France, 17–18, 120, 135, 139–142, 145, 151, 153–154, 158–160, 164, 166, 167–168, 177; and Second Empire, 126; and German occupation of, 139–147; and Third Republic, 126–127. *See also* Black markets; Classified advertising; Hidden markets; Offshore economy

Freed black people. *See* US South post Civil War

Geertz, Clifford, 212

General Corporation Act (1905), 109

George, Henry, 41

Germany, 18, 139, 149, 158–159, 161, 163–165, 177. *See also* Black markets; Hidden markets; Offshore economy

Gille, Zsuzsa, 76

Global South, 13–14

Goldman, Marshall, 220

Granovetter, Mark, 5

Habermas, Jürgen, 126

Haller, William, 246n58

Hedlund, Stefan, 213, 215–216

Helleiner, Eric, 158

Helper, Hinton, and *The Impending Crisis in the South*, 34, 36, 37

Hessler, Julie, 207

Hidden markets: black market, 1–2, 15, 17–18, 140–147, 155; counterfeit merchandise, 15; connectedness of formal/informal, 3, 7, 12, 15, 17, 20, 80, 84, 97, 115–116, 120, 129, 137, 246n58; gray economy, 2, 15, 155; licit/illicit, 1–3, 17, 80, 120, 145, 153, 155; moral/immoral, 120, 129, 137; visible/invisible, 1–3, 43, 115–116, 137, 151, 157. *See also* Black markets; Second-hand economies

Hispano borderlands: Colorado, 16; economic pluralism in, 102–103, 110; environmental issues in, 114–115; Euro-Americans in, 102, 105, 110, 113; geographical area of, 102; Las Gorras Blancas, 108, 245n36; MaCormick Cattle Company, 99–100; marginalization in, 101, 116; migration to "new" urban spaces, 110–111, 112, 114; Native American artisans in, 17, 100–102, 113; New Deal measures in, 114–115; New Mexico, 16–17; Nuevomexicanos, 16–17, 100–102; Nuevomexicano resistance in, 104–105, 106, 108–109, 114, 115;

Hispano borderlands (continued)
Nuevomexicano social networks, 107, 108, 116, 245n32; Pedro Perea and the "Free Home Bill," 103–104; poverty in, 114–116; shadow/hidden economies of sheep ranching and cutting in, 99–100, 101, 104–106, 114, 116. *See also* New Mexico (1890–1930)
Hochschild, Adam, 162
Hunt, Freeman, and *Hunt's Merchants' Magazine*, 35, 36, 37, 38

IG Farben, 174
Informal economy: percentage of unmeasured economic activity in, 1; ranges of, 1–2, 12–13
International Labour Organization (ILO): Development Alternatives with Women for a New Era (DAWN), 49, 62–63; Employment Branch (EMP), 47, 53; Employment/Rural (EMP/RU) section, 46; feminist development economists in, 2, 13–14, 44, 46–47; global research and findings, 57–59; Programme on Rural Women, 44–46, 52, 57, 63; reproductive labor in the Global South, 44–46, 50–52
Interracial economy, 82, 84–86, 88, 90–91, 93–95, 97–98. *See also* Deep South Piney Woods

James, Harold, 165
Jarvis, Edward, 32
Jewish artels. *See* Soviet Union
Jim Crow. *See* US South post Civil War
Johns, Anthony, 157
Joinovici, Joseph, 154

Kahan, Arcadius, 219
Kettell, Thomas, and the *New York Herald*, 35–36, 37
Killick, John, 68
Klochko, Mikhail, 191–192
Kondratjeva, Tamara, 213
Kornblith, Gary J., 97
Krueger, Ivar, 172–173
Kumair, Lalita and Krishna, 46

Lake Pontchartrain, 81–83, 86, 89
Laval, Pierre, 143
League of Nations, 160, 167, 175
Leet, John E., and *New Orleans Republican*, 86–88
Le Zotte, Jennifer, 11
Linebaugh, Peter, 68
Louisiana Cooperative Extension Service, 97–98
Loutfi, Martha, 47
Lumber: Banner Lumber Company, 95–96; Great Southern Lumber Company, 90, 92; Poitevent and Favre Lumber Company, 81–82, 86–88, 90, 95. *See also* Deep South Piney Woods
Lumber industry. *See* US South post Civil War
Luskey, Brian, 8
Luxembourg, 167

MaCormick Cattle Company. *See* Hispano borderlands
Malakhovka settlement, 205
Marshall Islands, 158
Marx, Karl, 4–5, 10, 223–224nn6–7
Mayo-Smith, Richard, 39, 40
McDermott, John, 176–177
McDowall, John, as moral crusader, 31
Mernissi, Fatima, 57
Metallgesellschaft, 162, 174
Mies, Maria, and *The Lace Makers of Narsapur*, 46, 57, 60
Moral statistics, early nineteenth century: insanity statistics, 32; in Lowell textile mills, 33; pauperism statistics, 30–31; prostitution statistics, 31–32; rise and fall of, 28–30; use of the word *priceless*, 33, 42–43. *See also* Economic indicators; Economic indicators in mid-nineteenth-century Northern US
Morgenthau, Henry, 172

Native American artisans. *See* Hispano borderlands
Naylor, Tom, 176
Nazi Germany. *See* Black markets

Neal, Larry, 164–165

New historians of capitalism, 6–7, 16, 84, 137, 224n12, 225n20, 225n23; and commodification/exploitation/profit, 6, 12, 225nn16–17, 225n22, 226n26; and US slavery, 6–7, 225nn18–19

New Mexico (1890–1930): Act Granting to Railroads the Right of Way Through the Public Lands (1875), 109; Court of Private Land Claims (CPLC), 106, 108, 112; decline in Santa Fe trade area, 101; deforestation in, 106; early twentieth-century tourism industry, 102, 113–115; *ejidos* (mixed-use spaces), 103, 105–106, 108; Panic of 1893, effect on, 107; Ralph E. Twitchell, and advertorial *Progress of New Mexico*, 111–112; Santa Fe railway and Fred Harvey company, 113; statehood (1912), 103, 110; state-sponsored capitalism/Anglo-American fee-simple property rights vs. Nuevomexicano Mercedes Reales (land grants), 103–105, 107–110; "squatters" in, 104–105, 107, 112; *United States* v. *Sandoval* (1897), impact of, 108. *See also* Hispano borderlands

New Orleans. *See* Cotton

Nikolaev, A.A., 207

Offshore economy: and *affaire Trémoille*, 166; and the Bahamas, 163–164; and the Cayman Islands, 155–158; and "cloaking," 173–174, 177; and covering legitimate and illegitimate markets, 157; definition of, 18–19, 157; development of, 158–160, 176–177; and "exchange controls," 165–166; "flags of convenience," 18, 157; and "flagging out," 163; and foreign trade zones (FTZs), 18, 175; and France, 158–160, 166, 167, 177; and Germany, 160–164, 173, 177; historiography of, 158; and Liechtenstein Anstalt (1926), 167; and Luxembourg "1929 holding company," 167; and Marshall Islands, 158; and "Muscat dhows" dispute, 159; and Panama, 164; and regulatory arbitrage, 157, 159, 176–177; and rise of protectionism (1930s), 174–175; and

Switzerland, 159, 166–167; and system of "imperial preference," 174–175; and tax evasion, 1, 12, 18–19, 166–168; and UK (and Channel Islands), 160–164, 167–172, 174–175, 177; and UK legislation of, 169–171; and UN sanctions, 176; and US, 160–164, 172, 175, 177; and World War I, 160–164, 176

Ogle, Vanessa, 158

Oubre, Claude F., 92

Palan, Ronen, 157

Palmer, Ingrid, 47, 52–56, 59

People's Republic of China (PRC) commercial system: and advanced producer cooperatives (APCs), 187; Beijing, 184, 187–188, 191, 199, 200–201; and China's cellular society, 186–188; the Cultural Revolution, 19, 188, 201; and first Five Year Plan, 182–183; Fujian Province, 187; and the Great Leap Forward, 188, 190, 191, 192, 193, 194, 201; and hardware fairs, 197–198; and Hundred Flowers campaign, 192–193; Jilin Province, 189–190; and "joint public-private enterprises," 182–183; and Municipal Vegetable Corporation (MVC), 188; and peoples' communes, 182, 188, 191; and pop-up restaurants, 183–184; and producer co-ops, 183, 188, 192, 193; and rail transport, 186, 190–191, 194; and reconstruction, 182; and road transport, 194–195; and rural fairs, 192, 197; Shanghai, 184, 187–188; Shanxi Province, 190; and *shock transport*, 191; and shops and stalls, 184, 198–200; and "specialized" corporations, 183, 189; and supply and marketing cooperatives (SMCs), 183, 185, 192–193, 197, 199; and trade warehouses, 184–185, 195–197; and urban peddlers, 184, 187–188, 200; Yunnan Province, 194

Pétain, Philippe, 142

Picciotto, Sol, 157

Piketty, Thomas, 38

Polanyi, Karl, 4–5, 218

Poor, Henry Varnum, and the *American Railroad Journal*, 36, 38

Portes, Alejandro, 246n58
Press in France. *See* Classified advertising

Railroad companies: East Louisiana
Railroad, 89, 90; Kentwood and Eastern
Railroad, 96–97; New Orleans Great
Northern Railroad (NOGN), 90, 238n2.
See also Deep South Piney Woods
Riello, Giorgio, and *Cotton*, 68
Rist, Charles, 154
Roosevelt, Franklin D., 164, 172

Saltykovka settlement, 205
Sanger, William, and *History of Prostitution*,
31–32
Santa Fe Trade Area. *See* New Mexico
(1890–1930)
Savené, Marie-Angélique, 57
Schmitz, Hermann, 174
Seamen, Ezra, and *Essays on the Progress of
Nations*, 34, 36
Second-hand economies, 8, 11, 76. *See also*
Cotton; Hidden markets
Sen, Gita, 49–52, 57
Shanghai. *See* People's Republic of China
(PRC) commercial system
Shattuck, Lemuel, 31
Shaxson, Nicholas, 158
Sherman Antitrust Act, 159
Simis, Konstantin, 214
Smith, Adam, 4–5, 10
Social history of capitalism, 8–13; bottom-up
agency, 8; as complex ecosystem, 10, 12; as
hybrid system, 9
Socialist commerce, 193–194, 199, 201–202.
See also People's Republic of China (PRC)
commercial system; Soviet Union, Jewish
artels
Société Suisse pour Valeurs de Métaux (SSM),
162–163
Soviet Union, Jewish artels in: clandestine
entrepreneurship and production in,
19–20, 203, 205, 211–216, 219–222, 271n100;
connection between economy and Jewish
ethnicity, 206, 216–221, 271n91; economically backward, 206–207, 210–211; invalid

artels, 212, 213–214; Jewish migration to
Moscow's suburbs, 203–205; Jewish shtetl
population in, 205–206; horizontal
economic exchange, 212, 219–220; Lenin's
"cooperative plan," 205; postwar anti-
Semitic campaigns, 217–218; protection
from local Soviet authorities, 212–213;
"shadow economy," 214–216; small-
medium cooperative producer units, 205,
208–210, 267n3; state abolishment of, 222;
statute and governance of, 209–210;
transition to socialism, 205–206; two
economic "orders" (*uklad*), 210–216;
vertical networking, 212–213
Spahr, Charles Barzilai, 38–39, 40
Standard Oil (NJ), 163
Stanley, Amy Dru, 137
Strasser, Susan, 76
Strathern, Marilyn, 219
Switzerland, 159–160, 165–167, 170, 174, 175
Szkolnikoff, Michel, 153–154

Teagle, Walter, 174
Thompson, E.P., and the eighteenth-century
moral economy, 27–28
Tranter, Victor, 176

Union of Radical Political Economists
(URPE), 49; value of rural women's hidden
economic activities, 44–46, 47; women and
development (WAD), 48; women in
development (WID), 48
United Kingdom, 18, 32–33, 67, 139, 158–162,
163, 167–171, 177. *See also* Black markets;
Cotton; Moral statistics, early nineteenth
century; Offshore economy
United Nations. *See* International Labour
Organization (ILO)
United States, 7, 18, 26, 28–29, 32, 34–43, 47,
67–68, 79, 86–87, 108–109, 114–116, 139,
158–164, 172–175, 177, 204. *See also* Cotton;
Deep South Piney Woods; Economic
indicators; Economic indicators in
mid-nineteenth-century northern US;
Hispano borderlands; Lumber; Moral
statistics, early nineteenth century;

Offshore economy; Railroad companies;
US South post Civil War
United States v. *Sandoval* (1897). *See* New
Mexico (1890–1930)
US South post Civil War: deforestation in,
15–16, 82, 84, 85, 97–98; freed black people
in, 15–16, 82, 85–86, 89–90, 91; Jim Crow
and illiteracy, 16, 82, 88, 92, 95, 96; lumber
industry, 15–16, 81–83, 85, 88, 95–96, 98;
sugarcane production, 15, 93–94. *See also*
Deep South Piney Woods

Van Bavel, Bas, 5
Verdery, Katherine, 214
Vernay, Alain, 158, 177

Wallerstein, Immanuel, 6; and world-systems
model, 7, 224n13
Walter, Ingo, 157
Wealth and inequality, viii, 12, 13, 26, 29–30,
34, 35, 37, 38–40, 41, 86, 88, 140, 153, 155,
166. *See also* Black markets; Deep South

Piney Woods; Economic indicators;
Economic indicators in mid-nineteenth-
century northern US; Moral statistics,
early nineteenth century; Offshore
economy
Weber, Max, 6
Woloson, Wendy, 8, 76
Women: economic opportunities for,
125–126, 133; and prostitution, 119, 121, 125,
127, 129–130; and rural women's economic
activities, 44–46, 47; and unpaid
reproductive labor, 44–45, 63. *See also*
International Labour Organization (ILO)
Woodman, Harold, and *King Cotton and His
Retainers*, 68, 79
Wright, Carroll, 41

Yunus, Muhammad, 20

Zakim, Michael, 32, 97
Zubkova, Elena, 207, 217
Zucman, Gabriel, 166

Acknowledgments

We would like to express our thanks to Roger Horowitz and the Hagley Museum and Library, Carol Lockman in particular, for sponsoring and organizing the conference, Hidden Capitalism: Beyond, Below, and Outside the Visible Market. Amyrs Williams at the Hagley and Wendy Woloson were part of the selection committee that chose the papers for the conference, and both offered valuable commentary and feedback that helped to shape the volume. We are especially grateful to Robert Lockhart at the University of Pennsylvania Press for shepherding this volume through the evaluation and publication process with such efficiency and graciousness. As well, we thank John Majewski, Roger Horowitz, and the two anonymous referees, whose insightful comments and suggestions improved this work. Finally, we thank Nelson Lichtenstein and the Colloquium on Work, Labor, and Democracy at the University of California, Santa Barbara, where the ideas that germinated into the conference and this volume were first discussed.

Lightning Source UK Ltd.
Milton Keynes UK
UKHW041525201219
355729UK00002B/226/P